GEORGE R. CRESSMAN
PROFESSOR EMERITUS
VILLANOVA UNIVERSITY

HAROLD W. BENDA
CHAIRMAN, DEPARTMENT OF EDUCATION
WEST CHESTER STATE COLLEGE

PUBLIC EDUCATION IN AMERICA

A Foundations Course

THIRD EDITION

NEW YORK

APPLETON-CENTURY-CROFTS

DIVISION OF MEREDITH PUBLISHING COMPANY

Preface

In the last five years, the extensive changes that have occurred in American life compel society to take a new and critical look at the whole program of public education. Reevaluation is a necessity, and the teacher, whether neophyte or one of long experience, must be familiar with the ways in which the forces of modernization affect his profession. There have been many innovations, but the ideas and accomplishments of the past in the field of education still provide us with inspiration today. Total rejection of traditional approaches in teaching can be folly, and many of the revised teacher preparation "programs" threaten to produce "educational illiterates" who will function in the schools of America.

It is not hard to prove that a person can be a more stimulating teacher if he has a knowledge of the democratic experiment to which he contributes. He must know the children in his classroom, certainly; he must be completely confident in his field of specialization, and he must be familiar with various methods of teaching. However, he should also be cognizant of his professional obligations, and thoroughly aware of the democratic structure within which the potentials of our youth may be more fully realized today than in the past.

Prospective teachers need the broad view which *Public Education in America* attempts to present. An examination of college and university catalogs indicates that its widest use may be in such courses as Educational Foundations, The Place and Purpose of Education in the Social Order, Social Foundations of Education, Principles of Education, and others. Because of the tendency to change the usual time of offering such courses from the first year to the third and fourth years of the undergraduate program, and considering the well-prepared college student, we have made a consistent attempt to present our material on a mature level.

In view of the broad acceptance of the first two editions of *Public Education in America* it has seemed best to follow the same general plan of organization for the third edition. However, a number of chapters in the third edition have been completely rewritten, several have been consolidated, and two present totally different content.

Where data are necessary the emphasis has been placed upon trends rather than upon data for a specific year in order that the material will not become so quickly outdated.

The chapter bibliographies are presented as *Further Readings.* Therefore, the material cited in the footnotes is generally not restated in these readings. The bibliographical sections may seem somewhat brief in view of the material available, but this should encourage the mature student to compile his own bibliographies in the periodical field. The prospective teacher must continually update his references. In Appendix D of this volume there is a general list of magazines in the educational field which should be available in the periodical rooms of any good college library.

We have had the benefit of the keen and able criticism of a number of people. We especially appreciate the invaluable assistance of Mr. George A. Harris, Chairman of the Department of Education at Villanova University, and of Dr. Charlotte E. King, Professor of Education at West Chester State College. We are also extremely grateful to the United States Office of Education and the National Education Association. The help from these sources has been significant.

G.R.C.
H.W.B.

Contents

III. THE EDUCATIONAL PROCESS AND THE CHILD

IV. EDUCATION AND SOCIETY

V. PROMISES AND PROBLEMS

APPENDICES

Tables

Figures

I

THE AMERICAN
SCHOOL SYSTEM

1

Education
in a Changing World

PREVIEW

▶ There is increased dependence today upon education as a major social force.
It has become a matter of national policy in many countries of the world.

▶ We are now in the midst of an educational revolution in America, involving widespread changes in educational practices and ideas.
Greater proportions of youth are continuing to the baccalaureate degree and beyond.
A significant part of the educational revolution is the increased emphasis upon sciences, mathematics, and languages.

▶ The fundamental values of the founders must still be cherished.
The Founding Fathers of the United States foresaw that an educated electorate was essential for a successful democracy.
It is necessary that in our devotion to curricular changes and related matters we do not lose sight of our basic purposes.
Democracy will persist only by devoted cultivation.

▶ Modern education must accept new responsibilities.
The danger of provincialism impels us to think of our educational responsibilities in an international framework.
America has yet to realize many ideals in the field of education, as well as in other spheres of interest.
Much remains to be done within our borders to minimize existing social inequalities.

3

▶ The urgency of our extensive social problems suggests that the development of effective national policy, democratically conceived, is necessary.

Even to the casual observer there is evidence of increased dependence upon education as a significant social force in the modern world. In the establishment of totalitarianism, a certain amount of literacy is essential for the use of propaganda to be effective. Upon a foundation of extensive literacy, it is possible to develop a highly organized system of education that can serve the national interests. This situation is characteristic of that evolving in the Soviet Union. On the other hand, it is the lack of any policy of general education directed toward national needs that is often responsible for major problems of the emerging nations. A newly independent country must have had preparation for that freedom, and preparation must come via an educational program which is accessible to a major part of the population. Otherwise, the survival of the country is jeopardized, and its subversion by other more powerful nations with ulterior designs is far more likely.

It is clear today that education must become a matter of national policy as never before. We are, indeed, in the midst of an educational revolution.

One may witness in America the concern for advanced technical training and the reorganization of curricula and technique in the secondary schools to provide for the gifted student. We see also many advanced placement programs with provisions for individual progress and with emphasis upon the opportunity for creativity, primarily in the technical and related fields. At present there is a widespread feeling that we have been overlooking too much potential talent, but the concern for this loss is not entirely recent. Terman called our attention to the problem many years ago, especially in his *Genetic Studies of Genius*. The renewed emphasis on this idea is a part of the revolution.

Conant [1] in his *Shaping Educational Policy* has suggested that in some countries education has been viewed as a means of "reducing social stratification," and generally it has been accepted that there is a direct relation between the level of education and the prosperity of a country. These are not new beliefs to many Americans, but they are new to much of the rest of the world, at least to the extent that they influence practice. Only recently the President of the United States pointed out the effect of the lack of education on the standard of living in underdeveloped areas.

[1] James Bryant Conant, *Shaping Educational Policy* (New York, McGraw-Hill, 1964).

A significant part of the educational revolution in America is evidenced by the increased proportion of eligible young people who are going to college and to graduate school. In many cases a bachelor's degree will merely admit a person to a profession; sometimes it will not even do that. One who scans the advertisements in such papers as *The New York Times* is impressed by the number of employers who wish to hire only chemists, physicists, and engineers with master's degrees and doctorates. The teaching profession as well is moving slowly in this direction.

This situation is occurring despite the increased costs of education at every level. Most colleges and universities are "bursting at the seams," and secondary schools can scarcely be provided rapidly enough. Although the population explosion has significantly affected this situation, there are other factors which must be considered.

Our outlook on the professions has changed. A generation ago a physics major among the graduating class at a college or university was considered an unusual individual with no way to make a living except by teaching. Now he is among the elite of the class. This is especially true if he has completed extensive graduate study. Other professions have been similarly metamorphosed.

These changes are factors in the educational revolution taking place in America and to a similar or lesser extent in many other countries. It has caused great reforms in secondary education; today there are strengthened courses in science which include up-to-date material, more intensive mathematics programs, courses advanced to the college level, and studies in modern languages including those not even considered a few years ago; courses in certain languages have been adopted by the elementary school, where oral use and intensive study is emphasized. Clearly the line between secondary and higher education is becoming obscured, and often the same may be said in reference to the elementary and the high school.

FUNDAMENTAL VALUES

In our evaluation of the educational program and its readjustment to a changing society, there is danger of losing sight of the ideals of the founders of our democracy. This we would do at our own peril.

That our early forefathers had a vision of the ultimate magnitude of a system of public education is doubtful. Monroe [2] thinks there is very little evidence of any conception of what was to come. Possibly this is true.

What is certainly clear, however, is that these early American leaders were very sure that the new form of government could not endure with-

[2] Paul Monroe, *Founding of the American Public School System* (New York, Macmillan, 1940), p. 201.

out an educated citizenry. Evidence of this type of thinking may be found in their writings and in their speeches. Washington, for example, in his Farewell Address of 1796 said:

Promote, then as an object of importance, institutions for the general diffusion of knowledge. In proportion as the structure of a government gives force to public opinion, it is essential that public opinion should be enlightened.

John Adams is credited with the statement:

Education is more indispensable, and must be more general under a free government than any other. In a monarchy, the few who are likely to govern must have some education, but the common people must be kept in ignorance; in an aristocracy, the nobles should be educated but here it is even more necessary that the common people should be kept ignorant, but in a free government knowledge must be general, and ought to be universal.[3]

Jefferson, the Virginian, in his later years wrote: "If a nation expects to be ignorant and free, it expects what never was and never will be." [4] On another occasion he advocated a general scheme of popular education.[5]

Madison, at one time, wrote: "A popular government without information or the means of acquiring it is but a prologue to a farce or a tragedy or perhaps both." [6] Monroe further notes that Madison argued for the support of education by general taxation and in this respect was "far in advance of the sentiment of his times." [7]

Reference must, of course, be made to Franklin, the distinguished Philadelphian and founder of the Academy for the education of youth. On one occasion, in his foresighted way, he said: "We must have a system of public education; its purpose must be to educate our people in their public duties." [8]

Other witnesses might be summoned, but enough has been said to demonstrate clearly the thesis that the founders were firm in their beliefs that any system of education, particularly at public expense, would have as its fundamental purpose that of making the new form of government work. They said little or nothing of what should be taught, how it should be taught, nothing of athletic teams, or school annuals and that sort of thing, but again and again expressed the belief that the *people must be educated in their public duties.*

A great many years ago James Russell Lowell, in Paris, was talking to Guizot, the statesman and historian. As one who knew intimately of the

[3] *The Works of John Adams* (Boston, Little, Brown, 1851), Vol. VI, p. 198.

[4] Ellwood P. Cubberly, *The History of Education* (New York, Houghton Mifflin, 1920), p. 526.

[5] Monroe, *op. cit.,* p. 199.

[6] *Ibid.*

[7] Monroe, *op. cit.,* p. 202.

[8] William McAndrew, *Ye Are the Salt of the Earth* (Philadelphia, University of Pennsylvania, Proceedings of Schoolmen's Week, 1928), p. 23.

rise and fall of empires and dynasties, Guizot turned to the American and said earnestly: "Lowell, how long do you expect that Republic of yours to last?" Lowell, after a moment's thought, said, "Our Republic will last as long as the ideals of the founders are observed." [9]

Is it too much to say, then, that it is the schools of America that can really make democracy work? If that is true, and the authors deeply believe that it is, then teachers are indeed important.

So it is that we must be conscious of the possibility that with devotion to curricular changes and related matters we may largely lose sight of our basic purposes—to make democracy work and to improve its functioning. Conflicting ideologies throughout the world only serve to make this more important. The development of more scientists, better linguists and the like must always be in the framework of democracy. Otherwise, education will have failed to serve its intended purposes.

Henry Steele Commager, [10] noted historian of Amherst College has pointed out that "No other people ever demanded so much of education as have the American. None other was ever served so well by its schools and educators." In addition, he states that there are four specific tasks of education. They are:

1. To provide an enlightened citizenry in order that self-government may work.
2. To create a national unity.
3. To Americanize—the first answer to a nation of immigrants was the public school.
4. To serve as an antidote to the forces of "riotous privilege and ruinous division."

He further suggests that the school has done well in the accomplishment of these purposes but now is faced with new demands and new duties. These, he insists, must be clearly defined and adequately supported by faith and money. If these are forthcoming the schools will justify our faith in education.[11]

Conant [12] has called attention to a not unrelated problem in this field, namely, that it is possible we may develop a surplus of scientists and technicians. He has stated, "It is strange that so little heed is given to the possibility of a recurrence of unemployment among certain groups of highly specialized persons." It may be pointed out that this condition did exist in pre-World War II Germany, and many think it may have been a very important contributing factor in the rise of Hitler. To apply these ideas to the educational process demands our best efforts, for the

9 McAndrew op. cit., p. 22.

10 Henry S. Commager, "Our Schools Have Kept Us Free" 1963 Edition, National School Public Relations Association, NEA (Washington). Original statement appeared as an editorial in a special issue of Life, Oct. 16, 1950.

11 Ibid.

12 Conant, op. cit., p. 2.

facts are exceedingly difficult to secure, and the application of them to education may demand a degree of centralization that, at present, the American people may vigorously resent. Some form of national policy may very likely be necessary.

Further, lest we become too provincial in our outlook, we must look beyond our national borders. An education that produces a narrow nationalism can be disastrous. The world in which we live must either become one world or none at all. The time may be long and the road difficult, but travel it we must.

In 1962 a conference was called by the United States Commissioner of Education to consider the pressing problems confronting the American schools in the years ahead. From this larger group, a committee consisting of practical educational leaders suggested in its report that "we see our fundamental goal as a world civilization and an educational system which in all ways supports human dignity for all races, castes and classes; self realization; and fullest vocational, civic, and social cooperation and service. In achieving this fundamental goal, there must be understanding and commitment to the proposition that education is a primary instrument of social change and welfare."

This statement, if implementation is achieved, could mark a great turning point in American education, for it could cause us to turn from nationalism to world needs and problems—internationalism. The purpose of the program, advises Brameld,[13] "is to channel and release the full resources of education in behalf of the creation of a world civilization." The forces now available for our destruction make necessary a real attempt to implement such a program.

DISCREPANCIES IN THE AMERICAN IDEAL

That the American ideal assumes equality of educational opportunity for all needs little substantiation. The emphasis here, it is agreed, must be upon *opportunity* rather than upon *equality*—every individual should have the opportunity to develop his abilities and capacities to the utmost.

Even though, as Commager states, we have done well in the larger tasks assigned to the schools, we still fall far short of attaining the ideal as we have stated it. Even with the better enforcement of compulsory attendance, too many drop out of school on both elementary and secondary levels, and in many areas opportunities are either insufficient or nonexistent.

Many children fail to get a decent minimum of education because of accidents of birth. They have been born in areas of low soil fertility where schools are poor; in slum areas where the same may be true, or they are of a race that has been discriminated against, as have Negroes

---

[13] Theodore Brameld, "World Civilization: the Galvanizing Purpose of Public Education," *Phi Delta Kappan,* Vol. XLIV, No. 2 (November, 1962).

in many parts of the nation. The result all too often has been a meager and inadequate schooling. Nevertheless, the median school years completed by persons 25 years old and over in the United States has increased from 8.4 percent in 1940 to 11.4 percent in 1962.[14] Local differences are, of course, of more significance than the national median.

That illiteracy (where illiteracy is defined as the inability to read and write a simple message either in English or in any other language) has dropped from 11.3 percent in 1900 to 2.4 percent in 1960 constitutes a very significant advance, but still leaves much room for improvement. Here again particularization is important.

We are indebted to the United States Office of Education for the following data and table on pupil retention. It will bear careful study.

A careful study of the table "Educational Differences among the States" will bring various aspects of the problem forcibly to the attention of every student.

The problem of the underprivileged in urban areas is outstanding today in any consideration of equality and is highly complicated by racial issues as well as others.

So-called blighted areas present new and different problems which must be solved to a considerable degree before we can view the scene with any degree of satisfaction. It is encouraging to note that nationwide attention is being given to this problem which is prominent in the larger cities. Similar conditions are found, however, in many rural areas.

The Higher Horizons program in New York City, the Ford Foundations Great Cities Grey Area programs, Houston's Talent Preservation project, Phoenix's Careers for Youth, and Seattle's Disadvantaged Student program are but a few of the challenging examples of efforts to contribute to the solution of the existing problems. A number of these approaches are promising attempts to insure further progress toward the American ideal of equality of opportunity.

Since education is largely considered a state function, our approach to these issues is a fragmented one. An experiment in one area, however, may serve as fertile ground for others concerned with similar problems. Successful projects may be adopted totally or partially, and the possibilities of failure thus lessened. It is slow—painfully slow—considering the urgency of our problems. This is in part why some sort of national policy, possibly developed through "interstate cooperation," as Conant suggests, may be the answer.

It is certain that some of our great social problems cannot wait interminably for their solution. To the attempts to resolve these we shall direct our attention, giving some thoughts to background, costs, organization, promising practices, and related problems.

[14] U.S. Department of Health, Education, and Welfare, *Progress of Public Education in the United States 1963–1964* (Washington, D.C., Office of Education, 1964) pp. 3–4.

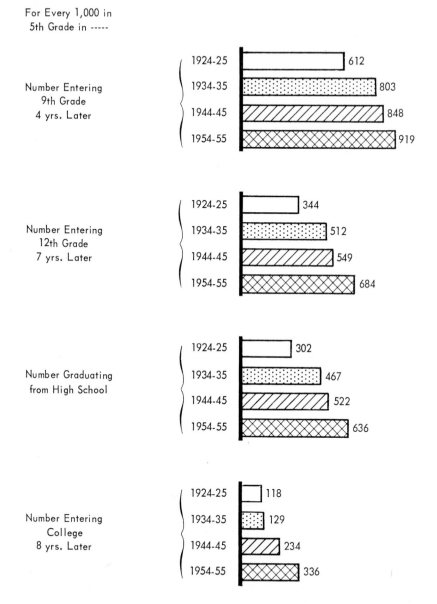

Figure 1-1. Estimated Retention Rates, Fifth Grade through College Entrance, in Public and Nonpublic Schools: United States, 1924–32 to 1954–62

For Every 1,000 in
5th Grade in -----

Number Entering
9th Grade
4 yrs. Later

1924-25 ... 612
1934-35 ... 803
1944-45 ... 848
1954-55 ... 919

Number Entering
12th Grade
7 yrs. Later

1924-25 ... 344
1934-35 ... 512
1944-45 ... 549
1954-55 ... 684

Number Graduating
from High School

1924-25 ... 302
1934-35 ... 467
1944-45 ... 522
1954-55 ... 636

Number Entering
College
8 yrs. Later

1924-25 ... 118
1934-35 ... 129
1944-45 ... 234
1954-55 ... 336

SOURCE: U.S. Department of Health, Education, and Welfare, Office of Education, *Biennial Survey of Education in the United States,* and *Digest of Educational Statistics.*

Table 1-1.   Educational Differences among the States

Estimated Average Salaries of Classroom Teachers in Public Schools, 1964-65		Personal Income per Child of School Age (5-17), 1963	
1. Alaska (16-$6,354)	$8,360*	1. New York	$13,218
2. California	7,900	2. Nevada	13,116
3. New York	7,800	3. Connecticut	12,922
4. Connecticut	6,975	4. Delaware	12,661
5. Massachusetts	6,950	5. New Jersey	12,106
6. Illinois	6,809	6. California	12,088
7. Maryland	6,727	7. Illinois	11,870
8. Delaware	6,700	8. Massachusetts	11,854
9. Michigan	6,700	9. Alaska (32-$7,985)	10,507*
10. New Jersey	6,698	10. Maryland	10,484
11. Arizona	6,670	11. Missouri	10,293
12. Indiana	6,530	12. Rhode Island	10,204
13. Nevada	6,530	13. Pennsylvania	10,114
14. Oregon	6,470	14. Washington	9,902
15. Minnesota	6,460	15. Ohio	9,649
16. Washington	6,400	United States	9,616
17. Rhode Island	6,251	16. Colorado	9,585
United States	6,235	17. Oregon	9,577
18. Pennsylvania	6,150	18. Michigan	9,513
19. Florida	6,140	19. Indiana	9,348
20. Wisconsin	6,125	20. Nebraska	9,149
21. New Mexico	6,085	21. New Hampshire	9,119
22. Hawaii	6,060	22. Wyoming	9,065
23. Ohio	6,050	23. Iowa	9,051
24. Colorado	6,025	24. Wisconsin	9,047
25. Wyoming	5,996	25. Florida	8,979
26. Utah	5,945	26. Hawaii	8,914
27. Iowa	5,747	27. Kansas	8,911
28. Missouri	5,660	28. Minnesota	8,766
29. Montana	5,635	29. Montana	8,131
30. Kansas	5,587	30. Oklahoma	8,017
31. Vermont	5,550	31. Virginia	7,996
32. Texas	5,461	32. Arizona	7,990
33. Virginia	5,450	33. Vermont	7,876
34. New Hampshire	5,435	34. Maine	7,853
35. Maine	5,200	35. Texas	7,801
36. Louisiana	5,175	36. North Dakota	7,303
37. Oklahoma	5,160	37. Utah	7,208
38. Idaho	5,150	38. South Dakota	7,202
39. North Carolina	5,052	39. Idaho	7,078
40. Georgia	5,050	40. West Virginia	6,833
41. Nebraska	5,000	41. Tennessee	6,743
42. Tennessee	4,850	42. Georgia	6,732
43. North Dakota	4,800	43. Kentucky	6,673
44. Alabama	4,775	44. New Mexico	6,643
45. Kentucky	4,750	45. North Carolina	6,591
46. West Virginia	4,590	46. Louisiana	6,286
47. South Dakota	4,475	47. Arkansas	5,996
48. South Carolina	4,450	48. Alabama	5,904
49. Arkansas	4,200	49. South Carolina	5,410
50. Mississippi	4,103	50. Mississippi	4,801
Canal Zone	8,142		
Guam	4,908		
Puerto Rico	3,940		
Virgin Islands	4,850		

* The purchasing power of $1 in four large Alaska cities averages about 76¢ as compared with the average purchasing power of $1 in areas covered by the Consumer Price Index of the U.S. Bureau of Labor Statistics. All dollar amounts shown for Alaska should be reduced by about one-fourth to make the purchasing power of Alaska figures comparable to figures reported for other states.

Table 1-1.   Continued

Estimated School-Age Population (5-17) as Percent of Total Resident Population, 1964*		Number of School-Age Children (5-17) per 100 Adults Aged 21-64, in 1964*	
1. Utah	29.9%	1. New Mexico	66
2. New Mexico	29.8	2. Utah	66
3. South Carolina	29.1	3. Mississippi	65
4. Mississippi	29.1	4. South Carolina	62
5. Louisiana	28.5	5. Louisiana	61
6. Idaho	28.2	6. North Dakota	61
7. Alabama	28.1	7. Idaho	61
8. North Dakota	28.1	8. South Dakota	60
9. Alaska	28.0	9. Alaska	59
10. Wyoming	27.7	10. Alabama	59
11. Georgia	27.6	11. Montana	58
12. Arizona	27.4	12. Minnesota	58
13. West Virginia	27.4	13. Arizona	57
14. Montana	27.4	14. Wyoming	57
15. North Carolina	27.3	15. Vermont	57
16. Michigan	27.3	16. Georgia	57
17. South Dakota	27.3	17. West Virginia	56
18. Vermont	27.1	18. Arkansas	56
19. Hawaii	27.1	19. Michigan	56
20. Minnesota	27.0	20. Kentucky	56
21. Texas	26.9	21. Hawaii	56
22. Maryland	26.9	22. North Carolina	55
23. Indiana	26.9	23. Wisconsin	55
24. Kentucky	26.8	24. Texas	55
25. Nevada	26.7	25. Indiana	55
26. Arkansas	26.5	26. Iowa	55
27. Delaware	26.5	27. Maine	54
28. Colorado	26.4	28. Nebraska	54
29. Wisconsin	26.4	29. Colorado	54
30. Ohio	26.4	30. Kansas	53
31. Tennessee	26.4	31. Delaware	53
32. Oregon	26.1	32. Maryland	53
33. Virginia	25.9	33. Ohio	53
34. Maine	25.9	34. Oregon	53
United States	25.8	35. Tennessee	53
35. Iowa	25.8	36. Washington	53
36. Washington	25.7	37. New Hampshire	52
37. Kansas	25.7	United States	52
38. Nebraska	25.6	38. Virginia	51
39. New Hampshire	25.5	39. Missouri	50
40. Illinois	25.3	40. Nevada	50
41. California	25.1	41. Illinois	50
42. Connecticut	25.1	42. Oklahoma	50
43. Oklahoma	24.7	43. Florida	49
44. Missouri	24.7	44. California	49
45. Pennsylvania	24.6	45. Connecticut	48
46. New Jersey	24.4	46. Massachusetts	48
47. Massachusetts	24.4	47. Pennsylvania	48
48. Rhode Island	24.1	48. Rhode Island	47
49. Florida	24.1	49. New Jersey	46
50. New York	23.2	50. New York	44

*Computation carried a sufficient number of places to give an exact ranking.

*Computation carried a sufficient number of places to give an exact ranking.

Table 1-1. Continued

Estimated Current Expenditures for Public Elementary and Secondary Schools per Pupil in ADA, 1964-65		State and Local Property Tax Collections as a Percent of Personal Income, 1963*	
1. New York	$790	1. South Dakota	6.3%
2. Alaska (19-$489)	643*	2. Kansas	6.3
3. New Jersey	607	3. Minnesota	6.3
4. Connecticut	593	4. Wisconsin	6.2
5. California	570	5. Montana	6.2
6. Oregon	569	6. Nebraska	6.2
7. Wyoming	554	7. Iowa	6.0
8. Illinois	551	8. New Hampshire	5.8
9. Delaware	536	9. Arizona	5.6
10. Washington	534	10. Wyoming	5.6
11. Wisconsin	532	11. Massachusetts	5.6
12. Minnesota	528	12. North Dakota	5.5
13. Montana	516	13. New Jersey	5.5
14. Rhode Island	514	14. California	5.4
15. Michigan	510	15. Maine	5.4
16. Nevada	505	16. Idaho	5.1
17. Maryland	503	17. Colorado	5.1
18. Massachusetts	502	18. Vermont	5.0
19. Indiana	490	19. Indiana	4.9
United States	483	20. Oregon	4.7
20. Pennsylvania	479	21. New York	4.7
21. Colorado	470	22. Michigan	4.7
22. New Mexico	470	23. Rhode Island	4.6
23. Ohio	469	24. Utah	4.5
24. Iowa	465	25. Connecticut	4.4
25. Kansas	462	26. Illinois	4.4
26. Arizona	451	United States	4.4
27. New Hampshire	448	27. Ohio	4.3
28. Vermont	438	28. Texas	4.1
29. Missouri	437	29. Florida	3.9
30. Hawaii	422	30. Maryland	3.6
31. North Dakota	422	31. Missouri	3.4
32. Louisiana	418	32. Washington	3.4
33. South Dakota	416	33. Oklahoma	3.1
34. Nebraska	407	34. Mississippi	3.1
35. Utah	407	35. Nevada	3.0
36. Florida	403	36. Pennsylvania	2.9
37. Texas	396	37. Tennessee	2.9
38. Virginia	380	38. New Mexico	2.8
39. Maine	371	39. Georgia	2.8
40. Oklahoma	366	40. Virginia	2.7
41. Idaho	332	41. Arkansas	2.7
42. Georgia	330	42. West Virginia	2.6
43. Kentucky	323	43. Kentucky	2.6
44. North Carolina	322	44. Louisiana	2.6
45. Arkansas	317	45. North Carolina	2.5
46. West Virginia	315	46. South Carolina	2.1
47. Tennessee	300	47. Hawaii	1.9
48. South Carolina	289	48. Alaska	1.8
49. Alabama	288	49. Alabama	1.7
50. Mississippi	273	50. Delaware	1.5
Canal Zone	617		
Guam	289		
Puerto Rico	204		
Virgin Islands	440		

*Computation carried a sufficient number of places to give an exact ranking.

Table 1-1. Continued

Median School Years Completed by Persons 25 Years Old and Older, 1960		Per-Capita Expenditures of State and Local Governments for All Education, 1963	
1. Utah	12.2	1. Alaska (10-$159.47)	$209.83*
2. Alaska	12.1	2. Utah	181.49
3. California	12.1	3. Wyoming	179.76
4. Colorado	12.1	4. California	178.29
5. Nevada	12.1	5. Washington	177.62
6. Washington	12.1	6. Colorado	176.66
7. Wyoming	12.1	7. New Mexico	172.97
8. Idaho	11.8	8. Oregon	170.89
9. Oregon	11.8	9. Arizona	161.82
10. Kansas	11.7	10. Delaware	160.22
11. Massachusetts	11.6	11. Nevada	157.93
12. Montana	11.6	12. Montana	154.56
13. Nebraska	11.6	13. Michigan	151.06
14. Arizona	11.3	14. Minnesota	149.04
15. Hawaii	11.3	15. North Dakota	148.97
16. Iowa	11.3	16. Kansas	147.64
17. New Mexico	11.2	17. Wisconsin	146.43
18. Delaware	11.1	18. Hawaii	146.25
19. Connecticut	11.0	19. South Dakota	144.06
20. Maine	11.0	20. Indiana	141.66
21. Florida	10.9	21. Iowa	141.23
22. New Hampshire	10.9	22. New York	138.38
23. Ohio	10.9	23. Idaho	128.09
24. Vermont	10.9	24. Vermont	128.01
25. Indiana	10.8	25. Maryland	127.32
26. Michigan	10.8	United States	127.31
27. Minnesota	10.8	26. Connecticut	127.26
28. New York	10.7	27. Nebraska	123.70
29. New Jersey	10.6	28. Illinois	122.25
United States	10.6	29. Oklahoma	121.20
30. Illinois	10.5	30. Louisiana	113.11
31. Maryland	10.4	31. Pennsylvania	112.92
32. Oklahoma	10.4	32. Texas	110.58
33. South Dakota	10.4	33. Missouri	110.27
34. Texas	10.4	34. New Jersey	110.05
35. Wisconsin	10.4	35. Maine	109.97
36. Pennsylvania	10.2	36. Ohio	109.66
37. Rhode Island	10.0	37. Florida	107.33
38. Virginia	9.9	38. Virginia	107.24
39. Missouri	9.6	39. New Hampshire	106.91
40. North Dakota	9.3	40. Massachusetts	103.00
41. Alabama	9.1	41. Kentucky	101.89
42. Georgia	9.0	42. North Carolina	101.21
43. Arkansas	8.9	43. Rhode Island	100.95
44. Mississippi	8.9	44. Georgia	97.08
45. North Carolina	8.9	45. West Virginia	95.83
46. Louisiana	8.8	46. South Carolina	88.36
47. Tennessee	8.8	47. Arkansas	87.49
48. West Virginia	8.8	48. Mississippi	87.18
49. Kentucky	8.7	49. Alabama	86.37
50. South Carolina	8.7	50. Tennessee	84.79
Puerto Rico	4.6		

SOURCE: All data in table extracted from Research Report, 1965-R 1, *Rankings of the States, 1965,* National Education Association (Washington) and used by special permission. Copyright © by the National Education Association. All rights reserved.

QUESTIONS AND PROJECTS

1. Arnold Toynbee has said that throughout history people have seldom examined the nature of their educational systems until their culture was well on the way to its decline. Comment upon this statement. How does it apply to our situation today?
2. Prepare a report for class presentation on the details of one of the current programs for disadvantaged youths.
3. Investigate various plans for teaching international understanding, and prepare an oral or written report as may be agreed upon.
4. Should schools indoctrinate for democracy? Discuss in detail.
5. Using the table concerning the ranking of the states, investigate the position of your state and be able to discuss in considerable detail the reasons for that position. Suggest what you think should be done to improve the situation.
6. Conduct a panel discussion on the proposals for developing a national policy for education as suggested by Conant.
7. Explain some secondary school program where great emphasis is put upon the development of creative ability. Try to find some evidence of its effectiveness.
8. Study carefully the data in Figure 1–1 on page 10. What percentage of high school graduates do you think should go to college? What is the percentage where you live?

AUDIO-VISUAL AIDS

MOTION PICTURES (16 MM)

Seminar on American Civilization: Life Goals and Democracy—NET, Indiana University, Audio-Visual Center, Bloomington, Ind. Presents a panel discussion on life goals and values in America. Dr. Max Lerner and five Brandeis University students explore the meaning of power, prestige, success, and security as life goals. They also question the value of freedom, solitude, and forces that pressure personality, as well as the problem of replacing unhealthy goals.

Democracy—Encyclopaedia Britannica Films, 1150 Wilmette Ave., Wilmette, Ill., 11 min., sd., b&w. (Companion film to *Despotism*.) The nature and meaning of democracy. Its two unique characteristics—shared respect and shared power—are defined and described. Then two important conditions are examined which have historically promoted the growth of democracy—balanced economic distribution and enlightenment.

Despotism—Encyclopaedia Britannica Films, 1150 Wilmette Ave., Wilmette, Ill., 11 min., sd., b&w. Illustrates the thesis that all communities can be ranged on a scale running from democracy to despotism. The two chief characteristics of despotism—restricted respect for the individual and concentrated power—are defined and illustrated. Two of the conditions which have historically promoted the growth of despotism are explained and exemplified. These are a slanted economic distribution and a strict control of the agencies of communication.

Nationalism—Encyclopaedia Britannica Films, 1150 Wilmette Ave., Wilmette, Ill., 20 min., sd., b&w. Defines nationalism and traces its development in modern times. Explains its changing aspects as revealed in three important phases: democratic, independence, and imperialist nationalism. Points up nationalism as a force both for progress and regress in the modern world; emphasizes today's need for directing constructive aspects toward world peace.

Basic Issues of Man: Return of Prometheus—NET, Indiana U., A-V Center, Bloomington, Ind., 30 min., sd., b&w. Discusses the question "Is science good or bad for man?" During a banquet in honor of a famed scientist, his lifelong friend delivers an accolade to science in general and a tribute to the distinguished guest. Rising to deliver his remarks, the scientist expresses his deep fears that science may well lead to the decline of civilization. The scientist's fears are symbolically illustrated by nightmarish scenes in which he despairs of scientific truth and man's inability to ever catch up with his own technological progress. Later, the scientist seizes upon the idea of the use of science for the benefit of man. His hopes are visualized in optimistic, dreamlike scenes.

Philosophies of Education—Education for National Survival—NET, Indiana U., A-V Center, Bloomington, Ind., 29 min., sd., b&w. Emphasizes the fact that our national strength depends more on a high level of educational achievement than on any other factor. We must come to realize this, and we must be willing to spend a larger proportion of our national income on education. We must provide an educational challenge for our young people, and we must discover the best talent and see to it that this talent is developed to the highest possible degree. Featured personality is Harold W. Stokes, president of Queens College in New York City.

Seminar on American Civilization—Do We Need a New Educational Revolution?—NET, Indiana U., A-V Center, Bloomington, Ind., 29 min., sd., b&w. Presents a panel discussion on the need for educational changes in America. Dr. Max Lerner and five Brandeis University students voice their views on what changes are needed and how they should be effected. They discuss the ends of education, the placement of the major emphasis, teacher training, and how to provide for all students regardless of special aptitudes and abilities.

FURTHER READINGS

American Association of School Administrators, *Educating for American Citizenship, Thirty-second Yearbook* (Washington, D.C., NEA, 1954).

Brameld, Theodore, and Stanley Elam, eds., *Values in American Education* (Bloomington, Indiana, Phi Delta Kappa, 1964).

Bishop, Hillman M. and Samuel Hendel, eds., *Basic Issues of American Democracy*, 4th ed. (New York, Appleton-Century-Crofts, 1961).

Brondy, Harry S., B. O. Smith, and J. R. Burnett, *Democracy and Excellence in American Secondary Education* (New York, Rand McNally, 1964).

Brookover, Wilbur B., and David Gottlieb, *A Sociology of Education* (New York, American Book, 1964).

Conant, James Bryant, *The American High School Today* (New York, McGraw-Hill, 1959).

Educational Policies Commission, *Public Education and the Future of America* (Washington, D.C., NEA, 1954).

Educational Research Service, *School Programs for the Disadvantaged* (Washington, D.C., 1963).

Kaplan, Bernard A., "Issues in Educating the Culturally Disadvantaged," *Phi Delta Kappan,* Vol. 45, No. 2 (November, 1963), pp. 72–76.

Mayer, Frederick, *American Ideas and Education* (Columbus, Ohio, Merrill, 1964).

Mercer, Blaine E., and Edwin R. Carr, *Education and the Social Order* (New York, Holt, Rinehart and Winston, 1957).

NEA Project on Instruction, *Schools for the Sixties* (Washington, D.C., NEA, 1946).

Neff, Kenneth L., *National Development through Social Progress: The Role of Education,* Bull. 1963, No. 8 (Washington, D.C., U.S. Office of Education, 1963).

Pounds, Ralph L., and James R. Bryner, *The School in American Society* (New York, Macmillan, 1959).

Rockefeller Brothers Fund, *The Pursuit of Excellence* (New York, Doubleday, 1958).

Shaw, Frederick S., "Educating Culturally Deprived Youth in Urban Centers," *Phi Delta Kappan,* Vol. 45, No. 2 (November, 1963), pp. 91–97.

Spindler, George D., *Education and Culture: Anthropological Approaches* (New York, Holt, Rinehart and Winston, 1963).

United States Office of Education, *Progress of Public Education in the United States of America,* 1963–1964 (Washington, D.C., 1964).

2

The Road We Have Traveled

PREVIEW

▶ Social institutions in the New World were strongly influenced by those of the "Old Countries."
The apprentice system was an important phase of early education, both in England and the colonies.

▶ Regional differences in attitudes toward education were the result of religious thinking, topography, distance, and social background. Early elementary schools were largely parochial in nature or partially or wholly supported by local governments, while some were entirely private.

▶ Highlights in the development of secondary education were: the Latin Grammar Schools, the Academies, and the English Classical High Schools.

▶ Early higher education was strongly influenced by European antecedents, with Harvard College founded in 1636 as the first in the colonies.
Higher education for women followed approximately 200 years after the establishment of the first college for men.

▶ The professional education of teachers had its real beginning in the first half of the nineteenth century.

When the emigrants from Europe came to the shores of the New World, they brought with them certain ideas and ideals to which they had aspired in the Old and which they had been denied because of poverty, religion, and other factors. Yet they were all, in varying degrees, products of the environment in which they had lived. This no one can escape completely, nor does one generally wish to do so.

Consequently, man's ideas regarding forms of government in general and social institutions in particular are transplanted. If a primary unit for government in the country from whence he came was the county, the easy and natural thing to do is to use the *county* in the new land. So it happened in America. Very often, indeed, actual names were transferred. Whether there was an element of nostalgia in this matters not. It was a common practice, and it was true of almost every country from which the colonists came.

What more natural thing, therefore, could be expected than the transplanting of the schools as they knew them in the homeland? They were set up with the limitations imposed by the frontier, of course, but they were largely transplants nonetheless.

THE APPRENTICESHIP SYSTEM

The system of training through apprenticeship was firmly established in England for a considerable period before the migration to North America began. At the time of the American Revolution it was still strong and was to continue so for a long time thereafter.

In the apprenticeship system, a youth was bound to a master for a specific term of years, usually seven, the period ending when the boy was 21 or the girl 18. This generally meant that a boy began his period of service at 14, although there were some variations for different occupations. The apprentice served without wage in the home of his master, learning the trade or craft and performing all the duties of a household servant in many cases. The youth was completely responsible to his master, who was obligated to furnish him with board and clothing and to give him such training in the trade as would make him a competent and independent workman when his period of service was completed.

Since many or most of these apprentices were children of the poor, it was not likely that they had any but the most meager literary education. An ancestor of one of the authors reports in his autobiography that he had but three terms of elementary education in a charity school in Warwickshire. Possibly this was more than usual for boys from a low economic status, since it was thought that this youth was too sickly to earn a living by manual work. It should be noted, however, that the children of the wealthy, whose parents were able to give them a literary education at their own expense, were not a part of this system.

So it was natural that this apprenticeship system should find a place in the colonies and continue in varying forms for generations. Monroe [1]

---

[1] Paul Monroe, *Founding of the American Educational System* (New York, Macmillan, 1940), p. 35.

points out that the indentured servants for the New World came from a variety of sources, largely poverty-stricken groups who saw opportunity abroad and certain ones who were politically oppressed. It might be added, too, that the simply restless young people also came in significant numbers. Monroe [2] specifically states: "Very few laborers of any standing came except under indenture. This was the customary way of paying for ocean passage." Even a schoolmaster occasionally sold himself into servitude in order to pay for his transportation to America. The aforementioned ancestor of the author came in this manner, although he had no idea of becoming a teacher until many years later.

Many of those who came as indentured servants were children whose services were sold until the indenture had been paid. In the course of time there developed a concern for the education of these apprentices. Monroe [3] further points out that in 1646 in Virginia a law was passed requiring that a school be established for them, and in 1701 a requirement was added that the masters of orphans must teach them to read and write.

The apprenticeship system was widespread throughout the colonies, but the concern became general that with vocational training must go at least some instruction in reading and writing. Thus was laid the foundation for later and more specific laws looking toward education for all children.

In later years, especially during the late eighteenth and early nineteenth centuries, the apprenticeship system declined to a marked extent, and a great part of vocational training has now been taken over by the public schools. All formal programs of vocational training, however, still require that a specific part of the educational time be devoted to fundamental education.

REGIONAL DIFFERENCES IN EDUCATIONAL THINKING

Differences in educational thinking and acting in colonial America cannot be understood without a brief discussion of the social, religious, and political differences that were then existent.

In general, it is true that the first motives in education were primarily religious. The followers of Luther and Calvin held that all children should have an opportunity for sufficient education to be able to understand the Scriptures. They must be able to read the word of God. It was also held this could best be accomplished by a system of schools supported, at least in part, by the state, but controlled by the church. With this policy the Anglican Church did not agree. Here, as in England, the Episcopal Church aided in the establishment of many "charity" or

[2] *Ibid.,* p. 38.
[3] *Ibid.,* p. 42.

Pictured here is the interior of an early American school, showing master's desk, pupils' benches, and a list of subscribers who contributed money to the building.

church-supported schools, but would go little farther than that so far as fundamental education was concerned.

Thus it came about that in regions settled by the various German or Dutch Reformed groups, the basic idea of *public* education developed. Naturally, there were differences within groups, as is still evidenced by the refusal of the Amish to go beyond a certain level of schooling and by their general resistance to centralization. After all, had they not suffered in the homeland at the hands of the state and of the educated?

As a result of these major differences in background, and of other minor ones, three more or less distinct types of education developed: (1) the parochial type of the Middle Colonies; (2) the local-government-controlled type in New England, and (3) what Graves has called the laissez-faire system in the South. These will be treated briefly in turn.

The Middle Colonies

There have been claims made by many historians that the first permanent school in the American colonies was founded in 1633 at New Amsterdam by the Dutch. Others seem to think that there is little real evidence of a school there at that time. Be that as it may, the records are clear that a school was in existence as early as 1642 with one Adam Roelansen the first schoolmaster. This school, as were others that followed, was typical of the parochial system in the mother country. The master was selected by the church authorities, certified by them, and recommended to the civil authorities who usually made the appointment. The company, that is, the local government, had the burden of financial support. Monroe [4] observes; "This obligation seems to have been assumed as one of the functions of government."

It was in 1664 that the English first took over governmental authority from the Dutch. This was followed by a brief restoration of Dutch rule and by the final re-establishment of the English in 1674. After this date the latter refused to recognize any responsibility for support of the school or the Dutch church. Thus the schools became private, with the local government empowered to license the schoolmasters.

It should be pointed out here that a most effective organization for the promotion of education in this area of the New World was the well-established missionary group, the Society for the Propagation of the Gospel in Foreign Parts. An organization of the Church of England, many of its efforts were devoted to the establishment and support of schools, churches, and libraries. Generally the schools so established were charity schools, but it must be remembered that the Society was working under the auspices of the Church of England.

The colony of Pennsylvania furnishes an excellent illustration of

[4] *Ibid.,* p. 77.

the development of a parochial system with many facets. It was in 1638 that the Swedes first landed at what is now New Castle, Delaware, and through the years they spread out along the river and inland as well. There were minor groups of Dutch and English settlers, but the Swedes were far in the majority. In Sweden the schools were largely in the control of the church, supplemented by considerable home instruction, in part by itinerant teachers. Sweden was, indeed, a literate country.

It was too much to expect, however, that in this wilderness far from home any formal system of schools should be established. Distances were great, and the population was spread out thinly. Some effort was made to associate schools with the churches, and it was at New Castle in 1656 that one of the earliest colonial schoolmasters, Everet Peterson, served both in that capacity and as an official in the church.[5] Home instruction was encouraged, and there was use made of the itinerant schoolmaster idea. This latter institution was not so novel, however, because in early America there were itinerant preachers, dentists, merchants, and others. The music teacher who comes to the home has not yet entirely disappeared from the scene.

In the end, however, the wilderness, lack of material for teaching, and lack of teachers themselves proved too much, so that when William Penn came in 1681 he found very little of anything remotely resembling a system of education. William Penn was a well-educated man. He has been described as an "executive and lawgiver" and expressed himself freely on the value of education. In his *Frame of Government* (1682), two sections illustrate his philosophy:

Twelfth: That the Governor and the Provincial Council shall erect and order all public schools. . . .

Twenty-eighth: That all children within this Province of the age of twelve years, shall be taught some useful trade or skill, to the end none may be idle, but the poor may work to live, and the rich, if they become poor, may not want.

In a farewell letter to his wife, he wrote:

For their learning be liberal. Spare no cost; for by such parsimony all is lost that is saved; but let it be useful knowledge, such as is consistent with truth and godliness, not cherishing a vain conversation or idle mind, but ingenuity mixed with industry is good for the body and mind too. I recommend the useful parts of mathematics, as building houses or ships, measuring, dialling, navigation; but agriculture is especially in my eye; let my children be husbandmen and housewives; it is industrious, healthy, honest, and of good example.[6]

Surely this is a broad and practical concept of education.

[5] James P. Wickersham, *History of Education in Pennsylvania* (Lancaster, Pa., Inquirer Publishing Co., 1886), p. 9.

[6] James Mulhern, *History of Secondary Education in Pennsylvania* (The Author, Philadelphia, 1933), p. 25.

An examination of the early laws of the Province of Pennsylvania indicates that the establishment of schools under public authority was contemplated.[7] Among other things, parents, guardians, and overseers were required to teach their children and those under their care to read and write, and it is a matter of record that penalties were assessed against those who failed to do so. No system of public schools as we know it was actually established in the early days, however, but a few schools under public direction were supported on a tuition basis.

Generally it was the Quaker "church" or meeting which fostered the school, establishing it and to some extent supporting it. The first such school in the Province appears to have been the "Friends' Public School" in Philadelphia (1689), known until this day as the "William Penn Charter School." In very many instances the school was built adjacent to the Meeting House, just "across the road," or not far away. Early ones were of logs; more permanent ones were of stone. Not a few were octa-

Early octagonal school in Pennsylvania about 1812 operated chiefly by the Friends or Quakers. The church or Meeting House was just across the road.

[7] Wickersham, *op. cit.*, pp. 38–39.

gonal in shape, a type of building apparently copied from England. Some of these persisted until well into the nineteenth century.

Other religious groups, of which there were many in Pennsylvania because of Penn's invitation to come and find the religious freedom which they were seeking, built schools of their own, generally by public subscription. Religious groups other than the Quakers most active in fostering education were the Lutherans, Moravians, and Mennonites. Many great colonial schoolmasters were those brought over by these churches. The schools were maintained largely on a rate or tuition basis, although a great deal of charity work appears to have been done. The law of 1809, sometimes called the "Pauper School Act," provided that the "poor should be taught gratis" with their tuition paid by the county. In part, it was dissatisfaction with the results of this Act that helped to bring about the Free School Act of 1834.

In New Jersey conditions and influences were generally similar to those in New York and in some areas resembled the Pennsylvania plans. Delaware was not radically different, being occupied by similar nationalistic groups. Private schools of various types flourished throughout the Middle Colonies, but the dominant pattern was still very largely parochial.

New England

Although it was true that the settlers in Massachusetts came for basic religious freedom, it was a freedom that too often they refused to extend to others. Partly as a result of this and partly from other causes, there was much greater homogeneity among those colonists than elsewhere. In Massachusetts, New Hampshire, Rhode Island, and Connecticut the people chose free, public, and government-supported schools.

In 1642 an act was passed in Massachusetts which, while it did not mention schools, clearly placed upon parents the responsibility for seeing that their children received the benefits of apprenticeship training and fundamental education that would enable them to understand the many capital laws of the colony. Penalties were provided for parents who neglected their duty in this matter. Here is at least the germ of later public education, although no schools were actually set up as a result of the law.

The famous law of 1647 was quite another story, however. Applying to both elementary and secondary education, it reflected the religious feeling of the time and clearly placed the responsibility for establishing schools upon the civil authorities of the local government, the "town." The New England town, which still stands unique as an efficient institution of democratic government, is usually made up of a small urban area or village and the rural area surrounding it. It has long been considered as the true community unit for school administration.

The law of 1647, known as the "Old Deluder Act," when put into modern English, reads:

. . . It being one chief project of the old deluder, Satan, to keep men from the knowledge of the Scriptures, as in former times by keeping them in an unknown tongue, so in these latter times by persuading from the use of tongues, that so at least the true sense and meaning of the original might be clouded by false glosses of saint seeming deceivers, that learning may not be buried in the grave of our fathers in the church and commonwealth, the Lord assisting our endeavors.

It is therefore ordered that every township in this jurisdiction, after the Lord hath increased them to the number of fifty householders, shall then forthwith appoint one within their town to teach all such children as shall resort to him to write and read, whose wages shall be paid either by the parents or masters of such children, or by the inhabitants in general, by way of supply, as the major part of those that order the prudentials of the town shall appoint; provided, those that send their children be not oppressed by paying much more than they can have them taught for in other towns; and it is further ordered, that where any town shall increase to the number of one hundred families or householders, they shall set up a grammar school, the master thereof being able to instruct youth so far as they shall be fitted for the university . . .[8]

The Act also provided that fines were to be assessed against those communities that failed to comply with the law, but for practical reasons the penalty was not effective. Compulsory attendance was not provided for and was not really required until 1852.

Early school buildings were, as might be expected, crude and in the simple architecture of the day. One interesting institution that was first set up in Connecticut in 1651 was known as the "dame school." Here a woman who may have had a little more education than was general, and probably not too many children of her own, received and taught the fundamentals to the children of other parents who would send them to her, at the same time trying to get her own housework done. Finney [9] states that these schools were frequently taught by "elderly women in straitened circumstances." Whereas some have described them as a sort of "glorified baby-sitting," they were characteristic of the colonial period and filled a real purpose for the education of the very young.

The South

It should be noted, first of all, that the great majority of those who settled in the southern colonies came primarily out of the desire to

8 Massachusetts (Colony), *Records of the Governor and Company of the Massachusetts Bay in New England,* Vol. II, p. 203.

9 R. L. Finney, *The American Public School* (New York, Macmillan, 1921), pp. 9–10.

better themselves economically and socially within the existing order of things. They were very seldom prompted by the spirit of reform or by the desire for religious freedom.

Early in the history of the South a type of agriculture developed that called for large farms or plantations. Since tobacco was at first the main crop, either fertilizer in large quantities or virgin soil had to be used for successive crops. It was the latter plan that was adopted. Large landholdings resulted in a widely scattered rural population and made necessary the recruiting of a large number of persons to work the estates. Consequently, there was gradually produced a sort of landed aristocracy and a large laboring or servant class, but no very significant middle class. These factors quite naturally had far-reaching results upon the growth of any type of organized education.

Some idea of early conditions in Virginia may be gained by the oft-quoted reply of Governor Berkley in 1671 as he answered certain questions submitted to him by the home government. In his reply to the question, "What course is taken about instructing the people within your government in the Christian religion?" he wrote:

The same course that is taken in England out of towns, every man according to his ability instructing his children. . . . But I thank God there are no free schools or printing, and I hope we shall not have them these hundred years, for learning has brought disobedience and heresy into the world and printing has divulged them and libels against the best government. God keep us from both.[10]

Monroe suggests that the first part of the reply is the most significant and that in general it was the English method of instruction at home that was transplanted. Actually, there probably were a few "free schools" in the colony at that time. Some private dame schools developed and here and there considerable tutorial education existed. Small school buildings were built on some estates and remain as points of interest today, as at Mount Vernon, Washington's home. No real "public" school, as such, was known for some time. Education was generally regarded as a special privilege, with charity or pauper schools not uncommon.

It must be noted, on the other hand, that from quite early times there was great interest in higher education, and in 1692 the College of William and Mary was established. In 1749 Washington College was founded. Here, after the Civil War, General Robert E. Lee became president and served with great distinction. The name was later changed to Washington and Lee University. The University of Virginia at Charlottesville had some of its buildings designed by Thomas Jefferson.

A few secondary schools were gradually founded, but many children of the aristocracy were sent either to England or to the North for their preparation for college or university.

Although so-called "free schools" increased in number as time went

10 Monroe, *op. cit.*, p. 53.

on, education continued to be regarded as a privilege, with the English "selective" idea predominating.

SECONDARY EDUCATION

In tracing very briefly the development of what is now American secondary education, three institutions stand out upon the ancestral tree. They are, in the order of their appearance: (1) the Latin Grammar School, (2) the Academy, and (3) the English Classical High School.

The Latin Grammar School

It is rather difficult to believe that it was just 15 years after the Pilgrims had landed upon the stern New England coast that they saw fit to establish what was clearly the first secondary school in the colonies, the Boston Latin Grammar School, which has existed to the present day. Many leaders in the Massachusetts Colony and elsewhere had been educated in the grammar schools of England, and the schools in the New World were modeled after them. Similar schools were organized in the other colonies, and nearly always the dominant purpose was preparation for college, although sometimes the colleges were not yet in existence. In this way the schools were an important step in preparation for the ministry. Their courses generally consisted of the study of much Latin, a reading of the classics, the New Testament, and grammar. A cogent and much criticized article in a popular magazine has described in glowing terms the "formal discipline" aspect of the Boston Latin School as it exists today.[11]

There were early Latin Schools in many other New England towns, as the law of 1647 required. They are found early (1697) in Pennsylvania. In New Jersey they appeared nearly 50 years later. The first grammar school in the South was founded in 1693 in connection with William and Mary College. In the early part or near the middle of the eighteenth century they appeared in Maryland and in certain other of the colonies. A few of these schools were supported entirely by taxation; more often partly by taxation and partly by tuition. It is likely that some were maintained entirely by tuition or by tuition combined with certain special funds.

Teachers in the Latin schools were generally men of character and ability, and they were held in high esteem by their fellow citizens. Many eminent men, Ezekiel Cheever, for example, are represented in the long roll of their teachers. However, not all were of the highest quality. A certain number, as might be expected, were more or less migratory, un-

[11] Howard Witman, "Our Schools—Afraid to Teach," *Collier's* (March 19, 1954), pp. 34–35.

stable personalities of somewhat questionable character. Every age seems to have its quota of such undesirables.

The Academy

It was not many years before there was a serious questioning of the value of the classical curriculum in a country and society so different from the homeland. Some schools failed because of lack of students and for financial reasons. After reaching a peak about 1700, the Latin Schools began to be less popular as the demand grew for a more useful type of education. Within the next 100 years nearly all of them had disappeared.

Near the middle of the eighteenth century in Philadelphia, Benjamin Franklin, already an influential citizen, began agitating for a different type of school. His ideas were set forth in his "Proposals Relating to the Education of Youth in Pennsylvania." He wrote of the "Education of Youth" as being "esteemed by wise men in all ages as the surest Foundation of Happiness both of private Families and the Commonwealths." He suggested that public-spirited people apply for a charter to form an Academy. His reasons may be summarized as follows:

1. It is better that children be educated at home and better facilities should be provided here than abroad.
2. The state needed intelligent public officers and native-born citizens should be educated for this purpose.
3. Good school teachers must be prepared at once.
4. A good school is a profitable institution.

He proposed a broad and practical curriculum that he felt would enable the school to accomplish its purposes. The school would be well equipped with maps, apparatus, and other necessary material. There would be physical exercises; there was to be emphasis upon written and spoken English; reading "was to be made serviceable"; the natural sciences were to be taught along with gardening and agriculture. Those who wished to study languages and the classics were to be given the opportunity.

Franklin's arguments and publicity must have been highly effective, because after only a few years the Academy was founded in Philadelphia in 1751, having received a cash grant of £200 from the City Council with a further promise of £50 per year for five years and an additional £50 for the right of sending one scholar each year from the Charity School to the Academy.

The school really began as three schools: one of Latin, one of English, and one of Mathematics. Children of the poor were taught gratis in a Charity School under the same management. Actually, the curriculum never did become as practical as Franklin had hoped, although the institution prospered greatly and in 1755 became a college, with a later development into the University of Pennsylvania.

The idea of the academy seemed to appeal strongly to people else-where, and very shortly it appeared in Massachusetts, prominent early ones being the Phillips Academies at Andover and at Exeter. Elsewhere, particularly in the Middle and New England colonies, the new schools spread like wildfire into every state. It is said that "by 1850 there were more than 6,000 academies with over a quarter of a million students." During the second quarter of that century they were almost exclusively the secondary schools of America. Wickersham points out that in Pennsyl-vania some counties had a score or more of academies within their borders. Some were entirely private; some received grants of money from the state. Some were for boys only; some were for young ladies only; others were co-educational. A number grew into colleges and normal schools; others simply closed for financial reasons. In a great many in-stances the academy property was taken over by the public school board for conversion into a high school. Soon after the middle of the century the academy had drifted away to some extent from its original practical purpose, but it is difficult to think of any other type of school which left so lasting an impression upon the life of a people.

The High School

As the years passed it began to be clearly seen that the acad-emy was not the ultimate institution for the new democracy, primarily for the following reasons:

1. It was not making secondary education available for all youth.
2. The curriculum was not practical enough to meet the changing times.
3. It was necessary for too many children to leave their homes and board at or near the academy they wished to attend.
4. It was not really an extension of the public school system but rather something separate from it.

Largely as the result of a desire to meet these shortcomings, the third ancestor of the modern American secondary school was established in Boston in 1821 and named the English Classical High School. According to Brubacher, the new institution had two notable additional functions, to furnish secondary education "(1) at public expense and (2) as the normal upward extension and completion of common school educa-tion." [12] It was not a school for boys who were going to college. Its chief purpose was described as "to fit them for active life or qualify them for eminence in private or public station." The word *classical* was shortly dropped, and it became just the *high school*. Then in 1826 a high school for girls was set up in the same city.

[12] John S. Brubacher, *A History of the Problems of Education* (New York, McGraw-Hill, 1947), p. 433.

The new institutions seemed immensely popular where they were established, yet they did not spread very rapidly for a good while. There was some opposition by the friends of the academy, but there was even greater opposition by those who felt that the high schools of America should not be tax-supported and free education thus provided for all. It was in Kalamazoo, Michigan, that the test case finally came, to reach ultimately the Supreme Court of that state in 1872. The historical and oft-quoted decision of Justice Cooley was that the Court did not "find the primary school districts restricted in the branches of knowledge which their officers may cause to be taught, or the grade of instruction that may be given, if their voters consent in regular form to bear the expense and raise the taxes for the purpose." So, "common schools" meant high school as well as elementary schools, and a great victory was won for free public education.

Shortly, the high schools began to grow with great rapidity. In the latter part of the nineteenth century, most high schools were offering two courses: one preparing for college and the other "preparing for life." Commercial courses were added as the century came to a close. It became clear, however, as the years were passing, that the function of college preparation was becoming a controlling factor. The colleges through their entrance requirements, it was alleged, were dominating the entire high school program.

Public and professional concern resulted in a serious study of the problem, and a number of committees were appointed to investigate. The Committee of Ten, a nation-wide committee, began its work as early as 1893, with a number of others following at intervals. Probably the most important was the Committee on the Reorganization of Secondary Education, which reported in 1918. Its recommended objectives for the American high school and its recommendations in many areas turned the course of secondary education and have been strongly influential ever since, even though further studies and reports have been highly significant.

An important change in the organization of secondary education appeared about 1910 when the first junior high schools were established in California. Primarily to meet the needs of adolescents more effectively and to reduce the excessive dropping out of pupils, the high school was extended downward.

The junior high school took a variety of forms. Changing from the original 8–4 plan, the most common was a 6–3–3 or a 6–6 organization; sometimes it was 7–5 or 6–2–4, as local needs and thinking seemed to determine.

Neither public nor private secondary education in the United States can be said to be of one type only. In a large country it must be varied, and it must change to meet changing needs. A high school education is

accepted in this country as almost a necessity as is shown by an enrollment that has doubled every decade from 1890. At present there are over
10½ million youth in our secondary schools.

HIGHER EDUCATION

In their thinking about higher education in America, the
colonists were strongly motivated by European attitudes and experiences.
The religious purposes of the older universities were strong in their
minds and were expressed quite definitely in their reasons for the founding of Harvard in 1636:

After God carried us safe to New England, and we had builded our houses,
provided necessaries for our livelihood, rear'd convenient places for God's worship, and settled the Civil Government: One of the next things we longed for,
and looked after was to advance Learning and perpetuate it to Posterity; dread-
ing to leave an illiterate Ministry to the Churches when our present Ministers
shall lie in the Dust.[12]

Although Harvard was established very early in the experience of
the colonists, it must be noted that it was not the first on the North
American continent. The University of Mexico was founded at Mexico
City nearly a century earlier, in 1553.

The Charter of Harvard as expressed in 1650 shows a fairly broad set
of purposes as follows:

The advancement of all good literature, arts and sciences.
The advancement and education of youth in all manner of good literature, arts
    and sciences.
All other necessary provisions that may conduce to the education of the English
    and Indian youth of this country in knowledge and godliness.

It was not until 1692 that the second college in the colonies was
started at Williamsburg, Virginia, as the College of William and Mary.
An original building of the college is still preserved as a most interesting
bit of Colonial architecture. Other colleges existing at present were
established in the following order: Yale (1701), Princeton (1746), Pennsylvania (1751), Columbia (1754), Rutgers (1766), Dartmouth (1769). All
of the above, except Pennsylvania, were sectarian in their support and
maintenance.

While the curricula of the earliest colleges were rather specifically
directed toward the preparation of young men for the ministry, it soon
became apparent that much more would be necessary. So it was that, just
as with the secondary schools, new curricula had to be added. Leaders
were vitally needed for the growing democracy; there were demands for

[12] Inscription on the west gate at Harvard.

doctors and lawyers and shortly for a number of other professional and technical leaders too.

At the time of the Civil War there were approximately 200 colleges in existence, but the war itself brought a temporary end to the expansion. Student bodies, particularly in the South, were decimated and property deteriorated rapidly. Even in some sections of the North this was also true to a very considerable extent. However, with the gradual recovery of the postwar period, expansion began anew, and by 1900 there were about 500 colleges in operation.

State Universities

The feeling that the work of the colleges should be more practical resulted in several more or less abortive attempts to change them into state institutions. A court case resulted when the state legislature in New Hampshire proposed to take such action at Dartmouth. The precedent-making decision of the United States Supreme Court in 1819 prevented the legislature from "altering the charter without the consent of the corporation." Nevertheless, this movement toward having state institutions that were more practical in nature did result in their establishment in a good many of the states, primarily those in the South and the new commonwealths that were being organized. Among those set up were North Carolina (1795), Georgia (1800), Ohio (1804), South Carolina (1805), Tennessee (1807), Indiana (1824), and Virginia (1825). Others were established in the states that were formed as the new nation pushed westward.

Professional Education

In addition to those providing theological training, professional schools or departments began to arise either independently or as a part of a college or university. At the University of Pennsylvania in 1765 the first school of medicine was established. Others followed shortly thereafter. The first private law school was established at Litchfield, Connecticut, in 1784, and other schools soon came into being at the larger universities. Pharmacy and technical education appeared in succession.

The Land-Grant Colleges

In 1862 the Morrill Act was passed by Congress and later signed by President Lincoln. This legislation appropriated lands in every state to promote education in the mechanic arts, agriculture, and the natural sciences. These grants came to be very significant in size as they

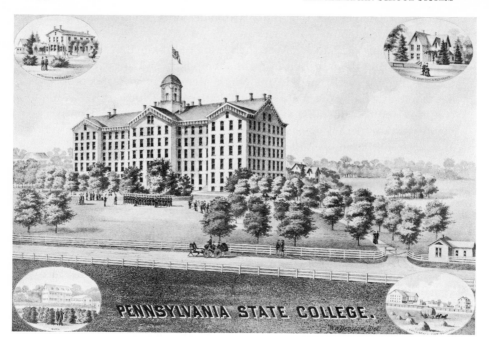

Courtesy: Department of Public Information,
The Pennsylvania State University.

An early engraving of Pennsylvania State College, now Pennsylvania State University. Chartered in 1855 along with Michigan State College, the two rank as the oldest of the Land Grant Colleges.

were supplemented from time to time. In about half of the states independent colleges were set up; in the remainder the funds were either used to expand the type of work mentioned above in existing state universities or used as a foundation for setting up new institutions. Most, if not all, of these have gone through periods of tremendous expansion, and the end surely is not yet in sight.

Higher Education of Women

It is sometimes forgotten that the early American colleges were originally for men only. In fact, higher education was considered to be for men only. Three distinguished women, Emma Willard, Catherine Beecher, and Mary Lyon, were influential in arguing that women could succeed in higher education as well as men. Mary Lyon founded Mt. Holyoke as a seminary in 1837, it becoming a college at a later date. Vassar, founded shortly after the Civil War, was the first women's college established as such.

Although the first colleges mentioned were exclusively for women, as many others were strictly for men, those in the western part of the country generally followed the pattern of co-education. Gradually women were admitted to more and more courses in the institutions that had not accepted them before, and the process is still continuing. Today all courses and professions are somewhere open to women.

TEACHER EDUCATION

Some special training for teachers was found in the medieval universities of the Old World but, as might be expected, in very early America it was entirely lacking. Colonial teachers came from several sources: (1) from the indentured servants, mentioned earlier; (2) from the clergy; and (3) from those who had had a considerable amount of education in Europe and who had been brought to this country specifically as teachers. A few of the early teachers in the colonies were held in high esteem and were quite competent, but lacking adequate preparation, the performance of all too many was at a low level. Teaching was either a part-time occupation or was a mere steppingstone to some profession. Washington Irving's caricature of the early American teacher was based on more than a fertile imagination.

It is not unusual, therefore, that we find a very considerable group of leaders who strongly urged that specific efforts be made to improve a situation that had deteriorated almost beyond endurance. Two early thinkers—Olmstead speaking at Yale in 1812, and later, a Yale man, Kingsley, urged that some specific intermediate institution be set up to do the job. Actually, Philadelphia established a "model school for the training of teachers" in 1818. Brubacher [13] states that this school was specifically set up, however, to prepare teachers for Monitorial Schools. These were institutions following a plan developed in England by Joseph Lancaster and brought over at the beginning of the century. In them, large numbers of children were taught by older pupils or monitors who had been instructed by the teacher in charge. For several decades they were common in both elementary and secondary education. Then, having served a real purpose, they and their highly formalized education passed from the scene.

It is true, of course, that many who wished to be teachers found their education in the academies. In fact, this was one of the purposes Franklin had in mind for them; however, this education was academic and in no sense professional. Thus, the concern mounted that without a specialized type of training, teaching would further decline.

In 1823 Samuel Hall set up a private seminary for teachers at Concord, Vermont. This made little contribution to the need, and the school lasted a relatively few years.

[13] Brubacher, *op. cit.,* p. 507.

Massachusetts was a leader in the movement for better teachers, as it had been in other educational areas. There the agitation grew, led by such men as Charles Brooks, Henry Dwight, Calvin Stowe, and by James Carter and the great Horace Mann (1796–1859). Mann had been appointed secretary to the Massachusetts State Board of Education and, with his brilliant oratory, campaigned most actively for better schools and better teachers. Finally, as a result of legislative enactment and some private contributions, the first state normal school was established at Lexington, Massachusetts, with Cyrus W. Pierce as its head. Later it moved to West Newton and to Framingham which became its permanent home.

Other state normal schools were established in Barre (1839), at Westfield (1844), at Bridgewater (1840), all in Massachusetts, and at Albany, New York, in 1844. These were followed by those in Connecticut, in Michigan, and in other states, so that the normal-school movement was firmly established. Lengths of the courses varied widely; some were private, some were state-aided, and some were publicly supported. In Pennsylvania private summer normal schools were not uncommon. There, as in other states, state-aided normal schools were finally purchased and operated as full "state normal schools." Rising standards for teachers caused the training period to be lengthened until many of them, the country over, became full four-year degree-granting institutions. At present a considerable number are offering work leading to the master's degree.

In addition to the normal schools, a great many colleges and universities added courses in preparation for teaching which have developed into the famous teachers colleges of today. A large number of these offer graduate work leading to the master's and doctor's degree, and no small number of their staffs render great service to school districts. Summer schools and correspondence courses have played their part in the developing program of teacher education.

We must not close this brief account without paying tribute to the work that has been done in training teachers-in-service by county and district superintendents and their staffs. Theirs has been the function of providing leadership in all phases of education, in certifying teachers as to their fitness, of trying to help them to improve by direct supervision, by teachers' meetings and other devices. The county officers especially, whose services were generally provided around the middle of the last century, sought out prospective teachers, examined them as to their probable ability, certified them, and usually tried to help them in their classrooms. Not the least important of teacher-training aids was the "institute," still adhered to in modified form in many areas. There, all the teachers in a county or city would be brought together for a week for inspiration, morale building, and instruction "in the art of teaching." Many of the famous educators in America thus made their influence felt upon the schools of the country. Now the lengthened periods of preparation, the summer schools, great conventions, conferences, workshops, and the like have caused the "institutes," as they were once known, to disappear. They form a significant landmark, however, on the road we have traveled.

QUESTIONS AND PROJECTS

1. Interview a labor leader or skilled craftsman, and find out the place of the apprenticeship system in the training of the modern worker. Report to the class on your findings.
2. Investigate in detail the Dame and Lancastrian or Monitorial Schools, and explain their contributions to American education. Secure, if possible, some early woodcuts or illustrations of these schools, and project them on the screen for the class, using the opaque projector.
3. Visit one or more historic old school buildings still standing in your community.
4. Study the development of the county superintendency in your state.
5. Appraise the contributions of the church or denominational college in America.
6. Why do so many colleges in the United States fear federal subsidies as an aid in their present financial distress? Do they not face the same dangers in accepting grants from business?

AUDIO-VISUAL AIDS

MOTION PICTURES (16 MM)

Design of American Education—McGraw-Hill Book Co., Text Film Dept., 330 West 42nd St., New York, N.Y., 16 min., sd., b&w. Explains the organization of the American democratic school system as opposed to an autocratic system; presents a philosophy of education which strives to develop responsible citizens in our democratic society.

Education in America: Seventeenth and Eighteenth Centuries—Coronet Film, 488 Madison Ave., New York, N.Y., 16 min., sd., b&w or color. Gives historical background to the early developments in American education—in New England, the South, and the Middle Colonies. Relates the character of the different schools—dame, latin grammar, private, parochial, pauper, academy and college—to prevailing social, economic, and cultural conditions.

Education in America: The Nineteenth Century—Coronet Film, 488 Madison Ave., New York, N.Y., 16 min., sd., b&w or color. Describes significant historical developments and the changing character of American education in the nineteenth century. Points out contributing factors of change, such as the establishment of the first high school, problems growing out of the Civil War, the teachings of Horace Mann, compulsory laws, the trend toward uniformity under state regulations, and the beginnings of teacher-training schools.

Education in America: Twentieth-Century Developments—Coronet Film, 488 Madison Ave., New York, N.Y., 16 min., sd., b&w or color. Reviews significant developments in American education in the twentieth century and relates these developments to the social, economic, and cultural life of the nation. Considers the influences of outstanding educators, educational theories and movements, and major trends and problems.

Philosophies of Education: Education as Intellectual Discipline—NET, Indiana
U., A-V Center, Bloomington, Ind., 29 min., sd., b&w. Comments on the importance of a disciplined mind and outlines the methods of obtaining intellectual discipline in a democratic society. Answers objections and comments
on a filmed illustration. Featured personality is Arthur Bestor, professor of
history at the University of Illinois.

Bill of Rights of the United States—Encyclopaedia Britannica Films, 20 min.,
sd., b&w. Explains the principles of the Bill of Rights and shows how the
English curbed civil liberties demanded by the Puritans. Presents a court case
in early American history involving freedom of the press and pictures events
leading up to the signing of the federal constitution and the drafting of the
amendments which became the Bill of Rights.

FILMSTRIP

Education in America—Museum Extension Service, 10 East 43rd St., New York
17, N.Y., 38 fr., si., color. An excellent presentation of many of the landmarks
discussed in this chapter. Valuable either as a summary or as an introductory
feature.

FURTHER READINGS

Butts, R. Freeman, *A Cultural History of Education* (New York, McGraw-Hill,
1947).

Cubberley, Ellwood P., *Public Education in the United States* (Boston, Houghton
Mifflin, 1934).

Douglass, Aubrey A., *The American School System* (New York, Farrar and Rinehart, 1940).

Eby, Fred, *The Design of Modern Education*, 2nd ed. (Englewood Cliffs, N.J.,
Prentice-Hall, 1952).

Edwards, Newton, and Herman G. Richey, *The School in the American Social
Order* (Boston, Houghton Mifflin, 1947).

Elsbree Willard S., *The American Teacher* (New York, American Book, 1939).

Graves, Frank P., *A Student's History of Education*, rev. ed. (New York, Macmillan, 1936).

Harper, Charles A., *A Century of Public Teacher Education* (Washington, D.C.,
NEA, 1939).

Knight, Edgar W., *Education in the United States*, 2nd rev. ed. (New York,
Ginn, 1941).

Krug, Edward A., *The Shaping of the American High School* (New York, Harper
& Row, 1964).

Mayer, Frederick, *American Ideas and Education* (Columbus, Ohio, Merrill,
1964).

Mulhern, James, *A History of Education*, 2nd ed. (New York, Ronald, 1959).

Noble, Stuart G., *History of American Education* (New York, Farrar and Rinehart, 1938).

Sizer, Theodore R., ed., *The Age of the Academies* (New York, Bureau of Publications, Teachers College, Columbia University, 1964).

3

The Organization
of Public Education

PREVIEW

▸ Although considering education a state function, the federal government has many times given it strong financial support.

▸ The courts have decided that legally the states have nearly full control over the educational policies within their own borders, being limited only by the federal Constitution.

▸ While the county is used as a strong unit for educational support and control in twelve states, most states use the city, township, or borough, or the still smaller individual school districts.

▸ The vertical organization of the schools reveals a wide diversity of practice.
1. The elementary school may begin with the nursery school or kindergarten and continue to include grades 6, 7, or 8.
2. The secondary school, generally covering grades 7 to 12, may be organized as separate junior and senior high schools, as a combined unit, or as a specialized school.
3. The junior college, covering grades 13 and 14, has had a rapid growth. It is sometimes a regular part of the secondary school but more often it is a separate unit, supported either publicly or privately, or some combination thereof.
4. Higher education in the college and graduate or professional school faces many serious problems in the years ahead.
5. Adult education, either public or private, is serving a definite need and is experiencing phenomenal growth.

ORGANIZATION IN TERMS OF THE UNIT OF CONTROL AND SUPPORT

Anyone who tries to describe the system of public education in English-speaking North America to a citizen of other countries soon becomes cognizant of the difficulties involved. This is true if one is speaking of the organization in the United States with its state by state variations or in Canada with the varying parts played by the central government and the provinces. Processes which on the surface seem relatively simple become tremendously complex when one attempts to clarify them. This task becomes even more complicated if one also considers nonpublic education. It has been described recently in an article in a metropolitan journal as follows; "American education is a vast sprawling enterprise without central direction or over-all organization." [1]

It is true that as a social organization moves from the simple to the complex so does the organization through which it educates its children. Growth and change are vital if education is to meet new needs and demands. In a very simple social order it may suffice to have the parents carry on the education of their children. However, such a method may become entirely untenable, and special individuals are entrusted with the task. These may be hired privately at first, but soon the social group—the church, village, and the like—will be responsible for education. Eventually special training is required for those who do the teaching, and an agency to control this training is needed. Thus the influence of the local governmental unit, such as the town, township, and later the state or the province (Canada), becomes necessary. As will be pointed out in more detail later, it was generally considered simplest to use as a unit the already existing local unit.

On this continent there has always been a deeply rooted desire to keep schooling as close to the people as possible. However, when it becomes impossible for the local unit to provide either the resources or the leadership needed in education, it is only natural to turn to the larger unit for assistance. New demands and the growing complexity of our needs are rapidly bringing about changes in our approach.

The Federal Government and Education

Those who take the time to examine the Constitution of the United States will find no mention therein of education. It is a result, however, of the Tenth Amendment in the Bill of Rights "package" that by implication education has come to be considered a function of the

---

[1] John W. Gardner, "Impact of Conant reforms felt across the country," *The New York Times* (Jan. 13, 1965), p. 79.

states individually. The Amendment reads as follows: "The powers not delegated to the United States, by the Constitution, nor prohibited by it to the States, are reserved to the States respectively, or to the people."

Why no specific mention was made in the Constitution has been the subject of much conjecture. It may be that some of those who framed the document did not think education of sufficient importance; it may be that a number intended it to be a private function or something to be conducted by the churches and similar groups. On the other hand, it may be that it was simply overlooked. A more likely answer is that those who were the leaders of the day feared that the inclusion of so controversial a matter might imperil ratification. Whatever the reason, by many legal decisions based on the Tenth Amendment, education has always been considered *primarily* a state function.

Ordinances of 1785 and 1787. In spite of these basic considerations, however, there is evidence that the Congress early felt a concern for giving education real encouragement. In the Ordinance of 1785, antedating the Constitution, provision was made for surveying the lands west of the Ohio River into townships six miles square. These were then subdivided into 36 sections, each one mile square. Evidence of this system can be noted by the traveler of today as he sees the farms laid out in this manner, with roads generally running straight across the landscape, turning at right angles when they do turn. The Ordinance further provided that: "There shall be reserved the lot No. 16 of every township for the maintenance of the public schools of the township."

The policies provided by the Ordinance of 1785 were put into effect by another passed in 1787 which laid down this important principle: "Religion, morality, and knowledge being necessary to good government and the happiness of mankind, schools and the means of education shall be forever encouraged." This same enactment authorized the Treasury to contract for the sale of lands to the Ohio Company, and it is from these pieces of legislation that the federal policy of reserving lands for educational use arose.

Much is sometimes made of the point that selfish interest motivated the actions described and that it was the need of the Continental Congress for money that brought the Ordinances into being rather than any real desire to aid education. To some extent this is true, but it is unfair to say that the other factors were not at work.

Swift observed in his *Federal Aid to Public Schools:*

The more important forces which originally influenced Congress in making reservations of school lands may be summarized as follows: (1) The precedents established by the American Colonies and by such a State as Georgia of reserving lands for schools in newly surveyed territory; (2) the need of selling the western lands; (3) the desire to make westward immigration attractive and (4) interest in the cause of education.

So significant was this act that it has been called "the endowment magnificent." As the years passed, however, the beneficent effect of the grants were reduced, in some cases by misuses of the monies received from the sale of the lands and in others by their use for current expenditures. In certain instances there are few records of what really happened to the money.

Other Federal Grants. However, precedent was established, and the record indicates a large and increasing number of financial grants to the states, frequently reaching down through the state governments to the local schools and school districts. A number were grants of land of various types or revenues from the sale thereof, as from the sale of "salt lands" (1796) and of "swamp lands" (1850). There was the distribution of "surplus revenues" in 1837, the money being used for schools in most states; a grant of a portion (25 percent) of the receipts from Federal Forest Reserves in states where the reserves existed (1908); and the Mineral Royalty Grants of 1920.

In speaking of the general uses of these federal grants Swift has further commented:

It is doubtful whether there is a single State in the Union which can point to an untarnished record. Despite all these facts, it is nevertheless true that, however badly managed, these permanent common school funds created out of Federal grants were the first stable sources of support given to free schools in more than half of the states.

In addition to the grants that have been mentioned, there is a growing list of federal activities in the educational field. Some of the more important ones may be noted:

The Morrill Act leading to the establishment of the Land Grant Colleges.
The education of the Indians.
Appropriations to the District of Columbia and territories.
The Smith-Lever Act (1914) providing federal aid to the states for promoting extension work in Agriculture and home economics.
The Smith-Hughes Act (1917) and subsequent acts providing federal aid for vocational work in the public schools.
The Civilian Conservation Corps.
The National Youth Administration.
Federal aid for school buildings as a result of the depression of the thirties.
Education of children of personnel on certain military reservations.
Aid to schools in critical defense areas.
Education of military and naval officers.
The establishment of the Air Force Academy (1954).
The federal school lunch programs.
Vocational Rehabilitation.
The G.I. Bill of Rights.
National Defense Education Act (1958).

Economic Opportunity Act (1964)
Higher Education Facilities Act (1965)
Elementary and Secondary Education Act (1965)

It would seem from this partial list that participation by the federal government in education is an accomplished fact. The question is seldom raised any longer as to the constitutionality of such action because it is admitted that justification is readily found in the so-called "general welfare" clause in the Preamble to the Constitution, which reads as follows:

We, the people of the United States, in order to form a more perfect Union, establish justice, insure domestic tranquility, provide for the common defence, promote the general welfare, and secure the blessings of liberty to ourselves and our posterity do ordain and establish this constitution for the United States of America.

Certainly it is clear that promotion of the "general welfare" includes the necessity of furthering public education. It is certain also that pressure for further participation in education by the federal government will be felt. The arguments for and against the greater use of federal funds will be presented at a later point.

The Federal Educational Agency. It was not until 1867 that there was any agency of the central government that had specific responsibility for education. Prior to this time, beginning with Horace Mann of Massachusetts, who led the public to an enlarged and revived thinking in regard to education, and with the assistance of Henry Barnard and others, there had been consideration given to the establishment of a national agency. The effects on education of the Civil War stimulated Congress to pass, and President Andrew Johnson to sign on March 2, 1867, the act creating a Federal Department of Education:

. . . for the purpose of collecting such statistics and facts as shall show the condition and progress of education in the several states and territories, and of diffusing such information respecting the organization and management of schools and school systems and methods of teaching as shall aid the people of the United States in the establishment and maintenance of efficient school systems, and otherwise promote the cause of education throughout the country.

The career of the Office has been a somewhat checkered one, and it was owing to some opposition from a few states that the title was changed from a "Department" to an "Office of Education," a subdivision of the Department of Interior. In 1870 it was changed to a "Bureau of Education" and so remained until 1929 when it reverted once again to an "Office of Education." In 1939 President Franklin D. Roosevelt moved the Office to the Federal Security Agency. In 1953 President Dwight Eisenhower created a Department of Health, Education, and Welfare, encompassing the former Office of Education. From the beginning the

Office has been headed by a Commissioner of Education appointed by the President and subject to Senatorial approval.

Although the duties and activities of the Office of Education have increased tremendously through the years, there has been no change in the three fundamental purposes:

1. To collect statistics and facts.
2. To diffuse information about schools.
3. Otherwise to promote the cause of education.

However, changing social and national and international needs have placed new obligations upon the federal government, and the Office of Education has had to grow to meet the demands made upon it. It is obvious that there is much latitude for growth in item 3 of the purposes above stated.

The programs of the Office as now carried out may be classified in six broad groups as follows:

1. The collection and analysis of statistics and facts.
2. The administration of grants.
3. Advice on school organization and administration.
4. Advice on methods of teaching.
5. Improvement of the teaching profession.
6. International relations in education.

The Office of Education employs a staff of approximately 2,000 persons who are regularly engaged in carrying out the programs mentioned. Requests for help and advice on a great variety of problems come in regularly, and replies of many sorts go back. Some are in the form of letters; some, telephone calls, and many as bulletins, pamphlets, and the like which are issued frequently. In addition, a new monthly magazine, *American Education,* is published by the Office. Many of the personnel serve frequently as consultants in surveys of building needs, studies of school district organization, and the like. They are also frequently found as speakers at important professional and lay meetings.

The financial grants administered by the Office are those to the states under the federal vocational acts and those to the land-grant colleges. As other federal aid is made a part of the national educational scene, it is almost inevitable that the monies will be allotted by the Office.

One of the newer services rendered by this division is the administration of the teacher exchange program between the United States and other countries. Assistance is also given in the broad student exchange program.

The publications of the Office are a rich library of information and inspiration as well. Some appear more or less regularly, as the *Biennial Survey of Education.* Others are published as the need arises and vary in

Figure 3-1. Organization of the United States Office of Education *

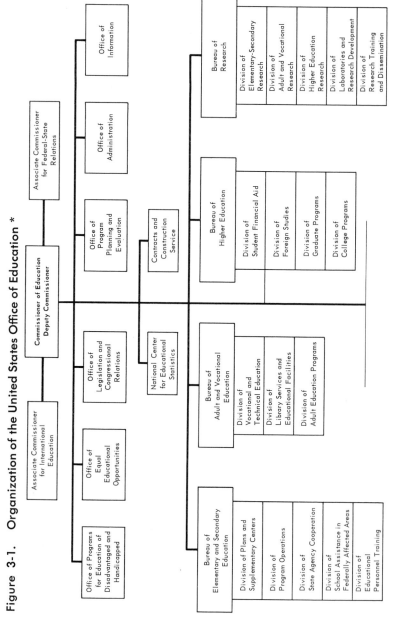

* Field: to be strengthened and placed under line control of chief OE official in each region.

46

form from mimeographed leaflets and circulars to large printed bulletins. A brief random sampling of the thousands of publications would include the following:

Radio and Television
Preparing Your Child for School
Offerings in Guidance Work in Colleges and Universities
Teaching as a Career
Life Adjustment Education for Every Youth
How Democratic Is Your School?
Evaluating Guidance Procedures
Motion Pictures on Democracy—a selected bibliography
Citizens Look at Education
Education of Negro Leaders
World Understanding Begins with Children
School Health Programs
The Education of Exceptional Children
Adult Education Activities
School Bus Maintenance
School and Work Programs
Education in China

Most of the small mimeographed publications may be secured from the Office itself, but printed ones should be ordered from the Superintendent of Documents, Government Printing Office, Washington 25, D.C. Although the publications are inexpensive, payment must be sent with the order, and stamps are not accepted. Partial lists of publications may be secured from the Superintendent of Documents. Other information as to new issues may be found in *American Education* and other periodicals.

These are but a few of the widespread and growing activities of the United States Office of Education, yet they will serve to give the student a fair idea of its functions and of its importance.

Education and the States

Since education, through the reasoning already shown, has been considered *primarily* a function of the individual states, it has seemed necessary in most cases to make constitutional provision there of, although this was not generally true in the earliest of such documents.

A few states made very early reference to education in their constitutions. Pennsylvania's Constitution of 1776 contained the following:

A school or schools shall be established in each county for the convenient instruction of youth at low prices, and all useful learning should be duly encouraged and promoted in one or more universities.

The revision of 1790 in the same state said:

The legislature shall, as soon as conveniently may be, provide for the establishment of schools throughout the State in such manner that the poor may be
taught gratis.

For lack of a time limit, this provision was more or less nominal and
nothing more than a loose statement of philosophy. A far more definite
mandate to the legislature, however, is found in the Pennsylvania Constitution of 1873 under which that state is now operating. Article X, section
1, reads as follows:

The General Assembly shall provide for the maintenance and support of a
thorough and efficient system of public schools wherein all children above the
age of six may be educated and shall appropriate at least one million dollars a
year for that purpose.

No state provides for the administration of its educational program
entirely by its constitution but rather through a growing body of enact-

Courtesy: The University of the State of
New York, The State Education Department.

State Education Building, Albany, New York.

ments by the legislature. In fact, it is widely recognized that constitutions should contain broad, general statements of policy likely to be more or less permanent. Details, on the other hand, that are more likely to be the subject of revision should be in legislative enactments or matters of policy delegated to boards or responsible officials.

Thus it has come about that the basis of state educational organization is, generally: (1) a state board or council of education; (2) a superintendent of education or official with some similar title; and (3) a department of education or public instruction.

The State Board of Education. The state board, sometimes called the State Council of Education, is generally a policy-making body of considerable importance. It serves, to some extent, the same purposes on the state level as the local school board does on the local level.

Forty-eight states have state boards of education, varying in membership from three in Mississippi to nineteen in Indiana. The remaining two states (Illinois and Wisconsin) have no state boards.[2]

Methods by which board members are chosen are:

1. Elected by people or representatives of people   12
2. Appointed by the governor   31
3. Ex officio, holding other state office at same time   4
4. Appointed by chief state school officer   1

Few require that the board members be professional educators, and if any general policy seems to exist at all, it is probably that of having appointees who are good citizens with a deep interest in education.

Boards for Vocational Education. The federal vocational education acts, which have been mentioned earlier and which provided for the distribution of funds to the states, required each of them to set up a state board to co-operate with the federal Board for Vocational Education. Each state complied with these laws and either designated the state board of education to serve as the board of vocational education as well or set up a separate organization for that purpose.

The Chief State School Officer. It has been well said that "in American education no position has greater potentialities for improving education in each of the states than that of the chief state school officer." These officers are provided for in all of the states, and their chief function is to furnish leadership for the educational program therein. They are designated by various titles. Thirty states use the appellation "superintendent of public instruction"; others use "commissioner of education," "superintendent of schools," or a similar title. The student will find the name of the official and his or her proper designation in the most recent edition of the *Educational Directory, Part I, State and County School Officers,* avail-

2 Robert F. Will, *State Education Structure and Organization,* Misc. No. 46 (Washington, D.C., U.S. Office of Education, 1964), pp. 15–18.

Figure 3-2. The University of the State of New York, The State Education Department

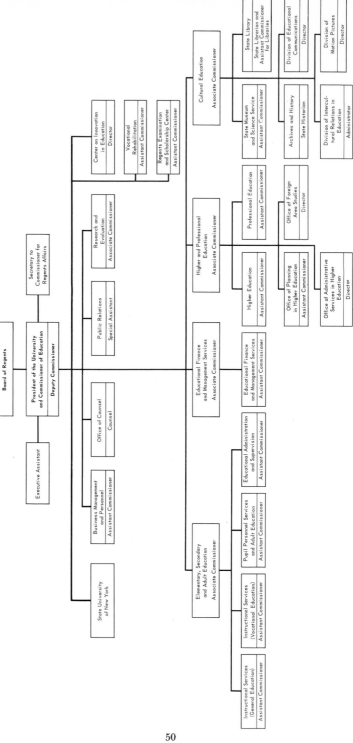

able in libraries and for sale from the Superintendent of Documents, Washington 25, D.C.

He is head of the staff of the state department of education and is either the executive officer, secretary, or a member of the state board of education in the states where such boards exist. Otherwise, he may be both policy-maker and administrator.

In twenty-two states, the chief school officer is elected by the people. In five states, including Alaska, he is appointed by the governor and in twenty-three states, including Hawaii, he is chosen by the state board of education.[3]

In view of the great possibilities for educational leadership, it is most important that the chief state school officer be a person of the highest qualifications, and most authorities are generally agreed that this is more likely to happen when the selection is made by the state board of educa-

Figure 3-3.   State of Alaska, Department of Education

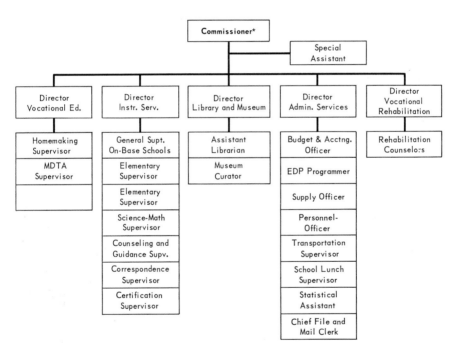

* Commissioner appointed by governor. State Board appointed by governor.

Reprinted by permission of Wm. T. Zahradnicek, Commissioner of Education.

   3 *Ibid.*

Figure 3-4. State of Florida, State Department of Education Organization (August, 1964)

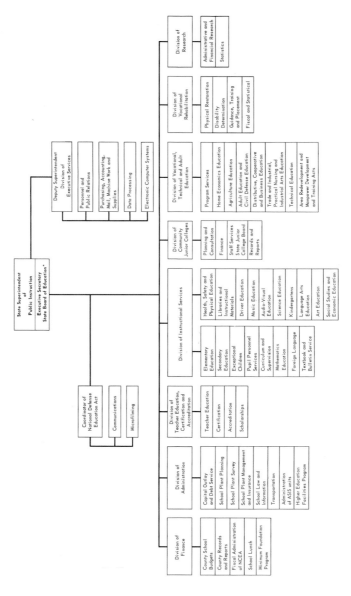

* Also serves as member of several commissions, boards and committees under cabinet system of state government. Superintendent elected by the people.

Reprinted by permission of J. K. Chapman, Deputy Superintendent.

Figure 3-5. Organization Chart, Nevada State Department of Education

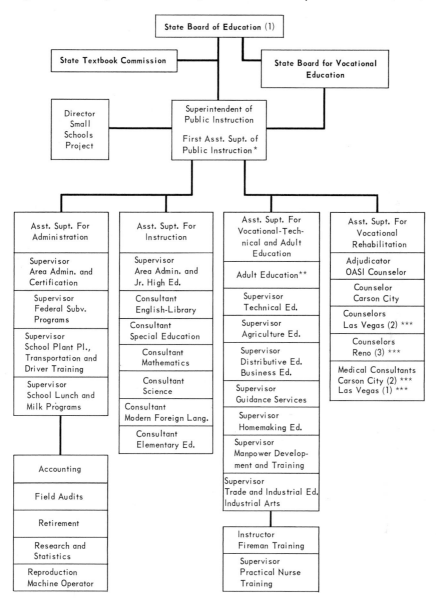

[1] State Board elected by people. State Superintendent appointed by State Board.
* Responsibility for Personnel & Publications is assigned to First Assistant Superintendent.
** Adult Education direction is performed by Asst. Supt. for Vocational-Technical Education.
*** Figures shown in circles represent number of employees of title in office.

Reprinted by permission of Byron F. Stetler, Superintendent of Public Instruction. February 1965.

tion for a rather long term. In this manner, too, the office is most likely to be divorced from politics. It almost goes without saying that the salary of the chief state school officer should be commensurate with the position, and such that it will command the services of the highest type of individual. Unfortunately, this has not been true in many of the states, the range in 1965 being from $9,000 per year in S. Dakota to $40,000 in New York.

State Departments of Education. Besides a state board of education and a chief state school officer, a third necessity for the proper administration of the educational program is a state department of education. The general organization of a state department of education varies greatly from state to state and is dependent upon such factors as: (1) the philosophy of the state board of education and the chief state school officer; (2) the amount of money available for salaries and expenses; (3) legislative enactments and mandates. No prevailing pattern of organization exists among the states.

If the full potentialities for service and leadership are to be realized by a state department of education, a sufficiently large and an especially competent staff must be available. This staff should be free of political pressures, and appointments should be on merit alone. This is not too often the case, and in very many states the salaries are too low to attract capable personnel. Dr. Conant [4] in summarizing his views on needed changes on the state level says: "What is needed are strong state boards of education, a first-class chief state school officer, a well-organized state staff, and good support from the legislature."

County and Local Units

The County. The next governmental unit in the United States, as far as size is concerned, is the county. It is an old unit, transplanted from England, and was generally in use before public schools were established. It was natural, therefore, in some states, that it came to be used more or less as a unit for the support and control of education. The extent of this control and support has varied considerably, much of the variation being due to the heterogeneity or homogeneity of the population. If there have been many different nationalistic and cultural groups in the population of the state, with a tendency to resist centralization, the county has occupied a weak position in the educational structure, as in Pennsylvania and in New England; if this has not been the case, the county has generally been stronger, as in Maryland.

There are those who argue that there is little need today for the county as a governmental unit; that this need was great when local units were small and transportation and communication poor, but that today

[4] James Bryant Conant, *Shaping Educational Policy* (New York, McGraw-Hill, 1964), p. 30.

Figure 3-6. Relationships of State, County, and Local Districts

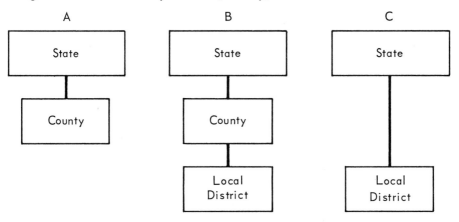

A—strong county unit state such as Maryland. See Chart.
B—state in which the county is an intermediate unit between the local district, which may be a township, town, borough, or city as in Pennsylvania and New Jersey.
C—state where the county is not used as an educational unit, as in New England. The local district may be the town, independent district, or variations thereof.

the state is able to carry on many functions of government far more efficiently. On the other hand, others point out that an intermediate unit such as the county is necessary because very many local units are still quite small and will continue to be so for a long time; that the county does tend to give the people more of a voice in their own government; and that it is, therefore an important link in the democratic process.

There are twelve states in which the county is the foremost or chief unit for educational administration below the state. They are:

Alabama	New Mexico
Florida	North Carolina
Georgia	Tennessee
Kentucky	Utah
Louisiana [5]	Virginia
Maryland	West Virginia

All states with a strong county unit of administration have a county superintendent of schools as the chief educational officer. A partial list of the powers and duties of a county board in a strong county unit state is shown by this list from a board in Maryland; it has the power and duty to:

Elect a county superintendent of schools, who serves as chief executive, secretary, and treasurer of the board.
Hold title of school property.

[5] The parish in Louisiana corresponds to the county in the other states.

Figure 3-7. Organization Chart, Board of Education of Washington County, Hagerstown, Maryland

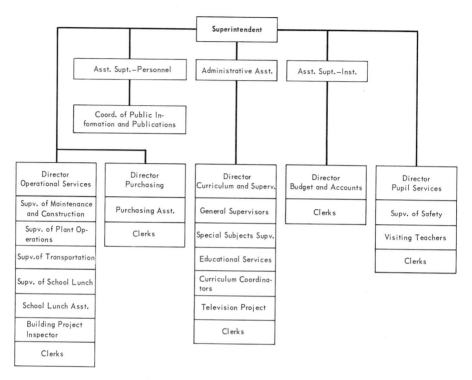

Reprinted by permission of County Superintendent of Schools, Washington County, Hagerstown, Maryland.

Determine educational policies for county.

Prescribe rules and regulations for conduct and management of schools.

Promote interests of schools.

Control and supervise public school system through the county superintendent and his professional assistants.

Divide county unit into school districts.

Purchase or sell school grounds, school sites and school buildings.

Rent, repair, improve and construct school buildings.

Employ school architects.

Receive donations of school property.

Obtain title before building upon a site or occupying donated house.

Condemn for school sites.

Maintain jointly schools on or near dividing line.

Provide proper water closets or outhouses.

Consolidate schools.

Purchase and distribute textbooks and other supplies and equipment.

Appoint teachers and fix salaries.

Suspend or dismiss teachers.

Prescribe and distribute county courses of study.

Grade and standardize schools.

Have school census taken.

Prepare county school budget with and on the advice of the county superintendent.

Have accounts audited and published.

Report to the State Board of Education.

Have annual report prepared and published.

Cause American flag to be displayed.

Provide and equip office of county superintendent.

Provide transportation for county superintendent and his professional assistants.

Recommend teachers for pensions.

Consent to dismissing pupils or closing schools during school hours.

Appropriate library money.

Consent to use of school plant for certain purposes.

Generally, in a state where the county is a strong unit the board will choose its superintendent. In such a case he is likely to be a real leader with high professional qualifications and with many powers and duties such as those to:

Attend meetings of the county board and its committees and act as its secretary.

Act as treasurer of the board.

Execute school laws, regulations, and policies.

Interpret school laws.

Decide controversies and disputes.

Supervise remodeling and construction of school buildings.

Recommend repairs, purchase, and sale of school sites and buildings and employment of architects.

Approve contracts.

Issue provisional and emergency certificates.

Nominate teachers for appointment, assign to positions, transfer or suspend for cause, recommend for promotion or dismissal.

Visit schools, advise with teachers and trustees.

Organize institutes.

Grade and standardize schools.

Prepare courses of study.

Cause examination of teachers to be held.

Prepare lists of books, supplies, and equipment.

Nominate professional, clerical, statistical and stenographic assistants.

Direct taking of school census.

Conduct correspondence, receive and verify all reports from trustees, principals, and teachers.

Prepare annual report.

Aid in organization of teachers' association.

Consent to dismissing pupils or closing schools during school hours.

Classify teachers' certificates.

In other states the county is not much more than an intermediate unit between the state and the smaller local districts. In such instances the county superintendent may be elected by the people, appointed by the state commissioner of education, or elected by all the school directors of the county. His powers and duties will vary from a mere nominal list with few leadership possibilities to those approximating closely the responsibilities of a strong county unit state. In some cases the qualifications set up for the professional staff of the county superintendent's office have been raised significantly, and the possibilities for educational leadership have grown accordingly.

In New England, it should be stated, the county has not been used as a governmental unit at all, while in New York it is an administrative unit for purposes other than schools. Much the same situation exists in Delaware, which has three counties, but does not use them in school administration.

The chief positions of the county in the educational structure as it operates in the various states are shown graphically on page 55.

The Township. In a few states, the prevailing type of local unit for school administration is the township, which is essentially a rural unit of government. In such instances it is likely that the co-ordinate urban unit will also be considered a school district. Such would be the city, borough, or, in some cases, the incorporated village.

Where the units above exist as separate school districts there will be found a board of school directors or board of education to bring the schools close to the public. Most of these boards will be elected by the people, but in certain other instances they may be appointed by the courts or occasionally by the mayor.

It is the local school board that really represents democracy at work and reflects the will of the people. These boards are created by the state and receive their powers from the state, yet this limits scarcely at all their power to carry out the sort of program the people wish and are willing to support. In general, it may be said that the powers and duties of the district school board are essentially those that have been listed as belonging to a strong county board *but* limited to the particular district. In the last analysis, the school board at its best is a policy-making body, with a superintendent of schools in charge of administration and supervision.

States in which the township may be considered the prevailing type of unit are:

Indiana   New Jersey   Pennsylvania

The Town. In a few states, chiefly in New England, the traditional "town" is the educational unit. Properly, the town may be considered to be a small urban area or village and the rural area round about. This is far more likely to be the true sociological unit than the township and, therefore, is generally more satisfactory. States where the town constitutes the school district are:

Connecticut	New Hampshire
Maine	Rhode Island
Massachusetts	Vermont

The Local School District. In by far the majority of states, the unit for educational administration is the local school district. Originally this was developed as the individual school and the area immediately surrounding it. Since the school was nearly always an elementary school, in later years it in no way solved the high school problem. As a result in a few states, California for one, special high school districts were organized and superimposed.

The local district was often small, inefficient, and expensive, and in such cases it has been almost impossible for it to be in any way adequate for meeting modern needs. Set up in the day when the horse was the chief mode of transportation, it is woefully inadequate for the age of the bus and the airplane.

States in which the district system prevails are:

Arizona	Iowa	Nebraska	So. Carolina
Arkansas	Kansas	Nevada	So. Dakota
California	Michigan	New York	Texas
Colorado	Minnesota	North Dakota	Washington
Idaho	Mississippi	Ohio	Wisconsin
Illinois	Missouri	Oklahoma	Wyoming
	Montana	Oregon	

Each of these districts will have a board of trustees or school directors with powers to operate the schools therein. Where the district is sufficiently large, there will be a local professional school officer who may be a superintendent, supervising principal, or principal.

It must be observed, too, that there are many states with a combination of several types of districts. For such information the student may wish to consult a specialized volume in school administration.

City Districts. Whether the township or the district, as it is usually considered, is the local unit for educational purposes, it is generally true that the city is set up as a separate school district. One sometimes finds this to be the case where the county is the unit of control, as in Maryland where Baltimore is a separate and independent unit or even in Delaware in which Wilmington is similarly set apart. This is frequently brought about by the concentration of wealth and the complexity of the organization required.

The size of the city or urban area is usually the determining factor

Figure 3-8. Wilmington Public Schools: A Large City System

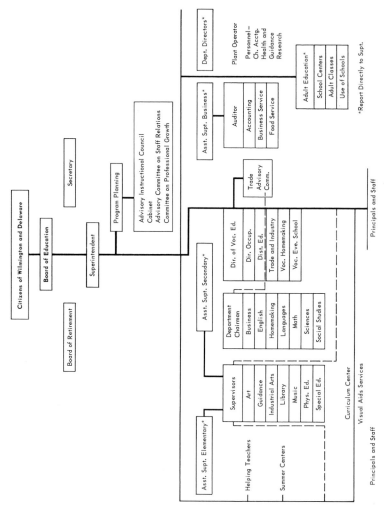

Reprinted by permission of Office of Superintendent of Schools, Wilmington, Delaware.

in deciding what services must be provided. In a large district a host of personnel, including assistant superintendents, specialists of many kinds, business managers, supervisors, principals, assistant principals, and others are likely to be found, all being under the professional direction of the superintendent of schools. Directing the entire system will be the lay board of education which will choose all personnel and determine policies. An excellent example of the organization of a large school district is shown in the illustration on page 60, representing the situation in Wilmington, Delaware.

A smaller city will generally have fewer services provided and fewer teachers with a smaller number of supervisory and administrative personnel. The school board will, however, exercise policy-making and directive powers of the same nature as if the district were larger.

Other Types of Districts. A few other specialized types of school districts may be mentioned before leaving the general topic.

In some states the elementary school district may include certain municipal units, and the high school district may be a much larger area with more governmental units involved. Such is the case in California.

In New England and in New York, the supervisory union may be found. In reality it is sort of an intermediate unit between the state and the local district and is formed of two or more local units or school districts. The superintendent of schools is the executive officer who thus administers the schools of two or more towns or villages which may not necessarily be adjoining.

Merged or consolidated districts are merely the result of the merging or grouping of small districts into larger and more efficient ones. Usually old municipal boundaries are erased for school purposes but not necessarily for other governmental functions. Such districts are found in Pennsylvania, where the entire state is being reorganized in this manner, and in a number of other states.

Toward Larger Units. In an age of rapid social change it must be obvious that these traditional school districts must be supplanted by larger ones which can better meet current and future needs. The problem, therefore has been studied in state after state, and various remedies have been suggested. In some cases it has meant changing to the county as the unit, as in West Virginia; in others it has been a plan of consolidation of schools; in still others it has meant the merging of small districts to form larger ones. Generally, it has been agreed upon that a school district should be large enough to support a complete educational program from the kindergarten through a sufficiently large high school. Indeed, some would have it large enough to support a junior college. Whatever the upper limit, few will deny that schools for a modern day demand a larger unit of control and support with a high quality of professional leadership and an intelligent, capable, and interested board of education.

ORGANIZATION IN TERMS OF THE VERTICAL STRUCTURE OF THE SCHOOLS

Because of the diversity of practice among the states, there have arisen so many methods of dividing the American educational system that at times it is rather difficult to see the real pattern. One is aware of the complexity of it when he tries to describe it to someone from another land.

Upon the major nomenclature there is general agreement. The divisions are: pre-elementary, elementary, secondary, and higher education. A brief description of each follows.

Pre-Elementary Education

Essentially, pre-elementary education consists of the nursery school and the kindergarten. The former is generally considered to cover the ages 18 months to 4 years, whereas the kindergarten accepts children between 4 and 6 years.

Nursery Schools. Nursery schools are mostly of four types: public, private, parochial, and beginning in the depression of the thirties, federally financed. Actually there are not many publicly supported nursery schools as yet. Most of them seem to be privately financed, although quite a few on college campuses are being used as laboratories for schools of education and homemaking. Nursery schools give a great deal of attention to the physiological development of the child while at the same time not neglecting his emotional, social, and moral development.

Although there is an increasing demand for more nursery schools, especially since more mothers are working outside of the home, no great probability exists that the number of publicly supported schools will increase in the near future. Already the great increase in general enrollment is stretching the cost of education to a critical point.

Kindergarten. Although theoretically the kindergarten is designed for children between 4 and 6 years of age, actually examples may be found where the extensions may be either upward or downward. Kindergartens are either supported by public funds, by private funds, or by church groups. Again, as with nursery schools, many exist in connection with colleges for practice or for research and study. Most kindergartens are found in the larger urban communities where transportation is no great problem. With the consolidation of rural schools, more kindergartens are being made available in rural areas, although distance presents a very difficult problem in many situations.

The kindergarten may properly be considered a transition between the home and the school. It strives to prepare the child for his smooth and effective progress in first grade. In the kindergarten he is taught how

Figure 3-9. The Structure of Education in the United States

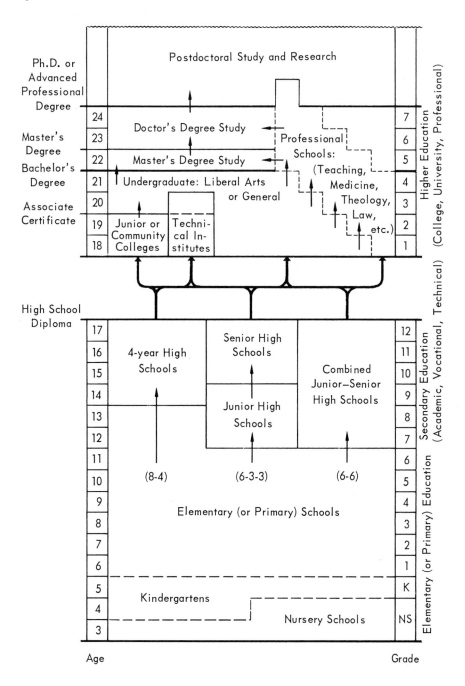

SOURCE: *Progress of Public Education in the United States of America, 1963–64* (Washington, U.S. Office of Education, 1964).

to care for his body, how to work and play with others. As in nursery school, his further emotional, social, and moral development will be fostered. Co-ordination of muscles and the development of skills in painting and working with elementary tools is stressed. Learning by doing is the motto of the modern kindergarten. DeYoung [6] says that "the phychological and physiological principle that colors most of the activities in the kindergarten is that of *readiness.*"

There is increasing pressure generally being felt by school boards to add kindergartens to the public school system or to increase the numbers of those now existing. As in the nursery school situation, the increasing numbers of children to be educated and the shortage of building space will be retarding factors. It does seem clear, though, that kindergarten experience is being widely accepted as a highly desirable part of the child's education.

Advantages of the Kindergarten. A great deal of research has been done on the effectiveness of the kindergarten, and at present the following seem to have been demonstrated:

1. Children who have had kindergarten experience make more rapid progress in the first five grades.
2. There are more repeaters in the first grade where no kindergartens exist.
3. Children in the first three grades who have had kindergarten experience show marked advantages in reading rate and comprehension.
4. Children who have attended kindergarten excel in rate and quality of handwriting.
5. Children with kindergarten experience tend to establish better person-to-person contacts.
6. Children with kindergarten experience tend to receive higher ratings in written and oral language.

Elementary Education

This division of education, as a rule, covers the ages from 6 to 12 or 14. However, practice varies so across the nation that it is difficult to describe it as a definite form. In terms of grades covered it may be:

1. Grades 1–8 inclusive.
2. Grades 1–6 inclusive.
3. Grades 1–7 inclusive.

The kindergarten, if a definite part of the public school system, might be included in each grouping.

A further division of the elementary school is to consider:

1. The kindergarten and grades 1 to 3, inclusive, as the primary unit.
2. Grades 4, 5, and 6 as the intermediate unit.
3. Grades 7 and 8, where a part of the elementary school, as the upper grades.

[6] Chris DeYoung, *Introduction to American Public Education,* 3rd ed. (New York, McGraw-Hill, 1955), p. 135.

There is, however, an increasing tendency to disregard grades and to consider the primary and intermediate units as separate entities. Thus, a child would progress through the primary unit as rapidly as his abilities would permit. There would be no failures, and it might take him three, four, or two years to finish the work provided in the organizational unit. Generally the teacher would have the same children for the time they would be in the unit. This, of course, has obvious advantages and disadvantages that will not be discussed in detail here. The success of the plan presupposes a superior teacher and a reorganized curriculum, the essentials for a successful school of any type.

There are those who presume to see in the ungraded units an answer to many of the ills of modern education. They suggest that it is a sort of return to the old one-teacher school. To this we should like to take vigorous opposition. The evils of the one-teacher schools were so many and so obvious to those who were familiar with them that for the past half century the efforts of educators throughout the land have been devoted to getting rid of them. However, if the proposed reorganization tends to have us put less reliance on grade levels and more on the proper progress of children, to that extent it will surely be to the good.

In size, elementary schools vary tremendously—from those with one teacher and one pupil, to thousands of one-room schools with generally small enrollments, and to large urban schools with many hundreds of students. Through consolidation and the merging of districts, and the demands of the public for a more efficient and better type of education, the small one-teacher schools are disappearing at a rapid rate.

The chief function of the elementary school is considered to be the development of the tools of learning. Its more specific aims, however, will be discussed in a later chapter and will be seen to be far broader than expressed in this simple statement.

In addition to the tendency to eliminate or minimize grade divisions,

Figure 3-10.   Organizational Pattern of Elementary Education

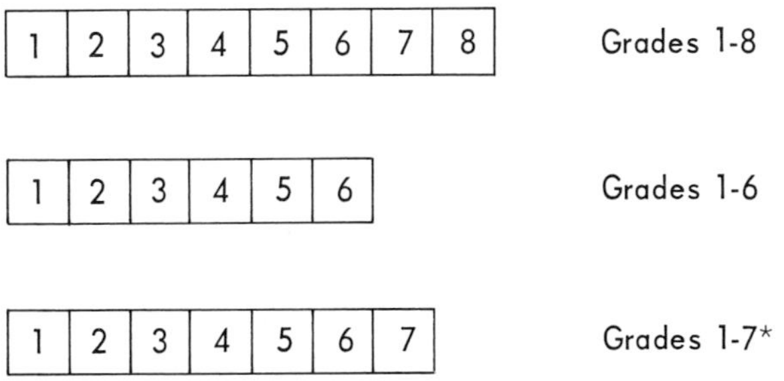

| 1 | 2 | 3 | 4 | 5 | 6 | 7 | 8 | Grades 1-8

| 1 | 2 | 3 | 4 | 5 | 6 | Grades 1-6

| 1 | 2 | 3 | 4 | 5 | 6 | 7 | Grades 1-7*

* Mostly in parts of the South. To each of the above patterns may be added a kindergarten and a nursery school (more commonly kindergarten only).

various other modifications of organizations have been used. Some of the more common are:

1. Ability grouping, where children of similar ability are grouped for teaching and learning.
2. Departmentalization, a plan whereby certain teachers teach certain subjects or groups of subjects.
3. Plans of individualized instruction, such as that originally used at Winnetka, Illinois, and later adapted in varying degrees by other districts.
4. The platoon organization, where a teacher stays with one group for a half day, and the rest of the time the pupils go to special classes.
5. The block system, where specific classes are taught for more or less indefinite periods and several subjects are scheduled in one large block of time. Considerable flexibility is thus provided for the teacher.
6. Team teaching, a more and more popular form of recent organization that will be described in Chapter 16.
7. The ungraded school, a form of organization committed chiefly to the stimulation of individual progress, also to be described in greater detail in Chapter 16.

There are also in many areas special schools for various types of atypical groups, such as crippled children, the deaf or blind, and those who are mentally retarded. Much instruction also is now being given for homebound children when special schools are not available because of distance, lack of numbers, or lack of financial support.

One of the most striking phenomena of recent years has been the enormous increase of enrollment in the elementary schools. With the low birth rate of the 1930's, plenty of classrooms and teachers were available. This birth rate produced a new low enrollment in the schools during the 1940–50 decade. Then with the war years came a rising birth rate that during the mid-years of the fifties caused the elementary schools literally to "burst at the seams," and the shortage of teachers became extremely serious. It is estimated that by 1970 the enrollment in the elementary schools will exceed 31 million as compared with a low of 19 million in the 1940–50 decade.

Secondary Education

Traditionally, American secondary education or the American high school has covered grades 9 to 12 inclusive, although in quite a few of the southern states it has included grades 8 to 11 inclusive, the elementary school consisting of but seven grades.

However, with an increasing knowledge of psychology and with an ever-increasing percentage of eligible youth going to high school in the first half of the present century, the concept of secondary education has been enlarged. Now it has come to mean the education provided for the years of adolescence and pretty generally includes grades 7 and 8 in a reorganized program.

The basic result of the reorganization of secondary education is to divide or regroup the high school grades into two institutions, a senior high school and a junior high school. The common pattern is to consider grades 7, 8, and 9 as the junior high school and 10, 11, and 12 as the senior high school, although there are many regional variations as shown in the diagram below. In addition there are a number of specialized schools, including vocational, technical, continuation, evening high schools, and others. A more recent tendency is to include as a part of secondary education grades 13 and 14, the junior college.

Growth in Numbers and Size. The amazing growth of secondary education is one of the outstanding phenomena of the present century. From 6,000 high schools in the United States in 1900 to more than 26,000 in 1960 is but a part of the story. In an endeavor to provide high

Figure 3-11. Organizational Pattern of Secondary Education

Types of Schools

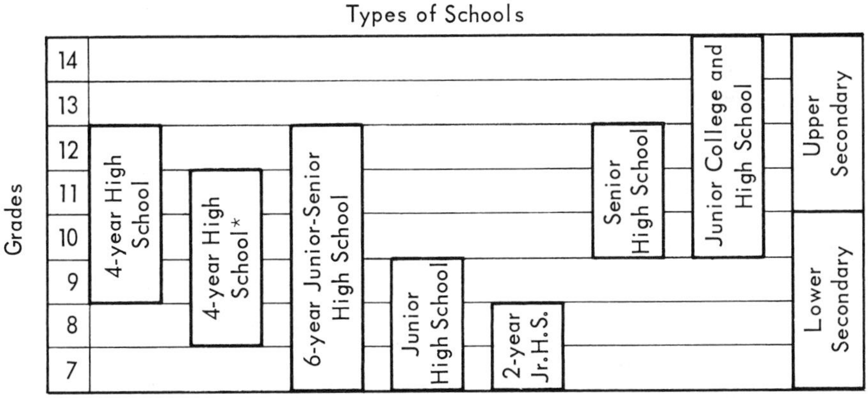

* Found mostly in certain Southern states.

school education for as many youths as possible, a great many very small organizations were established. Many had far too few pupils and teachers who had to teach too many subjects. As a consequence, much work of the last several decades has been devoted to the elimination of small high schools through consolidation and through the enlargement of districts.

Far more significant than the numbers of high schools is the greatly increased enrollment. The figures showing the numbers enrolled doubled every decade in the century until the 1940's when 7 million were on the rolls. High school enrollment figures totaled nearly 12 million in 1962–63, and projections of educational attainment predict that nearly six out of ten adults in the U.S. will have a high school diploma by 1980. If these predictions are correct it will mean that in 1980 over 75 million persons in the United States will have completed at least four years of high school. This figure is two-and-one-half times higher than the number of high school graduates in 1950.

Not only is it true that the high school enrollment has significantly increased, but the holding power of the institution has more than doubled in the last thirty years. Whereas only 27 percent of those who were in high school remained to graduate in 1931, by 1960 the figure had increased to approximately 65 percent, and it is still rising. This fact alone is highly significant.

A recent report of the Commission on Life Adjustment Education for Youth calls attention to many surveys that have been made throughout the country to try to determine how the secondary schools can best attempt to cope with their problem. The report suggests the following areas to which educators should give attention in the years ahead:

1. The secondary school staffs must continue to give special attention to the problem of the number of students who still drop out before graduation.
2. Educators should work to establish a fourteen-year sequence of educational experience instead of the present twelve-year program. This would mean the equivalent of two years of college for all students.
3. An appropriate balance should be developed between required and elective subjects or areas of learning.
4. Continued experimentation is needed to provide for greater individualization by a wide range of methods.
5. An adequate program for appraising the educational development of individual pupils must be prepared.
6. There is need for more experimentation to build a program of work experience.
7. Secondary school teachers and principals have a contribution to make toward improving programs of teacher preparation.
8. The problem of finance remains critical even after the adoption of state equalization programs.
9. The whole question of home-community-school responsibility should be reexamined.

Doubtless, no study of the American high school has caused so much discussion among the public and the profession as has the recent investigation of Dr. Conant, formerly president of Harvard University and later ambassador to Germany. His report [7] will undoubtedly affect the thinking of all those interested in education for many years to come, and it deserves the careful study of every student. It will not be presented here in

[7] James Bryant Conant, *The American High School Today* (New York, McGraw-Hill, 1959).

full but in a considerably condensed form. Further attention will be given to certain sections at various points in this volume where they have relevance.

Among the more significant recommendations for the improvement of the American high school are the following:

1. A greatly strengthened counseling system is needed.
2. Individualized programs for all students instead of the usual classifications, as college preparatory and the like, should be set up.
3. A basic required program for every student is essential. (See Chapter 10.)
4. Students should be grouped according to ability in each subject, not in general.
5. An adequate record of courses studied and grades attained should be given to each student at graduation.
6. A much greater proportion of the time in English should be given to composition.
7. Diversified programs that will produce marketable skills must be provided.
8. Special programs of required subjects should be established for the academically talented. (See Chapter 10.)
9. Special classes or tutors should be provided for the *highly gifted.*
10. The school board should be supplied regularly with an inventory of what is being done for the talented.
11. A six-period day should be provided in every high school.
12. Only those students should be chosen for advanced courses who have demonstrated an ability to handle them.
13. Students should not be given a rank in all subjects taken together, but at each marking period a list should be published indicating those who have made a B or better.
14. A developmental reading program should be established.
15. Summer schools should be set up for the talented.
16. A third and fourth year of foreign languages should be available.
17. Much greater emphasis should be placed upon science and the scientific approach. (See Chapter 10.)
18. Home rooms should be kept together for the entire high school course and should represent a cross section of the student body.
19. American government and economics should be required in 12th-grade social studies.

Most important, Dr. Conant feels that in order to attain these ends the high school must, in very many cases, be made larger through the reorganization of school districts. No high school, he thinks, should have a graduating class of fewer than 100 students. At present about 70 percent of our secondary schools do not meet this standard. He is convinced that American secondary education can be made satisfactory without any radical changes in the basic pattern.

While most of the recommendations in the above-mentioned report concern the four-year and senior high schools, actually many of them pertain to all the grades making up secondary education. The 1960 report, *Education in the Junior High School Years*, calls for a minimum of 125 pupils in each of grades 7 and 8 and an optimum of 750 pupils for a separate junior high school of three years.[8] He further suggests a minimum goal of 50 teachers for 1,000 pupils and especially decries the emphasis upon interscholastic athletics and upon social affairs for children of the junior high school grades. He warns against making the junior high school "a replica of the senior high school with its attendant social pressures." The most desirable situation, the report indicates, would be a

*Courtesy: James Weakley, Director of Public
Relations, St. Petersburg Junior College.*

St. Petersburg Junior College, St. Petersburg, Florida, is one of the new junior colleges, the number of which is increasing rapidly.

8 James Bryant Conant, *Recommendations for Education in the Junior High School Years* (Princeton, N.J., Educational Testing Service, 1960).

seven-period day with a teacher teaching five periods with 125 to 150 pupils daily. The report should be studied in some detail by all students.

The Junior College

The junior college was first conceived around the middle of the last century and involved little more than a slight reorganization of the first two years of the usual college. Earliest definitive organizations existed in Illinois, Georgia, Texas, and Wisconsin. In a very few communities the junior college was blended with the last two years of the usual high school, and the pattern of public education became 6–4–4. This type of organization, however, is far from common.

The greatest development of the junior college has been since 1920. From 52 such institutions in that year the number has risen to 577 reported for the fall of 1963 by the United States Office of Education. It has been estimated that one student in every four beginning his program of higher education during 1963 in the United States was enrolled in a junior college.[9] The tuition in these schools varied widely, from none to $3,000.

Methods of Control. The usual method of classification of junior colleges is based upon the types of control which may be listed as follows: (1) public; (2) proprietary-controlled or supported by local groups but really private; (3) parochial or church. At the present time there are twenty-two denominational or religious groups that control and support junior colleges. Since 1947–48 the public institutions have been established more rapidly.

Many of the colleges usually considered as "public" are really off-campus centers of four-year colleges or universities as previously mentioned; also some of those classed as "private" bear the same relationship to private colleges or universities. Naturally many of these are in no sense terminal institutions but act as part of the regular college course.

It is generally assumed that a junior college, to meet community needs completely, should be both terminal and preparatory. From the terminal type of institution has grown the community college and the technical institute. The question is still debated as to whether the junior college is a part of the secondary school or a part of higher education. Actually it is both.

It should be noted at this point that in 1962 the President's Committee on National Goals made the following significant statement: [10] "Two-year colleges should be within commuting distance of most high school

9 Edmund J. Geazer, ed., *American Junior Colleges,* American Council on Education (Washington, D.C., 1963), pp. 3–6.

10 *Goals for America,* Report of the President's Committee on National Goals (New York, Prentice-Hall, 1961), p. 7.

*Courtesy: W. A. Kamrath, Co-ordinator of
Public Relations. Photograph by Julius Schuman.*

El Camino College, California. Architecturally, the College follows low, smooth lines; simplicity is emphasized. The Commerce Building pictured here is enhanced by landscaping which features palms and other tropicals.

graduates." It is highly probable that most of these new institutions will be mainly technical schools. Recent estimates indicate that by 1970 at least 600 junior colleges will be in operation.

Higher Education

At the present time the young people who are seeking admission to the colleges and universities are representative of the post-war high birth rate. This fact plus the increasing desirability of a college education has taxed the facilities of nearly all institutions of higher education. In the last 15 years the enrollment in such schools has more than doubled. A reasonable estimate would place the current figure at more than 5 million with the end nowhere in sight. All this has taken place in spite of constantly rising tuition and maintenance costs.

The United States Office of Education [11] has reported the following figures representing the numbers of various types of institutions for the fall of 1963:

[11] United States Office of Education, *Circular No. 728* (Washington, D.C., 1964), p. 5.

Four-Year Institutions

Universities	146
Liberal Arts Colleges	788
Independently organized	
Professional Schools	
Teachers Colleges	186
Technological Schools	57
Theological, religious	201
Schools of Art	46
Other professional	79

Two-Year Institutions

Junior Colleges	577
Technical Institutes	21
Semi-professional schools	39
Total	2,140

Any figures such as those presented above must be subject to constant revision. New institutions are being formed continually, such as community colleges with two- or four-year curricula. Many of these may be supported and operated by municipalities, and they are generally concerned with meeting various educational needs of the community. Teachers colleges tend to become general colleges and later universities. Junior colleges and other two-year organizations may not infrequently develop into four-year institutions. As a result the entire situation is more or less in a state of flux.

One of the most recent developments in the field of higher education is the formation of a new institution that will consist of the last two years of college and two years of graduate school. The first of such organizations, called a "senior college," was opened at Boca Raton, Florida, in 1964 and dedicated in October, 1964, by President Johnson. It has no freshmen or sophomores but will concentrate on juniors, seniors and graduate students. In this case it is set up primarily to meet the demands for advanced scientific training. It is highly likely that this school will be followed by similar institutions elsewhere.

The proliferation of institutions engaged in higher education, their growth in size and functions, and the new demands made upon them necessitates comprehensive planning at least on the state level. It is only in New York and California that anything of real significance has been accomplished in this direction. Pennsylvania is in the process of developing a comprehensive master plan, and this is being considered in certain other states as well. Some such state-wide planning is essential if social

A modern community college near Binghamton, New York. Technical training is emphasized. The college is a division of the State University and brings higher education to the community level, gearing it to community needs.

needs are to be met and foolish competition and waste avoided. The educational revolution makes wise planning doubly necessary.

Some of the more serious problems that face higher education today are the following:

1. How will it be possible to provide the physical plant and professional staffs that will be needed to take care of the greatly increased number of young people who will wish to attend college in the years ahead?
2. Shall the federal government be encouraged to assist in the financing of higher education or will this lead to some type of federal control?
3. How can endowment funds be invested to provide higher returns?
4. Is it wise to urge business and industry to contribute larger sums to higher education or will this lead to another type of control?
5. How can the institutions best fit into the program of national or military service that will likely continue to be demanded of young people?
6. What type of program can be carried on to recruit and educate a high type of personnel for college teaching?
7. What alterations or changes of the curricular offerings will be needed to meet the new demands?

Most of the colleges and universities throughout the land have found it necessary to increase their tuition and other costs quite substantially.

The crux of the problem now is whether they have not reached the "all the traffic will bear" point. Surely there is a point of diminishing returns, a serious result of which will be that very many more capable young men and women will be denied a college education.

One possible approach to the crisis is the granting of many additional scholarships by the states and loans by the federal and state governments. These could be used at all types of approved institutions of higher education and, where made available by the federal government, would operate similar to the G.I. grants except that they would be available only to the most capable.

Another avenue of assistance has been recently noted in which several large corporations have offered to match contributions made by any of their employees to colleges or universities. Thus if the vice-president donates $1,000 to his alma mater, the corporation will tender a like amount. If this practice spreads to any great extent, it can be of material assistance to many institutions.

It should be pointed out as well that many industries, foundations, service clubs, parent teacher associations, and other organizations are increasing the scholarships they grant to worthy students who are pursuing specific courses. The spreading of this movement can also be of material help.

Adult Education

The education of adults is nothing new in America. Far back in the early nineteenth century "singing schools" were quite common, even in rural areas. In 1950 the great Philadelphia Evening High School marked its 100th anniversary and noted that over 40,000 people had taken advantage of its services the preceding year—services which were rendered free of cost to residents of the city. Offering well over 100 courses with many discussion groups and co-operating with other community groups, such as PTA's, community councils, labor unions, and the like, the Evening High School has been very effective in adult education.

It is estimated that expenditures for public school adult education reach $100 million annually. If all other types of adult education are considered, it is likely that the total cost will exceed a billion dollars. This sort of education is big business in the full sense of the word. Indeed, it is worthy of note that one of every thirteen high school diplomas given in 1963 in Los Angeles was earned by an adult and that in many communities full-time day schools are being established for the growing number of adults who seek to further their education.

In addition to the many programs of adult education carried on by local school districts there may be added many other types, such as the following:

1. Programs by such community organizations as the YMCA, YWCA, Boy and Girl Scouts, etc.
2. Programs by nonprofit co-operative groups such as The Institute of Lifetime Learning in Washington, D.C.
3. Programs carried on by colleges and universities both on and away from the campus and through the medium of television.
4. Programs carried on by museums, libraries, and the like.
5. Programs set up by churches and other religious groups.
6. Programs by corporations and labor unions.

To this list may be added such activities as public lectures, concerts, counseling, Americanization classes, certain television programs, and in-service training in industry.

Much of adult education stems from the realization that education does not end when a public school or college career has been finished, and that community responsibility for providing opportunities for education and growth is a lifetime matter. This is true in both large and small communities. In fact, some of the most interesting programs are found in rural areas, as in New York where the emphasis has been put upon current affairs and the development of an informed citizenry.[12]

Some schools seem to concentrate on recreational and social activities; others run the gamut from fly-tying to philosophy and the "Great Books." The Ford Foundation, which established the Fund for Adult Education, suggests the following definition of education which some localities find acceptable for their program:

Education must meet the needs of the human spirit. It must assist persons to develop a satisfactory personal philosophy and a sense of values; to cultivate tastes for literature, music, and the arts; and to grow in ability to analyze problems and arrive at thoughtful conclusions.

Modern psychology teaches that learning can go on as long as life goes on and that people at any age can learn new things. The acceptance and implementation of this concept can mean much for our democracy.

[12] A. P. Crabtree, "Adults Keep Up with the Times in Rural Areas," *NEA Journal*, Vol. 43 (February, 1954), pp. 94–95.

QUESTIONS AND PROJECTS

1. Examine the educational program in one of the dependencies of the United States.
2. Prepare an exhibit of the publications issued by the United States Office of Education.
3. Examine the offerings of a vocational school or department. Investigate the part the federal government plays in the work of the school or department.
4. Compare the organization of education in some foreign country with that of the United States.
5. Examine the organization of the State Department of Education in your own state.
6. Discuss the arguments for and against the state adoption of textbooks.
7. Compare the county as an educational unit with the smaller district.
8. Visit the office of the county superintendent in your county, and investigate the nature of his work.
9. Secure the data on the progress being made in the elimination of one-teacher schools in your state.
10. What are the advantages of the consolidated school as compared with the one-teacher school?
11. List the disadvantages of the small district.
12. Prepare an exhibit of Manuals for Teachers in large or medium size school districts.
13. If possible, visit as a class a fairly large consolidated school and a one-teacher school.
14. Prepare a panel discussion on the questions relative to the qualifications of school boards.
15. Have a superintendent of schools talk to the class about the administration of schools.
16. Compare the democratic and undemocratic organization of schools.
17. Have a group of students visit a nursery school, public or private, and report to the class on the activities observed.
18. Do the same for each of the other units of the school system that you have studied.
19. Write to a superintendent of schools in a district not having a kindergarten, and ascertain why none has been established.
20. What arguments can you give for the establishment of community colleges?
21. What weaknesses have resulted from the emphasis upon the local control of schools?
22. How do you account for the fact the public junior colleges have developed so much more rapidly in the west than in the east?
23. Organize a panel discussion or symposium on the place of the private and parochial school in America.
24. Discuss the ways in which the colleges and universities can meet the anticipated very large enrollments of the next decade.
25. Debate the issues involved in the "comprehensive" high school *versus* the schools for separate purposes such as vocational, technical, etc.

26. Compare the high school you attended with the standards suggested in the Conant reports.

AUDIO-VISUAL AIDS

MOTION PICTURES (16 MM)

Design for American Public Education—McGraw-Hill Book Co., Text-Film Dept., 330 West 42nd St., New York, N.Y., 20 min., sd., b&w. The organizational structure of American public education, first, as it might be if it were an "assembly line" educational process controlled centrally and, second, as it actually is in a democratic society.

Fight for Better Schools—March of Time, distributed by McGraw-Hill Book Co., Text-Film Dept., 330 West 42nd St., New York, N.Y., 18 min., sd., b&w. How the schools of Arlington County, Virginia, were raised from among the nation's poorest to among the best.

How Good Are Our Schools?—National Education Association, 1201 16th St., N.W., Washington, D.C., 27 min., sd., b&w. This is a film report of Dr. Conant's two-year study of American public secondary schools. After presenting his findings he recommends certain changes which he believes would improve the secondary school curriculum.

Right Angle—National Education Association, 1201 16th St., N.W., Washington, D.C., 28½ min., sd., color or b&w. A newspaper reporter finds the public school doing a good job educating all children, regardless of family backgrounds or abilities.

School Board in Action—National School Boards Association, Inc., 1940 Sheridan Road, Evanston, Ill. What the school board does, how it does it, and why it does it.

School and Community—McGraw-Hill Book Co., Text-Film Dept., 330 West 42nd St., New York, N.Y., 14 min., sd., b&w. Shows the benefits which school and community obtain when they co-operate.

Schools March On—March of Time, distributed by McGraw-Hill Book Company, Text-Film Dept., 330 West 42nd St., New York, N.Y., 18 min., b&w. The story of what happened in Woodford County, Illinois, when the one-room schools were consolidated.

FILMSTRIPS

Bringing the Community to the Classroom—Wayne University, Detroit, Mich., 50 fr., si., b&w. Shows how various members of the community may come into the classroom to add vitality to learning.

Design of American Public Education—McGraw-Hill Book Co., Text-Film Dept., 330 West 42nd St., New York, N.Y., 35 fr., si., b&w. Cartoons and diagrams illustrate the organization of public education in the United States.

Kindergarten and Your Child—Wayne University, Detroit, Mich., 36 fr., si., b&w. Discusses the values of the kindergarten.

RECORDINGS

The Community School. Dr. Maurice Seay of the University of Chicago presents seven characteristics of the community school. Included are the teachers, the plant, the instructional materials, and the atmosphere.

*The Core Program in the High School—*Educational Recording Services, 5922 Abernathy Dr., Los Angeles, Calif., 33⅓ r.p.m. microgroove. Harold Alberty discusses: Part I—Types of core programs and correlations in high schools. (15 min.) Part II—Discussion of the "type 5" or "problems-of-living" core and its advantages. (15 min.)

*The High School Curriculum for Life Adjustment—*Educational Recording Services, 5922 Abernathy Dr., Los Angeles, Calif., 33⅓ r.p.m., microgroove. Harl R. Douglass discusses: Part I—History of the curricula on the secondary school level and a discussion of present conditions indicating new changes. (15 min.) Part II—Curriculum changes dictated by modern conditions. (15 min.)

*The Community College and Its Functions—*Educational Recording Services, 33⅓ r.p.m. Jesse P. Bogue, Executive Secretary, American Association of Junior Colleges, discusses the functions of the institutions.

FURTHER READINGS

Barker, Roger G., and Paul V. Gump, *Big School, Small School* (Stanford, Calif., Stanford University Press, 1964).

Brown, B. Frank, *The Nongraded High School* (Englewood Cliffs, N.J., Prentice-Hall, 1963.)

Campbell, R. F., and G. R. Sproufe, "Toward a Rationale for Federal-State-Local Relations in Education," *Phi Delta Kappan,* Vol. 47 (September, 1965), pp. 2–7.

Conant, James B., *Slums and Suburbs* (New York, McGraw-Hill, 1961).

Cressman, George R., *Local Units for Educational Administration* (West Chester, Pa., published by the author, 1932).

Dean, Stuart E., *Elementary School Administration and Organization,* Bull. 1960, No. 11 (Washington, D.C., U.S. Office of Education, 1960).

Fields, Ralph R., *The Community College Movement* (New York, McGraw-Hill, 1962).

Hanna, Paul R., ed., *Education, an Instrument of National Goals* (New York, McGraw-Hill, 1962).

Hobson, C. J., and Samuel Schloss, *Statistics of State School Systems, 1961–62,* Circular No. 751 (Washington, D.C., U.S. Office of Education, 1964).

Knezevich, Stephen J., *Administration of Public Education* (New York, Harper & Row, 1962).

Land, William G., "The Shakeout in USOE," A report on the reorganization of the U.S. Office of Education, *Phi Delta Kappan,* Vol. 47 (September, 1965), pp. 31–33.

McConnell, T. R., *A General Pattern of American Public Higher Education* (New York, McGraw-Hill, 1962).

Medsker, Leland L., *The Junior College* (New York, McGraw-Hill, 1960).

Morphet, E. L., R. L. Johns, and T. L. Reller, *Educational Administration: Concepts, Practices and Issues* (Englewood Cliffs, N.J., Prentice-Hall, 1959).

Morrison, D. G., and S. V. Martorana, *The 2-Year Community College: An Annotated List of Studies and Surveys* (Washington, D.C., U.S. Office of Education, 1958).

National Association of Secondary School Principals, *Junior High School Development, Practices, and Research* (Washington, D.C., NEA, 1962).

National Education Association, *Rankings of the States, 1965,* Research Report 1964 R 1 (Washington, DC., 1965).

Reeves, Charles E., *School Boards: Their Status, Functions, and Activities* (Englewood Cliffs, N.J., Prentice-Hall, 1954).

Rosencrance, Francis C., *The American College and its Teachers* (New York, Macmillan, 1962).

Trump, J. Lloyd, *Images of the Future* (Washington, D.C., NEA, 1959).

United States Office of Education, *Adult Education in the Public Schools* (Washington, D.C., 1960).

Will, Robert F., *State Education, Structure and Organization,* Misc. No. 46 (Washington, D.C., U.S. Office of Education, 1964).

Wynn, D. Richard, *Organization of Public Schools* (Syracuse, Center for Applied Research in Education, 1964).

4

Providing the Funds
for Education

PREVIEW

▶ In a rising economy the costs of education at all levels are certain to rise proportionately.

Expenditures per pupil in average daily attendance have risen nearly five times since 1929–30.

Inflation has been a major cause, but a number of other factors have contributed also.

▶ Rising educational costs are probably best considered in relation to the Gross National Product (GNP).

The ratio of educational expenditures to the GNP has increased threefold since the mid-1940's.

▶ The federal government, under heavy pressures to aid education, has increased the amount of its support greatly.

However, the proportionate share of its distribution has not yet changed very significantly.

▶ Over a considerable number of years the state has tended to bear a larger share of the total cost of education.

More or less of a plateau has been reached in regard to the state's contribution during the last few years, and wide variation exists among the states.

▶ Much effort is being made to find new sources of revenue and to broaden the tax base.

Increasing use has been made of sales and income taxes.

▶ In the distribution of state funds great stress is being put upon the principle of equalization.

▶ The proportionate share of the costs of education borne by the local districts, while decreasing significantly during the last 20 years, has held rather constant in more recent years.
Careful budgeting and accounting is necessary by the local districts for the efficient and proper expenditure of funds and is generally required by the states.

▶ Many unsolved problems in the field of educational finance demand further careful study.

The cost of public education in America does not remain static any more than does that of any other service. In a rising economy it is inevitable that such charges should rise to an extent and in a manner reasonably proportionate to other rising costs. This would be expected even if the demands upon the schools had not greatly increased. However, a birth rate that has grown far beyond nearly all predictions has placed unprecedented loads upon the schools, and the problem of providing funds to meet the most urgent of needs takes on a new acuteness.

It is extremely difficult if not impossible to get an accurate measure of the increased cost of our national expenditures for education. In 1929–30 the total expenditure per pupil in average daily attendance in public elementary and secondary schools in the United States was $108 while in 1963–64 it was $559, an increase of nearly five times. (See Table 4–1 on page 83.) If we use as a base the figure for 1919–20 of $64, the increase is more than eight times.

Expenditures have, of course, been affected by inflation, and it is likely that this will be influential in the future. Also responsible for rising costs are factors such as: (1) more children are remaining in school longer; for example, in 1890 only 3 percent of our young people were graduating from high school while now more than 70 percent are completing secondary education; (2) more and better buildings are being built and will continue to be needed; (3) the school year is longer; (4) more attention is being given to the gifted and the handicapped and the underprivileged; (5) auxiliary services, such as school nurses, transportation, and the like have been increased; (6) better equipment of all sorts is desirable; and (7) higher salaries must be paid for more fully prepared personnel.

Table 4-1.   Total and Per-Pupil Expenditures for Public Elementary and
Secondary Education: United States, Selected Years from
1919–20 to 1963–64

School Year	Total	Total Expenditure per Pupil in Average Daily Attendance
1919–20	$ 1,036,151,000	$ 64
1929–30	2,316,790,000	108
1939–40	2,344,049,000	106
1949–50	5,837,643,000	259
1951–52	7,344,237,000	313
1953–54	9,092,449,000	351
1955–56	10,955,047,000	388
1957–58	13,569,163,000	449
1959–60	15,613,255,000	472
1961–62[1]	18,169,057,000	515
1963–64[2]	21,201,199,000	559

[1] Data from *Preliminary Statistics of State School Systems, 1961–62.*
[2] Data from *Estimates of School Statistics, 1963–64,* Copyright 1963 by the National Education Association. Used by permission.

NOTE.—Beginning in 1959–60, includes Alaska and Hawaii.

SOURCE of final data: U.S. Department of Health, Education, and Welfare, Office of Education, *Biennial Survey of Education in the United States,* and *Statistics of State School Systems, 1959–60.*

Probably, the best way to ascertain the extent to which our educational costs have risen is to compare them with the general prosperity of the country, measuring them against the gross national product, frequently listed as GNP. A careful examination of the table on page 84 will indicate that in 1962–63 for education on all levels we spent approximately $32 billion which was 5.76 percent of the gross national product. Compared with the middle 1940's this ratio of expenditures for education to the GNP has increased approximately three times. In terms of dollars it is nearly eight times larger.

It is almost useless to speculate upon what this percent ought to be in a democratic society. It will have to be considered in relation to the percent of the national budget necessary or considered necessary for defense. Whether the gross national product will continue to increase sufficiently so that a fairly constant percentage available for education covers the needed services for young people is for the future to determine.

Table 4-2.   Gross National Product Related to Total Expenditures [1] for Education: United States, Selected Years from 1929 to 1962

Calendar Year	Gross National Product	School Year	Expenditures for Education	
			Total	As a Percent of Gross National Product
1929	$104,436,000,000	1929–30	$ 3,233,601,000	3.10
1931	76,271,000,000	1931–32	2,966,464,000	3.89
1933	55,964,000,000	1933–34	2,294,896,000	4.10
1935	72,502,000,000	1935–36	2,649,914,000	3.65
1937	90,780,000,000	1937–38	3,014,074,000	3.32
1939	91,095,000,000	1939–40	3,199,593,000	3.51
1941	125,822,000,000	1941–42	3,203,548,000	2.55
1943	192,513,000,000	1943–44	3,522,007,000	1.83
1945	213,558,000,000	1945–46	4,167,597,000	1.95
1947	234,289,000,000	1947–48	6,574,379,000	2.81
1949	258,054,000,000	1949–50	8,795,635,000	3.41
1951	328,975,000,000	1951–52	11,312,446,000	3.44
1953	365,385,000,000	1953–54	13,949,876,000	3.82
1955	397,469,000,000	1955–56	16,811,651,000	4.23
1957	442,769,000,000	1957–58	21,119,565,000	4.77
1959	482,704,000,000	1959–60	24,722,464,000	5.12
1961	518,173,000,000	1961–62	29,430,000,000	5.68
1962	554,894,000,000	1962–63	31,980,000,000	5.76

[1] Includes expenditures of public and nonpublic schools at all levels of education (elementary, secondary, and higher education).
[2] Estimated.

Note.—Beginning with 1959–60 school year, includes Alaska and Hawaii.

Sources: U.S. Department of Health, Education, and Welfare, Office of Education, *Biennial Survey of Education in the United States,* and *Digest of Educational Statistics,* 1963 edition; and U.S. Department of Commerce, Office of Business Economics, *Survey of Current Business,* July 1958 and July 1963.

Figure 4-1.   Educational Expenditures *

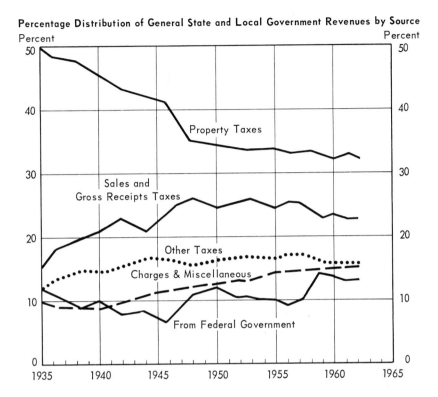

Percentage Distribution of General State and Local Government Revenues by Source

* Expenditures for education are estimated at $33.7 billion ($27.1 billion public and $6.6 billion private) for the school year ending in 1964. Between 1954 and 1964 educational expenditures increased by 142 percent, and in the school year 1961–62 they comprised 5.5 percent of gross national product.

SOURCE: 1964 Edition, *Health, Education, and Welfare Trends.*

SOURCES OF THE SUPPORT FOR PUBLIC EDUCATION

By Unit of Government

In the first place, the funds for the support of public education in America must inevitably come from three areas of government: (1) the national unit, (2) the state unit, and (3) the local unit (intermediate or local district). Secondly, from whatever area of government the funds are raised and spent, they must be derived from taxation. Other sources are almost negligible. In a few cases contributions may be made locally by wealthy individuals, or occasionally by industries or foundations, but in the total picture these are insignificant and will not be discussed further.

It will be well to note at this point what the trends have been in the changing distribution of support. This will be revealed in the table below.

Table 4-3.   Public Elementary and Secondary School Revenue Receipts from Federal, State, and Local Sources: United States, 1919–20 to 1961–62

School Year	Total	Federal	State	Local (including inter-mediate)[1]
		Percentage Distribution		
1919–20	100.0	0.3	16.5	83.2
1929–30	100.0	.4	16.9	82.7
1939–40	100.0	1.8	30.3	68.0
1941–42	100.0	1.4	31.5	67.1
1943–44	100.0	1.4	33.0	65.6
1945–46	100.0	1.4	34.7	63.8
1947–48	100.0	2.8	38.9	58.3
1949–50	100.0	2.9	39.8	57.3
1951–52	100.0	3.5	38.6	57.8
1953–54	100.0	4.5	37.4	58.1
1955–56	100.0	4.6	39.5	55.9
1957–58	100.0	4.0	39.4	56.6
1959–60	100.0	4.4	39.1	56.5
1961–62	100.0	4.3	38.7	56.9

[1] Includes a relatively minor amount from other sources (gifts and tuition and transportation fees from patrons), which accounted for 0.4 percent of total revenue receipts in 1961–62.

NOTE.—Beginning in 1959–60, includes Alaska and Hawaii. Because of rounding, detail may not add to totals.

SOURCE: U.S. Department of Health, Education, and Welfare, Office of Education, *Statistics of State School Systems, 1961–62.*

A study of the figures presented in the table above will indicate, among other things, that for the United States as a whole there has been little change in the relative distribution of school revenue by source since

1956. In round numbers the figures are: from the federal unit, 4 percent; from the states, 40 percent; and from local sources, 56 percent.

Estimates of the distribution for 1963–64 indicate that for that period they would be: federal 3.5 percent; state, 40.1 percent; and local, 56.4 percent.[1] The student will find it advisable to study carefully in Table 4–4 the figures for his own state in light of the national picture and to be able to explain the deviations that are evident. What changes may be made in the figures presented in the table above by new legislation at the federal level remains to be seen. It is inevitable that the major sources of funds will still continue to be the state and local units.

FEDERAL SUPPORT

The background of the pattern of federal support has been developed in Chapter 2, and it is becoming quite clear that the significant increase of such support for education is becoming an accomplished fact. There appears to be general acceptance of the theory that the central government's role in financing education must increase. Examples of this point of view may be found in:

The Vocational Education Act of 1963
The Elementary and Secondary Education Act of 1965
The Higher Education Facilities Act of 1965

Actually this legislation provides vastly increased federal support for varied aspects of education on all levels and makes funds available in many cases for non-profit private schools as well as public schools.

The traditional arguments used for and against direct federal aid to education may well be noted at this point. They still should be evaluated and discussed by mature students, especially in light of recent developments. The arguments generally offered in support of so-called "federal aid" may be listed as follows:

1. Education is sufficiently important in relation to the general welfare to be included among the fields of support by the federal government.
2. Education is "national defense" and as such has a just claim on the resources of the national government.
3. Broad federal educational aid has ample precedent behind it.
4. The states vary widely in their ability to support an adequate educational program, and federal aid is, therefore, needed to equalize educational opportunity (see table *Educational Differences Among the States,* pp. 11–14).
5. It is an accepted principle of American government that wealth should be taxed where it is found and such revenue expended in proportion to need. Only the federal government can do this.
6. Our population is now highly mobile, and many do not remain in the states

[1] Research Division, National Education Association, *Estimates of School Statistics, 1963–64* (Washington, D.C., NEA, 1963), p. 16.

Table 4-4. Estimated Revenue and Nonrevenue Receipts, 1965–66

Region and State	Revenue Receipts by Source (in thousands)				Percent of Revenue Receipts by Source[a]		
	Federal[b]	State	Local and Other[c]	Total	Federal[b]	State	Local and Other[c]
50 states and D.C.	$1,920,303	$9,675,177	$13,123,323	$24,718,803	7.8%	39.1%	53.1%
New England	97,466	322,094	809,334	1,228,874	7.9	26.2	65.9
Connecticut	19,800	127,000	240,000	386,800	5.1	32.8	62.0
Maine	11,300	30,500	63,200	105,000	10.8	29.0	60.2
Massachusetts	52,000	119,000	368,000	539,000	9.6	22.1	68.3
New Hampshire	4,200	7,424[d]	57,634	69,258[d]	6.1	10.7	83.2
Rhode Island	6,200	25,750	49,500	81,450	7.6	31.6	60.8
Vermont	3,946	12,420	31,000	47,366	8.3	26.2	65.4
Mideast	379,639	2,268,134	3,216,559	5,864,332	6.5	38.7	54.8
Delaware	4,500	60,000	15,000	79,500	5.7	75.5	18.9
Maryland	36,139	158,134	299,171	493,444	7.3	32.0	60.6
New Jersey	40,000	190,000	667,000	897,000	4.5	21.2	74.4
New York	175,000	1,285,000	1,448,000	2,908,000	6.0	44.2	49.8
Pennsylvania	98,000	575,000	707,388	1,380,388	7.1	41.7	51.2
District of Columbia	26,000	...	80,000	106,000	24.5	...	75.5
Southeast	502,290	2,277,323	1,363,134	4,142,747	12.1	55.0	32.9
Alabama	49,000	194,000	76,000[e]	319,000	15.4	60.8	23.8
Arkansas	34,521	74,650	62,781	171,952	20.1	43.4	36.5
Florida	61,850	320,177	274,153	656,180	9.4	48.8	41.8
Georgia	52,000	266,500	115,500	434,000	12.0	61.4	26.6
Kentucky	40,000	146,000	95,000	281,000	14.2	52.0	33.8
Louisiana	24,119	278,880	100,000	402,999	6.0	69.2	24.8
Mississippi	41,500	106,000	60,500	208,000	20.0	51.0	29.1
North Carolina	57,000	319,016	108,200	484,216	11.8	65.9	22.3
South Carolina	42,000	145,000	56,000	243,000	17.3	59.7	23.0
Tennessee	40,300	170,100	133,000[f]	343,400	11.7	49.5	38.7
Virginia	48,000[g]	170,000	214,000	432,000	11.1[g]	39.4	49.5
West Virginia	12,000	87,000	68,000	167,000	7.2	52.1	40.7
Great Lakes	285,754	1,523,683	3,115,500	4,924,937	5.8	30.9	63.3
Illinois	81,000	324,000	1,007,000[h]	1,412,000	5.7	22.9	71.3[h]
Indiana	38,754	254,083	392,500	685,337	5.7	37.1	57.3
Michigan	70,000	500,000	570,000	1,140,000	6.1	43.9	50.0
Ohio	61,000	333,000	821,000	1,215,000	5.0	27.4	67.6
Wisconsin	35,000	112,600	325,000	472,600	7.4	23.8	68.8

* Estimated by NEA Research Division.
N.A. = Not available.
a/ Distribution may not add to 100.0% because of rounding.
b/ Includes all federal grant programs to state and local school systems, including aid to federally affected areas, NDEA, manpower development and retraining, vocational education, etc. Estimates of federal revenues under "The Elementary and Secondary Education Act of 1965" have been included on the basis of anticipated expenditures during the 1965–66 school year. The money value of commodities under the School Lunch Program may be incomplete.
c/ Includes revenue receipts from local and intermediate sources, gifts, and tuition and fees from patrons.

Table 4-4.　Continued

| Region and State | Revenue Receipts by Source (in thousands) | | | | Percent of Revenue Receipts by Source[a] | | |
	Federal[b]	State	Local and Other[c]	Total	Federal[b]	State	Local and Other[c]
Plains	$ 148,388	$ 507,113	$ 1,316,550	$ 1,972,051	7.5%	25.7%	66.8%
Iowa*	15,500	45,000	272,000	332,500	4.7	13.5	81.8
Kansas	25,000	65,000	211,000	301,000	8.3	21.6	70.1
Minnesota	35,000	205,000	300,000	540,000	6.5	38.0	55.6
Missouri	40,888	152,113	286,000	479,001	8.5	31.8	59.7
Nebraska	11,000	9,000	133,000	153,000	7.2	5.9	86.9
North Dakota	6,000	20,500	52,050	78,550	7.6	26.1	66.3
South Dakota	15,000	10,500	62,500	88,000	17.0	11.9	71.0
Southwest	168,770	881,260	776,600	1,826,630	9.2	48.2	42.5
Arizona	25,000	68,400	95,000	188,400	13.3	36.3	50.4
New Mexico*	20,500	99,000	31,600	151,100	13.6	65.5	20.9
Oklahoma	37,270	77,860	150,000	265,130	14.1	29.4	56.6
Texas[i]	86,000	636,000	500,000	1,222,000	7.0	52.0	40.9
Rocky Mountain	57,333	231,178	394,819	683,330	8.4	33.8	57.8
Colorado	25,000	69,000	186,000	280,000	8.9	24.6	66.4
Idaho	6,000	30,700	43,000	79,700	7.5	38.5	54.0
Montana*	8,600	30,000	69,000	107,600	8.0	27.9	64.1
Utah[i]	13,833	75,478	64,819	154,130	9.0	49.0	42.1
Wyoming	3,900	26,000	32,000	61,900	6.3	42.0	51.7
Far West	255,700	1,574,102	2,091,500	3,921,302	6.5	40.1	53.3
California[k]	200,000	1,200,000	1,713,000	3,113,000	6.4	38.5	55.0
Nevada	4,500	28,602	22,000	55,102	8.2	51.9	39.9
Oregon	23,200	78,000	193,000	294,200	7.9	26.5	65.6
Washington	28,000	267,500	163,500	459,000	6.1	58.3	35.6
Alaska	13,000	24,300	10,000	47,300	27.5	51.4	21.1
Hawaii	11,983	65,990	29,327	107,300	11.2	61.5	27.3

d/ Excludes state's share of teacher retirement and social security.

e/ Includes funds not handled by custodian of school funds.

f/ Includes funds of city and county governments for debt service for school buildings amounting to $22,000,000.

g/ Adjusted by NEA Research Division to include estimated revenues under Public Law 89–10.

h/ Local sources do not include receipts from students, etc., for athletics, book rentals, and other student and community services.

i/ Does not include revenues for kindergartens; also excludes revenues for public junior colleges which are no longer under local school systems.

j/ Adjusted by NEA Research Division to include revenues covering deficits in School Lunch Program; federal revenues also adjusted to include funds of approximately $3.6 million potentially available under Public Law 89–10.

k/ Data supplied by California Teachers Association.

Source: NEA Research Division, Copyright © 1965 by the National Education Association. All Rights Reserved. Reprinted by permission.

where they have been educated. Therefore, the quality of such education is a matter of national concern.

There is also a considerable number of citizens and organizations who oppose federal aid to education chiefly for the following reasons:

1. States which are having difficulty in supporting an adequate program of education, such as certain ones in the South, are those who have not made a conscientious and sincere effort to do so. It is not totally a question of financial ability.
2. Federal participation will inevitably lead to federal control, something contrary to our democratic ideals.
3. Constitutionally, education is and should remain a dominant obligation of the states.
4. Avoidance of or reduction in many avenues of waste in state and local educational practice would result in greater efficiency and materially lessen the need for federal participation.
5. A good many persons and groups oppose federal aid unless at the same time funds can be given to parochial and possibly private schools. It is highly questionable if such action would not be considered unconstitutional.
6. It is unfair and undemocratic to take money from one state and give it to another.

In speaking of the importance of education to the nation, President Johnson on July 28, 1964, made the following statement:

If we are learning anything from our experiences, we are learning that it is time for us to go to work, and the first work of these times and the first work of our society is education.

STATE SUPPORT

As may be implied from the statements briefly presented on page 87, strong efforts are being made to have the states assume a somewhat larger share of the total cost of education. This is desired in order to reduce the part of the cost borne by the local unit where the real estate tax becomes most burdensome, as well as to enable the state to use the broader tax area of the entire state, thus more nearly equalizing the burden of cost.

The state, therefore, is becoming somewhat more important as a provider of funds for public education on the elementary and secondary levels. Strong legal support for this trend may be found in the significant number of court decisions affirming that education is constitutionally a state function.

In the table on page 86 are indications that the *share* of the cost of education borne by the state has risen from 16.5 percent in 1919–20 to 38.7 percent in 1961–62, whereas the *share* borne by the local governments decreased from 83.2 percent to 56.9 percent in the same period. Although there are presently ten states in which more than 60 percent of the total revenues for education comes from state sources, it seems in the last few years that more or less of a plateau has been reached in the movement. Of course, it is obvious that the dollar expenditures are quite another matter.

Sources of State Funds

The states secure their funds for educational purposes from taxes either specifically designated or those not so set apart and from which the revenue may be used for the general operating expenses, including education, of the state government. At present, approximately one-half of the states are using taxes earmarked for education with the money not entering the "general fund" at all.

One of the arguments generally raised against the use of taxes earmarked for schools is that when revenue from that source falls, the schools may suffer severely. Proponents of this type of tax argue that education is nearly always assured of reasonable support, because the funds cannot be diverted to other purposes.

The more common and important taxes in the various states that are used either directly or indirectly for education are as follows:

General sales taxes

Selective sales taxes and gross receipts, as alcoholic beverages, tobacco, insurance, soft drinks, public utilities

Income taxes, graduated or flat

Property taxes

Severance taxes, as coal, silver, oil

License and privilege taxes, as motor fees, alcoholic beverages, parimutuel, insurance premiums

Inheritance and estate taxes

A chart prepared by the United States Office of Education is presented on page 92, indicating trends in the use of the more common and important sources of revenue for state and local governments. It will be noted that revenues from property and sales, and gross receipts taxes have reached a somewhat stable position.

The National Education Association [2] has pointed out that for 1964 general sales and gross receipts taxes were the best revenue producers in 30 states while the personal income tax was the leading producer in 13 states.

Today it is becoming more accepted that a satisfactory tax system

[2] NEA Research Bulletin, Vol. 43, No. 2 (Washington, D.C., May, 1965), pp. 48–49.

Figure 4-2.   General Revenues of State and Local Governments by
              Source *

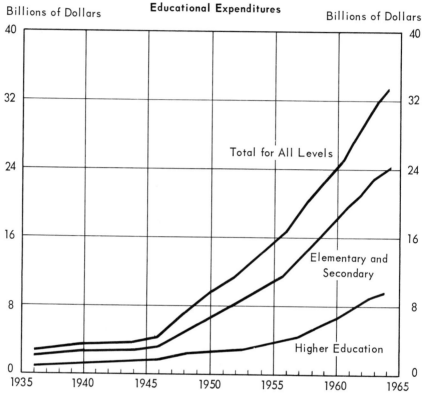

* Property taxes, which are the principal revenue source of local governments, yielded
$19.1 billion in fiscal year 1962. Sales and gross receipts taxes, a principal source of State
revenues, yielded $13.5 billion. Of combined State and local revenues in FY 1962, prop-
erty taxes accounted for 32.7 percent; sales and gross receipts taxes, 23.2 percent; other
taxes and charges, 30.6 percent; and the Federal Government, 13.5 percent.

SOURCE: 1964 Edition, *Health, Education, and Welfare Trends.*

should have a reasonably broad base. Taxes, either local or state, should
not be based on one source alone, such as property, but upon a fair number of other sources. It is, in effect, a method by which all of the eggs are
not placed in one basket and by which all or *very nearly all* persons are
reached in one form or another. Looking at the *broad tax base* in another way it may be said to consist of "taxes reaching new sources of
revenue, levied by the state and shared in one way or another with the
communities, more or less roughly in proportion to the amount of such
taxes paid by the residents of the community." Sales and income taxes

could well be part of a broad tax base and are finding wide use throughout the nation.

The Distribution of State Funds for Education

It is pretty generally agreed that the chief financial interest of the state, as far as the schools are concerned, is to guarantee to every child, wherever he may live, a certain foundation program. This foundation program is variously construed and may consist of all or parts of the following:

1. Properly qualified teachers for every child.
2. A safe, sanitary, and adequate school building.
3. A minimum school term.
4. Free textbooks and supplies.
5. Free transportation beyond a reasonable distance.

A standard per pupil cost of the foundation program may then be set. While such a figure would vary from state to state, it would undoubtedly be far in excess of $200 per year even in the poorest state. It is estimated that by 1970 the actual United States average cost per pupil for current expenses will rise 110.9 percent over the figure of $472 for 1959–60.

There are very few who will not agree that local districts vary widely in their ability to support such a foundation program as described. Ability, as used in this sense, is considered to be some measure showing a relationship of resources to load, resources usually being thought of as taxable possibilities or wealth.

A district or state with large taxable resources, for example, would be one with fertile soil, with prosperous industries, or with a people who had high incomes and who owned relatively good homes. Conversely, unproductive soil, industries with low earning possibilities, as in many of the coal-producing areas of Pennsylvania, and a people with low incomes and living in poor housing would have greatly reduced possibilities for supporting education or any other governmental service, for that matter.

Load, as the term is used here, means the number of teachers in relation to the number of pupils. Here again there is wide variation. Many areas have a much larger number of children in proportion to the number of adults (those who pay the taxes) than others. A locality with a smaller number of children and with other factors, such as wealth and number of earning adults equal, can support a much better program of education than can a district with the opposite conditions.

Thus it comes about that the state can best distribute its money on the equalization principle, which means allocating the money according to ability and need. In such a plan, however, each district is usually required to levy a certain minimum tax rate of its own, thereby exerting a reasonable effort. Then the state must assist by giving its funds to districts to make up the difference between the amount this reasonable effort will yield and the cost of the foundation program. Various formulas have been developed to provide a means of determining how much money each district should receive under such a plan, the formulas differing from state to state.

In addition to funds distributed by the equalization formula, money may be allocated for a number of other purposes, as the following:

1. To assist in providing better schools.
2. Vocational education.
3. Education of the handicapped.
4. Education of atypical children of other types.
5. Transportation.
6. To encourage the elimination of small schools.
7. For partial assistance in building new schools.

SUPPORT BY THE COUNTY AND LOCAL DISTRICT

Whether the local district is the county or the smaller municipal unit or both, it is there that the balance of the money needed to operate the schools must be raised after revenues from the federal government and the state have been deducted.

With the state carrying an increased share of the total cost of education and with the share of the federal government not changing materially, it follows that the proportionate parts borne by the county and local units have decreased over the last 20 years. In 1945–46 these units provided 63.8 percent of the total school revenue receipts from all sources, while in the last several years the percent borne by them has been more or less constant at 56.5 to 56.9 percent. It is obvious that the local and intermediate units still furnish more than half of the total revenue receipts. The table on page 92 presents the most recent data available on this matter.

If the county is a strong unit for school support, then it is likely that it will provide either all or a large part of the funds needed on the local level. Such is the case, for example, in Maryland. In the United States as a whole, however, the county is not a very significant source of revenue for schools.

LOCAL FINANCING

The local government, representing units smaller than the county, as has been pointed out in a previous chapter, bears the real burden of supporting education below the state level. The chief reason for this seems to be that the people locally can have the sort of schools for which they are willing to pay. On the other hand, the smaller the districts, the more likely there is to be inequalities among them. In general, the larger the area of support, the greater the chances of reducing the inequalities existing as a result of local conditions.

The great source of revenue at the local district level, as in the county, is the general property tax, usually meaning real estate, but in some cases including personal property as well. In a good many states the property tax is the sole source of revenue for education locally. The real estate or general property tax is not without a number of serious weaknesses. In general practice, the property is assessed (has a value placed on it) by local elected officials who, except in the rarest of cases, are not real estate experts. The results are the accumulation of wide inequalities and thus an unfair distribution of the tax burden. Recent tendencies have been in the direction of establishing some nonlocal agency as a state or county board of tax equalization to adjust many of the inequalities that are a part of the politically dominated local-assessment system. Some progress is being made in this direction; more is urgently needed.

Since World War II there have been some attempts toward enlarging the taxing powers of the local districts and permitting them to use a good many other sources than the property tax. In Pennsylvania, for example, the so-called "Tax Anything" law illustrates the point. This act in substance permits a local district to tax anything not already taxed by the state. It may to some extent be considered a scheme that encourages the state to shift its own responsibility.

The property tax, as previously stated, is the source of many financial inequities; and with shifting populations and changing industrial patterns, difficult problems arise in providing funds for education at the local level. In fact, the problems are very similar for all the functions of local government. Certainly a significant part of the answer lies in shifting a greater share of the cost to the state, possibly even to the national government.

It is widely agreed that in the financing of public education the local school board, representing the school district, should have a large amount of fiscal independence. Operating under constitutional and legal limitations, the board should be able to form its budget with the professional assistance of the superintendent and his staff, set its tax rates, oversee the collection of its funds and direct their expenditure. This can be done best if the board of education is independent of other politically chosen local bodies or officials. However, since the state pays so large a share of the total cost of education, some supervision from that source is in order. This may take the form of approval of the budget and/or of the final report for the fiscal year.

Many districts with low borrowing capacities have found themselves at an impasse in regard to providing the funds for necessary school construction. The only alternatives seem to be: (1) To enlarge the borrowing capacity by raising the limitations. Care must be taken here, however, not to reach the point of confiscatory taxation. (2) To provide legal means of circumventing the limitations, as represented by the "authority" method of financing. This is a plan to by-pass the low borrowing capacities of states or municipalities by setting up an independent body chosen in accordance with the laws of the particular state. This "authority" then issues bonds, builds and equips the buildings, and rents them to the governmental units. The state or municipality becomes full owner after a fixed period of years since the annual payments include amortization as well as rent. (3) To receive help for this purpose from the state or federal governments. Both of these sources are now entering the school building picture in a limited way.

ISSUES TO BE FACED

In a brief summarization of the difficulties ahead in the problem of school support, Morphet and Lindman [3] suggest that among the most important issues that must be faced are the following:

1. How much should the citizens of each state and community invest in the support of their schools?
2. To what extent should the taxpayers of one area be expected to make a greater effort than those of another area to provide a reasonably adequate educational program?
3. To what extent should control be permitted or encouraged to follow the school dollar?
4. To what extent should local initiative and responsibility be encouraged?
5. What proportion of the funds for school support should come from state sources?
6. Should there be a "partnership" program of school support, or should the state undertake to support a foundation program entirely from state revenues?
7. Should the taxpayers of an entire state be expected to help pay the extra expenses of operating numerous small schools or maintaining small inefficient districts?
8. Can adequate educational opportunities be assured by providing state support for only certain portions of the program?
9. What should be the place of the general property tax in the school support program?
10. What steps should be taken to improve state school finance programs?
11. What is an adequate foundation program of education?

[3] Edgar Morphet and Erick L. Lindman, *Public School Finance Programs of the Forty-eight States,* Circular 274 (Washington, U.S. Office of Education, 1950), pp. 4–8.

All of these problems present matters of unusual importance to the American people. There is no doubt but that it is going to be increasingly difficult to find the larger and larger funds that must be found if our children's needs are to be met.

All too often the classroom teacher, and particularly the beginning teacher, is inclined to say that matters of securing and using funds for education are complicated and must be left to administrators alone. Nothing could be farther from the truth. Detailed studies of finance *are* complicated, it is true, but the basic elements and principles presented in this chapter are matters that can be understood by anyone. Far too many teachers become suddenly interested in money matters when their requests for highly desirable equipment are turned down or when salary checks are not paid on time. This is much too late. Every teacher should be able to talk over the financial needs of the schools with the parents of his students and he should be so well informed that he can effectively counsel with lay groups whenever the occasion presents itself.

We have not done a good job of public relations on the need for school funds, and the time to begin is now, both for the beginning teacher and for all those in service, for no matter how strong the facts in favor of increased support for education may appear, there will be no action unless the public is sincerely convinced.

QUESTIONS AND PROJECTS

1. Conduct a debate on the question: Resolved, that the federal government should provide greater financial aid to public education.
2. Investigate the taxes used for the support of education in your own state, both on the state and district levels.
3. Secure data on the relation of good education to good business.
4. Compare your state with other states and with the national average as far as expenditures for education and efforts to support education are concerned.
5. Investigate the national expenditures for education and for luxuries—tobacco, liquor, etc.
6. Organize a panel discussion around the following major topic: Wealth in all forms should be taxed for the support of the public schools.
7. Clarify what is meant by the phrase *long-term financial planning.*
8. Investigate the extent to which your state has a broad tax base.
9. Study some possible areas of economy which should be considered for public education.
10. Be able to explain to a family having no children why they should pay their share of the cost of education.

AUDIO-VISUAL AIDS

MOTION PICTURES (16 MM)

Education is Good Business—General Picture Productions, Inc., 621 Sixth Ave., Des Moines, Iowa, 10 min., sd., b&w and/or color. Contrasts a community in which business and industry proudly support their schools, with another in which business and industry are less alert.

Investment in Youth—Hollywood Film Enterprises, Inc., 6060 Sunset Blvd., Hollywood 28, Calif., 22 min., sd., b&w. Develops the theme that youth is Canada's most natural resource, and that public expenditure for their development is a sound investment.

Pop Rings the Bell—National School Service Institute, 27 East Monroe St., Chicago 3, Ill., 23 min., sd., b&w. Emphasizes the need for adequate financial support to meet the new educational needs.

The Sixth Chair—National School Service Institute, 27 East Monroe St., Chicago 3, Ill., 18 min., sd., b&w. Highlights such problems in education as building construction and modernization, class size, more teachers, up-to-date educational tools, and portrays the dangers of the public's complacency towards education. A picture that will help to put the public squarely behind a better financial program of action.

A Way of Life—International Harvester Co., 180 No. Michigan Ave., Chicago, Ill., 25 min., sd., color. The story of school at Beaverton, Michigan, and how the problem of finance for educational purposes was solved, providing broader educational opportunities for the young and new ideas and better living for the whole community.

National Goals, No. 5: Education—NYU-TV, 29 min., sd., b&w. Presents a discussion of educational problems including the question: "Whom shall we educate, how, and for what?" Proposes: early testing for abilities, special training, more creative teaching, less administrative and clerical burdens on the part of the teacher, and the evaluation of new teaching techniques. Discusses the need for new schools, salary increases, and federal aid to education.

RECORDING

Education the Foundation of Business—Educational Recording Services, 5922 Abernathy Drive, Los Angeles, Calif., 2 sides, 33⅓ r.p.m. microgroove. Address by Willis A. Sutton. Discussion of the relation between the level of education and the circulation of newspapers, life insurance, savings accounts, grocery and department store sales in the local area and in the nation.

FURTHER READINGS

Burke, Arvid J., *Financing the Public Schools,* rev. ed. (New York, Harper & Row, 1957).

Clayton, A. Stafford, "The Effects of Public Support of Church-Related Schools," *Phi Delta Kappan,* Vol. 47 (September, 1965), pp. 19–24.

Committee for Economic Development, *Paying for the Public Schools,* A statement on National Policy by the Research and Policy Committee on Education for Economic Development (Washington, D.C., 1959).

Garber, Lee O., and Newton Edwards, *The Law Governing the Public Financing of Education* (Danville, Illinois, Interstate Printers and Publishers, 1964).

National Education Association, *Ranking of the States, 1965,* Research Report 1965 R 10 (Washington, D.C., 1965).

Rockefeller Brothers Fund, *Pursuit of Excellence and the Future of America* (Garden City, N.Y., Doubleday, 1958).

Special Project on School Finance, *Financing the Public Schools 1960–1970* (Washington, D.C., NEA, 1962).

"The Elementary and Secondary Education Act of 1965," *American Education,* Vol. 1 (April, 1965).

United States Office of Education, *Digest of Educational Statistics, 1964 Edition* (Washington, D.C., 1964).

United States Office of Education, *Financing Public Education, Special Features of a Satisfactory State Plan* (Washington, D.C., 1947).

United States Office of Education, *Progress of Public Education in the United States of America, 1963–1964* (Washington, D.C., 1964).

United States Office of Health, Education, and Welfare, *Health, Education, and Welfare Trends, 1964 Edition* (Washington, D.C., 1964).

United States Office of Health, Education, and Welfare, *Vocational Education Act of 1963* (Washington, D.C., 1964).

II

THE PROFESSION OF
EDUCATION

5

The Work of the Teacher

PREVIEW

▸ Teaching is a complicated task with new responsibilities being added continually.

▸ Within the school there are:
   1. Regular teaching duties which involve the direction of learning and working closely with children as well as the study and evaluation of new techniques.
   2. Nonteaching duties which include guidance of many types and many activities outside of the classroom.

▸ Teaching also involves working with the community.
   Community attitudes, expectations, and requirements vary widely.

▸ The teacher has many obligations to his profession.
   No member of a professional group can stand alone. He has obligations to his local group and to the membership at large.
   The modern teacher actively participates with his fellows in all group efforts for the improvement of the educational processes, the profession itself, and the community.

▸ A major responsibility of a professional group is the development of standards for its members and the maintenance of provisions attainment and enforcement of these standards.
   Here the Code of Ethics is of major consideration. Professional organizations become a major force in these efforts and demand the concern and cooperation of all teachers.

▸ As in other major professions, the problems involved in the continuing of education are of great significance and should be a concern of every teacher.

It is the thesis of the authors of this volume that the function of the teacher in the American democracy is far more important than that of any other group. If the ideas of the founders are to be preserved and if education is as closely linked to national security as we believe it is, then the work of teachers is of great significance. Other services are of great value, of course, but it should be emphasized that good teachers are absolutely necessary for the development of every other profession. There is no satisfactory alternative to this.

Of course, in many fields the results of effort are seen much sooner. In a relatively short time the doctor's patient may recover; at the end of the day the carpenter can look back with satisfaction upon what he has done, but all too often the results of the teacher's labors are seen only in the long run. Sometimes they are seen at once, as when a child's face shows his satisfaction with some accomplishment, however small, or when the countenance of a college student glows when he comes to understand a great principle. Very often, however, the effectiveness of a teacher's work is seen in the later accomplishments of his students, and this is natural because education does not take place overnight. The intellectual curiosity that a teacher generates, the abilities he stimulates, and the character that he helps to form take time to reach fruition.

Many of the rewards of teaching appear when students return to speak to a former teacher and tell of the vital contributions made to their lives. Another reward is the satisfaction expressed by parents whose children have been profoundly influenced by a devoted teacher. These are but a few of the compensations which result from the work of a good teacher.

Certainly there is no monotony in teaching. All children are different, and every good teacher knows this. Nor are children the same day after day any more than adults are. Some are hard to understand and difficult to reach; others are easy to know well and need only occasional guidance and encouragement. The teacher who is really interested in children as people—and no one else should be teaching—can thus find in his group far more challenges than he can ever meet to his satisfaction. If a teacher is truly concerned with the progress of his students, he will find variety and stimulation in his work.

In every school, teachers are confronted with some disinterest and antagonism, for there are students who have neither the aptitude nor the enthusiasm for schooling. Generally, these are in the minority, but they do create difficulties, and it is well for the teacher to realize that such situations exist. It should be clear that if one understands the frustrations involved in teaching, there is less chance of disillusionment. An idealistic approach is most effective when tempered with a consciousness of the nature of the problems—real, and sometimes insolvable—which are likely to occur.

In very recent years the changing nature of our population has brought new problems and new challenges to the classroom. Generally fluctuations of population in cities are due largely to mass migration from one part of the country to the urban and suburban areas of other sections. Classroom problems result from underprivilege, lack of education, segregation, and language difficulties. Such situations present teachers with tremendous problems that require excellent preparation and considerable experience. The needs here are urgent and demand the best in buildings, equipment, and personnel.

Teachers must not lose sight of the fact that both actually and legally they are acting in place of parents during many—if not most—of the children's waking hours. They are concerned with their students' social, emotional, physical, and moral growth as well as their intellectual development. Whether the children and their parents wish it or not, teachers are guides and examples to the young people entrusted to them. What more worthy task can there be?

With this background then, it will be helpful if we make a careful and realistic analysis of the many activities in today's schools that concern the teachers as they are involved with their challenging responsibilities and the satisfactions which result from their daily work.

THE ACTIVITIES OF THE TEACHER

The real duties of the effective modern teacher are much broader and much more complicated than the average layman believes. Far too many individuals still think the teacher works only between the hours of 9 and 3 or 3:30, during which time he is "hearing lessons" and disciplining children, and when *they* go home his day is over.

Nothing could be farther from the truth, for it seems that each year the teacher's task becomes a more complicated one. More and more of the responsibilities that were formerly accepted by the home are being transferred in whole or in part to the school. Beyond this, additional services are expected from the teacher as a member of the community in which he lives and in which he teaches.

Consequently, it may be well for us to look at the teacher's work from three different points of view: (1) teaching duties and nonteaching duties within the school; (2) activities within the community; (3) activities as a co-worker with other teachers.

ACTIVITIES WITHIN THE SCHOOL

The Teaching Process

Without question, it is accepted that the main task of the teacher on either the elementary or the secondary level is that of guiding the children in the learning process. At the elementary level the teacher is generally associated with a smaller number of pupils for a longer period of time each day and is more likely to work with small groups within his entire grade. In both high and elementary schools, however, the conducting of many formal classes is involved.

The modern teacher is a guide and a friend to children; he stimulates and directs their learning toward the end of truly democratic living. He is neither taskmaster nor driver, although that type of discipline or control must be maintained which will permit the effective performance of the activities that are supposed to be carried on. The teacher who cannot get his students to attain this standard of behavior in the classroom can in no sense become effective.

In addition to the guiding and directing of learning in groups or classes, the good teacher will continually be working with individuals, studying their needs and assisting them where individual help is necessary. For the elementary school much of this can occur in the classroom, but it is inevitable that some of it will also have to be done outside of the formal school hours both before the session starts and after it closes.

Preparation for Daily Teaching

It goes without saying that any good teacher will need to do much planning for the work of the classroom. Lesson plans must be made either roughly outlined or planned in detail. For the beginning teacher this will have to be done more carefully and thoroughly than will be necessary as one grows in experience and in ability. In some schools, these plans will have to be available for the supervisor for inspection and approval. Then there are other materials to be prepared, such as photographs, various audio-visual aids; bulletin boards must be planned, and other material looked after.

The increased use of television as a teaching tool requires much study and preparation outside of regular school hours; it is a mistake to think that the television teacher replaces the classroom teacher. Indeed, it places new responsibilities upon him. It means that the regular teacher must familiarize himself with lessons to be presented, with related reading material, and with additional stimulation and follow-up resources.

In like manner the use of teaching machines and programmed learning presents new challenges to the teacher assisting pupils through new techniques. The mastering of new techniques involves intensive study and preparation by the teacher.

No small part of the teacher's work is that of keeping informed of new developments, evaluating them, and using those of promise. All of this is a matter of keeping techniques up-to-date and is no more than what is expected of an alert member of any profession.

Kindergarten children study nature. Upper Merion Township Public Schools, Pa.

Testing Pupil Achievement

Not the least important part of teaching is the measurement of pupil progress and growth. This involves the preparation of tests, examinations, and other written work, and it should be noted that the preparation of good, valid tests and examinations is a time-consuming task but an important one. Few teachers like to correct written work and tests, but it must be done fairly and well. It has been said that "correcting papers is the dishwashing of school teaching," but students who turn in written work have the right to expect that it will receive the best attention of the teacher.

NONTEACHING DUTIES

The things teachers do that are not directly related to the teaching process are, indeed, many and are a cause of some concern to administrators and to teachers themselves. There are attendance records to be kept; if they are not approached in the proper spirit they are likely to become a considerable chore. A careful accounting is necessary, however, in the gigantic business of public education. Supplies and equip-

Courtesy: School District of Philadelphia.
Joesph L. Pollock, Director of Informational Services.

A teacher in the elementary schools of the city of Philadelphia works with
a small group of third graders. Emphasis is upon pronunciation.

ment must be looked after also, and inventories kept, as well as new
materials requisitioned.

Parents too must be apprised of the progress of their children. No
completely satisfactory type of report has as yet been found; in many
communities school people, with frequent parental co-operation, are
studying how to improve report cards which have varied from the formal
letter-grading cards of yesteryear to personal letters and oral conferences
with parents. All of this takes a considerable amount of any teacher's
time.

Care of the Classroom and Other Duties

Then, too, the room which the teacher uses must be kept in
good condition. This may range from the actual janitorial service per-

formed in the old one-teacher, one-room school to the rearranging of furniture, pictures, bulletin boards, and the like in a school with superior custodial service. An attractively arranged classroom is an asset to any school, and for this the teacher should gladly accept a major responsibility.

Many schools have banking or thrift systems in which the children are encouraged to make regular deposits. However, the teacher must oversee the operation of the program and accept considerable responsibility for an accurate accounting.

Then in nearly all secondary schools there are homerooms, with programs to be planned and carried out, and frequently there are study halls to be supervised and hall duties. Now that transportation to and from school is becoming such an important part of education, teachers are frequently assigned duties in connection therewith. Children need to have directed activities when they get to school early in the morning and while waiting for the bus to take them home. On occasion some teachers are expected to ride on transportation vehicles and exercise some control and discipline en route. Generally though, this is the responsibility of the bus driver.

In both elementary and high schools there are co-curricular activities to be directed or sponsored. Of course, these are more varied for the secondary school, but the elementary teachers also have traffic patrols, citizenship clubs, and the like for which responsibility must be assumed. Everyone of these may be justified and thoroughly worthwhile, yet they are a significant part of his day.

Some fairly definite idea of the division of the teacher's time may be seen in a study made by the NEA [1] in 1961 which uses a scientifically determined sample of the nation's public school teaching population. Teachers were asked to give their best judgment of the time spent in an average week on each of seventeen activities other than classroom teaching. Seasonal activities were prorated over the weeks of the school year. Graphic results of the distribution for elementary and high school teachers separately follow:

There is considerable feeling at the present time that the teaching load must be lightened and more relaxation provided during the day. The tendency in the high school has been to have more and more of the so-called extraclass activities on school time through the use of an activity period.

In the elementary school the modern self-contained classroom seems to have accentuated the problem. Here the teacher is with the children constantly from the time they arrive in the morning until they leave at the end of the day. Not only is he with them in the classroom, but usually

[1] "Time Devoted to School Duties," *NEA Research Bulletin*, Vol. 40, No. 3 (February, 1962) pp. 83–88.

Figure 5-1. How the Elementary School Teacher Divides the Week (Average Work Week of 48 Hours, 30 Minutes)

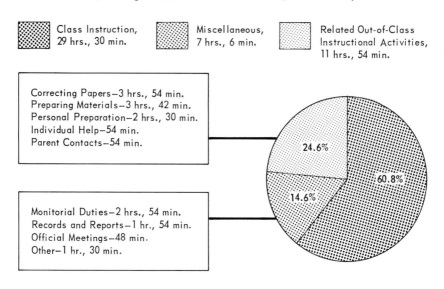

Class Instruction, 29 hrs., 30 min.

Miscellaneous, 7 hrs., 6 min.

Related Out-of-Class Instructional Activities, 11 hrs., 54 min.

Correcting Papers—3 hrs., 54 min.
Preparing Materials—3 hrs., 42 min.
Personal Preparation—2 hrs., 30 min.
Individual Help—54 min.
Parent Contacts—54 min.

Monitorial Duties—2 hrs., 54 min.
Records and Reports—1 hr., 54 min.
Official Meetings—48 min.
Other—1 hr., 30 min.

24.6%

60.8%

14.6%

Figure 5-2. How the High School Teacher Divides the Week (Average Work Week of 45 Hours, 54 Minutes)

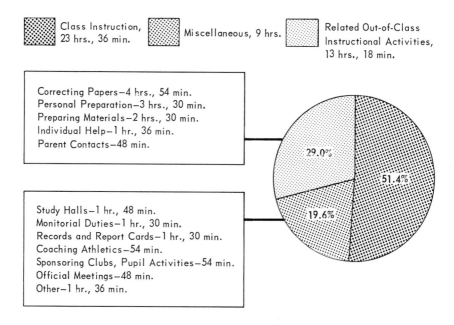

Class Instruction, 23 hrs., 36 min.

Miscellaneous, 9 hrs.

Related Out-of-Class Instructional Activities, 13 hrs., 18 min.

Correcting Papers—4 hrs., 54 min.
Personal Preparation—3 hrs., 30 min.
Preparing Materials—2 hrs., 30 min.
Individual Help—1 hr., 36 min.
Parent Contacts—48 min.

Study Halls—1 hr., 48 min.
Monitorial Duties—1 hr., 30 min.
Records and Report Cards—1 hr., 30 min.
Coaching Athletics—54 min.
Sponsoring Clubs, Pupil Activities—54 min.
Official Meetings—48 min.
Other—1 hr., 36 min.

29.0%

51.4%

19.6%

Source: Figures 5–1 and 5–2 from *NEA Research* Bulletin, Vol. 40, No. 3 (October, 1962), pp. 86–87. Copyright NEA and used by special permission.

he directs their activities on the playground and eats lunch with them as well. There are many who feel very strongly that by some methods, not yet clearly determined, ways must be found for the teacher to be free from responsibility for his children for at least short periods during the day.

Every modern school should provide an attractive lounge or teacher's room for women and for men where some relaxation may be found when time permits. In many instances these rooms are furnished by the board of education. In other situations the parent-teacher association has found this to be a worthwhile project.

Working with the Community

It will be most helpful to the teacher who is considering entering upon service in a new community if he will gather all the information possible about it before accepting appointment. This will be useful to an applicant trying to find out if it is a desirable place in which to work. The author remembers well two college seniors who accepted appointments in a rather large town and signed the usual contracts after an interview with the superintendent. Several weeks later they visited the community, decided they didn't like it, and repudiated their contracts. Such performance quite obviously fosters bad relations on all sides, even though no penalty may be legally provided.

After a teacher has accepted appointment in a district, he will be a better teacher if he has gotten all available facts concerning it. Many data may be gathered from the United States census reports, particularly the bulletins *Characteristics of the Population,* published for each state. Facts about the industrial nature of the community and of the agriculture in the surrounding territory may also be secured from publications of the Census Bureau and possibly from the local Chamber of Commerce or Board of Trade. It goes without saying that the new teacher will surely wish to spend quite a few days in the community where he expects to teach before entering upon his duties. A compilation of items upon which data may be secured would include the following:

Population
Area
Racial and nationalistic characteristics of the population
Growth of the community
Historical background
Industrial nature
Professions and occupations
Housing
Business status
Size of the school system

Recreational facilities
Social service agencies
Religious organizations
Possible future growth

Attitudes Toward Teachers. Communities differ very greatly in their attitudes toward teachers because of many factors which will be taken up elsewhere in this volume. In some places educators are highly respected, just as are certain members of the older professions of medicine and law. Here they will be welcomed into all of the various community organizations and enterprises and expected to share community responsibilities. They will be granted the same rights and privileges as are members of the other professions. On the other hand, in some places they will not be a very highly respected group, and they may be surrounded with restrictions, some of which seem petty and ridiculous. The day of these unreasonable requirements is passing rapidly in most of the country, but no teacher can escape the fact that much is required of him in the way of patterns of behavior and of moral conduct. The teacher, man or woman, is in a strong position of leadership in regard to the youth of the community; the same does not hold true for all professional people. This fact cannot be ignored or wished away. While this may be more obvious in small communities than in large ones, it is always present to a considerable degree. It should be considered a challenge rather than a handicap that teachers are generally expected to be examples of fine living.

Richey [2] comments as follows here: "If you were to call upon a lawyer or a medical doctor for business reasons, either would likely appear before you carefully groomed and would display behavior appropriate to his profession. The same should be expected of teachers."

It will be well for the new teacher to find out what the local requirements or expectations are and honor them. Simon,[3] in his *Preface to Teaching,* has suggested that if the teacher respects the standards of the community on small things which are really symbolic, such as not eating in certain restaurants, he will be in a far better position to win a victory on such important matters as the freedom to teach controversial issues and to carry on the full duties of citizenship.

Special Requirements and Expectations. In some communities, unfortunately, although it is generally illegal, there may be discrimination against the members of certain religious groups. It is encouraging to note, however, that such practices seem to be decreasing.

In some localities membership in some church or at least active participation in the work of some church is expected. Some superintendents

[2] Robert W. Richey, *Planning for Teaching* (New York, McGraw-Hill, 1952), p. 247.
[3] Henry W. Simon, *Preface to Teaching* (New York, Oxford University Press, 1938).

think that such a person will be a better teacher and more truly interested in the community where he teachers. Possibly this is a sort of carry-over from the days when it was common practice to require the teacher also to teach a Sunday School class. Today it is rather widely held that this should be a matter for the teacher's own conscience and that many will probably do better work if they have a respite from formal teaching over the weekend.

This discussion naturally leads to the problem of where the teacher should live. Although it is true that most school boards prefer to have a teacher live in the community, modern transportation has made commuting much more common than it was a few years ago. Many boards of education set up local residence as a condition of employment; others suggest that the teacher stay in the community on frequent or, at least, occasional weekends, and on rare occasions it will be officially suggested that residence elsewhere will be preferred. Certainly it will be clear to almost anyone that only a teacher who knows the community, who participates in its activities, and who is really a part of it can be sensitive to its problems and its needs and thus be more likely to do an effective teaching job. The teacher who knows the community merely as a location for his school can hardly win the complete respect of those who live there and support it, nor can he attain his full potentialities as a leader and guide of children. Writing on this general problem, the Commission on Teacher Education of the American Council on Education [4] has said:

Simulation of an unfelt degree of community interest, either for protective purposes or in a grimly "professional" spirit will not do. On the other hand, friendliness and a sense of the value of community relations will lead teachers to take steps appropriate to themselves, and to the situations in which they find themselves, that will speed the day when a genuine community membership has been acquired.

Only as one becomes a part of the community itself can this result be attained.

It is an encouraging sign that in most communities teachers are being sought for membership in local service clubs for men and women. They are asked to give leadership to many enterprises, such as the Community Chest, and to national movements of significance—the Red Cross, and other agencies devoted to health and welfare.

More and more, too, the school children are being asked to aid in the solicitation of funds for these organizations. No one can deny that, properly administered, this can be excellent practice in good citizenship which is surely worthwhile. On the other hand, many teachers and administra-

[4] Commission on Teacher Education, *Teachers for Our Times* (Washington, American Council on Education, 1944), p. 159.

tors are profoundly disturbed at the multiplicity of "drives" and similar occasions in which the school is asked to participate. Quite a few have met the problem by organizing a "chest" or "United Drive" for the particular school, allocating funds to all groups on some agreed basis and then prohibiting all other appeals, a procedure which has met with general satisfaction. In matters such as these and in other similar situations, such as essay contests, a clear-cut policy of the board of education will be invaluable to the teacher, who should make certain that he is familiar with any policy that exists.

In more than a few communities people look to the teachers for leadership in the Boy and Girl Scout movements and the like, and to these requests many respond willingly. In fact, in a good many teacher-preparation programs, training is given in these areas. The same may be said for such work as playground direction and other areas of recreational activity. Some of this, of course, involves much time outside of school hours, and on occasion extra compensation is given for it. A question that must be faced is how much outside work may be properly expected of a teacher beyond regular classroom duties before extra pay is justified. A recent case in Pennsylvania, for example, resulted in a court decision that denied the right of a school board to require a high school teacher to collect tickets at a football game on Saturday without additional compensation.[5] Where somewhat similar cases have reached the courts in other states the school boards have been upheld. The pattern of decisions indicates that boards have the right to require of their teachers adherence to "reasonable" rules and regulations pertaining to duties outside of the classroom. The key to justifiable requirements seems to be in their reasonability, a matter which will frequently have to be determined by the courts in specific situations.

An illustration of the type of legislation covering this matter is found in the Pennsylvania School Laws where Section 510 reads in part as follows.

The board of school directors in any school district may adopt and enforce such reasonable rules and regulations as it may deem necessary and proper, regarding the management of its school affairs and the conduct and deportment of all superintendents, teachers, and other appointees or employes during the time they are engaged in their duties to the district, as well as the conduct and deportment of all pupils attending the public schools in the district, during such time as they are under the supervision of the board of school directors and teachers, including the time necessarily spent in coming to and returning from school.[6]

[5] 78—D and C. 266, Delaware County (Pa.) Reporter, 38 Delaware County, Pa., 406.

[6] *School Laws of Pennsylvania, 1951* (Harrisburg, Pa., Department of Public Instruction), Section 510.

Parent-Teacher Organization

One type of nonteaching activity in which most teachers are expected to engage, at least to some extent, is that of the parent-teacher association. From holding office, to serving on committees of various sorts, to talking with parents on regular meeting nights, teachers have a vital part to play in this co-operative work of the home and the school. Such organizations must not be teacher-dominated, but certainly the teacher may be expected to exert some reasonable amount of leadership. Few groups can do more good for the welfare of the children of any community than a well-planned and well-directed parent-teacher association; few can do more harm than one that fails to get a proper perspective of its program and one which is badly led.

A word of caution to the teacher about community activities may not be amiss at this point. It should be kept in mind that it is easier for most people to say "yes" than to say "no" to the things that one may be asked to do. What, then, is a desirable optimum?

Obviously, a teacher's first obligation is to be a *good* teacher in the most complete sense of the word. Certainly a new teacher in any community must choose wisely those activities which will make him a better teacher and which will not take so much time as to make it impossible for him to do a first-class job in his school. He needs time to prepare his work, to counsel with students, and to carry out effectively all the many professional tasks that are a part of good teaching. He needs time for relaxation and recreation too. To the extent that these goals are made too difficult or impossible, he is undertaking too much. It is not out of place to say that a teacher as well as anyone else must "develop the gentle art of saying 'no.' "

THE TEACHER AND THE PROFESSION

In the early days of American education when schools were small—very many having but one room—the teacher was, in most cases, isolated. He worked alone, removed from other colleagues, and without supervision or direction except that from the parents of his children and from the local trustees. The teacher of today, on the other hand, is far more likely to find himself in a large building, and often there is a superintendent not far away. There are principals, department heads, special teachers of many kinds, supervisors, consultants, health and social workers, custodians, members of the business staff, and of course, many other teachers of the same subject, field, or grade with whom proper working relationships may or must be established.

A teacher today, more than ever before, must realize that he is a member not only of a single school system but also of a very large professional group of more than 1¾ million members in the United States. With the recognition of this fact comes the realization that he cannot possibly stand alone. He needs the help of all his fellow members and to them he owes his support and contributions.

One cannot completely ignore the debate over whether or not teaching is really a profession rather than a trade or a craft. A good bit of agreement seems to have been reached on this question, but the rather fruitless argument will likely continue for some time to come. We should like to support at this point the specific statement of the Commission on Teacher Education and Professional Standards (TEPS) [7] as set forth in their recent *Position Paper:*

Teaching is a profession to the degree that its members are professional. A person who qualifies as a professional in any field:

Is a liberally educated person.
Possesses a body of specialized skills and knowledges essential to the performance of his job.
Makes rational judgments and acts accordingly; accepts responsibility for the consequences of his judgments and actions.
Believes in his service to society.
Assumes responsibility with his colleagues in developing and enforcing standards and abides by these standards in his own practice.
Seeks new knowledge and skill in order to improve his practice.

It is a basic assumption that the work of the teacher is made up of those activities that are largely intellectual. This does not mean that he does nothing with his hands any more than this may be said of doctors or of other commonly recognized professional groups. The point is that one cannot "teach by the book" or "by the rule" any more than a surgeon can operate in such a way. There are recommended procedures, it is true, but people are different, and the selection of procedures, materials, and their adoption must be the result of intellectual activity. Herein is the essence of a profession.

Such an outlook and recognition of need requires that careful attention be given to the type of education and background that will be most likely to bring about the sort of practitioner and the type of practice desired. It is in this field where controversy still exists. There seems to be little disagreement over the point that the teacher should be a liberally educated person. The area of nonagreement lies in determining how much of a liberal education is necessary and what its relation should be to the professional education that seems to be desired.

Now, of course, this concern is not pertinent to teaching only but may be considered relevant to other professions too. It probably ought to be a matter of continuing concern for all professional groups.

[7] National Commission on Teacher Education and Professional Standards, *A Position Paper* (Washington, NEA, 1963).

Courtesy: Senior High School, Oneonta, N.Y.
Architect: Warren H. Ashley, West Hartford, Conn.

The comprehensive high school curriculum affords students an opportunity to develop salable skills.

It is generally agreed that the candidates for entrance to a teacher education program should be the more intellectually capable high school graduates, and there is considerable evidence that this is the case more than ever before. Recently, many teacher education institutions have been raising their admission requirements—a procedure that will be more feasible as the supply of teachers more nearly approximates the demand.

The Commission on Teacher Education and Professional Standards [8] has pointed out that:

Students wishing to enter and remain in teacher education programs should meet high standards on the following counts; intelligence, academic achievement, physical stamina and health, emotional stability, moral and ethical fitness, knowledge of current spoken and written English, and ability to work with others. Evaluation should be continuous.

There are those who think that teacher education programs must encompass a fifth year if they are to be satisfactory; others suggest that all

[8] *Ibid.*, p. 7.

professional work in education be on the graduate level, and still others feel that the program can be carried out by eliminating many of the current professional courses.

This is illustrative of the ferment in the field of teacher education. If vested interests are not overly influential and if the thinking of disciplined minds is applied to our current and future needs, much good may result.

RESPONSIBILITY FOR THE DEVELOPMENT OF STANDARDS

A further reference at this point to the previously mentioned *Position Paper* (TEPS) will indicate the importance of joint responsibility by the members of the profession for the setting of standards for conduct and practice as well as for their enforcement. Most groups of workers, professional or otherwise, find that standards must be set up covering conditions for entrance and practice, obligations to the other members and to society, remuneration, and the like. Early illustrations of such provisions are found in the old trade guilds and the apprenticeship system with which the student is very likely familiar.

The earliest acceptance of a code of conduct is found in the use of the Hippocratic Oath by the medical profession. Actual codes of ethics, though, are quite recent in origin, a few of them having been adopted during the first half of the last century. Most of them are a product of the past 50 or 75 years.

Although it is still debated whether standards for professional status should be set by law or by voluntary action of the group itself, the majority will agree that the most effective policy is for the members themselves to be directly responsible for the enforcement of the standards which they have established. Certainly this is the most likely way to stimulate individual interest and responsibility. It may be charged that this represents the work of "establishment"—a term somewhat derisively used in recent studies of teacher education.[9] This is, however, characteristic of the policies for setting standards in nearly every major profession.

THE TEACHERS' CODE

The Code of Ethics of the Education Profession—the teachers' code—has been revised several times, most recently in 1963 when it was approved by the Representative Assembly of the National Education Association at its meeting in Detroit. The student considering education for a career should study the Code carefully so that he may know the obligations he assumes. Certainly no one should enter teaching without

---

[9] James B. Conant, *op. cit.*

being in sincere agreement with the principles accepted by the profession at large.

A code of ethics is not a series of laws. It was never intended to be such. Not many teachers do wrong "by degree" or on purpose, but errors of judgment are likely to happen unless a well-known set of standards is available as a guide. It is a sort of light along the way for the professional conduct of members, and where personal judgment is uncertain, a code of ethics will often help the teacher to do the right thing deliberately. For the very few who do wrong by design, some measures of enforcement are necessary in order that both the children and the members will be protected. As in other phases of human living, it is true in teaching that wrongdoing by one individual can bring disrepute and injury to many who are innocent.

THE CODE OF ETHICS OF THE EDUCATION PROFESSION

Adopted by the NEA Representative Assembly, July 1963

Preamble

We, professional educators of the United States of America, affirm our belief in the worth and dignity of man. We recognize the supreme importance and the pursuit of truth, the encouragement of scholarship, and the promotion of democratic citizenship. We regard as essential to these goals the protection of freedom to learn and to teach and the guarantee of equal educational opportunity for all. We affirm and accept our responsibility to practice our profession according to the highest ethical standards.

We acknowledge the magnitude of the profession we have chosen, and engage ourselves, individually and collectively, to judge our colleagues and to be judged by them in accordance with the applicable provisions of this code.

Principle I

Commitment to the Student

We measure success by the progress of each student toward achievement of his maximum potential. We therefore work to stimulate the spirit of inquiry, the acquisition of knowledge and understanding, and the thoughtful formulation of worthy goals. We recognize the importance of cooperative relationships with other community institutions, especially the home.

In fulfilling our obligations to the student, we—

1. Deal justly and considerately with each student.
2. Encourage the student to study varying points of view and respect his right to form his own judgment.
3. Withhold confidential information about a student or his home unless we deem that its release serves professional purposes, benefits the student, or is required by law.
4. Make discreet use of available information about the student.
5. Conduct conferences with or concerning students in an appropriate place and manner.
6. Refrain from commenting unprofessionally about a student or his home.
7. Avoid exploiting our professional relationship with any student.
8. Tutor only in accordance with officially approved policies.
9. Inform appropriate individuals and agencies of the student's educational needs and assist in providing an understanding of his educational experiences.
10. Seek constantly to improve learning facilities and opportunities.

Principle II

Commitment to the Community

We believe that patriotism in its highest form requires dedication to the principles of our democratic heritage. We share with all other citizens the responsibility for the development of sound public policy. As educators, we are particularly accountable for participating in the development of educational programs and policies and for interpreting them to the public.

In fulfilling our obligations to the community, we—
1. Share the responsibility for improving the educational opportunities for all.
2. Recognize that each educational institution may have a person authorized to interpret its official policies.
3. Acknowledge the right and responsibility of the public to participate in the formulation of educational policy.
4. Evaluate through appropriate professional procedures conditions within a district or institution of learning, make known serious deficiencies, and take any action deemed necessary and proper.
5. Use educational facilities for intended purposes consistent with applicable policy, law, and regulation.
6. Assume full political and citizenship responsibilities, but refrain from exploiting the institutional privileges of our professional positions to promote political candidates or partisan activities.
7. Protect the educational program against undesirable infringement.

Principle III

Commitment to the Profession

We believe that the quality of the services of the education profession directly influences the future of the nation and its citizens. We therefore exert every effort to raise educational standards, to improve our service, to promote a climate in which the exercise of professional judgment is encouraged, and to achieve conditions which attract persons worthy of the trust to careers in education. Aware of the value of united effort, we contribute actively to the support, planning, and programs of our professional organizations.

In fulfilling our obligations to the profession, we—

1. Recognize that a profession must accept responsibility for the conduct of its members and understand that our own conduct may be regarded as representative.
2. Participate and conduct ourselves in a responsible manner in the development and implementation of policies affecting education.
3. Cooperate in the selective recruitment of prospective teachers and in the orientation of student teachers, interns, and those colleagues new to their positions.
4. Accord just and equitable treatment to all members of the profession in the exercise of their professional rights and responsibilities, and support them when unjustly accused or mistreated.
5. Refrain from assigning professional duties to non-professional personnel when such assignment is not in the best interest of the student.
6. Provide, upon request, a statement of specific reason for administrative recommendations that lead to the denial of increments, significant changes in employment, or termination of employment.
7. Refrain from exerting undue influence based on the authority of our positions in the determination of professional decisions by colleagues.
8. Keep the trust under which confidential information is exchanged.
9. Make appropriate use of time granted for professional purposes.
10. Interpret and use the writings of others and the findings of educational research with intellectual honesty.
11. Maintain our integrity when dissenting by basing our public criticism of education on valid assumptions as established by careful evaluation of facts or hypotheses.
12. Represent honestly our professional qualifications and identify ourselves only with reputable educational institutions.
13. Respond accurately to requests for evaluations of colleagues seeking professional positions.
14. Provide applicants seeking information about a position with an honest description of the assignment, the conditions of work, and related matters.

Principle IV

Commitment to Professional Employment Practices

We regard the employment agreement as a solemn pledge to be executed both in spirit and in fact in a manner consistent with the highest ideals of professional service. Sound professional personnel relationships with governing boards are built upon personal integrity, dignity, and mutual respect.

In fulfilling our obligations to professional employment practices, we—

1. Apply for or offer a position on the basis of professional and legal qualifications.
2. Apply for a specific position only when it is known to be vacant and refrain from such practices as underbidding or commenting adversely about other candidates.
3. Fill no vacancy except where the terms, conditions, policies, and practices permit the exercise of our professional judgment and skill, and where a climate conducive to professional service exists.
4. Adhere to the conditions of a contract or to the terms of an appointment until either has been terminated legally or by mutual consent.
5. Give prompt notice of any change in availability of service, in status of applications, or in change in position.
6. Conduct professional business through the recognized educational and professional channels.
7. Accept no gratuities or gifts of significance that might influence our judgment in the exercise of our professional duties.
8. Engage in no outside employment that will impair the effectiveness of our professional service and permit no commercial exploitation of our professional position.

This new Code of Ethics of the Teaching Profession has now been adopted by every state teachers' association in the nation. The 100 percent mark was reached when the Vermont Education Association adopted the code in April, 1965. This should make unnecessary the use of any individual state codes in the future.

Enforcement

There is little doubt that members of certain other professions, such as medicine and law, are more strict in the enforcement of their particular codes than are teachers. One of the chief problems confronting us, therefore, is the attainment of better compliance. Much can be done by familiarizing those in the teacher-education institutions and in the field with the provisions of the Code. Of value are official interpretations of applicable situations; the *NEA Journal* and such pamphlets as *Interpretations of the Code of Ethics* [10] informatively treat specific problems. If the ultimate enforcement is to be in the hands of the members—which is certainly where it should be—the procedure now in effect is about all that may be expected under present conditions. Local ethics committees can be of great help in correcting local violations and misunderstandings. Persistent and flagrant violations can result in expulsion from membership in the NEA.

TEACHERS' ORGANIZATIONS

The National Education Association, the major professional organization for teachers, had its origin in Philadelphia in 1857. The American Medical Association was founded ten years earlier in 1847 and the American Bar Association in 1878, so it may be said that our Association was not late in beginning but came into existence at about the same time as did the organizations of a number of other important professions.

Courtesy: Michigan Education Journal.

New home of the Michigan State Education Association, East Lansing, Michigan.

[10] *Interpretations of the Code of Ethics* (Washington, NEA, 1963).

Early membership in the Association was limited to men, probably because most of the teachers of the day were men. It was only a very few years, however, until women were admitted. Chartered by an Act of Congress in 1906, the NEA grew rather slowly for many years, but not long after a reorganization in 1920 the membership gains were very marked. Membership as of May 31, 1965, was 943,581 out of an estimated total number of teachers of 1,807,466. While the percentage of teachers belonging is now over 50, it is far short of what it ought to be and is nothing short of a disgrace. We will never attain complete professional status until a much greater number of those engaged in teaching belong to the largest of all professional organizations in the world. Present dues in the NEA

Courtesy: National Education Association.
Photograph by Louis Checkman.

Model of the new building of the National Education Association, Washington, D.C.

are $10.00 annually, with life membership at $225. Especially for young teachers, life membership, which may be paid at the rate of $25.00 a year, is highly desirable because of the increased benefits and the resulting financial saving.

Figure 5-3.   Organization Chart

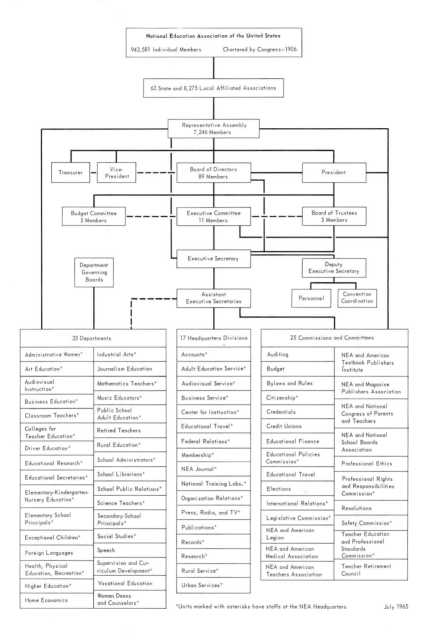

National Education Association of the United States
943,581 Individual Members   Chartered by Congress—1906

63 State and 8,275 Local Affiliated Associations

Representative Assembly
7,246 Members

Treasurer

Vice-President

Board of Directors
89 Members

President

Budget Committee
5 Members

Executive Committee
11 Members

Board of Trustees
5 Members

Executive Secretary

Department Governing Boards

Deputy Executive Secretary

Assistant Executive Secretaries

Personnel

Convention Coordination

33 Departments		17 Headquarters Divisions	25 Commissions and Committees	
Administrative Women*	Industrial Arts*	Accounts*	Auditing	NEA and American Textbook Publishers Institute
Art Education*	Journalism Education	Adult Education Service*	Budget	
Audiovisual Instruction*	Mathematics Teachers*	Audiovisual Service*	Bylaws and Rules	NEA and Magazine Publishers Association
Business Education*	Music Educators*	Business Service*	Citizenship*	NEA and National Congress of Parents and Teachers
Classroom Teachers*	Public School Adult Education*	Center for Instruction*	Credentials	
Colleges for Teacher Education*	Retired Teachers	Educational Travel*	Credit Unions	NEA and National School Boards Association
Driver Education*	Rural Education*	Federal Relations*	Educational Finance	
Educational Research*	School Administrators*	Membership*	Educational Policies Commission*	Professional Ethics
Educational Secretaries*	School Librarians*	NEA Journal*	Educational Travel	Professional Rights and Responsibilities Commission*
Elementary-Kindergarten-Nursery Education*	School Public Relations*	National Training Labs.*	Elections	
Elementary School Principals*	Science Teachers*	Organization Relations*	International Relations*	Resolutions
Exceptional Children*	Secondary-School Principals*	Press, Radio, and TV*	Legislative Commission*	Safety Commission*
Foreign Languages	Social Studies*	Publications*	NEA and American Legion	Teacher Education and Professional Standards Commission*
Health, Physical Education, Recreation*	Speech	Records*	NEA and American Medical Association	
Higher Education*	Supervision and Curriculum Development*	Research*	NEA and American Teachers Association	Teacher Retirement Council
Home Economics	Vocational Education	Rural Service*		
	Women Deans and Counselors*	Urban Services*		

*Units marked with asterisks have staffs at the NEA Headquarters   July 1965

The National Education Association is the only organization that represents or has the possibility of representing the great body of teachers in the United States.

Source: National Education Association.

The Association has for many years maintained headquarters in Washington, D.C. at 1201 16th Street, N.W., and is at present located in the beautiful new building at the same address shown herein on page 124.

The purposes of the NEA, as defined in the charter, are: "To elevate the character and advance the interests of the profession of teaching and to promote the cause of education in the United States."

The organizational chart of the Association presented on page 125 shows 17 heaquarters divisions, 33 departments, and 25 committees and commissions. The large Representative Assembly, made of up delegates from the state and local associations, constitutes the real governing body, thus giving it democratic form. Stinnett [11] has described the services of the NEA as falling into the following categories:

Professional growth
Promoting conferences, workshops, and meetings.
Public Relations
Furnishing data to citizens groups, preparing radio and TV programs, motion pictures and the like.
Defending the teaching profession
Making investigations of situations where teachers are unjustly accused and trying to correct such situations.
Research
Carrying on pertinent research studies and answering questions from members where objective data are desired.
Professional standards
Through staff members, committees and other means working for higher standards for all aspects of teaching, especially trying to secure an adequate supply of good teachers.
Teacher welfare
Working for high teachers' salaries and improved retirement systems.
Federal relations
Attempting to secure desirable new educational legislation and preventing the passage of undesirable types.
Curriculum and instructional development
Trying to encourage continuous study of curricula and better teaching methods.
International education
Co-operating with other agencies in support of the United Nations, UNESCO and the WCOTP.
Selective teacher recruitment
Through FTA and many other agencies trying to secure an adequate supply of properly qualified young people to prepare for teaching.
Publications
Publishing professional journals, yearbooks, books, research abstracts, and the like. The *NEA Journal* is the official organ of the Association.

[11] T. M. Stinnett, *The Teacher and Professional Organizations* (Washington, NEA 1953), pp. 88–91.

The influence of the NEA has grown very rapidly in recent years, and its growth and ability to serve and to lead will increase largely in proportion to the increase in membership and the interest of those who belong.

No organization can ever be better than the members who are a part of it. No organization is perfect. The only way, however, in which it can be kept to a high standard and democratic in its operation is through the continuous and active participation of its members. Both from quality and quantity of membership, leaders take courage to fight aggressively for things that are vital. Thus the individual plays his part.

It is the strong feeling of the authors that it should very soon be unthinkable that any teacher should fail to join his National Education Association and become *actively* interested in it. That will be a major step toward true professional status and toward a better tomorrow for education in America.

State Associations

Actually, as might be expected, a good number of state education associations were formed before the NEA came into existence. Now

Courtesy: the Association.

Headquarters of the Texas State Education Association, Austin, Texas.

every state, together with the District of Columbia, and Puerto Rico, has its own association.

The organization of the state associations varies. The common pattern consists of subdivisions usually affiliated with the NEA. Most have local units; most are controlled by a delegate body; most hold state-wide conventions; some have district meetings as well; most have divisions, sections, and committees which carry out the work of the associations. Dues vary widely in the state associations, while local units may or may not have dues of their own. Generally they are found to be necessary. Many of the states have excellent headquarters buildings with staffs to carry on the association's activities.

The services of the state associations may be classified into categories quite similar to those performed by the NEA on the national level. Some associations are, as might be expected, more active than others. Some are more democratically organized than are others. A number of the state associations, as the one in Pennsylvania for example, are effective agencies for securing the adoption of progressive educational legislation and for gaining improved salaries and working conditions for teachers. Through its many meetings, both state-wide and district, professional improvement is stimulated, selective teacher recruitment is sponsored, and individual participation in professional matters encouraged. Active cooperation with the State Department of Public Instruction is sought continually in matters that are for the advancement of education.

Associations that are dominated by administrators alone and those which are involved in partisan politics are not good representatives of a great profession. Where any such condition exists, the active interest and participation of individual teachers can correct it.

Local Associations

Actually, the local association is the foundation of all professional activities. No state or national association can be effective unless the local branches are strong, functioning, and active. Stinnett [12] cites the difficulty of defining "local association" and suggests six types: (1) a unit, including all teachers in a small school district or in a city school system, that is an all-inclusive organization of teachers employed by one school board; (2) a unit, including teachers with common interests in a city school system; (3) a unit, including the teachers in a whole county; (4) a unit, including the teachers in a district, region, or zone of the state; (5) a unit, including the faculty members of a college, or (6) a unit made up of a high school FTA club or a college student NEA chapter.

The local association will have a constitution and bylaws, and its structure will greatly resemble that of a state association, with committees

[12] *Ibid.*, p. 64.

suggested by that group and others that local conditions may seem to require. Activities of local groups are related to the professional welfare of the members, cultural activities, social and recreational endeavors, and are dedicated to improving professional standards. All of these serve worthwhile purposes. Many local associations also publish newletters or other publications for the membership.

Student NEA and Future Teachers of America

The newest nation-wide professional organization, originally called the Future Teachers of America, was established in 1937 as a result of the efforts of the NEA. It has been described as "a practice school for the training of leaders."

More recently major changes have taken place in the group's organization. On the college level the name Student National Education Association is used with the individual units known as chapters. On the state levels the organization is called Student (Name of State) State Education Association, as the Student Pennsylvania State Education Association and the Student Idaho State Education Association. The name Future Teachers of America is still retained for the secondary school organization, and the individual units are known as clubs. In the college each student member pays dues of $1 to the NEA and usually $1 to the state association. There are no student dues in high school clubs, although a $2 annual charter fee is charged. In the college chapter each member receives the journals of the national and state association.

The work of the college chapter is specifically designed to give practice in regular professional activities. Programs might include such topics as the professional Code of Ethics, the Exchange Teacher program, organization and functions of professional organizations, the importance of public relations, suggestions for beginning teachers and the like. Typical projects would be sponsoring American Education Week, sponsoring career days, acting as hosts for conventions, establishing FTA clubs in high schools and many others.

What the Student NEA on the college level actually does is to provide a sort of "activity program" in the work of professional associations.

The real purposes of the high school clubs are (1) to search out capable people for teaching, and (2) to give them some actual experience in working with children. Thus they serve both guidance and exploratory functions.

Both chapters and clubs are organized on a local, state, and national basis, generally paralleling the regular organization of the profession. In 1955 by official action both became a part of the National Commission on Teacher Education and Professional Standards. Surely this is a significant step in the growth of teaching toward professional status. At

Courtesy: National Education Association.
Photograph by Carl Purcell.

Teaching is a rewarding experience for this young man and thousands more like him. Here a former Student NEA president has an opportunity to make application of his college preparation as he functions as a student teacher.

present the Student NEA has more than 103,000 members in colleges and universities while the FTA has more than 258,000 in high schools. There is a deep conviction that out of this movement must come the professional leaders of tomorrow.

World Organizations of Teachers

It was on August 1, 1952, that a number of different international groups of teachers decided to give up their separate identity and form the World Confederation of Organizations of the Teaching Professions, abbreviated as the WCOTP.

If education is as important as many think it to be, and if it has a real part to play in the maintenance of peace in the world, then the place of a strong international organization which can speak for education universally is obvious.

The aims of the WCOTP are as follows:

a. To foster a conception of education directed toward the promotion of international understanding and good will, with a view to safeguarding peace and freedom and respect for human dignity.

b. To improve teaching methods, educational organization and the academic and professional training of teachers so as to equip them better to serve the interests of youth.

c. To defend the rights and the material and moral interest of the teaching profession.

d. To promote closer relationships between teachers in the different countries.[13]

The WCOTP is a young organization, and there are many difficulties ahead, but the possibilities of developing understanding among the teachers of all nations are great indeed. At present the teachers' organizations from approximately 78 countries hold membership in the WCOTP, and it is hoped that more will decide to play an active role in the near future. Already an opportunity is provided for many of the world's teachers to keep themselves and others informed as to educational needs, problems, and opportunities everywhere. Surely this can be a major contribution toward world peace.

The American Federation of Teachers

The American Federation of Teachers, with a total membership of more than 100,000, is affiliated with the American Federation of Labor-Congress of Industrial Organizations (AFL-CIO). Its slogan is "Democracy in Education and Education for Democracy." School administrators may not belong to the Federation, since it is an organization for teachers only.

The Federation publishes a monthly journal, *The American Teacher*, which contains articles on teaching methods, protective measures for teachers, means of improving salaries and working conditions, problems of academic freedom, and the like.

It may be said, in general, that the program of the Federation has been somewhat more militant than have been those of the other teachers organizations. Its activities have been largely aimed at securing increased support, better salaries, good working conditions, and academic freedom. Probably the difference between the Federation and the NEA is more of method than of goals. Elsbree [14] writes: "It seems probable that the society's contribution in the future is going to continue to be that of a mi-

13 *NEA Handbook, 1964–1965* (Washington, NEA, 1964–1965), p. 334.

14 W. S. Elsbree, *The American Teacher* (New York, American Book, 1939), p. 512.

nority group, stimulating and spurring on to action larger professional organizations."

Whether or not this prophecy proves to be correct, an intensive struggle is now in progress between the Federation and the National Education Association. Currently the issue concerns who has the right to act as sole bargaining agent for the local teachers in negotiations with the school boards over salaries, working conditions, and related matters. Recent successes by the Federation in New York and Philadelphia seem to indicate that the aggressive tactics of the union are likely to be more effective in getting results. The meaning of these and other victories have not been lost on the NEA, which has attempted to strengthen its efforts for better service to local groups, especially in large urban areas. It is possible that this controversy will be all to the good and that it will not be easily resolved.

Teachers must make their own decision as to which organization will serve them best. It seems to most professional people, however, that the majority of teachers will wish to be allied with an organization that is independent of all specialized groups. Labor has long been a friend and strong supporter of education and teachers; this fact should not be ignored. Professional people are likely to be best served, however, by an independent organization.

The Commission on Teacher Education and Professional Standards

A significant aspect of the way in which the members of the educational profession are trying to work together to raise standards has been the development of the National Commission on Teacher Education and Professional Standards. It was in 1946 at a meeting of the NEA Representative Assembly in Buffalo, New York, that the formation of the new body was authorized. It was directed "to carry forward for the profession a continuing program for the improvement of standards for the selection, preparation, certification, and in-service growth of teachers, as well as standards for institutions which prepare teachers."

In support of the National Commission, which reports annually to the Representative Assembly, there have been developed state councils and state commissions on teacher education and professional standards. The councils are organizations of agencies dedicated to the improvement of teacher education, and the state commissions are agencies of the state education associations. There are now 54 state commissions in 50 states, and the District of Columbia, a few states having two commissions. These parallel the National Commission in function and purpose.

The National and State Commissions have been constant and earnest in their efforts to raise the sights of all in education to the achievement of higher standards. Through national, state, and regional conferences, through a magazine, the *Journal of Teacher Education,* published by the National Commission, through newsletters and miscellaneous publications the commissions have been responsible for significant progress toward real professional status. To quote the National Commission,[15] "These organizations make possible continuous, co-ordinated efforts to solve the problems of professionalization."

ACCREDITATION

The term *accreditation,* as here used, refers to the setting of standards for educational institutions and, through evaluation, to ascertaining the extent to which these standards are met. Those institutions that meet them to a high degree are then "accredited" or approved. This process has been going on for many years by means of voluntary associations for secondary schools and for general colleges. There has also been some additional accreditation of institutions that prepare teachers. It was long felt, however, that the organization known as the American Association of Colleges for Teacher Education did not have a sufficiently broad backing for its work.

Therefore, in 1948 a movement was begun to establish an agency for this purpose that would be more broadly representative of the whole profession. Consequently, there was organized the National Council for Accreditation of Teacher Education frequently designated NCATE. This has been described as "an independent, autonomous, voluntary accrediting body devoted exclusively to the evaluation and accreditation of teacher education programs." Formal work was begun by the Council in 1954, but it was evident that considerable difficulty was still ahead before full support of all interested bodies was assured.

A large number of people feel that this movement toward the full and uniform accreditation of institutions that prepare teachers is one of our most promising efforts toward the attainment of professional status. To quote the Commission on Teacher Education and Professional Standards further: "Teaching is the last of the great professions to achieve an effective accrediting agency, broadly representative of the profession and dedicated to improving the quality of professional services provided the public." [16]

The careful student of education will not be unaware of the fact that considerable opposition has developed recently to the growing role of NCATE in the field of professional growth and accreditation. It is felt in some quarters that the Commission is coming to be a sort of quasi-legal

[15] National Commission on Teacher Education and Professional Standards, *A Note of Optimism* (Washington, NEA, 1954), p. 5.

[16] *Ibid.,* p. 6.

body in the field of certification, for example, and in setting itself up as an organization that accredits institutions it improperly exceeds its purposes.[17] The extent to which this is true is a matter for debate. Few will deny, however, that the influence of TEPS and NCATE in the general upgrading of professional education has been all to the good. Mistakes have been made, it is true, but where these have produced conflict cooperative study has brought about cooperation and improvement. Certainly there seems to be no other similar movement so full of promise on the horizon.

CONTINUING EDUCATION

One cannot adequately discuss the work of the teacher without giving more than passing attention to his obligation to continue his professional growth after his formal entry into the profession.

No profession can afford to take any other than a positive attitude in this matter. For example, an attorney who has no knowledge of the increasing body of new legislation and the developing pattern of court decisions would find himself losing cases that he might otherwise win as well as being guilty of giving his clients bad advice. The physician who, after receiving his license to practice, fails to inform himself of the newer drugs and of better methods of diagnosis and treatment, inevitably stagnates; his patients suffer, and his position is thoroughly inexcusable. Many medical schools in the United States and Canada are providing abundant opportunities through meetings, discussion groups and short courses for physicians who need and desire such services.

Teaching, in this respect, is surely no different from other professions. We are learning more about the mind and its functioning; our understanding of the whole field of human relations is growing rapidly; new methods of teaching are being developed, and the body of knowledge in many specialized areas has increased almost beyond belief. It is difficult to realize, for example, that all children in the elementary and junior high schools in 1960 were born since the first atomic bomb was dropped on Hiroshima and are children of the atomic age. This fact alone places tremendous obligations upon the teaching profession. If they are to serve well, teachers must constantly prepare themselves to live in the world as it is today and as it will be tomorrow.

Avenues of Growth

The means by which professional growth may be attained in education are not very different from those of other similar groups.

[17] James Bryant Conant, *The Education of American Teachers*, (New York, McGraw-Hill, 1963), Ch. 2.

There are quite naturally one or two avenues which are particularly used by teachers, as the following will indicate.

Meeting Increased Certification Requirements. Here is a field which rather specifically belongs to teaching. Other professions do not generally receive temporary licenses to practice. Teachers do, and in order to meet additional requirements two standards must usually be met, whether the goal is a higher type of certificate, a renewal of a temporary one, or complete permanent certification. The first requirement is, quite universally, evidence of successful teaching experience and, secondly, evidence of professional growth, as shown by the attainment of a certain number of college credits or by a variety of other means. There is a growing feeling that, if granted at all, the permanent certificate should not be issued until quite late in one's educational experience.

Already there are approximately 32 states that do not grant life certificates. Delaware, for example, requires that each certificate be renewed every five years on evidence of successful experience and professional growth. Others, at the very least, require evidence of growth or a refresher course or courses for a teacher who has left the service for a period of years and then wishes to return. Teachers will, indeed, be very unwise if they resist such tendencies or fail to take the lead in their attainment. Our record here is not too good.

Of course, growth by compulsion, or by law, as the foregoing represents to a considerable degree, may not be the best. Almost everything depends upon the spirit with which it is approached and carried out. Some would chide us severely because so much professional education has thus come about. It should be remembered, however, that to no small degree this is true of other groups, such as medicine and law. State requirements are operative there, very effectively operative. Neither should teachers be criticized too much because they seek more education to improve their incomes, because for these same reasons many physicians and others specialize.

Summer Sessions. Primarily because of the long vacation which is peculiar to teaching, the summer session has been the traditional device by which teachers seek to improve their professional status and to grow. No other professional group has anything quite like it. Whether it is the traditional six-weeks session, the still shorter one of two or three weeks, or the summer quarter of many colleges and universities, the summer school is chiefly a special session for teachers. For this development, teachers and administrators alike should receive much credit.

The usual summer session today tries to combine recreation with academic work of a high quality, and many institutions provide practice or laboratory schools in order to furnish practical experience for those attending.

A recent tendency has been noted in the increased number of teachers who attend summer schools in Europe, thus combining study with foreign travel and broadening their horizons in that manner.

Graduate Work. Here again we find that higher certification requirements for positions of greater responsibility have been a motivating factor. Then, too, it is now common practice to tie up higher salaries with higher qualifications and higher degrees. Thus graduate work begins to pay, and the ambitious teacher goes off to the graduate school, in summers, after school hours, or on leaves of absence.

The master's degree is becoming far more common in classroom teaching and the doctor's degree, either the Ph.D. or Ed.D., is appearing more and more frequently. In the field of the specialist and in administrative and supervisory positions it is becoming increasingly common. Certainly in the classrooms of the secondary school of the future the doctor's degree will not be at all unusual.

Workshops. While the so-called workshops may well be considered a type of graduate work in many instances, it is also serving as a device for professional improvement in many larger school systems. Here teachers come together for shorter or longer periods to work co-operatively on their own problems, under the guidance of a director and with the co-operation of specialists. Frequently teachers are paid for participating in these efforts as a part of the local program of professional growth. In many instances they have been highly effective, whereas in others they have been workshops in name only.

Teachers' Meetings. Probably no device intended for professional growth has been more maligned than has this. Most school systems consider regular teachers' meetings necessary and require the attendance of all teachers. In a very few cases teachers may be paid extra for attending, especially when such meetings are not held during the regular school day.

Undoubtedly teachers' meetings have justly deserved in many instances the condemnation heaped upon them. All too often they have been administration-dominated and run in a dictatorial fashion with nothing to stimulate interest and with little or no help given to teachers. Little wonder they are so generally disliked!

On the other hand, there have been many instances of inspiring, democratically planned and conducted meetings—meetings showing a purpose and spirit of helpfulness. Where these have been based on needs and teachers have been able to turn the results to better teaching, professional growth has resulted to a marked degree. There is little excuse for any other type of teachers' meetings.

As has been suggested, other professional groups have used many of the same means and methods of continuing education as we have mentioned for educators. Other professions have their great conventions, their graduate work, their institutes and short noncredit technical courses. Motion pictures, television, clinics, and numerous other devices are widely used. Professional education is probably second to none in its use of modern methods for in-service growth. To participate in these is a professional obligation.

Some of the most vocal critics of education have alleged that there is far too much "working for credits" among educators. A close examination of the situation would seem to indicate that there is only limited validity to this charge.

It is true, certainly, that steps on most salary schedules are geared to better preparation, more credits, if one wishes to put it that way. To say that this is wrong is to ascribe an ulterior motive to those who seek to grow. It is also true that in very many cases these advanced courses are approved by administrators where the teacher works or by the college or university advisor assigned to the student. One can very well seek more adequate preparation for the job and a better salary at the same time. What is wrong about this?

A teacher should be able to go into a field of specialization, as guidance, speech therapy, and others without his motives being challenged. There is little doubt that much specialization takes place in medicine for better service and, at the same time, better incomes. There is little about such action that can be rightfully questioned.

More and more advanced work for teachers is being financed by foundations, by local school districts, and by government. School boards are granting leaves of absence to teachers who may wish to work on the curriculum, such as has been done in the sciences and foreign languages. All of this is especially commendable for a group whose personal incomes are not as high as in other vocations.

On the whole, teaching ranks fairly high in the extent to which there has been developed programs of continuing education.

THE NEW TEACHER

The new teacher in a large organization will not always find getting off to a good start an easy matter. Sometimes very little is done to help him. All too frequently he is given the textbooks, the roster, the list of students assigned, and perhaps the course of study. That may be all. On the other hand, in some schools there is a carefully planned orientation program with special meetings and activities for new teachers. Elsewhere, schools, in addition to this, assign the new teacher more or less closely to another experienced person as a sort of big brother or sister. Here friendly counsel and advice can easily be found. Some communities also bring in members of the parent-teacher association and on rare occasions business people to make the new teacher feel at home.

In far too many schools, though, the new teacher gets the heaviest load and the worst assignments, but more and more superintendents are realizing that this is bad administration. The first task of any teacher is to do an outstanding piece of work in the classroom. One's record in this matter spreads quickly and respect grows among one's colleagues. Hence, it is well to keep other aspects of one's work in positions of relative importance, doing first things first. In this manner, progress toward the attainment of the goals of the schools can best be achieved.

QUESTIONS AND PROJECTS

1. Write to the best teacher you have had asking him his reasons for choosing teaching as a career. A summary report based on answers by a large number of teachers will be valuable for the class.
2. Try to persuade one of your former teachers, either elementary or secondary, to keep a record of his activities for one week. Compare your report, or better the combined report of the class with some accepted research.
3. Interview some older teachers, trying to find out whether the so-called nonteaching duties of teachers are increasing.
4. What do you think of the use of teacher's aides, comparable to nurse's aides, as a solution to the problem of nonteaching duties and the long-term teacher shortage?
5. Prepare an exhibit of report cards now in use by various school systems to report pupil progress to parents.
6. What do you think of the personal interview as a means of reporting pupil progress?
7. Ascertain whether teachers in your state may be required legally to visit the homes of their children.
8. What is the role of the visiting teacher in modern school systems?
9. What differences would you expect to find in the work of a teacher in a small high school and one in a large high school?
10. Check with several teachers to find what differences are made in their work by the self-contained classroom and the modern acoustical treatment of school buildings.
11. How do the expectations held for teachers by communities today compare with those held a century or more ago? (See Elsbree.)
12. Check a modern community to ascertain the type of relationships existing between such out of school agencies, as the Scouts, Y.M.C.A., and others and the schools. How might these relationships be improved?
13. Debate the question: Resolved, that the legal working week for teachers in the public schools should be 40 hours with extra pay for overtime.
14. Study the codes of ethics of several other professions and compare them with the NEA Code.
15. Investigate the curricula for teacher education in a small liberal arts college, a large university, and a teachers college. What are the advantages and disadvantages of each?
16. What are the advantages and disadvantages of doing graduate work as soon as the undergraduate work has been completed?

AUDIO-VISUAL AIDS

MOTION PICTURES (16 MM)

American Teacher—March of Time, distributed by McGraw-Hill Book Co., Text-Film Dept., 330 West 42nd Street, New York, N.Y., 15 min., sd., b&w.

Directs attention to the importance of the teacher in the American way of life. Contrasts the education of yesterday with that of today. Brings out the many activities in which a teacher participates, both in and out of school, the importance of the teacher's recognition of individual differences in students, and the attempt in classes to develop thinking rather than an accumulation of facts.

A Desk for Billie—National Education Association, 1201 16th St., N.W., Washington, D.C., 1957, 57 min., sd., b&w and/or color. An excellent film showing dramatically the effect of good schools and teachers on the child of a migrant family.

And Gladly Teach—National Education Association, 1201 16th St., N.W., Washington, D.C., 28 min., sd., b&w and/or color. Shows effectively the satisfactions and opportunities in teaching. The film is "about teachers and the company they keep."

Camping Education—Outdoor Education Association, Inc., 369 Lexington Ave., New York 17, N.Y., 35 min., sd., b&w and/or color. Presents experiences in organized camping activities for elementary grades. Each sixth-grade child experiences one week of camping education as part of the school program.

Field Trip—Virginia Department of Education, Richmond, Va., 10 min., sd., b&w. Instructions on how to plan and take a field trip, using a trip to Dismal Swamp as an example. Made for parents and teachers with the co-operation of the Norfolk County School Board.

Insuring Our Investment in Youth—Carl F. Mahnke Prod., 16 min., sd., b&w. Discusses the need for a guidance program in the secondary schools and describes the operation of such a program. Points out the cost to industry and the frustrations of people who are not in suitable positions of employment. Shows how the school guidance program correctly places a graduate in industry through the use of cumulative records and tests of scholastic ability, aptitudes, and interests in guiding his vocational training.

Freedom to Learn—National Education Association, 1201 16th St., N.W., Washington, D.C., 27½ min., sd., b&w and/or color. Shows that modern schools prepare our children to assume their responsibilities as good citizens. It explains that respect for facts, constant search for the truth, and knowledge of the world are essential in this preparation.

How Good Are Our Schools?—National Education Association, 1201 16th St., N.W., Washington, D.C., 28 min., sd., b&w. An excellent documentary film produced by CBS and narrated by Ralph Bellamy. Highlights the findings of the 1959 Report of Dr. James B. Conant.

Maintaining Classroom Discipline—McGraw-Hill Book Co., Text-Film Dept., 330 West 42nd St., New York, N.Y., 14 min., sd., b&w. Explores the fundamentals of controlling class conduct and developing attitudes. Contrasting methods of handling a class are demonstrated.

Near Home—International Film Bureau, 57 East Jackson Blvd., Chicago, Ill., 25 min., sd., b&w. Illustrates several basic principles of good teaching. A class and teacher study the community in which they live. Shows pupils and teacher in a learning situation that capitalizes on an inherent interest in things near by and approaches the learning through problem solving. Some difficulties may be noted with the British accent.

Skippy and the Three R's—National Education Association, 1201 16th St., N.W.,

Washington, D.C., 29 min., sd., b&w and/or color. Follows a first grader from his first day at school, through his school experiences as guided by the teacher and her teaching methods, to the point where he is learning through self-motivated endeavors and interests. Shows the method of motivating the desire to read, write, and do number work and illustrates how a teacher utilizes the interests of pupils to encourage the learning of fundamental skills in school work along with the social skills of living.

Teacher and Pupils Planning and Working Together—McGraw-Hill Book Co., Text-Film Dept., 330 West 42nd St., New York, N.Y., 19 min., sd., b&w. Students are shown learning to work together. They organize themselves into functional groups to make and carry out plans for investigation and to present their findings and recommendations in a group report.

What Greater Gift—National Education Association, 1201 16th St., N.W., Washington, D.C., 28 min., sd., b&w. and/or color. Presents the teacher as a professional person and shows something of the nature of teaching. Stresses that today's teacher needs professional preparation to acquire the understanding and skills essential to good teaching.

FILMSTRIP

Let's Take a Look at Teaching—Wayne University, Detroit, Mich., 50 fr., si., b&w. An overview of the teaching profession and of what it has to offer in terms of salary, tenure, working conditions, opportunity for travel, and individual interests. Pictures a typical school day showing the varied demands on the teacher and her responsibilities.

RECORDINGS

Teachers Are People Too—Indiana University, Audio-Visual Center, Bloomington, Ind., 15 min., tape recording. One of a series of radio programs on guidance. Dramatizes the fact that teachers are human beings too! Represents them as sincere, hardworking individuals who have devoted a long time in training and preparation. Teachers are called "co-operators" because their jobs require them to co-operate with students, parents, and community.

A Forward Look for the Teaching Profession—Educational Recording Services, 5922 Abernathy Dr., Los Angeles, Calif., $33\frac{1}{3}$ r.p.m. microgroove. Discussion by W. S. Elsbree. Part I—Comparison of teaching with other professions (15 min.). Part II—Professional aims of successful teachers (15 min.).

Characteristics of a Good Teacher—Educational Recording Services, 5922 Abernathy Dr., Los Angeles, Calif., $33\frac{1}{3}$ r.p.m. microgroove. Discussion by A. S. Barr. Part I—Personal qualities and competencies of the good teacher. (15 min.) Part II—Difficulties in rating teaching and some available evaluation scales and techniques. (15 min.)

FURTHER READINGS

"Albuquerque's Climate for In-Service Education," *NEA Journal,* Vol. 54 (March, 1965), pp. 26–27.

"A Series on Teacher Organizations," Five articles on current problems of teachers and their organizations, *Phi Delta Kappan,* Vol. 45 (March, 1964), pp. 269–296.

Barr, A. S., and others, "The Measurement and Prediction of Teaching Efficiency; A Summary of Investigations," *Journal of Experimental Education,* Vol. 16 (June, 1948), pp. 203–283.

Barzun, Jacques, *Teacher in America* (Boston, Little, Brown, 1945).

Highet, Gilbert, *The Art of Teaching* (New York, Knopf, 1950).

Laux, Dean M., "A New Role for Teachers," *Phi Delta Kappan,* Vol. 46 (February, 1965), pp. 265–268.

Lieberman, Myron, "Professional Ethics and the NEA," *Phi Delta Kappan,* Vol. 44, (April, 1963), pp. 310–312.

Lieberman, Myron, "Who Speaks for Teachers?" *Saturday Review,* Vol. 48 (June 19, 1965) pp. 64–66+.

National Association of Manufacturers, *Your Career in Teaching* (2 East 48th St., New York, 1955).

National Commission on Accrediting, *Accreditation in Teacher Education, Its Influence on Higher Education* (Washington, D.C., 1965).

National Commission on Teacher Education and Professional Standards, *Invitation to Teaching* (Washington, D.C., NEA, 1958).

National Education Association, "Implementing the Code of Ethics of the Education Profession and Strengthening Professional Rights" (Washington, D.C., 1964).

NCTEPS, *Milestones in Teacher Education and Professional Standards* (Washington, D.C., NRA, 1964).

Reader's Digest Association, *I Am a Teacher,* Reprints of articles from *The Reader's Digest* (Pleasantville, N.Y., 1957).

Rugg, Harold, and B. Marion Brooks, *The Teacher in School and Society* (Yonkers, N.Y., World Book, 1950), pp. 273–477.

Sizer, Theodore R., "Classroom Revolution, Reform Movement or Panacea," *Saturday Review,* Vol. 48 (June 19, 1965), pp. 52–54.

Snow, Robert H., "Anxieties and Discontents in Teaching," *Phi Delta Kappan,* Vol. 44 (April, 1963).

"Status of the American Public School Teacher," *NEA Research Bull.,* Vol. 35, No. 1 (February, 1957).

Teaching as a Man's Job (Homewood, Illinois, Phi Delta Kappa, 1938).

United States Office of Education, *Teaching as a Career* (Washington, D.C., 1963).

Willett, Henry I., "Public Schools Under Pressure," *Atlantic,* Vol. 194, No. 4 (October, 1954), pp. 57–62.

6

The Preparation of Teachers

PREVIEW

▶ It is clear that the demand for teachers will far exceed the supply in the foreseeable future.
Detailed study of the matter, however, indicates that the problem today involves the need to have trained teachers in a wide variety of fields of preparation so that their distribution throughout the educational levels and fields will be a balanced one.

▶ It is most important to secure *good* teachers for our children.
Research has not yet produced a clear picture of the good teacher although considerable progress has been made.

▶ Certification and legal requirements have been rising rapidly in recent years, but wide variations still exist among the states.

▶ While there is much ferment in the whole field of teacher preparation, certain trends may be noted.
1. There is at least a strong commitment to the "approved program approach."
2. Much effort is being given toward strengthening the academic preparation of prospective teachers.
3. Requirements for certification in the various fields are being increased.
4. Increased use of the National Teacher's Examination is evident.
5. More efforts are being made to secure reciprocity in certification among the states.

▶ The effect of the so-called Conant Report has been widespread, but no strong new pattern has as yet developed.

▶ Among other major problems in the area of teacher education are:
1. The question of proportion of general to professional education in the program.
2. The need for greater contact with schools and children for those preparing to teach.
3. The controversy over whether the teacher education program should be four or five years in length.
4. The problem of attracting more competent young people to the profession.

Any discussion of the topic of this chapter must be concerned to some extent at least with each of these items:

1. The supply and demand.
2. The quality of teachers needed.
3. The methods of preparation.

SUPPLY AND DEMAND

While details of the problems in this subheading will be discussed in the following chapter, the major trends must be presented here because a relationship exists between them and the matter of teacher preparation.

It is far from easy to predict how many teachers will be needed in the years ahead. Short range predictions are, of course, more reliable than long range ones. The children who will be in school during the next six years are already a part of the population, so a minimum of guesswork is involved here. What happens thereafter is largely dependent upon the birth rate which is not likely to decrease very markedly. Minor fluctuations are to be expected, but population growth of the past predicts that the future birth rate will be kept on a rather high plateau. A rapid population growth now indicates continued high, if not increased, pressure upon the schools for teachers, space, and equipment.

Estimates of the number of teachers needed are determined not only by the number of children to be taught, but by the number of teachers who leave the profession annually. Estimates must also take into consideration the need for teachers to relieve overcrowded conditions, to introduce new subjects and methods, to provide special services and to replace poorly trained personnel.

Problems of supply and demand inevitably affect the teacher education process. There are those who argue that high standards of entrance and preparation will attract more students and better ones. Others affirm with equal conviction that this will cut down the supply and increase the existing shortages in the field. The high standard versus the low standard approach to the preparation of teachers will no doubt continue to be argued with adequate facts leading to a resolution being immediately available. It is true, however, that throughout the nation, standards for entrance into and continuance in the profession are being raised. This is evident in other professions as well as in teaching.

THE QUALITY OF TEACHERS NEEDED

The Analyzation of Teachers

In the profession of teaching, we do not want people who will merely "keep" school, but those who will be most effective in guiding children and youth toward the attainment of the goals we have set for our educational system.

A main source of concern as we approach this topic is that we find ourselves so far from agreement as to what constitutes an effective teacher. Considerable research has been done on the problem; more is currently under way. Certainly the institutions that prepare teachers for the public schools cannot do so most effectively until we know more surely what the critical and contributing factors are for successful teaching.

The fact that so little progress has been made in determining the distinguishing characteristics of competent teachers is not surprising because teaching is a complex process involving many aspects of a person's total being. It involves the reactions of one human being upon other human beings. It concerns many aspects of the behavior of these individuals, not just at the time the action is observed but years later as well. Children may learn a particular skill on a particular day, but what they do with this skill at some future time may be far more important.

In writing of the complexities of the problem, Ryans[1] pointed out, in a preliminary study in referring to teacher competencies:

In general, these traits and abilities may be grouped into two categories: (1) Those having to do with the teacher's mental abilities and skills, his understanding of psychological and educational principles, and his knowledge of general and specific subject matter to be taught, and (2) those qualities having to do with the organization of the teacher's personality, his personal adjustments, his effectiveness in maintaining good working relationships with pupils and other individuals, and the patterns of his interests.

Of course, while the qualities mentioned under (1) are necessary for successful teaching, there is no guarantee that knowledge itself will make a good teacher. A person may know the elements and principles of psychology and the details of subject matter but lack the ability and know-

[1] David G. Ryans, "The Investigations of Teacher Characteristics," *Educational Record*, Vol. 34 (October, 1953), p. 372.

how to apply them. This comes from practice and association with children and is related to the qualities mentioned under (2).

Ryans goes on to say that on category (2) we have relatively little information. Many of the investigations have indicated also that what constitutes good teaching varies in different fields of subject matter and at different levels in the school. Although there are certain principles which are common, good teaching in grade 1 may mean one thing and quite something else in the 6th; it may mean one thing in algebra and something else in the social studies. Possibly later research may provide the answer to some of our difficulties here.

All this, of course, does not mean that there is nothing but chaos now, and that there is no general, if subjective, agreement on what is involved in good teaching. Ryans [2] offers us this guide: "Teaching is effective to the extent the teacher does things or behaves, in ways that are favorable to the development of skills, understandings, work habits, desirable attitudes, and adequate personal adjustment on the part of the pupils or students." The difficulty, of course, lies in what is meant by *desirable, good,* and *adequate.* Sincere people differ on these matters. Continued research may give us more definite answers.

Various Approaches to the Study of Good Teaching

The usual approaches that have been made to the evaluation of teaching competencies have been from that of evaluation or measurement of:

1. Personal qualities.
2. Performance or behavior and actions in teaching-learning situations.
3. Mental prerequisites.
4. Pupil growth and achievement.

Obviously there cannot be a single approach to the problem of teaching competencies. Rather it must be a many-sided one.

A. S. Barr [3] has pointed out, as he summarized over 150 studies relating to the measurement and prediction of teaching efficiency, that generally they fall under the following groups, according to the criterion employed:

1. Student-teaching rating.
2. In-service ratings.
3. College grades.
4. Pupil growth.
5. Consensus of opinion.
6. Miscellaneous.

[2] *Ibid.,* p. 375.
[3] A. S. Barr and others, "The Measurement and Prediction of Teaching Efficiency," *Journal of Experimental Education* (June, 1948).

It would be valuable at this point for the student to hear the recording listed among the audio-visual aids at the end of the chapter. Here Dr. Barr summarizes briefly the basic areas of agreement and disagreement as revealed by the large number of studies that have been made, some good, others not so good. On the whole, there seems to be a rather high correlation among the many studies of the personal qualities that make for successful teaching and fair agreement on certain of the competencies or abilities involved, although the latter are very far from being as definite and valuable as one might hope. The beginning student will do well to consider as worthwhile those standards on which there is general agreement.

A very large number of the studies that have attempted to evaluate the factors of teaching success have approached the task from one of the following aspects:

1. Personal and social traits.
2. Knowledge of the subject.
3. Professional preparation.

A brief discussion of each of these will be pertinent at this point.

Personal and Social Traits. Teaching is in large part the reaction of one personality with another. These reactions are highly complex, making accurate analysis difficult. Reactions may be as varied as there are pupils in a classroom, and they may be affected by environmental conditions, such as competitive situations, racial and religious relationships, and even the weather and climate. In spite of the difficulties involved, personal and social qualities have been extensively studied. One of the early and more extensive investigations was a part of the Commonwealth Teacher-Training Study, directed by Charters and Waples. From the judgments of administrators, teachers, parents, pupils, and professors, a ranking of significant traits of teachers—in a variety of academic situations—was developed. This list, as would any so developed, has questionable validity, but it does represent collective judgment, as it intends.

Barr and his associates [4] later took the average rankings of the traits and compared them with an analysis of the rankings of the same traits on a large number of teacher-rating scales. Although there were similarities, the significant differences between them effectively suggests that many teacher-rating devices do not properly weigh what a number of those intimately concerned with the profession consider important. Later studies tend to confirm this idea.

The variables and complexities involved in the area of evaluation necessitate further research in order to develop a reasonably accurate system of teacher-rating. The public will demand—and rightly so—that some form of merit rating be developed to be used in promotions and salary

4 Barr and others, *op. cit.,* p. 214.

classifications. Although there are, of course, many considerations which involve subjective appraisals, there is a real need for an efficient and objective method of teacher-evaluation.

The Subject-Matter Approach. Those who approach the problem of teaching competency from the standpoint of subject matter are on firm ground when they say that no one can teach what he does not know. A broad knowledge of subject matter is vital and no amount of personality, no amount of bluffing, can make up for the lack of it. Young persons soon find this weakness in a teacher. Then all too often poor discipline results, and the teacher fails. A strong personality can no more compensate for lack of knowledge in a teacher than can good "bedside manner" compensate for lack of knowledge in a physician. One of the purposes of the National Teachers' Examinations is to give the prospective employer the opportunity to check the extent to which a candidate has the subject-matter knowledge necessary. The other opportunity besides examinations to ascertain such status is by consideration of marks made in high school and college.

On the other hand, knowledge alone surely does not make a person a good teacher. There are many illustrations of brilliant men who cannot teach. They may dislike people; they may lack patience and understanding, or they may not understand how children and young people learn. They might be eminently successful in a laboratory or in a research division of industry, but teaching involves working with people and not only with objects. The true test of a teacher must be how his students grow, mentally, physically, and morally, not merely how well they are entertained or how much they admire his own learning.

The Professional Approach. So the professional side is important too, and there is surely a partial fallacy in the statement, "Teachers are born not made." The growing field of knowledge of psychology, the increasing complexity of the problems of growth and learning, the multiplication of the tools of teaching with their possibilities for use and misuse, the heritage of our educational past and the challenges of the future, all point to the importance of the professional side of teacher education. More will be said of this matter when we consider specific teacher-education programs later in this chapter. It is important to point out here, however, that the professional aspect of the teacher's background *is* important. Can it be tested by examination? Possibly it can, to some extent. It can perhaps best be evaluated by an observation of the student teaching and later by observation of the techniques of the teacher in the classroom and in the community.

Critical Factors

It must be obvious to the student, as he recalls his own experience, that there is no one way to evaluate the competencies of teaching.

It is a complicated and complex process which must eventually be analyzed more effectively. Therefore, the search for "critical" factors must be continued. One of the most significant studies of recent years has been carried out by Ryans [5] under the sponsorship of the American Council on Education. The following excerpt is from the summary chapter of the final report.

After having identified teachers who qualified for membership in each group, an attempt was made to determine some of the distinguishing characteristics of the high, middle, and low groups, as revealed by Teacher Characteristics Schedule responses. Of particular interest were responses of teachers generally assessed high which distinguished them from those generally assessed low.

For elementary and secondary teachers combined, some of the more notable characteristics which distinguished the high group from the low and the low group from the high are those which follow.

There was a general tendency for the high teachers to: be extremely generous in appraisals of the behavior and motives of other persons; possess strong interest in reading and literary affairs; be interested in music, painting and the arts in general; participate in social groups; enjoy pupil relationships; prefer non-directive (permissive) classroom procedures; manifest superior verbal intelligence; and be superior with respect to emotional adjustment. On the other hand, low teachers tended generally to: be restrictive and critical in their appraisals of other persons; prefer activities which did not involve close personal contacts; express less favorable opinions of pupils; manifest less high verbal intelligence; show less satisfactory emotional adjustment; and represent older age groups.

It is as difficult to describe *briefly* a good teacher as it is to try to describe an outstanding physician. Some, teachers and physicians, are superior in one phase of their activities and average or less in others. But it is the totality of the individual—his services, his personality, his abilities, and the *results* of all these—that constitutes success, mediocrity, or failure.

Sometimes it is said that almost anyone knows a good teacher when he sees one, but the facts of even elementary research do not bear this out. There are too many borderline cases; personal and professional judgments are not enough. They can be grossly in error, and further research to standardize somewhat the process for which every administrator and supervisor must exercise responsibility is an urgent necessity.

LEGAL REQUIREMENTS FOR TEACHING

The Background

In the earliest days of the development of the American public school system there were very few, if any, requirements for teachers

[5] David G. Ryans, *Characteristics of Teachers: Their Description, Comparisons and Appraisal* (Washington, D.C., American Council on Education, 1960), pp. 397–398.

actually set down in the laws of the various states. Few persons had any real vision of the future extent of public education and the great part the state would play in the control and direction of it.

On the other hand, in the early days many local communities through their boards of trustees, boards of control, or similar bodies set up widely varying local requirements. These had largely to do with such matters as ability to discipline the school, the possession of sufficient knowledge to teach the fundamentals or the so-called "3 R's," and on occasion, certain standards of character. The first and third of these were generally investigated merely by questions asked by the employing body of laymen and sometimes by a specially appointed committee. A few questions involving problems in arithmetic would probably suffice to determine the applicant's fitness to teach the required amount of that subject while the reading of certain selections and a demonstration of handwriting ability generally were sufficient to teach in those areas. Written recommendations of former employers would also be of help.

This was, it is true, a crude way to determine a candidate's ability and desirability, but it was the only safeguard the parents had of protecting their children against incompetent and unworthy individuals. A part of the process of securing better teachers, therefore, lay in having individuals of a high caliber on the boards of trustees, selectmen, or the examining committees. It is well to point out here that even today this is a *sine qua non* for securing good teachers. Ultimately, it is still the school board that determines standards above the state minimums.

Although there was some gradual improvement in required teacher qualifications prior to the Civil War, the real advances did not begin until sometime thereafter. As the appointment of local professional school officers, both county and local superintendents of schools, became more common, ascertaining the fitness of teacher candidates and licensing them came to be placed in their hands. The effectiveness of this procedure was, of course, limited by the availability of properly trained persons, as has always been the case, but it was at least the beginning of the professional selection and certification of personnel. Elsbree [6] points out:

As a result of the concentration of the functions of examining teachers in the hands of professional educators, two important changes occurred in the appointment of teachers to public school posts. The first was the modification of the examination procedure used in selecting teachers, including a tendency to substitute written for oral examinations in determining the academic fitness of candidates. The second change involved an extension of the original certification plans to include a greater variety of certificates and a wider validity to those granted.

[6] Willard S. Elsbree, *The American Teacher* (New York, American Book, 1939), p. 185.

Gradually there developed, mostly during the latter half of the nineteenth century, the plan of centralizing the granting of teachers' certificates in the hands of state departments of education. This was done sometimes by mere suggestions to local officers, sometimes by general and detailed instructions to be followed, and later in many states by the complete taking over of the function. A teacher's certificate is a license to practice, and since public school teachers are, to a considerable extent, employees of the state, there is much logic for the acceptance of the function of certification by that unit of government.

Table 6-1.   Summary of Minimum Preparation Required by States for Lowest Regular Initial Certificates (as of January 1, 1964)

College Years of Preparation Required	Number of States Requiring	
	Elementary School Teachers	Secondary School Teachers
5 years	1	3
4 years	45	49
3 but less than 4 years	0	0
2 but less than 3 years	5	0
1 but less than 2 years	1	0
Less than 1 year	0	0
Totals	52	52

Note: Inclusion of District of Columbia and Puerto Rico makes total of 52.

SOURCE: Data are from *A Manual on Certification Requirements for School Personnel in the United States,* 1964 Edition, by W. Earl Armstrong and T. M. Stinnett. Copyright by the NEA and used by special permission.

Trends in Certification

Certification practices in the various states are far from uniform. Significant differences exist in the amount and types of training required for a certificate, in the kinds of certificates granted, in the provisions for their renewal, and in the extent of their validity. Some progress, although small, does seem to have been made toward a more or less common requirement of the degree as a minimum attainment for the issue of the lowest form of regular certificate. Armstrong and Stinnett [7] report that "as of January 1964 a total of 46 states, including the District of

[7] W. Earl Armstrong and T. M. Stinnett, *A Manual on Certification Requirements for School Personnel in the United States, 1964 Edition,* National Commission on Teacher Education and Professional Standards (Washington, D.C., NEA, 1964), pp. 5–6.

Table 6-2.   Minimum Requirements for Lowest Regular Teaching Certificates *

State	Elementary School			Secondary School		
	Degree or Number of Semester Hours Required	Professional Education Required, Semester Hours (Total)	Directed Teaching Required, Semester Hours (Included in Column 3)	Degree or Number of Semester Hours Required	Professional Education Required, Semester Hours (Total)	Directed Teaching Required, Semester Hours (Included in Column 6)
Alabama	B	30	3	B	24	3
Alaska	B	24	C	B	18	C
Arizona	B	24	6	5[a]	22	6
Arkansas	B	18	5	B	18	5
California	5	20[b]	180CH	5	15[b]	120CH
Colorado	B	AC	AC	B	AC	AC
Connecticut	B	30	6	B	18	6
Delaware	B	30	6	B	18	6
District	B	24	6	5	18	6
Florida	B	20	6	B	20	6
Georgia	B	18	6	B	18	6
Hawaii	B	18	AC	B	18	AC
Idaho	B	20	6	B	20	6
Illinois	B	16	5	B	16	5
Indiana	B	27	8	B	18	6
Iowa	B	20	5	B	20	5
Kansas	B	24	5	B	20	5
Kentucky	B	24	8[c]	B	17	8[c]
Louisiana	B	24	4	B	18	4
Maine	B	30	8	B	18	6
Maryland	B	26	8	B	18	6
Massachusetts	B[d]	18	2	B[d]	12	2
Michigan	B	20	5	B	20	5
Minnesota	B	30	6	B	18	4
Mississippi	B	36	6	B	18	6
Missouri	B	20	5	B	20	5

LEGEND: AC means approved curriculum; B means a bachelor's degree of specified preparation; 5 means a bachelor's degree plus a fifth year of appropriate preparation, not necessarily completion of the master's degree; C means a course; CH means clock hours.
* Professional requirements listed are the basic requirements for degree or lowest regular certificates. Some variation from the professional requirements as stated in this table may be found in the requirements for specific certificates listed for the respective states in Chapter II.
[a] Arizona secondary certificate: master's degree or 30 semester hours of graduate credit. Secondary-temporary: bachelor's degree and completion of an approved program; valid for five years only (grades 7–12).
[b] Includes an 8-semester-hour (elementary) and 6-semester-hour (secondary) unit for directed teaching. The requirement is actually stated in clock hours, however.
[c] A teacher who has taught successfully for four or more years is required to take only 4 semester hours of practice teaching or a seminar of 4 hours. A teacher who has had two years of successful experience may take a seminar dealing with professional problems instead of the 8 hours in practice teaching.
[d] Completion of the bachelor's degree or graduation from an approved four-year normal school.
[e] The Montana provisional certificate is based on graduation from an approved two-year program and is renewable only by scheduled training toward the bachelor's degree.

Table 6-2. Continued

State	Elementary School			Secondary School		
	Degree or Number of Semester Hours Required	Professional Education Required, Semester Hours (Total)	Directed Teaching Required, Semester Hours (Included in Column 3)	Degree or Number of Semester Hours Required	Professional Education Required, Semester Hours (Total)	Directed Teaching Required, Semester Hours (Included in Column 6)
Montana	64[c]	AC	AC	B	16	AC
Nebraska	40[f]	8	3	B	AC	AC
Nevada	B	18[g]	4	B	18	4
New Hampshire	B	30	6	B	18	6
New Jersey	B	36[h]	6[h]	B	24[h]	6[h]
New Mexico	B	24	6	B	18	6
New York	B	36	12	B[i]	18	6
North Carolina	B	18	3	B	18	3
North Dakota	64	16	3	B	16	3
Ohio	B	28	6	B	17	6
Oklahoma	B	21[i]	6	B	21[i]	6
Oregon	B	20	4	B[k]	24	6
Pennsylvania	B	36[l]	6	B	18	6
Puerto Rico	68	53	6	B	29	5
Rhode Island	B	30	6	B	18	6
South Carolina	B	21	6	B	18	6
South Dakota	60	15	3	B	20	6
Tennessee	B	24	4	B	24	4
Texas	B	18	6	B	18	6
Utah	B	30	8	B	22	8
Vermont	B	18	6	B	18	6
Virginia	B	18	6	B	15	4-6
Washington	B[m]	AC	AC	B[m]	AC	AC
West Virginia	B	20	6	B	20	6
Wisconsin	64	26	8	B	18	5
Wyoming	B	20	C	B	20	C

[f] Provisional teaching certificates are issued for specifically endorsed grades, subjects, fields, and areas in designated classes of school districts upon evidence of partial completion of an approved teacher education program, generally 40–60 semester hours including specified amounts of general and professional education.

[g] For a three-year certificate; for a five-year certificate, the requirement is 30.

[h] The practice-teaching requirement is 150 clock hours, 90 of which must be in actual classroom teaching.

[i] A provisional high school certificate is issued for the academic fields based upon completion of the bachelor's degree with 18 semester hours in education, including 6 in supervised practice teaching (including 80 class periods of supervised instructional experience); valid for five years; nonrenewable; holder must complete requirements for the permanent certificate.

[j] For the standard certificate; for the temporary certificate, the requirement is 12.

[k] Provisional certificate only; for standard certification, a fifth year must be completed within five years after provisional certification.

[l] Eighteen in professional education and 18 in elementary content subjects.

[m] Provisional certificate only; for standard certification, a fifth year must be completed within six years after provisional certification.

SOURCE: Data are from *A Manual on Certification Requirements for School Personnel in the United States*, 1964 Edition, by W. Earl Armstrong and T. M. Stinnett. Copyright by the NEA and used by special permission.

Table 6-3. General Requirements for Teaching Certificates

State	U.S. Citizenship	Oath of Allegiance or Loyalty	Must Secure Employment	Recommendation (College or Employing Officer)	Minimum Age Required	Fee Required for Certificate	General Health Certificate Required	Chest X-ray Required	Special Course Required
Alabama	No	No	No	Yes	17	$2.00	No	Yes	No
Alaska	Yes	No	No	No	18	5.00	No	No	No
Arizona	Yes	Yes	No	No	18	4.00	No	Yes	Yes
Arkansas	No	No	No	Yes	18	none	Yes	Yes	No
California	Yes[1]	Yes	No	No	18	8.00	Yes	No	Yes[2]
Colorado	No	Yes	No[3]	Yes	none	5.00	No	No	No
Connecticut	Yes	No	No	Yes	18	none	Yes	No	Yes[4]
Delaware	No	Yes	Yes[5]	Yes	none	none	Yes	Yes[6]	No
District	Yes	Yes	No	Yes	none	none	Yes	Yes	No
Florida	Yes	Yes	No	Yes	20	5.00	Yes	No	No
Georgia	No	No	No[7]	Yes	none	none	No	No	No
Hawaii	Yes	Yes	Yes	Yes	none	none	Yes	Yes	No
Idaho	Yes[8]	Yes	No	Yes	18	5.00	No	No	No
Illinois	Yes	Yes[9]	No	No	19	4.00[10]	No	No	Yes[11]
Indiana	No	Yes	No	Yes	none	1.00	Yes	No	No
Iowa	No	No	No	Yes	18	2.00	No	No	Yes[12]
Kansas	No	Yes	No	Yes	none	5.00	No	No	No
Kentucky	No	No	No	Yes	18	none	No	No	No
Louisiana	No	No	No	Yes	none	none	No	No	Yes[13]
Maine	No	No	Yes[14]	Yes	17	none	No	No[15]	No
Maryland	Yes	Yes	Yes	Yes[16]	18	none	No	No	No
Massachusetts	Yes	No	No	No	none	none	Yes	No	No
Michigan	Yes	Yes	No	Yes	18	none[17]	No	No	No
Minnesota	No	No	No	Yes	none	3.00	Yes	No	No
Mississippi	Yes	Yes	No	Yes	18	none	Yes	No	No
Missouri	No	No	No	Yes	none	none	Yes	No	No

1 Filing for declaration of intention will qualify for citizenship.

2 A course in the Constitution of the United States is required for renewal of the standard certificate.

3 Except for vocational and some special service certificates.

4 History of the United States.

5 Except for graduates of Delaware colleges or high schools.

6 Not prerequisite but required by law sometime during the first year and each year of employment.

7 Evidence of employment is now required for issuance of the provisional four-year certificate based on the bachelor's degree, unless the applicant has been certificated previously in Georgia.

8 Must be a citizen or have taken out first papers.

9 An oath is required before teaching is begun but not before issuance of the certificate.

10 $4 to the state, $1 to the county superintendent for issuance, and $2 for registration, making a total of $7.

11 American history and/or government.

12 American history or government.

13 American history, biological and physical science; Louisiana history for upper-elementary teachers only.

14 Required only of out-of-state, initial applicants who apply under reciprocity.

15 Not required for certification, but the law requires a chest x-ray every two years; responsibility of employing superintendent.

16 Recommendation of employing officer.

17 Out-of-state applicants are charged a fee of $3 for investigating credentials.

18 A registration fee of $2 is charged for initial certification and $1 for each year of validity.

19 Can use Mantoux test.

20 Or have filed declaration of intention.

Table 6-3. Continued

State	U.S. Citizenship	Oath of Allegiance or Loyalty	Must Secure Employment	Recommendation (College or Employing Officer)	Minimum Age Required	Fee Required for Certificate	General Health Certificate Required	Chest X-ray Required	Special Course Required
Montana	Yes	Yes	No	Yes	18	2.00[18]	Yes	Yes[19]	No
Nebraska	Yes	Yes	No	Yes	none	2.00	Yes	No	No
Nevada	Yes[20]	Yes	No	No	18	$1.-$2.	Yes	Yes	Yes[21]
New Hampshire	No	Yes	Yes	Yes	none	none	No	No	No
New Jersey	Yes	Yes	No	No	18	$5.00	No	No	No
New Mexico	Yes	No	No	Yes	18	1.00	Yes	Yes	No
New York	Yes	No	No	No	18	5.00	No	No	No
North Carolina	No	No	Yes[22]	No	18	none	Yes	Yes	No
North Dakota	Yes[23]	Yes	No	Yes	18	$3.-$5.	No	No	No
Ohio	No	No	No	Yes	none	2.00	No	No	No
Oklahoma	Yes[24]	No	Yes[25]	Yes	none	1.00	Yes	No	Yes[26]
Oregon	Yes	Yes	No	No	18	5.00	No	Yes	No
Pennsylvania	Yes[27]	No	No	Yes	18	none	Yes	No	Yes
Puerto Rico	Yes	Yes	Yes	No	18	none	Yes	Yes	No
Rhode Island	Yes	Yes	Yes	Yes	19	none	Yes	No	Yes[28]
South Carolina	Yes	No	No	Yes	18	none	Yes	Yes	No
South Dakota	Yes	Yes	No	Yes	18	5.00	No	No	No
Tennessee	No	No	No	Yes	18	2.00	No	No	No
Texas	Yes	Yes	No	Yes	18	$2.-$3.	No	No	Yes[29]
Utah	No	No	No	Yes	none	none	No	No	No
Vermont	No	Yes	Yes[30]	Yes	19	none	No	No	No
Virginia	Yes	No	Yes	Yes	18	none	No	No	No
Washington	Yes[31]	Yes	No[32]	Yes	18	1.00	No	Yes	Yes[33]
West Virginia	Yes	No	No	Yes	18	1.00	No	No	No
Wisconsin	No	No	No	Yes	none	2.00	Yes[34]	Yes[34]	Yes[35]
Wyoming	Yes[36]	No	Yes	Yes	none	none	No	No	Yes[37]

21 Nevada school law and Constitution and U.S. Constitution (by credit or examination).

22 Applies only to out-of-state applicants.

23 Must be a citizen or have declared intention.

24 Must be a citizen or have taken out first papers.

25 For temporary certificate only.

26 Oklahoma history and 6 semester hours of American history and government.

27 Citizenship may be waived for exchange teachers and teachers of foreign languages.

28 Rhode Island education; may be completed within three years of initial teaching in the state.

29 Texas and federal governments.

30 Required of nonresidents.

31 Must be a citizen or have declared intention.

32 Required of nonresidents.

33 Washington State history and government or Pacific Northwest history and government (may be satisfied by examination).

34 Required for employment in public schools.

35 Cooperatives required of teachers of economics, social studies, and agriculture. Conservation required of teachers of science and social studies.

36 Must be a citizen or have taken out first papers.

37 United States and Wyoming Constitutions (may be satisfied by credit course or examination).

SOURCE: Data are from *A Manual on Certification Requirements for School Personnel in the United States,* 1964 Edition, by W. Earl Armstrong and T. M. Stinnett. Copyright by the NEA and used by special permission.

Columbia, were enforcing the requirement for regular certificates." This gain of only two states over 1961 is rather surprising but may be due in part to the continuing shortage of teachers.

Armstrong and Stinnett [8] state that according to reports from the various states the following trends seem to be evident:

1. There is a commitment to the principle of using the "approved program" approach as now seen in some 40 states. Approval may come from the state department of education, NCATE, or both.
2. There is a definite trend toward strengthening the academic preparation of prospective teachers in the areas of general education. There is, further, a growing number of states that require an "area of concentration" for elementary school teachers.
3. Another obvious and marked trend is that of increasing the requirements in the various teaching fields.
4. There appears to be an increased use of the National Teachers' Examinations.
5. It may be added too that there is a growing feeling that there should be greater reciprocity in certification standards and procedures among the states. Some progress seems to have been made in this matter in certain areas of the country, but it is extremely slow.

The last few years have been ones of unusual controversy in the teacher education field primarily because of the suggestions made in the much quoted Conant Report.[9] For many years the teaching profession has been striving to get a good measure of control "over its professional house," that is, of teacher education, certification, and accreditation. Although this has been achieved to a considerable extent for medicine, law, and other professions, it is difficult to understand why it should be so strongly resisted for education. An illustration of the struggle over the present structure was shown in the virulent attack upon NCATE previously discussed briefly in this volume.

It remains to be seen how the "approved program" will develop. Will it result in the colleges and universities having a much larger share in the certification of teachers with the state yielding much of its present authority in the field? This should be clarified in the years immediately ahead.

Other requirements prescribed by law in the various states are shown in the table on pages 154–155.

With the period of required preparation being extended, there is less need for adhering to the minimum age requirement. On the other hand, because of the increasing emphasis upon loyalty for public service, a great many states are requiring all teachers and prospective teachers to take the oath of allegiance or the equivalent thereof. Evidence of good

---

[8] *Ibid.*, p. 3.

[9] James B. Conant, *The Education of American Teachers* (New York, McGraw-Hill, 1963).

character is widely required and is generally included in the recommendation of the college official.

In view of the fact that requirements are changing rapidly, it will be well for the teacher contemplating employment in a particular state to write to the Department of Education inquiring as to the legal requirements in effect at that particular time.

As a final word on the matter of the certification of teachers, it should be stated that most authorities agree it is not good policy to write the regulations into statutory law. It is better by far to delegate the power of setting standards to the state board of education—which can carry on or sanction studies to indicate possible changes and authorize them when the need is demonstrated. It is assumed further that in the ideal situation the board will look for leadership to the state superintendent and the professional staff of the state department of education and will act upon their recommendations. Then when standards are set and policies adopted, it will be the task of the superintendent and his staff to administer them.

PROBLEMS IN TEACHER EDUCATION

General Versus Professional Education

In this area of what constitutes a first-class program of teacher education there has been a long and at times bitter controversy. Occasionally there seems to have been more heat than light involved in the discussion. It is proper that curricula should be continually examined and revised by "men of good will." Too often differences of approach to the problems have resulted from the various backgrounds of the academician and those who have been more directly involved in public education. It is time that this conflict should be minimized and the issues resolved as much as possible without bitterness. Undoubtedly there are several different ways, not producing vastly different results, by which good teachers may be educated, but in the search for common grounds vested interests and professional jealousies ought to be put aside. Then, out of controversy beneficial results may arise.

Numerous conferences have been held, studies made, and reports issued treating the problems suggested. A few of these which have been most effective have been:

Harvard University Committee on *The Objectives of Education in a Free Society* (1945).
The Improvement of Teacher Education, Commission on Teacher Education, American Council on Education (1946).
Various Conferences and Reports on Teacher Education held by the Commission on Teacher Education and Professional Standards (TEPS), NEA.

Significant studies carried out by numerous colleges and universities and financed largely by the Ford Foundation during the past ten years.

Report on *The Education of American Teachers* by Conant—Report of a two-year study financed largely by the Carnegie Foundation (1963).

It is possible to say now that out of these studies have come a number of conclusions and recommendations that have had fairly wide acceptance. The major ones may be set down as follows:

1. It is generally agreed that teachers should have a broader background of general education. Quantitative recommendations vary, but the most widely discussed ones may be found in the above mentioned Conant Report.
2. Some consolidation or reduction of professional courses may be necessary if the first requisite is to be implemented. There is as yet no general agreement upon details, and none is presently in sight.
3. The development of the Master of Arts Program in Teaching has found fairly wide acceptance as a way
    a. To secure teachers with a broader cultural background.
    b. To provide liberal arts graduates with methods and techniques of teaching.
    c. To improve the source of supply of teachers.
4. There is no general agreement on whether the teacher education program ought to be four or five years in length. The Commission on Teacher Education and Professional Standards (TEPS) thinks it should be five years while Conant insists that four are sufficient. There is a marked tendency evident in a number of states to require the acquisition of the fifth year or its equivalent at the end of several years of teaching experience.
5. A conclusion seldom questioned is that there should be more contact and experience with children on all levels prior to the initial teaching activity. Practice teaching or student teaching, as it is frequently called, thus becomes the most important part of the pre-professional experience. Out of this belief has come the development of the internship period now a specific part of the program at some universities.

Some feel, however, that an increasing association with children and young people should be required of all teacher education students *throughout* their college course. This has been strongly recommended by some studies and certainly has much merit.

The question of what extent all professional education should be on the graduate level is receiving much attention, but it is certain that this is presently impractical and inadvisable, for should graduate programs be limited to a few institutions in each state, there would quickly develop a teacher shortage of monumental proportions. One thing is certain: the ultimate pattern of teacher education in America is not yet formed. It may well be that from the conflicting theories and points of view an entirely new and different institution will grow to supersede those now in existence. At least it seems clear that there will be radical changes in

Photograph by Robert Galbraith,
Jamaica, N.Y. Courtesy: The Board of
Education of the City of New York.
Architects: Katz, Waisman, Weber, Strauss,
and Joseph Blumenkranz, consultant.

P.S. #197, Queens, New York. Teachers gain much knowledge about
their pupils while observing them on the playground.

programs of teacher education. The student will do well to familiarize himself with the reports and studies mentioned herein.

Attracting Competent Young People

Even if the problems we have discussed are well resolved, it will be to no avail unless we have young people of high quality who wish to enter the profession. Consequently the problem of great urgency is that of selective recruitment, and with more and more people being attracted to the profession as current data indicate, the time may be now when we can seriously devote more attention to the question of quality.

At present no definite cut off point can be accepted below which applicants for teacher education should be disqualified, but Conant [10] suggests that applicants should be limited to the upper thirty percent of the graduating classes of the secondary schools. Possibly so, but it is hard to say, for there undoubtedly should be many exceptions for individual institutions and individual students. Stinnett,[11] in commenting upon this position says,

I heartily concur with the thesis that the basic approach to the massive improvement in teacher education which this nation must achieve lies in discriminating selective admission to preparation programs. I am not prepared to say that the cut off point should be the upper thirty percent, in part because we have not yet perfected selective admission and screening procedures. But the cut off point should be high, I believe this to be the single most crucial weakness in teacher education—the failure to enforce careful selection.

It is only fair to say that Conant is now proposing the thirty percent be used "on a national basis." To apply it currently to every single institution or to every high school graduate seeking admission surely would be impractical and unwise. There are many factors other than high scholastic aptitude that are part of the successful teacher's equipment. However, if the intellectual level of the teacher education program is to be raised, the candidates for the program must come from the upper levels of the preparatory school classes. An *automatic* cut off point of 30 percent, however, may be effectively questioned.

How is it possible to get more young people of high academic quality to become teachers? One of the best methods has always been the influence of good teachers in service. Impressed by their devotion and interest, young people have wished to become teachers themselves.

Conversely, it must be regretfully admitted, many promising young people have been detoured from a career in education by poor teachers

---

[10] James Bryant Conant, *The Education of American Teachers* (New York, McGraw-Hill), pp. 81–82.

[11] T. M. Stinnett, in a symposium on James Bryant Conant's *The Education of American Teachers, Journal of Teacher Education,* Vol. 15 (March, 1964), pp. 45–49.

who are disgruntled and disgusted. "If that is what teachers are like," they think, "teaching is not for us." Unfortunately, neither teaching nor any other profession will ever be entirely free of that sort of influence. Not much can be done about it on a short-term basis, at least.

Professional organizations, such as the National Education Association and the various state associations, have been devoting earnest efforts to the problem. Committees have been studying the demand and supply and suggesting ways of meeting the shortage. Probably the most prominent movement has been the Future Teachers of America, organized in 1937 by the National Education Association. At present there are more than 6,000 high school clubs. The FTA clubs are exploratory in nature and are designed in part to attract the best young people into their activities. Here it is hoped that through such things as studying what teaching is like through visits to schools and colleges, by associations with children, through actual temporary teaching experience in the classroom, and in other ways, interest will be stimulated, knowledge will be broadened, and many worthy young people will be guided into preparation for a career in teaching.

Literature having guidance value for those interested in teaching as a life career is available from many sources. A few recent examples may be listed as follows:

Teaching Career Fact Book——National Education Association
Teaching as a Career——United States Office of Education
Invitation to Teaching TEPS Commission——NEA
The Good Life–College Teaching——NEA
Our Teachers: Their Importance to Our Children
        and Our Community——National Association of Manufacturers
Should You be a Teacher?——New York Life Insurance Company

Many groups, such as service clubs, parent-teacher associations, and some Future Teachers of America clubs are offering scholarships to worthy students who wish to enter teaching. Indeed, such activities are helpful contributions.

Many institutions concerned with the preparation of teachers hold Career Days or Career Forums on the campus for those who may be interested. At such events information is presented on the profession and on the particular college; preliminary study seems to indicate that these functions are quite effective.

Of course, guidance directors and counselors have—or should have—a deep interest in this problem, and through the usual techniques available can be of great service to young people and to the profession.

QUESTIONS AND PROJECTS

1. Prepare a report on two or more of the separate research studies treating the effectiveness of teaching, and present this to the class for discussion.
2. Investigate the patterns of behavior expected of teachers in your home community, and report to the class upon them.
3. Debate the question: "Resolved, that the maintenance of higher standards will bring more good teachers into the profession than will lowered standards."
4. Conduct a round-table discussion on the way in which motion pictures and radio affect the recruitment of teachers.
5. Conduct a discussion on the use of "teacher's aides" in the classroom to make it possible for the teacher to devote more time to so-called teaching duties. Teacher's aides as used here may be compared to nurse's aides in the nursing field.
6. Evaluate the probable effectiveness of a Career Conference as it has operated in a particular high school of your knowledge.
7. Investigate the work of several FTA clubs in high schools as to their effectiveness in influencing desirable candidates to enter teaching.
8. Make a list of the personal characteristics of the best teacher you have ever had. List his teaching techniques or methods and have them summarized by a committee.
9. Do the same as in Question 8 for the worst teacher you have had. Compare the results with those obtained from standard research, such as is reported in this chapter.
10. Discuss all the possible ways of using more of the teacher's time for actual classroom teaching rather than for nonteaching duties.
11. Arrange for a committee to collect and to evaluate critically some of the pamphlets and material aimed at encouraging individuals to enter the teaching profession.
12. Conduct several panel discussions on various aspects of the Conant report.

AUDIO-VISUAL AIDS

MOTION PICTURES (16 MM)

Elementary Teacher: Beginning Student Teaching—Indiana University, Audio-Visual Center, Bloomington, Ind., 10 min., sd., b&w. Discusses the training and functions of the teacher in a world of rapid change. Shows Janet, a student teacher, as she acquaints herself with a classroom, the school, and its program and experiences of practice teaching. Uses flashbacks to emphasize the points being discussed by the teaching supervisor and Janet during an evaluation of the latter's progress.

Freedom to Learn—National Education Association, 1201 16th St., N.W., Washington, D.C., 27½ min., sd., b&w and/or color. Shows that modern schools prepare our children to assume their responsibilities as good citizens. It explains that respect for facts, constant search for the truth, and knowledge of the world are essential in this preparation.

Horace Mann—Encyclopaedia Britannica Films, 1150 Wilmette Ave., Wilmette, Ill., 19 min., sd., b&w. Portrays important episodes in the life of Horace Mann, the "father of the common schools." Reviews his activities as teacher, lawyer, state senator, board of education member, and college president. Emphasizes Mann's work in pointing up the need for well-built schools, good textbooks, democratic methods of learning, schools for teachers, and universal education in the United States.

Introduction to Student Teaching—Indiana University, Audio-Visual Center, Bloomington, Ind., 20 min., sd., b&w. Shows the activities of Bill, Nancy, and Carol during the early weeks of their student teaching experiences. We see how they get acquainted with the school personnel and policies, become accustomed to handling routine classroom matters, become familiar with a wide variety of instructional materials, and learn as much as they can about the pupils. Designed primarily for student teachers on the secondary level.

Preparation of Teachers—United World Government Films, 1445 Park Ave., New York, N.Y., 20 min., sd., b&w. Shows teacher training at Ball State Teachers College, Muncie, Indiana. Emphasizes learning to understand children and providing for individual differences. Stresses the need for desirable personality traits in teachers.

The School and the Community—McGraw-Hill Book Co., Text-Film Dept., 330 West 42nd St., New York, N.Y., 14 min., sd., b&w and/or color. Discusses the problem of separation between the school and the community. Indicates that teachers, parents, school officials, and the citizenry share responsibility for bringing them together. Shows the benefits which the school and the community gain when they co-operate.

The Teacher—Child Education Foundation, 535 E. 84th St., New York 28, N.Y., 25 min., sd., color. Shows the process by which a student is prepared to teach the child from 2 to 8 in a modern professional college. You see college students going about their normal activities—in class sessions, seminars, and conferences, working with children, having dates, leading the pleasant, stimulating college life of the future teacher today. Portions of the film were used on the American Inventory TV Program of *The Teacher*.

Teachers for Tomorrow—University of Wisconsin, Madison, Wis., 22 min., sd., b&w. Shows how students are trained to become teachers in courses and practice work at the School of Education at the University of Wisconsin. Stresses the importance of proper selection and training of prospective teachers; examples of the kind of program student teachers will follow and the outlook for the future in the teaching profession.

Teaching—Mahnke Productions, 215 E. Third St., Des Moines, Iowa, 11 min., sd., b&w. Shows the contributions of teachers to American democracy and presents the traits of a good teacher, the attractions in teaching, the educational requirements, and the various types of teaching jobs.

What Greater Gift—National Education Association, 1201 16th St., N.W., Washington, D.C., 28 min., sd., b&w and/or color. Presents the teacher as a professional person and shows something of the nature of teaching. Stresses that today's teacher needs professional preparation to acquire the understanding and skills essential to good teaching.

FILMSTRIPS

Let's Take a Look at Teaching—Wayne University, Detroit, Mich., 50 fr., si., b&w. An overview of the teaching profession and of what it has to offer in terms of salary, tenure, working conditions, opportunity for travel, and individual interests. Pictures a typical school day showing the varied demands on the teacher, and her responsibilities.

Focus on the Future—National Education Association, 1201 16th St., N.W., Washington, D.C., 70 fr., color, with tape and/or script. A story of how Future Teachers of America Clubs are organized and operate in one of the larger states. Emphasizes programs, activities and values of the Clubs as a means of securing high quality candidates for the profession.

RECORDING

Characteristics of a Good Teacher—Educational Recording Services, 5922 Abernathy Dr., Los Angeles, Calif., 15 min., 33⅓ r.p.m. microgroove. Discussion by A. S. Barr: Part I—Personal qualities and competencies of the good teacher. (15 min.) Part II—Difficulties in rating teaching and some available evaluation scales and techniques. (15 min.)

TAPE

How Should America's Teachers Be Educated?—Teachers College, Columbia University. Two tapes 20 minutes long. Two speakers, with opposing points of view, each make 20 minute presentations. Speakers are Prof. Arthur Bestor, Jr. and Prof. Karl W. Bigelow. Order for recording on your tape from: National Tape Repository, Bur. Audio-Visual Instruction, Stadium Building, Room 348, University of Colorado, Boulder, Colorado.

FURTHER READINGS

Armstrong, W. Earl, "National Council for Accreditation of Teacher Education," *NEA Journal,* Vol. 43, No. 9 (December, 1954), pp. 571–574.

Barzun, Jacques, *Teacher in America* (Boston, Little, Brown, 1945).

Bellack, A. A., *Theory and Research on Teaching* (New York, Teachers College, Columbia University, Bureau of Publications, 1963).

Biddle, Bruce J. and William J. Ellena, eds., *Contemporary Research on Teacher Effectiveness* (New York, Holt, Rinehart and Winston, 1964).

Combs, Arthur W., "Can We Measure Good Teaching? Objective Measurement is Impossible," *NEA Journal,* Vol. 53 (January, 1964), pp. 34–73.

Conant, James B., *The Certification of Teachers: The Restricted State Approved Program Approach* (Washington, D.C., The American Association of Colleges for Teacher Education, 1964).

Conant, James B., *The Education of American Teachers* (New York, McGraw-Hill, 1963).

Denemark, George W., ed., *Criteria for Curriculum Decisions in Teacher Education*, (Washington, D.C., Association for Supervision and Curriculum Development, 1963).

Fattu, N. A., "Research on Teacher Evaluation," (bibliography), *National Elementary Principals*, Vol. 43 (November, 1963), pp. 19–27.

Gage, N. L., *Handbook of Research on Teaching* (New York, Rand McNally, 1963).

Highet, Gilbert, *The Art of Teaching* (New York, Knopf, 1950).

Hodenfield, G. K., and T. M. Stinnett, *The Education of Teachers* (Englewood Cliffs, N.J., Prentice-Hall, 1961).

Howsan, Robert B., "Teacher Evaluation—Facts and Folklore," *National Elementary Principals*, Vol. 43 (November, 1963), pp. 6–18.

Kinney, L. B., *Certification in Education* (Englewood Cliffs, N.J., Prentice-Hall, 1964).

"Legal Status of the Public School Teachers," *NEA Research Bull.*, Vol. 35, No. 1 (February, 1957).

Long, Sr., M. Brideen, O.S.F., "A Synthesis of Research Studies on Predicting Teaching Success," *Catholic Educational Review*, Vol. 55, No. 4 (April, 1957), pp. 217–230.

Mitchell, Harold E., "Can We Measure Good Teaching Objectively? Recent Research Holds Promise That We Can," *NEA Journal*, Vol. 53 (January, 1964) pp. 35–36.

National Commission on Teacher Education and Professional Standards, *The High-Standard Approach to Teacher Supply*, Report of the Albany Conference (Washington, NEA, November, 1954).

National Education Association, *Teaching Career Fact Book* (Washington, D.C., 1963).

Rath, L., "What is a Good Teacher," *Childhood Education*, Vol. 40 (May, 1964), pp. 451–6.

Ryans, David G., "Assessment of Teacher Behavior and Instruction," *Review of Educational Research*, Vol. 33 (October, 1963), pp. 415–441.

"The Postwar Struggle to Provide Competent Teachers," *NEA Research Bulletin*, Vol. 35, No. 2 (October, 1957).

Trump, J. Lloyd, "The Education of a Professional Teacher," *Phi Delta Kappan*, Vol. 45 (June, 1964), pp. 448–9.

Trump, Lloyd, *Focus on Change—Guide to Better Schools* (Chicago, Rand McNally, 1961).

Wiggins, Sam P., *Battlefields in Teacher Education* (Nashville, George Peabody College for Teachers, 1964).

7

Fields of Service and
Professional Opportunities

PREVIEW

▸ Opportunities for employment and service in education are better
than ever.

In the elementary school, even in the nursery school field, growth
is likely to continue at a high rate and teacher demand will be great.

In the secondary school the most urgent need is for a better distribution of new teachers among the various subject fields.

In many special fields there is now an urgent need for good teachers,
and the demand is certain to increase.

Real opportunities exist also in supervision and administration for
properly qualified individuals.

As the wave of students engulfs the colleges and universities, it appears inevitable that the demand for good teachers on this level
will far exceed the supply.

▸ The attractions of teaching have increased because of:
1. Salary schedules that are being improved constantly.
2. Adequate retirement systems.
3. Sick leaves and sabbatical leaves.
4. Other fringe benefits designed to improve teacher welfare.

Seldom in our history have the opportunities for service and
advancement in education been as exciting as they now are, and there is
every indication that this will continue. At present there simply are not
enough properly qualified teachers in both the elementary and the
secondary schools.

From the teacher's standpoint, however, the situation can have a silver lining. He need not take the first position he is offered. He can do some choosing of locality, such as that near a college or university where he can do graduate study; this is an important consideration. He also has the opportunity to choose between various salaries and working conditions. All of these factors have the potential for bringing better service to the public as well as opportunities to the individual.

For the teacher who wishes to advance in his profession, the chances were never better. Increased numbers of teachers means more demands for consultants, supervisors, principals, and administrators at all levels. The young teacher who wishes to prepare himself for broader responsibilities may advance rapidly. True, it may not be as rapid as in some industrial fields, but for the person with integrity, ideas, and ambition, there is in education a promising future.

In the following material, we shall try to indicate for the student the specific nature of the opportunities in a good many different fields of service, as these circumstances exist today and as they are very likely to be in the years ahead.

POSITIONS IN THE VARIOUS FIELDS

Pre-Elementary and Elementary Education

In the nursery schools opportunities for employment, while not abundant, are growing in a limited way. Covering ages 1½ to 5, this institution has not been widely adopted as part of the public school system. However, a great many nursery schools are operated in connection with the experimental or child welfare work of the larger colleges and universities. It is probable that by far the largest number are privately operated by individuals, in many cases in their own homes.

In the late 1930's, nursery schools received a considerable impetus, with partial financial support being furnished by the federal government. This program continued in varying degrees into the early war years, and later a considerable number of the schools were transferred to public support and control. Although it is likely that in the years ahead most large cities will make the nursery school a part of their program, at present the opportunities for employment are not great and are best in privately operated institutions.

Possibilities for future employment in public kindergartens seem to be very good indeed. In 1963–64 there were 2,211,000 children enrolled at this level, and while most institutions were in the larger cities, the demand for kindergartens in smaller communities has materially increased. Because of the rapid growth of the population and other factors mentioned earlier, the demand for teachers of 4- and 5-year-olds will undoubtedly continue at a high level.

The increased cost of public education generally will likely prevent a more rapid growth of public kindergartens than would otherwise take place. In many places it will be all too difficult to meet building needs for children who are in the compulsory attendance ages. Space for kindergartens may have to wait. In spite of this, there is no reason why anyone properly trained for kindergarten work should not find very satisfactory employment.

Photograph by Richard L. Strayer.

Westtown-Thornbury School: More and more young men are entering the profession for work in the elementary school.

In the grades usually considered more specifically the elementary school (grades 1–6 or 1–8) the possibilities of finding highly desirable positions are excellent. From one point of view, it is now and will continue to be a "teachers market." Sufficient data is available to indicate that more than 100,000 new teachers will be needed annually for the elementary schools. These needs are results of the following:

1. Teachers leave their positions for various reasons.
2. In most schools there is increased enrollment.
3. There is a need to relieve overcrowding and to eliminate short sessions.
4. Instruction and services not now provided are desired.
5. The unprepared teacher must be replaced.

It will take a phenomenal growth of the supply of teachers to anywhere nearly meet the demands, and such growth is nowhere in sight at present. Opportunities at this level for professional advancement and for securing a position commensurate with one's abilities are all that could be desired. Maul [1] has pointed out the idea that "the greatest challenge to the profession, therefore, is how to attract a far greater proportion of new teachers for service in the elementary grades."

In a later report the National Education Association [2] confirms this statement made two years earlier, but adds another of special significance for secondary education: "The lack of balance between elementary and high-school teaching fields overshadows all else. . . . The largest need is in the elementary classrooms." Since the needs represented in several of the above areas, notably 3, 4, and 5, are more or less chronic and little is likely to be done about them soon, it should be clear that there will be little diminution in the demand in the foreseeable future.

Secondary Education

The children of the post-war high birth rate have been moving through the secondary schools of America for some time now. They have entered colleges and universities and continue to knock at their doors as a part of the expected "tidal wave." At the same time there is nothing to indicate that the high school enrollment will move in any direction but upward. The general population increase is bound to have this effect which will likely be bolstered by the attempts to keep youth in school longer and to provide broader services.

Recently there has been a pronounced increase in the number of young people preparing for secondary teaching. Actually the problem now seems not to be one of the total supply but rather one of distribution; the supply of new teachers does not match the needs as far as subject matter demands are concerned. In some fields there will continue to be a shortage; in others, an oversupply.

This brief analysis refers to the country as a whole, but there are wide variations among the states and within each state as well. Certain teacher preparation institutions, for example, report a continuing heavy

---

[1] Ray C. Maul, "Changing Nature of the Teacher Shortage," *NEA Journal,* Vol. 52 (November, 1963), pp. 41–42.

[2] *Teacher Supply and Demand in Public Schools, 1965,* Research Report 1965 R 10 (Washington, D.C., 1965) pp. 12–13.

demand for teachers of the social sciences, while for the country at large there is a definite surplus. Likewise, the state-wide regulation in California requiring the teaching of foreign languages in the upper elementary and junior high school grades is likely to result in a mammoth shortage of teachers in the languages in that state even if existing standards are lowered. Thus, local demands and limitations modify any generalized statements of demand and supply. The prospective teacher as well as those in service will find it necessary to keep in touch with professional journals for current information on these matters. The Report to which reference has been made several times in this chapter is thoroughly up-to-date and helpful; the student should be familiar with it.

It must be obvious to the reader that an unusual responsibility rests upon the guidance staffs of the secondary schools, and indeed, upon the entire teaching personnel for an updated program of counseling—one that will bring before interested students adequate facts that may be helpful to them in the preparation for the teaching profession.

It is obvious too that the student in the teacher education institution should receive similar help during his freshman and sophomore years. There seems to be no other really effective way of correcting the subject matter field imbalance.

OPPORTUNITIES IN SPECIALIZED FIELDS

No attempt is made here to treat all of the special fields in which one may find opportunities for service. Every teacher knows, however, that children differ widely in many respects, and it is difficult or impossible for the typical classroom teacher with 25-30 pupils, to handle many individual types properly. He may not be trained for it, and he surely does not have the time.

In the interest of the democratic principle, however, all children have the right to the type of education suited to their needs and their abilities. This necessitates special classes, special programs, and special teachers.

Exceptional Children

One of the earliest attempts to provide better education for exceptional children has been that of special classes or even special schools for the *mentally retarded*. The larger cities have long provided such services, and now it is quite common to find excellent work being done in cities and towns of 5,000-10,000 people.

Teachers in this field must have considerable training in the education of the mentally retarded, and special state certification is usually necessary. Salaries frequently are higher than those for regular classroom teachers. Work of this type is rewarding, but it requires a deep concern for such children on the part of the teacher, with probably somewhat more than the usual amount of patience. Excellent preparation for teaching the mentally retarded is provided in quite a few of the state colleges and in most of the large universities.

Another very important group of exceptional children is composed of the *physically handicapped*. In the large cities are usually found special schools for these children—schools built with ramps instead of steps, with special furniture, textbooks, and equipment. Outside of the large cities physically handicapped children will usually be taught in their homes by teachers of homebound children.

There are special schools exclusively for the deaf and the blind. Many of these are wholly or partially state-supported, although a few are privately operated.

Some special training is needed for the teaching of the physically handicapped, but devoted teachers will find abundant opportunities here.

Courtesy: Division of Public Relations,
Public Schools of Pittsburgh.

A group of gifted children at work in the public schools of Pittsburgh, where special provision is made for their development.

Another type of exceptional children is represented by the *mentally gifted*. This is an exceedingly important group which has been greatly neglected. The more usual approach, where there is any serious attempt to meet the problem, has been through the enriched curriculum or accelerated progress. In some cities the mentally gifted have been put into special classes with a special curriculum and special teachers. Occasionally special high schools for the gifted have been established in some of the largest cities. Few teachers have had adequate preparation for working in this field, and it is highly probable that if more teachers were available there would be a great deal more active work carried on. An earnest person who wholeheartedly prepares himself should have very little difficulty in finding satisfactory opportunities for service.

Subject-Matter Specialists

In the last few years subject-matter specialists have been developed in very many fields. The tendency has been to designate these individuals as consultants rather than supervisors. Possibly this development has been stimulated mostly by the following:

1. The enlargement of school districts.
2. The changing nature of curricula and the complexity of subject-matter in various fields.
3. The changing philosophy of supervision and the consequent use of the term "consultant" implying a more or less cooperative relationship.

Specialists are needed today in all fields. Reading and speech accounted for most of the earlier use of such personnel, but needs have developed in recent years in practically all subjects. Emphasis upon the development of elementary school libraries with the strong stimulus of the Federal government has indicated need for consultants and specialists in this area.

Consultants attempt to help teachers individually. They help to develop courses of study, assist in the introduction of new material, direct workshops for both elementary and high school teachers, serve as advisors to the administration, and carry out a host of other services as needed.

For those who are willing to devote themselves to graduate study in these areas and who secure the master's degree or better, employment opportunities with higher salaries than those of regular teachers are indeed excellent.

Guidance

Another specialized field where the need is great at present is that of guidance. Although guidance is usually thought of in connection with the secondary school, considerable emphasis is laid at present upon extending it to the elementary school. An illustration of this may be seen in the 1955 Yearbook of the Association for Supervision and Curriculum Development, bearing the title *Guidance in the Curriculum.*

Certification in guidance is usually in teaching guidance or counseling or both. Generally the equivalent of the master's degree is advisable for specialization. The demand is strong, and salaries paid are generally well above the average.

Other Specialized Fields

Among other fields in which there is an increasing demand is that of school psychologists. A very large number of school districts and a good many counties are now employing such specialists, and the need is growing rapidly. The positions are well paid and generally require considerable education above the bachelor's degree. Psychologists perform such services as directing the work in many fields of educational measurement, administering psychological tests, directing programs for the retarded and gifted, and advising teachers on psychological and behavioral problems arising in their classrooms.

Such other opportunities as the following may be suggestive of broad areas that are likely to be of interest to the beginner or those who have been in service for some time:

Visiting Teacher
School Nurse
Athletic Coach
Business Manager
Audio-Visual Director
Director of Research
Curriculum Specialist
Director of Public Relations
Deans of Boys and Girls
Placement Director

There are, of course, many other areas of specialization where there is considerable demand and opportunity. The whole field of vocational education might be included because in most areas thereof real shortages exist. In some cases the shortages are acute. It is unnecessary, however, to discuss these in detail.

Richey [3] has drawn up a rather exhaustive list of positions for teachers which the student may find it profitable to examine. In an expanding school system there are ever-growing opportunities and abundant avenues of service for those with special interests and aptitudes.

[3] Robert W. Richey, *Planning for Teaching* (New York, Mc-Graw-Hill, 1963), pp. 138–141.

OPPORTUNITIES IN ADMINISTRATION AND SUPERVISION

Because of the more or less autocratic connotation of the word supervisor, it has been replaced to a considerable extent by words that at least have more democratic implications. Examples are: directors of elementary education, curriculum specialists, advisors, and consultants (as previously discussed). This can be all to the good, of course, but here and there the word supervisor still finds common use.

It is true that the best-paid positions in education are in these and similar fields and in the general administrative levels. These latter include principals, directors of various sorts, and superintendents. The distinctions between supervision and administration have always been hazy and incomplete, and the new vocabulary does not bring about any greater clarification.

Whereas the ability to be a successful teacher is a prerequisite to becoming a successful administrator, supervisor, and director, it is not true by any means that a successful teacher always makes a successful administrator or supervisor. The latter positions involve working with adults and with the general public a great deal more than with children—a change that many do not find to their liking.

On the other hand supervisory and administrative personnel are in positions of leadership, and if they are democratically minded individuals motivated by a democratic philosophy, through cooperative effort they may inspire teachers to do their best. Such work can be satisfactory and far-reaching. Positions such as we have mentioned are available to both men and women, but on the higher administrative levels it must be noted that men are definitely in the majority.

To become a supervisor, director, or principal, experience and graduate work are usually required, with specialization in administration generally being mandatory for principals. Likewise in all of the areas under discussion state certification is being required by more and more states.

Sometimes supervisors, consultants, and similar personnel will work under the direction of the principals. It is more usual, however, for them to work out of the superintendent's office. Always, though, in the latter situation the line of responsibility should be through the principal's office. In some smaller schools the building principal is the only consultant or supervisor available to the teachers there; whether or not supervisors are available, the principal is responsible for what goes on in his school. Good principals are well paid, and as numbers of schools grow and as the organization becomes more complex, more principals will be constantly needed. Both men and women with tact and understanding, with the ability to inspire and lead others, and with experience and good training in the field will find opportunities for leadership.

The superintendency is generally considered the top position in public school work. The superintendent is the executive officer of the school board, responsible to them. He must provide leadership for the entire school system, carry on a well-planned program of public relations, and he should be an individual with vision as well.

The superintendent today both in cities and counties is a far better-trained person than was the case a decade or more ago, the doctorate being quite common. Many graduate schools of education are setting up special provisions for the training of superintendents, a field of activity in which financial assistance was made available by the Kellogg Foundation.

The way to the superintendency is generally through the principal-ship, either elementary or secondary. Superintendents of the larger cities are commonly chosen from those who have been successful in smaller systems. Good superintendents will always be needed but, as might be expected, competition becomes keener as the salaries get better. Although by far the greater number of superintendents are men, there is no reason that this need be the case. A significant number of women have become highly successful superintendents of schools.

EDUCATION ON THE COLLEGE AND UNIVERSITY LEVEL

The tidal wave of students which has engulfed the elementary and secondary schools of the nation is beginning to be noticeable in higher education as well.

More than 40 percent of the college-age youth are now receiving college and university education. The figure has increased from 4 percent of college-age youth in 1899–1900 to 40 percent in 1963–1964.[4]

One may assume that this percentage of increase will continue to 1970–71 when we should have nearly 50 percent of college-age youth, or nearly 6,000,000 in institutions of higher education. If we think this proportion will not be reached and the figure should remain at around 40 percent where it is now, the enrollment should reach 4,500,000. Whatever figure we accept, the result is bound to be amazing.

Preparation for college teaching takes a considerably longer time, is more expensive, and can best be obtained in the graduate schools of the larger universities. Most institutions seek candidates with the master's or doctor's degrees or require that they be secured in service. In many fields, particularly mathematics and the sciences, the competition of industry for highly trained persons, to whom better salaries may be offered, accentuates the problem for the educational institutions. The securing of properly qualified personnel is probably the greatest challenge faced by the colleges and universities of today and tomorrow. Indeed, if the figure of

[4] United States Office of Education, *Digest of Educational Statistics,* Bulletin 1964, No. 18 (Washington, D.C., 1964), pp. 75–76.

6,000,000 is selected as the likely enrollment for 1970, approximately 337,000 additional qualified staff members will be necessary, and they simply are not in sight. The opportunities in college teaching, therefore, are almost without limit.

College teaching sometimes may not be as well paid as public school teaching, but the situation is improving very rapidly, and there is always opportunity for advancement to positions with abundant financial rewards. In addition, the field of the college and university professorship usually carries considerable prestige and in many institutions furnishes opportunity for study, research, and consultative work.

Young people who wish to prepare for college teaching may find it desirable to begin graduate work in their field rather early. The expense of this study can frequently be met by scholarships and fellowships which require an individual to do some teaching or research and permit him to carry on his graduate work at the same time. The attainment of the master's degree is an essential for college teaching, and the doctorate is highly desirable. In the field of education, actual teaching in the public schools is rather generally a definite requirement.

AVENUES OF PROMOTION AND ADVANCEMENT

Higher Standards of Preparation

Undoubtedly the usual way for teachers to advance themselves financially is to secure better preparation for their work. Since salary schedules generally pay additional increments or increases for the attainment of higher degrees or for progress toward them, this has become common practice. Some states or school districts reward teachers for other means of preparation, such as travel, writing, and experimental work.

From Small to Larger Districts

A study of salary schedules will generally show that the larger systems pay more money than smaller ones and, of course, the ones with more wealth (not always large) will pay higher salaries than the less wealthy districts. As a consequence, a very common line of promotion is for teachers to move from the smaller to the larger and wealthier districts. Higher state-wide salary schedules only mean that the larger districts will raise their schedules sufficiently high to attract teachers with experience from the smaller centers. Very likely this will always be the case.

Preparation for Positions of Greater Responsibility

Of course, it will be obvious from what has gone before that a common line of promotion is from teacher to specialist or to supervisory or administrative positions. If it is the desire of the teacher to advance in this manner, then his graduate work should be pointed in the right direction, and every opportunity should be sought to secure experience of even a minor type that will better qualify him for the position he seeks. The pattern of the future may well be that of providing a sort of internship for advancement to administrative and supervisory responsibilities. It is being done at present in a number of localities.

SALARIES AND FRINGE BENEFITS

It is a known fact that, as far as financial rewards are concerned, teaching has a low placement in the list of professions. Indeed, there are a number of skilled trades that have for some time had higher average wages than teaching. The situation, however, is not as dark as it may seem to appear at first study. The rise of teachers' salaries during the last ten years has been encouragingly rapid. They have, in fact, been rising faster than the cost of living and faster than the average wages and salaries of other employed persons. They are now about 14 percent above the earnings of all wage and salary workers.[5]

Available data indicate that in the ten-year period of 1953–54 and 1963–64 the average annual salary of the instructional staff increased 61.1 percent but in terms of the purchasing power of the dollar in 1963 prices, the increase has been but 32.7 percent.[6] Significant progress since 1950 is shown in the table on page 178.

The attention of the student should be called at this time to the mistake of putting too much emphasis upon the "averages" in salaries. Certainly they are significant, but more important questions are: "Where can one go salary-wise?" "Are career salaries available?" Answers to these questions are definitely encouraging.

If significant progress is to be made, however, teaching cannot be a part-time job. Absorption in one's work, continued study, travel where possible, and the seeking of various avenues of professional growth are necessary if advancement is to be made by the young teacher. This may involve some self-denial, especially in the early years of service, but it cannot be overemphasized—*teaching cannot be a part-time job if it is to command career salaries.*

In 1964 the Representative Assembly of the National Education Association recommended that in order to compare favorably with incomes from other professions requiring comparable preparation, starting salaries for qualified degree teachers should be at least $6,000, and for those with experience and holding the master's degree should range at least to

[5] NEA, *Teaching Career Fact Book* (Washington, D.C., 1963), p. 39.
[6] NEA, *Economic Status of Teachers in 1963–1964,* Research Report 1964, R 7, Research Division (Washington, D.C., April, 1964).

Table 7-1.   Average Salaries Paid Total Instructional Staff, School Years
              1929–30 through 1963–64, in Current Dollars and in Terms
              of 1962–63 Purchasing Power *

School Year	Average Annual Salary		Indexes of Average Salaries 1953-54 equals 100.0	
	In current dollars	Purchasing power in 1962-63 prices	In current dollars	Purchasing power in 1962-63 prices
1950-51	3,126	3,753	81.7	86.5
1951-52	3,450	3,984	90.2	91.9
1952-53	3,554	4,062	92.9	93.7
1953-54	3,825	4,337	100.0	100.0
1954-55	3,950	4,499	103.3	103.7
1955-56	4,156	4,701	108.7	108.4
1956-57	4,350	4,770	113.7	110.0
1957-58	4,702	4,997	122.9	115.2
1958-59	4,939	5,193	129.1	119.7
1959-60	5,174	5,362	135.3	123.6
1960-61	5,449	5,577	142.5	128.6
1961-62	5,710	5,785	149.3	133.4
1962-63	5,921	5,921	154.8	136.5
1963-64	6,164[a]	5,755[b]	161.1[a]	132.7[b]

Sources: Column 2 from U.S. Office of Education and NEA Research Division. Figures
for all years ending in even numbers through 1959–60 and figures for 1950–51 from the
U.S. Office of Education. Figures for other years are interpolations or estimates by the
NEA Research Division.
Columns 3, 4, and 5 computed by the NEA Research Division.
a/ Preliminary estimates.
b/ Based on prices as of September 1963.

* SOURCE: *Economic Status of Teachers in 1963–64*, Research Report 1964, R 7 (Washington, NEA, 1964), p. 8.

$13,000 followed by continuing scheduled increases for career teachers of
advanced qualifications.

The Resolutions further state that a professional salary schedule
should:

a. Be based upon preparation, teaching experience and professional growth.
b. Provide a beginning salary schedule adequate to attract young people into
   the profession.

c. Provide increments sufficient to double the bachelor's degree minimum within ten years for professionally qualified teachers with the master's degree, with further salary increases for additional preparation and experience.

d. Recognize advanced education by providing specific salary classes for successive levels through the doctor's degree.

e. Be developed cooperatively by school board members, administrators, and teachers.

f. Permit no discrimination as to grade or subject taught, residence, creed, race, sex, marital status, or number of dependents.

g. Recognize, by salary ratios, the responsibilities of administrators and other appropriate school personnel.

h. Be applied in actual practice.

An example of a good salary schedule is found in that of Cheltenham Township, Pennsylvania, a district suburban to Philadelphia. Outside of a beginning salary somewhat lower than called for in the NEA Resolutions, it meets the standards remarkably well. The schedule is really in operation, and actually there is no upper limit to the top salary a classroom teacher may obtain. In addition certain important fringe benefits are provided as noted. This makes the salary program particularly attractive.

The preceding table is a brief and selective presentation of minimum and maximum salaries from a number of districts in different parts of the country. They vary in numbers of teachers employed, from 75 in a district to over 2,500 in others. Salaries do not seem to depend so much on size as they do on the wealth of the district, its location, and the willingness of the people to support a program that will attract quality teachers. These are not isolated cases. There are a great many of them, and these few are presented to the student contemplating education as a career so that he can see that there is opportunity for a good life economically— opportunity to provide a thoroughly satisfying living for himself and his family if he will devote himself wholeheartedly and thoroughly to his task. So it is, indeed, with every profession.

A significant movement in providing better salaries for teachers is the granting of additional payments for work which is considered outside of the regular classroom or not closely allied to the duties of a particular teacher. For example, in the Abington Township, Pennsylvania School District, an elaborate "Extra Duty and Responsibility Pay Program" has been adopted after co-operative efforts by the board and the teachers. This plan begins by setting up certain guiding principles, then defines the contractual duties for each member of the staff and the so-called "extra duty and responsibility pay activities." Each activity, such as Athletic Manager, has a careful qualitative analysis made of the duties involved, and then a certain number of "units" is assigned to represent a quantitative measure.

Table 7-2.   School District of Cheltenham Township, Pa., Teachers Salary
Program

Steps	Bachelors	Masters	Masters + 12	Masters + 24	Masters + 40
1st	$5000	$5300	$5400	$5500	$5700
2nd	5300	5600	5700	5800	6000
3rd	5600	5900	6000	6100	6300
4th	5900	6200	6300	6400	6600
5th	6200	6500	6600	6700	6900
6th	6500	6800	6900	7000	7200
7th	6800	7100	7200	7300	7500
8th	7100	7400	7500	7600	7800
9th	7400	7700	7800	7900	8100
10th		8000	8100	8200	8400
11th		8200	8300	8400	8600
12th		8400	8500	8600	8800
13th			8700	8800	9000
14th			8900	9000	9200
15th			9100	9200	9400
16th				9400	9600
17th				9600	9800
18th					10000
19th					10200

I   The salary of a currently employed teacher will advance only one step for a year of satisfactory service.

II   Teacher raises for 1965–66 shall not exceed $500 unless the teacher qualifies for the next highest column or education category.

III   A Bachelor's Degree is a prerequisite for employment as a regular teacher. However, the salary of a currently employed teacher with less than a Bachelor's Degree will be the same as a salary of one who holds a Bachelor's Degree.

IV   The salary of a teacher who holds an earned doctorate shall be $200 more than that shown on the corresponding step for 40 credits beyond a Master's Degree.

V   Teachers who have completed three years of teaching in Cheltenham Township shall be eligible for merit increments which shall be over, above and beyond the regular increment and salary shown on the scale. A teacher rated *outstanding* by the administration may be granted a $400 merit increment and become eligible for another merit increment in three years.

Table 7-3.

I   Salary Scale for Teachers 1965–1966

The [previous] page shows the salary scale. Every word on that page is important as are certain deletions from the 1964–65 schedule. Please study it carefully and be correctly informed.

II   Health Insurance

Effective July 1, 1965, the school district will pay seventy-five percent (75%) of the employee individual rate premium for Blue Cross, Blue Shield, and Major Medical insurance for each regular employee who wishes such coverage in the school district. The current rate schedule produces the following amounts.

Table 7-3

	Paid by District Monthly		Paid by Employee Monthly	
Blue Cross				
Single	$2.63		$0.87	
Widow(er) & Child(ren)	2.63		4.37	
Family	2.63		7.37	
Blue Shield	Plan "A"	Plan "B"	Plan "A"	Plan "B"
Single	$0.95	$1.41	$0.31	$0.47
Widow(er) & Child(ren)	0.95	1.41	1.61	2.96
Family	0.95	1.41	2.88	4.66
Major Medical				
Single	$0.97		$0.32	
Dependents	0.97		2.02	
Total for all three	$4.55	$5.01	$1.50	$1.66
			8.00	9.35
			12.27	14.05

III   Graduate Study Grants

100% Reimbursement will be paid for graduate study tuition costs up to $200 per year for approved courses not needed to qualify for provisional or permanent certification. $20,000 will be budgeted for 1965–66 and pro rated if the total requests exceed that amount.

IV   Religious Holiday has been added as one of the reasons a teacher may be absent with pay for one day per school year. The one day may be for graduation or legal business or religious holiday or etc.

V   Jury Service has been approved without loss of pay. The district will pay the difference between the salary and compensation paid by the court.

All salary data used through the courtesy of and by the special permission of Dr. Edwin B. Keim, Principal, Cheltenham High School.

Such a scheme or system is developed for all situations that are common or anticipated. Payment is then made as an addition to the regular salary of the teacher according to definite action of the board. Currently each teacher is paid an additional $50 annually * for each unit allowed. Thus the Athletic Director in the senior high school is granted ten units and receives $500 in addition to the amount to which he is regularly entitled in the salary schedule. The Yearbook Financial Director is allowed two units or $100, the Senior Class Play Coach four units or $200. Such an arrangement seems highly reasonable and contributes to good morale on the staff. The principle involved is finding rather wide acceptance.

Table 7-4.   Selected School Systems Reporting Maximum Salaries of $11,000 or More in 1963–1964

District	Scheduled Salaries 1963-1964		
District	Minimum B.A.	Maximum M.A.	Top Maximum
Long Beach, Calif.	$5,325	$ 9,860	$11,150
Sacramento, Calif.	4,875	9,653	11,775
Palo Alto, Calif.	5,400	9,100	11,050
Greenwich, Conn.	5,350	10,025	11,250
Oak Park, Ill., Elementary.	5,000	9,328	11,776
Lower Merion, Pa.	5,000	10,700	12,000
White Plains, N.Y.	5,300	9,900	11,200
Bronxville, N.Y.	5,400	10,625	11,875
Upper Darby, Pa.	4,600	9,650	11,200
Ladue, Mo.	4,600	12,600	12,600
Newton, Mass.	5,000	10,700	11,600
Glen Ridge, N.J.	4,900	11,100	11,500
Scarsdale, N.Y.	5,200	11,200	12,000
Niles Twp, Ill. High School.	5,300	10,200	12,100
Bloomington, Ind.	4,500	8,100	11,100
Wazata, Minn.	4,900	10,296	11,682
Westside, Neb., Dist. No. 66.	4,900	8,340	11,120

SOURCE: Adapted from "High Level Scheduled Salaries, 1963–64," *NEA Research Bulletin,* 41:100–103 (Washington, December, 1963).

Merit Rating

The pressure is mounting for school districts to provide salary schedules that will in some effective way recognize superior teaching. It

* This amount may, of course, be changed to meet changing economic conditions.

may be in the form of a super maximum at the top of the schedule or a system whereby "merit" may be rewarded each year.

Any system of rewarding superior teaching involves the use of some type of rating system by which teachers are evaluated in terms of their relative effectiveness and salaries adjusted accordingly. It certainly is difficult to find fault with the principle involved here. Surely better teachers should be encouraged in part by the payment of better salaries. The difficulty arises when a satisfactory scheme or device is sought for determining the relative effectiveness of teaching. The fact must be faced that no single reliable instrument has been developed. The measurement of effective teaching is a far more difficult task than measuring individual productivity in the industrial field.

Merit rating is not new. A few attempts may be noted nearly 50 years ago. Indeed, a good many districts have tried some sort of merit system and quite a few have discontinued it in view of teacher and, very frequently, administrative opposition. There exists a real fear that favoritism, human weakness, and even politics may creep into the picture and teacher morale be shattered. This indeed is not without foundation.

Careful study of situations where merit systems have been successful reveals that the following conditions must be met:

1. A high basic salary for all teachers must be in effect.
2. The principles involved and the details of operation must be co-operatively decided with teachers playing a dominant part.
3. There must be maintained a high degree of trust in the sincerity, fairness, and efficiency of those who do the evaluating.
4. There must be no limitations to the number of teachers who attain the super maximums or merit raises.

At the time of writing there have been quite a few increases in attempts to award higher salaries for superior teaching. Public pressure in the matter will undoubtedly increase, and much further study is needed. It will be a grave mistake if the profession itself does not take the lead. The student will find a vast amount of material on the subject in current periodical literature and in a goodly number of pamphlets and books.

Retirement

In these times when the span of life has so significantly increased, it is quite proper for all of us to be concerned about adequate financial provision for old age. Pension plans of many kinds have become an important part of the American economic picture. Social security, as set up by the federal government, has been extending and improving its coverage and its benefits for the great mass of citizens.

A considerable time before the advent of social security and the rapid growth of group pension plans, retirement systems had been set up for many thousands of teachers. Some of these plans were not altogether

sound in the beginning, but revisions were made, systems were recon-
structed so that pretty generally they have been greatly strengthened. The
earliest teachers' retirement systems were found in the cities and, indeed,
a good number of the larger cities still maintain those systems or plans
which they have had for many years. All states except Idaho now provide
for mandatory membership in the retirement system for all new entrants
into the profession. Membership in Idaho is voluntary for such persons.[7]

In the recent modification of the national social security laws, legislation was enacted making it possible for the teachers of a state or a subdivision to decide (voluntarily) to come under social security coverage.
The extent to which this will happen is a matter of some concern because:
(1) social security is not nearly as good as many, if not most, teachers'
retirement systems; (2) the fear is that social security will eventually lead
to the abandonment of long-established liberal retirement plans. This
would surely be highly unfortunate.

At the present time "some or nearly all of the teachers in 37 states"
are now covered by social security. In all of these social security supple-
ments existing retirement systems or is integrated with them.

Types of Provisions for Older Teachers

Two general types of provisions for aged and disabled teachers
exist: (1) pension plans, and (2) retirement plans. In the pension plan the
teacher makes no contributions of his own, all costs being paid by the
state or local municipality, as the case may be. This type of provision,
with modifications, is found in Delaware and New Mexico. In such plans
there are no legal guarantees that the benefits will not be changed or even
withdrawn at any time.

The rest of the states use the joint-contributory system in which the
teacher contributes a certain percentage of his salary. This is then usually
matched by the local school district or the state or by each of these units
contributing the matching share together. Funds received from the teacher
are then invested in securities, preferably bonds, and the proceeds credited
to his account. Similar investments must be made of the monies received
from the other sources mentioned. In all of these investments it is of the
highest importance that supervision and direction be given by boards or
individuals of top character, for it is from the proceeds of such investments that future benefits must be paid.

Regulations of existing retirement systems provide generally for a
minimum age (usually around 60) at which a teacher may retire and a
maximum age (usually 65–70) at which retirement is compulsory. In some
systems, length of service may be substituted for the minimum-age provision, thus making earlier retirement possible.

[7] *NEA Research Bulletin,* Vol. 41, No. 4 (Washington, D.C., 1963), p. 119.

A good retirement system provides also for an adequate allowance for the teacher in case of total disability and for return of the teacher's contributions with interest in the event of his leaving the profession before retirement is possible.

In most systems the amount the teacher will receive annually is determined by a set formula, both in case of retirement for age or for disability. Also it is the usual practice for the member to select a beneficiary who may share in the retirement benefits in a manner determined by local or state laws.

Adequate provisions are not commonly available for those who change their service from one state to another. It is highly desirable that constructive efforts be devoted to the solution of this problem in more satisfactory ways than now exist.

Characteristics of a Good Retirement System

The NEA [8] has been an important factor in providing leadership for the establishment of sound retirement systems and has formulated the following principles by which adequacy and soundness may be measured:

1. Membership required of new teachers; voluntary for those in service.
2. Guarantees to both teacher and public.
3. Cost shared by teacher and public.
4. Amount of deposits and payments stated in enactment.
5. Deposits of teacher and payments by public concurrent with service.
6. Individual accounts kept.
7. System on reserve basis.
8. Periodic actuarial investigations.
9. Provisions for disability retirement.
10. Teacher's accumulated deposits returnable in case of withdrawal from service, or death prior to retirement.
11. Choice of options offered upon retirement.
12. Credit allowed for past service.
13. Rights under previous retirement systems safeguarded.
14. Reciprocal relations between systems.
15. Retirement board in control.

Future Problems of Retirement

One of the most acute problems of nearly all, if not all, retirement systems is to keep the allowances in line with the cost of living. An annuity established in 1940, for example, is wholly inadequate when received now. Various proposals have been made to meet this situation, but

[8] "Analysis of Local Provisions for Teacher Retirement," *NEA Research Bulletin,* Vol. 18, No. 3 (May, 1940), p. 128.

they boil down to two general considerations: (1) liberalizing the plans by increasing benefits, which must inevitably increase the cost to the contributing parties, and (2) changing the major part of the investments from bonds to common stocks which are likely to be more responsive to changing conditions in the economy. This latter plan is surely not without hazard, but is being used in many industrial pension plans. It is a matter of great interest to every teacher.

As has been suggested earlier, the problem of the relationship between national social security and teachers' retirement plans will become one of increasing urgency, because of the rising costs of local and state retirement systems and because of the demand for increasing existing retirement benefits through supplementing them by those of social security. The teacher of tomorrow will need to keep in very close touch with such matters.

Sick Leaves

It is certainly recognized today that a condition of fair employment makes it very necessary that competent employees be allowed a reasonable amount of sick leave without loss of pay, at least without *full* loss of pay. Such sick leaves, in the case of school districts, may be either specified in state law or may be a definite part of a teacher's contract. All sick-leave policies should, of course, be protected against abuse by either party.

Most common procedures in the larger districts seem to be the granting of sick leaves will full pay for periods of from five to ten days. There appears also to be a tendency to make the amount of sick leave to which a teacher is entitled in any one year cumulative. This trend is eminently desirable.

In a great many of the smaller districts of the country, no set policies for sick leaves exist, and it is for that reason that teachers through their professional associations have worked for legislation making a minimum sick leave with full pay mandatory for all districts. Gradually, laws are appearing upon the statute books, and the probability is that the number of states with such legislation will increase.

With the threefold purpose of protecting the children, the school district, and the employer, a good many school systems are requiring that teachers take regular physical examinations every year or every few years. In many instances these examinations are provided either at the expense of the school district or the state. Such examinations may possibly reduce the need for the taking of prolonged leaves of absence.

In accepting employment it is desirable for the teacher to ascertain policies and procedures in regard to the granting of such leaves as are discussed here.

Maternity Leaves

As more and more married teachers are being kept on payrolls throughout the country, it becomes increasingly important for boards to adopt realistic and reasonable policies for granting leaves for child-bearing. Otherwise, the services of many competent teachers may be lost to the school.

Actually the situation in regard to this matter is far from satisfactory. A fair number of the larger cities have made maternity leaves a matter of policy for a good many years, and there has been a substantial increase in satisfactory regulations in districts of this type. In far too many school systems, however, married women who seek such leaves are summarily dismissed. A good case can be made for establishing the fact that such procedures are contrary to public interest.

Where maternity leaves are granted, they are generally for a year or longer without pay.

Sabbatical Leaves

Extended leaves of absence for a semester or full year are often desirable for the improvement of the teacher's services to the school system. Probably the most frequent purpose for which leaves of this type are granted is for graduate or further study or for travel. Other reasons noted are for restoration of health, recreation, or "other purposes satisfactory to the school board," as in Pennsylvania. Sometimes full salary may be paid, but more often it is half salary or thereabouts. Sometimes no salary is given; the position is merely held open. Where leaves are granted, it is the general policy for the teacher to be required to return to the district for at least a year. It is safe to say that the experiences of districts or states with a sound sabbatical-leave policy have been on the whole very favorable.

Other Benefits

With the widespread and increasing concern for the welfare of the employee and the recognition of the practical value of this concern to the employer, there has been a marked increase in such "fringe benefits" as group insurance, hospitalization, medical-surgical plans, and the like. In some instances these are joint-contributory plans, and in other instances they are not. Where such schemes are in operation and where they are administered fairly, relations between teachers and employer seem to be on a higher level; this surely is an end to be desired. They can very definitely be morale builders, and the prospective teacher may well concern himself with them as he considers employment.

QUESTIONS AND PROJECTS

1. Interview school administrators in a number of communities having no kindergartens. Ascertain from them why no kindergartens are maintained at present and what plans exist for their establishment.
2. Discuss the problems involved in making kindergartens compulsory on a state-wide basis.
3. Assume that a high school friend of yours wishes to major in health and physical education and asks your advice as to a desirable minor. What facts would you gather in order to advise him?
4. Consult various college catalogs in your region and suggest those which would prepare you for becoming: (a) a reading specialist, (b) a speech specialist, (c) a guidance director, (d) an elementary school principal, (e) a teacher of the mentally retarded, (f) a teacher of gifted children.
5. Present a report to the class on the experimental work in the education of teachers now being carried on by the Ford Foundation.
6. Investigate one of the programs now being developed for the education of college teachers.
7. Secure from the Admissions Office at your college or university a record of admissions over the past ten years and also the predictions for the next decade. What steps are being taken to meet the influx of students?
8. Make a careful study of the teachers' retirement system in your own state. What changes do you think need to be made?
9. Investigate the so-called "fringe benefits" that exist in one large and one smaller school system.
10. What constitutes a desirable sick-leave plan?
11. A businessman in an address recently made the statement that teachers' salaries are low primarily because they have a very poor type of public relations. Discuss this topic.
12. Evaluate the arguments for and against the single salary schedule.
13. Debate the problems involved in the employment of married teachers in the public schools.
14. What are the arguments for and against making teachers eligible for social security benefits?
15. Explain the meaning and use of the term *Index Salary Schedules*.

AUDIO-VISUAL AIDS

MOTION PICTURES (16 MM)

A Class for Tommy—Bailey Films, Inc., 6509 De Longpre Ave., Hollywood, Calif., 20 min., sd., b&w. Typical day in the life of a mentally handicapped child; includes a visit with Tommy's parents showing the close cooperation and understanding between the school and the home.

And Gladly Teach—National Education Association, 1201 16th Street, N.W.,

Washington, D.C., 28 min., sd., b&w and/or color. This film is about teachers and "the company they keep." It points out the satisfactions and opportunities in teaching.

Appointment with Youth—McGraw-Hill Book Co., Text-Film Department, 330 West 42nd Street, New York, N.Y., 26 min., sd., b&w. A dramatic picture of the work of a teacher, the film concludes that teaching is a good profession, not just for its good working hours, salary, and vacations, but more importantly, for the deep personal satisfaction it gives.

Education for Democracy—Missouri State Teachers Association, Columbia, Mo., 22 min., sd., color. Sets forth the purposes behind current methods and practices of the public schools at all levels.

Teaching—Mahnke Productions, 215 E. Third St., Des Moines, Iowa, 11 min., sd., b&w. Shows the contributions of teachers to American Democracy and presents the traits of a good teacher, the attractions in teaching, the educational requirements, and the various types of teaching jobs.

FILMSTRIP

Teaching as a Career—National Film Board of Canada, Room 658, 630 Fifth Ave., New York, N.Y., 47 fr., si., b&w. Examines the pros and cons of teaching as a career with special reference to educational requirements, personal aptitudes, specialized training, remuneration and opportunities for advancement.

RECORDINGS

Teacher Salary Schedule—Minnesota State Dept. of Education, St. Paul, Minn., 15 min., tape. A school board will seek to establish a salary structure that will induce the right type of teachers to gravitate toward their school. The cost of education rests on society as a whole. Presented by Walter E. Englund.

Teacher Tenure (Fair Dismissal)—Minnesota State Department of Education, St. Paul, Minn., 15 min., tape. Avoiding the fear that results when cheap politics invade the classroom. Presented by Walter E. Englund.

FURTHER READINGS

American Federation of Teachers, *Merit Rating* (Chicago, the Federation, 1958).

Castetter, William B., *Administering the School Personnel Program* (New York, Macmillan, 1962).

Cooke, Blaine, "Merit Pay for Teachers," *Saturday Review* (December 16, 1961), pp. 46–47, 61–62.

"Fringe Benefits for Teachers," A discussion by NEA consultants, *NEA Journal*, Vol. 52 (November, 1963), pp. 17–18.

"High Level Scheduled Salaries, 1963–64," *NEA Research Bulletin,* Vol. 41 (December, 1963), pp. 100–103.

Hodenfield, G. K., and T. M. Stinnett, *The Education of Teachers* (Englewood Cliffs, N.J., Prentice-Hall, 1961).

Keppel, Francis, "Master of Arts in Teaching," *Saturday Review,* Vol. 44 (June 17, 1961), pp. 63–65.

Kvaraceus, W. C., "Mental Health Hazards Facing Teachers," *Phi Delta Kappan,* Vol. 32 (April, 1951), pp. 349–350.

National Education Association, *NEA Handbook* (Washington, D.C., published annually).

National Education Association, "Salary Schedules," *Classroom Teachers: 1963– 64* (Washington, D.C., 1964).

National Education Association, *Who's a Good Teacher* (Washington, D.C., 1961).

Nolte, M. Chester, and John P. Linn, *School Law for Teachers* (Danville, Illinois, Interstate Printers & Publishers, 1963).

Rhodes, Eric, "What Index Scheduling Means," *Phi Delta Kappan,* Vol. 46 (May, 1965), pp. 459–460.

Thompson, Ronald B., *The Impending Tidal Wave of Students,* American Association of Registrars and Admissions Officers (Columbus, Ohio, Ohio State University, 1964).

"Trends in Salary Schedules and Roadblocks to Progress," *NEA Research Bulletin,* Vol. 41 (December, 1963).

United States Office of Education, *Employment Outlook for Teachers* (Washington, D.C., 1964).

III

THE EDUCATIONAL
PROCESS AND
THE CHILD

8

Goals of Education
for America's Schools

PREVIEW

▶ A clear sense of purpose is important for all human activities; this is especially true in education.

Early education was chiefly concerned with the acquisition of knowledge which, it was assumed, led to power and produced the virtuous person.
Faith in the power of education to make men good was strong in western culture.
In early America, religion and the removal of illiteracy were dominant purposes.
Formal discipline found its place in the New World too.

▶ The most important sets of objectives in the last fifty years have been:
   1. The Cardinal Principles of Secondary Education.
   2. The Objectives of the Educational Policies Commission.
   3. The Imperative Needs of Youth.

▶ To be valuable, objectives must be stated in terms of specific pupil behavior and adjusted to various grade levels.
Continuity of purpose between elementary and secondary education becomes unusually important in today's world as revision of curricula proceeds.

IMPORTANCE OF GOALS

Probably nothing is more important to an individual—or to groups—than a sense of purpose. Without this there is aimless wandering which may lead to degeneration. History has shown this to be true again and again. Even an unworthy goal or purpose, once it has general acceptance, can weld a people together as was shown in Nazi Germany in the 1930's and early 1940's. It can also drive them to supreme effort if there is complete belief in the cause.

All this may be truly said of education, and it is noteworthy that through the years study has been devoted to the broad and detailed objectives, aims, or goals (for these terms are used more or less synonymously) of the work of the schools. There has been a fascinating evolution of thought on this matter as changing conditions have demanded reexaminations of earlier goals.

Far too many people think of the study of educational objectives as pure theory. Nothing, however, can be farther from the truth. The acceptance of sound aims gives all phases of the educational system a *raison d'être*—the school board a basis for the formulation of policies, the superintendent a sound background for his administrative and supervisory practices, the teachers a reason for the specific things which they do from day to day—and even further, the students when they are conscious of purposes are likely to respond more readily to the teacher's guidance. Everyone likes to understand why he is required or encouraged to do things. It is essential both to good human relations and to progress.

Although, as has been stated previously, the major and fundamental purpose of public education is that of promoting the development of the type of citizenry that will insure the perpetuation and improvement of our democratic form of government, this purpose must be analyzed much more carefully in order to give it meaning and practical value.

THE BACKGROUND

In the earliest days of organized knowledge, men were concerned with the proper ends of learning. The most commonly accepted goal came to be acquisition of knowledge itself, and, of course, this has been a constant beacon through the centuries. Socrates and Plato thought that knowledge was the way to virtue, and today the inscription, *Knowledge Is Power,* is found over the doors of many schools and libraries. Almost anyone will admit that there is truth in this position, but that it is surely not true without serious limitations.

At the beginning of the Renaissance it was thought that all that was necessary was to rediscover and teach the wisdom of Aristotle. Man's expanding horizons, however, and his inquisitive nature soon made it necessary to change this point of view.

John Locke (1632–1704), distinguished philosopher in the late seventeenth century, was concerned primarily with the education of the gentleman when he wrote of "four things: virtue, wisdom, breeding, and learning." These he thought must be the necessary acquisitions of that privileged individual, "the gentleman's son."

Later Johann Friedrich Herbart (1776–1841) again spoke of virtue as that which "expresses the whole purpose of education." Mort and Vincent [1] write of both Locke and Herbart, separated by more than a century: "They saw education as the great power to make men good. This education could change the world."

Others, as Comenius, Rousseau, Pestalozzi, and many more, expressed this common belief in varying degrees but with their own specific contributions as to method. Again Mort and Vincent [2] point out, "Indeed, faith in education as a power to make men good and to provide a full life is a prominent characteristic of Western culture."

No review of the background of the goals of education would be complete without reference to the brilliant English philosopher, Herbert Spencer (1820–1903),[3] who asked the question, "What knowledge is of most worth?" and answered it first by stating his premise that education must be for "complete living." It is to this "complete living" that knowledge must contribute and education be directed. Influenced by the growing knowledge of science in his day he put much emphasis upon it, without however, discarding what had been accepted previously. He refers to the following as specific goals:

1. Those activities which lead directly to self-preservation.
2. Those activities which by securing the necessaries of life directly minister to self-preservation.
3. Those activities which have for their end the rearing and discipline of offspring.
4. Those activities which are involved in the maintenance of "proper social and political relations."
5. Those miscellaneous activities which make up the leisure part of life, devoted to the gratification of tastes and feelings.

It will be interesting to note a bit later what a debt certain students of educational objectives in the United States owe to this Englishman.

EDUCATIONAL GOALS IN AMERICA

Throughout our brief survey of the developing educational goals in America there will be evidence of our borrowing from European antecedents. This was as natural in education as in other social areas, and it should be expected that a significant interchange of ideas should continue right down to relatively recent days. Since World War II, however,

[1] Paul R. Mort and William S. Vincent, *Introduction to American Education* (New York, McGraw-Hill, 1954), p. 25.

[2] *Ibid.*

[3] Herbert Spencer, *Education* (New York, D. Appleton and Co., 1880), pp. 31–34.

the flow of educational influence has been *from* America to the West and to the East. This is, as anyone may know, more the result of victory in war than of any philosophical movement, but it is a fact that it has happened just the same.

Early American Objectives

The student will recall from his study of Chapter 2 the early emphasis upon *religion* as a specific aim of colonial education. From the definite purpose of the Latin Grammar Schools to the almost exclusive use of religious material, such as the catechism and the Bible, as teaching material, there is evidence that religion was an outstanding goal.

Literacy, of course, was a concomitant purpose of the lower or elementary school. The "3 R's"—"readin', 'ritin', and 'rithmetic"—were the vehicles by which it was hoped this would be accomplished.

The idea of *formal discipline,* largely borrowed from Europe, appears rather continuously as an important objective on all levels. This means that training of the mind can be effectively accomplished by such things as grammar, mathematics, languages, and the classics generally, whether they have any practical value or not. Then, claim its advocates, this "trained mind" will function in other areas possibly unrelated. Therefore, the harder a thing is the better. Utility does not matter at all. Although modern psychology has strongly disproved the validity of this idea, it still has its adherents, and no one seriously studying the objectives of education can ignore it.

Education for Today and Tomorrow

It will be noted by the student that what we have been saying is concerned largely with the assumption that education is *preparation for life.* It has meant that eyes must be upon the future; that what we have our students study today must be in light of what they will need and do tomorrow. Now it does not take a very wise person long to see that this must put the teacher in the role of the prophet. It is impossible in anything but a static world to know what tomorrow will be like and to prepare children for the roles they will play. Fortunately, of course, in ordinary human living there are things that will concern almost everyone. Health is a matter of constant concern for every individual; most girls will eventually marry and have children; most boys will need education for making a living. People generally will have a reasonable amount of leisure time. These and other areas to which we shall refer, we know; and to these education must be directed.

As a result of our thinking, we have pretty generally come to believe that education can better prepare young people for life tomorrow by teaching them to live today. *Education is life,* not just a preparation for it. The best way to prepare children for family living tomorrow is to help them to play their parts in their families today—learning by living, it may be said. But it is easy to dwell on methods, and we are talking about objectives and goals. It is not difficult to see, though, that our objectives, if really put to use, must determine our methods.

RECENT SIGNIFICANT STUDIES

As mentioned earlier, by the end of the nineteenth century the secondary schools of America had accepted as their dominant purpose the preparation of students for college. In fact, it was strongly alleged that the colleges were dominating the high schools and controlling what they taught and did. To this there was much more truth than fiction, and it was clear that something had to be done.

The Seven Cardinal Principles

What was certainly one of the most important reports ever made in the field of education in America was brought out in 1918 by the Commission on the Reorganization of Secondary Education of the NEA. The report, resulting from a long study, was published as a government bulletin, and the Commission [4] stated therein as the objectives of secondary education the following which have come to be known as The Cardinal Principles of Secondary Education:

1. Health.
2. Worthy home membership.
3. Command of the fundamental processes.
4. Vocation.
5. Civic education.
6. Worthy use of leisure.
7. Ethical character.

The student may readily see how these were what might be called "intellectual descendants" of Herbert Spencer. The Commission modified and added to his proposals, adjusting them to the needs of the postwar day. These "principles" or objectives became the basis to a large extent for the reorganization of the whole secondary school program in the United States. It was a new outlook that was called for. Says French,[5] a long-time student of education:

Here for the first time in American education, a responsible professional body declared that the curriculum should be based upon an analysis of the life needs

[4] *Cardinal Principles of Secondary Education,* Bureau of Education Bulletin No. 35 (Washington, Government Printing Office, 1918).
[5] William M. French, *Education for All* (New York, Odyssey, 1955), p. 43.

of adolescent youth and upon the needs of society rather than upon a traditional body of subject matter which had been transmitted as a part of our common cultural heritage.

The Commission discussed each of these objectives in considerable detail, pointing specifically to their meaning for the youth of the day and suggesting how the high school program should be organized about them. The entire report is well worth reading today as an educational classic.

Actually the effect of this study was felt not only in the field of secondary education but in the elementary schools as well. All of the objectives mentioned, with the possible exception of vocational preparation, can be considered as belonging in the grades below the high school.

Of course, not all schools fully took the Commission's report to heart and really did something about it. Many did but some ignored it entirely, whereas others merely tried to justify their present offerings by showing how they were meeting the Cardinal Principles. On the whole, however, the effect has been very real and far-reaching.

Work of the Educational Policies Commission

A number of other sets of educational objectives have been prepared during the last half-century, some of which have been of much value. In 1924, for example, Franklin Bobbitt [6] developed a tenfold classification. These have been helpful in curriculum building but will not be presented in detail here. Students may, however, wish to consult them.

One of the most recent lists of carefully formulated objectives for education is that developed by the Educational Policies Commission,[7] the original pronouncement being issued in 1938.

The Commission, organized and sponsored by the NEA and the American Association of School Administrators, is probably the most important single educational body of its kind in the world. From time to time highly significant policy-making statements and reports are issued. Many of them have been outstanding. Not the least have been the publication already referred to and the later one, entitled, *Policies for Education in American Democracy.*[8]

The Commission suggested what the schools ought to try to accomplish and what they thought should be done to try to fulfill these aims of *democratic* education, for it was the democratic processes and values which were always kept in mind.

After formulating certain broad generalizations regarding the mini-

[6] Franklin Bobbitt, *How to Make a Curriculum* (Boston, Houghton Mifflin, 1924), p. 8.

[7] Educational Policies Commission, *The Purposes of Education in American Democracy* (Washington, NEA, 1938).

[8] Educational Policies Commission, *Policies for Education in American Democracy* (Washington, NEA, 1946).

mum essentials of a democracy, the Commission [9] listed its proposed objectives, dividing them into four large groups:

1. Self-realization.
2. Human relationships.
3. Economic efficiency.
4. Civic responsibility.

In the publication to which reference has just been made, a chapter is devoted to each of these large areas, and specific aims or objectives are developed. Thus clarification is given to the more general statements which are often of little value for the individual teacher or student.

The Objectives of Self-Realization

Here the Commission was concerned with the "personal development, growth and learning" of the individual. These objectives are essential for success in all phases of modern living. The detailed goals follow:

The Inquiring Mind. The educated person has an appetite for learning.
Speech. The educated person can speak the mother tongue clearly.
Reading. The educated person reads the mother tongue efficiently.
Writing. The educated person writes the mother tongue effectively.
Number. The educated person solves his problems of counting and calculating.
Sight and Hearing. The educated person is skilled in listening and observing.
Health and Knowledge. The educated person understands the basic facts concerning health and disease.
Health Habits. The educated person protects his own health and that of his dependents.
Public Health. The educated person works to improve the health of the community.
Recreation. The educated person is participant and spectator in many sports and other pastimes.
Intellectual Interests. The educated person has mental resources for the use of leisure.
Esthetic Interests. The educated person appreciates beauty.
Character. The educated person gives responsible direction to his own life.

The Objectives of Human Relationships

Here the Commission was concerned with the activities of the individual affecting "home and family relationships" with their extension to others in the community. The specific aims expressed were:

[9] *Ibid.,* pp. 185–253.

Figure 8-1. Objectives of Education (Educational Policies Commission)

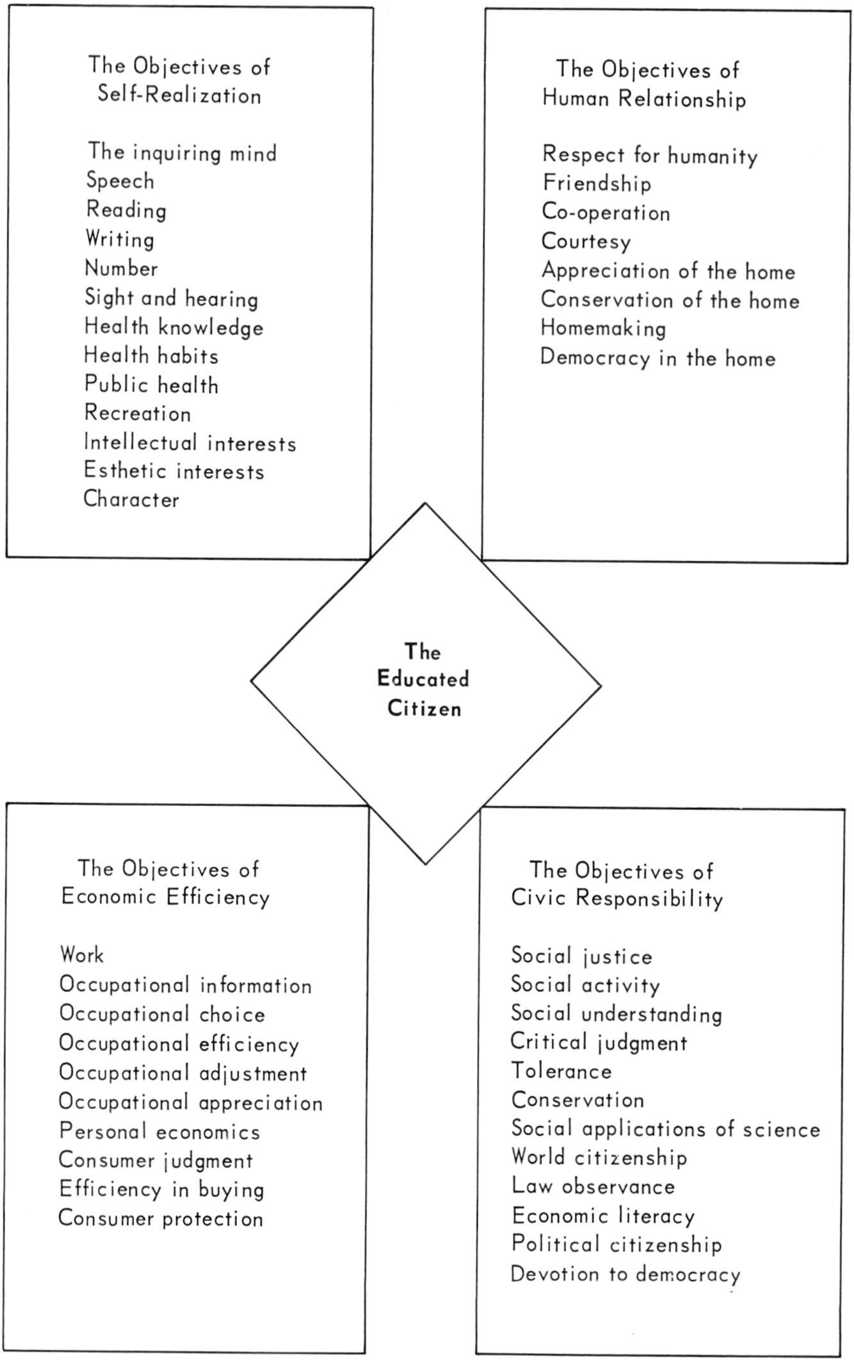

The Objectives of
Self-Realization

The inquiring mind
Speech
Reading
Writing
Number
Sight and hearing
Health knowledge
Health habits
Public health
Recreation
Intellectual interests
Esthetic interests
Character

The Objectives of
Human Relationship

Respect for humanity
Friendship
Co-operation
Courtesy
Appreciation of the home
Conservation of the home
Homemaking
Democracy in the home

**The
Educated
Citizen**

The Objectives of
Economic Efficiency

Work
Occupational information
Occupational choice
Occupational efficiency
Occupational adjustment
Occupational appreciation
Personal economics
Consumer judgment
Efficiency in buying
Consumer protection

The Objectives of
Civic Responsibility

Social justice
Social activity
Social understanding
Critical judgment
Tolerance
Conservation
Social applications of science
World citizenship
Law observance
Economic literacy
Political citizenship
Devotion to democracy

Respect for Humanity. The educated person puts human relations first.
Friendships. The educated person enjoys a rich, sincere, and varied social life.
Co-operation. The educated person can work and play with others.
Courtesy. The educated person observes the amenities of social behavior.
Appreciation of the Home. The educated person appreciates the family as a social institution.
Conservation of the Home. The educated person conserves family ideals.
Homemaking. The educated person is skilled in homemaking.
Democracy in the Home. The educated person maintains democratic family relationships.

The Objectives of Economic Efficiency

Emphasizing that the roles of the consumer and producer were "equally dependent upon education," the Commission listed the following objectives for economic efficiency:

Work. The educated producer knows the satisfaction of good workmanship.
Occupational Information. The educated producer understands the requirements and opportunities for various jobs.
Occupational Choice. The educated producer has selected his occupation.
Occupational Efficiency. The educated producer succeeds in his chosen occupation.
Occupational Adjustment. The educated producer maintains and improves his efficiency.
Occupational Appreciation. The educated producer appreciates the social value of his work.
Personal Economics. The educated consumer plans the economics of his own life.
Consumer Judgment. The educated consumer develops standards for guiding his expenditures.
Efficiency in Buying. The educated consumer is an informed and skillful buyer.
Consumer Protection. The educated consumer takes appropriate measures to safeguard his interests.

The Objectives of Civic Responsibility

Finally, the goals here involve the dealings of the educated person with his government at all levels and his relationships with peoples of other nations. They are:

Social Justice. The educated citizen is sensitive to the disparities of human circumstance.
Social Activity. The educated citizen acts to correct unsatisfactory conditions.
Social Understanding. The educated citizen seeks to understand social structures and social processes.
Critical Judgment. The educated citizen has defenses against propaganda.
Tolerance. The educated citizen respects honest differences of opinion.
Conservation. The educated citizen has a regard for the nation's resources.

Social Applications of Science. The educated citizen measures scientific advance by its contribution to the general welfare.

World Citizenship. The educated citizen is a co-operating member of the world community.

Law Observance. The educated citizen is economically literate.

Devotion to Democracy. The educated citizen acts upon an unswerving loyalty to democratic ideals.

A vocational class may involve students in meaningful activities. Vocational Department, West Chester High School, West Chester, Pennsylvania.

The Imperative Needs of Youth

The most recent large scale study of the objectives of secondary education in a changing society has been sponsored by the National Association of Secondary School Principals.[10] Although definitely for the high school, it is of importance for the elementary school also. The list has gained wide acceptance and has been influential in helping to bring about certain modifications in the curriculum of American secondary schools.

[10] National Association of Secondary School Principals, *The Imperative Needs of Youth of Secondary School Age,* Bulletin No. 145 (Washington, D.C., NEA, 1947).

The objectives follow, stated as the basic needs of youth:

1. All youth need to develop salable skills and those understandings and attitudes that make the worker an intelligent participant in economic life. To this end, most youth need supervised work experience as well as education in the skills and knowledge of their occupations.
2. All youth need to develop and maintain good health and physical fitness.
3. All youth need to understand the rights and duties of the citizen of a democratic society, and to be diligent and competent in the performance of their obligations as members of the community and citizens of the state and nation.
4. All youth need to understand the significance of the family for the individual and society and the conditions conducive to successful family life.
5. All youth need to know how to purchase and use goods and services intelligently, understanding both the values received by the consumer and the economic consequences of their acts.
6. All youth need to understand the methods of science, the influence of science on human life, and the main scientific facts concerning the nature of the world and of man.
7. All youth need opportunities to develop their capacities to appreciate beauty in literature, art, music, and nature.
8. All youth need to be able to use their leisure time well and to budget it wisely, balancing activities that yield satisfactions to the individual with those that are socially useful.
9. All youth need to develop respect for other persons, to grow in their insight into ethical values and principles, and to be able to live and work cooperatively with others.
10. All youth need to grow in their ability to think rationally, to express their thoughts clearly, and to read and listen with understanding.

The careful student will note that the more specific and definite objectives are, the more useful they are likely to be. General statements are necessary as guides and have their place. To be worthwhile in the classroom, however, they will have to be tailored to fit local situations and to be stated in terms of specific pupil behavior.

Two examples will point this out. If by way of illustration we choose *citizenship* from the Cardinal Principles, this must be broken down in terms of many subitems of behavior which have real meaning. Too many persons jump to the conclusion that citizenship means voting regularly and not much else. It means, among many other things: *attitudes* of obedience to laws, *appreciations* of the worth of democracy, *ideals* of honesty in community and state and national affairs, *knowledge* of how local government operates, and *habits* such as not throwing paper on the streets or refuse in the glorious geyser basins of Yellowstone Park. Only when objectives are so brought down to earth in terms of the individual can they have much practical value.

Then, taking an illustration from the objectives of the Commission, merely saying, "The educated citizen is economically literate," means nothing unless it is pinpointed to the pupil in terms of expected behavior —habits, knowledge, attitudes, appreciations, ideals, and skills at various age levels. Does being economically literate mean the habit of studying the stock market reports daily; a knowledge of how foreign exchange operates; an appreciation of the gold standard; or what does it mean really? This particularization of objectives by members of a local school system is what must be done if objectives are to be useful.

When this has been accomplished then a group of teachers will know where they are going. Carried out in such a manner, objectives will determine the curriculum to be adopted, the activities to be chosen, textbooks and materials to be purchased and used, and finally they will give direction to the measurement and evaluation of results. Only then will the public be getting what it has a right to expect of its schools.

DIFFERENTIATION OF ELEMENTARY AND SECONDARY GOALS

The constantly changing international situation and the rapidly broadening extension of knowledge have tended to make us think more definitely of the unifying purposes of our entire educational system. We tend to think less today of dividing lines between the elementary and the secondary schools. Foreign languages have been extended far down into the elementary grades, and in doing so it has been found imperative to revise the courses in those fields in the secondary schools. Continuity thus becomes a matter of the highest importance. The sciences have been extended downward too, and mathematics of greater complexity has become common place in the lowest grades.

Of course, these are largely curricular changes but they can only be justified if we consider them in the light of the broad view of our goals and purposes. The major goals of public education become more unified, and this is as it should be. No longer may it be truly said that the chief purpose of the elementary schools is to prepare for secondary education. They are both a part of one great whole.

Shane [11] has pointed out that "During a span of sixty years our objectives . . . have shifted from a narrow concept of formal instruction stressing the '3 R's' to an era in which the schools attempted to assume responsibility for total human development."

This is not the first time in educational experience that the pendulum has swung from one side to the other, and it is to be hoped that once again this action will result in a desirable middle ground position.

It will take teachers and administrators of great skill to see that the

[11] Harold G. Shane, "Elementary Education: Objectives," *Readings in Curriculum,* Glen Haas and Kimball Wiles, eds. (Boston, Allyn and Bacon, 1965), p. 317.

emphasis on academic excellence does not result in over-burdening busy work. We need to hope that in striving for academic excellence we do not lose the concern for the prime importance of the development of the whole child. There *can* be a proper blending of the two, but it will require educational statesmanship of a high order.

THE BROADER VIEW

The fundamental objectives of education in our democracy should change very little through the years. Points of emphasis change, of course; weak areas need to be strengthened, and broader outlooks replace more provincial ones.

The Rockefeller Brothers Fund Report,[12] for example, stresses the need for education to emphasize excellence in all phases of human living. To quote from the Report; "Excellent performance is a blend of talent and motive, of ability fused with zeal. Aptitude without aspiration is lifeless and inert." The Report [13] emphasizes both intellectual and moral excellence and closes with the following significant paragraph:

In short we will wish to allow wide latitude in the choice of values, but we must assume that education is a process that should be infused with meaning and purpose; that everyone will have deeply held beliefs; that every young American will wish to serve the values which have nurtured him and made possible his education and his freedom as an individual.

Such a goal, of course, can be a constant guiding star for education on all levels. According to Mayer [14] "A lasting culture demands more than academic ornamentation. It demands more than orthodox scholastic ritual. It certainly demands more than efficiency. A great culture demands boldness of insight, a dedicated leadership, and, above all, a cordial hospitality to new ideas."

[12] Rockefeller Brothers Fund, *The Pursuit of Excellence* (New York, Doubleday, 1958).

[13] *Ibid.,* p. 49.

[14] Frederick Mayer, *American Ideas and Education* (Columbus, Ohio, Merrill, 1964), p. 580.

QUESTIONS AND PROJECTS

1. Consult businessmen and labor leaders about their ideas of the purposes or aims of education. Discuss these with the class.
2. Divide the class into committees or groups, having each take one of the Cardinal Principles and analyze it into specific subobjectives for certain grade levels of children.
3. How can a proper balance be obtained between the individual and social purposes of a democracy?
4. Conduct a panel discussion on how the objectives of education would differ in an authoritarian type of government and in a democracy. This may also be done in the form of individual papers.
5. Examine the recent publication of the Educational Policies Commission and then see if you would modify any of the objectives previously set up by that same body and discussed in the chapter.
6. Comment upon the statement by T. H. Briggs: "We must teach pupils to do better the desirable things that they will do anyway."
7. Examine a course of study in your major field. Note the general and specific aims and objectives stated and how they are used in curriculum-building.
8. Visit a classroom on either the elementary or secondary school level. Ascertain, if possible, how the material being taught fits into the specific aims of education for that grade level. Is the teacher conscious of these aims?
9. Are you conscious of the objectives in your own particular class? If not, ask your teacher to help you get them clearly in mind.

AUDIO-VISUAL AIDS

MOTION PICTURES (16 MM)

Importance of Goals—McGraw-Hill Book Co., Text-Film Dept., 330 West 42nd St., New York, N.Y., sd., b&w. Case of 13-year-old Tommy illustrates the principles that all education is essentially a process of attaining basic, meaningful goals.

Freedom to Learn—National Education Association, 1201 16th St., N.W., Washington, D.C., 28 min., sd., b&w and/or color. Shows why students in a democracy must be allowed to study all sides of controversial issues.

Practicing Democracy in the Classroom—Encyclopaedia Britannica Films, 1150 Wilmette Ave., Wilmette, Ill., 24 min., sd., b&w. Shows teaching methods which not only develop subject matter but also provide opportunity for practicing democratic processes. Stresses methods which develop and draw upon the knowledge, skills, and attitudes of the students.

FILMSTRIP

Objectives of Education—Erle Press, 43 fr. Explains the four areas of development and living which serve as objectives of education as stated by the Educational Policies Commission of the NEA.

TAPE

Goals of Education: Doorway to the Future—ABC Radio, National Citizens Commission for the Public Schools. Story on the goals of education and a young girl who has great aims for teaching drama. Educational Recordings Service, Univ. of Colorado, Boulder, Colorado. Recorded on your tape.

FURTHER READINGS

Alexander, William M., and J. Galen Saylor, *Secondary Education, Principles and Practices* (New York, Holt, Rinehart and Winston, 1950).

Brameld, Theodore, "World Civilization: The Galvanizing Purpose of Public Education," *Phi Delta Kappan,* Vol. 44 (November, 1962) pp. 58–68.

Brammell, P. Roy, *Your Schools and Mine* (New York, Ronald, 1952).

Conant, James B., *Shaping Educational Policy* (New York, McGraw-Hill, 1964).

Conant, James B., *The Child, the Parent, and the State* (Cambridge, Mass., Harvard University Press, 1959).

Educational Policies Commission, *Public Education and the Future of America* (Washington, D.C., NEA, 1955).

Educational Policies Commission, *The Purposes of Education in American Democracy* (Washington, D.C., NEA, 1938).

Mursell, James L., *Principles of Democratic Education* (New York, Norton, 1955).

Rockefeller Brothers Fund, *The Pursuit of Excellence: Education and the Future of America* (Garden City, N.Y., Doubleday, 1958).

9

The Curriculum
and Curricular Activities

PREVIEW

▶ Specific objectives stated in terms of child behavior form the starting point for curriculum-building.

In the elementary school the curriculum, under the influence of reformers in Europe and America, has rather quickly adjusted to social needs.

The high school curriculum has been largely influenced by the addition of new subjects and the removal of few.

▶ Major attempts to revise the secondary curriculum have been, among others:
1. The report of the Committee of Ten.
2. The report of the Commission on the Reorganization of Secondary Education.
3. The work of the Educational Policies Commission.
4. The report of the Commission on Life Adjustment Education.
5. The Conant Report.

▶ Changing approaches to the organization of subject matter involve the concepts of:
1. Correlation.
2. Integration.

▶ The four chief types of curricula now in use in both elementary and secondary schools are:
1. The subject-matter curriculum.
2. The broad-fields curriculum.
3. The core curriculum.
4. The experience or activity curriculum.

The use of a modern curriculum involves the construction of "units of work."

▸ The building of a modern curriculum should make use of the efforts and resources of many persons, including: teachers, pupils, supervisors, administrators, curriculum experts, and community representatives.

▸ Curricula should be undergoing continuous revision.

A changing world such as there is today necessitates a changing pattern for achieving educational goals. The school population will be the adult citizens of tomorrow; they will see society move into the twenty-first century. What the year 2000 will be like depends to a great extent upon what qualities our schools choose to have the children and youth develop through experiences provided in the school's curriculum.

In recent years much discussion and debate have centered on answering the question, "What shall the schools teach?" When this question is answered and a pattern for organizing the knowledge to be taught is decided, then a curriculum can be developed.

What knowledge students are expected to attain and what qualities a good citizen should possess must, of course, be based upon the objectives of education which have been established. The student will do well to keep in mind these goals as discussed in the preceding chapter. Although the goals are *general* in scope they serve as a framework for deriving more *specific* and *immediate* goals. These are the objectives of teaching and learning which must be very definite and must be stated in terms of possible attainment for children of specific interests and abilities. When that is done, a beginning can be made in the building of the learning experiences through which children and young people may make the desired ultimate growth.

The statement of these goals is not easy if real value can be attached to them. For example, general and specific goals are often confused with one another as are remote and immediate goals. On occasion they are stated in terms of an adult need or point of view while neglecting the needs of the younger person in the position of learner.

Some of the learning activities pursued by the pupil may fill an immediate need, and at the same time serve to reach a remote future objective. For example, a child is taught to read and write in order that he can progress in the required experiences of the school or for his own immediate satisfaction and pleasure. On the other hand, literacy will have a strong influence on the individual's future and the future of his nation and the world, so this objective which seems remote is as valuable as the more immediate goal. Burton [1] refers to four levels of objectives which help clarify the foregoing statement:

1. The broad social purposes or objectives of society (in so far as society can be thought of as having objectives) and hence the remote, general aims or purposes of education.

    [Examples of these might be character, morality, citizenship, democracy, etc.]

2. The more specific social purposes or objectives of given social groups.

    [Examples of these might be the Cardinal Principles or the Four Major Objectives of the Education Policies Commission 1938] referred to in Chapter 8.

3. The teacher's purposes or objectives.

    [Examples of these are the certain skills, understandings, attitudes, behavior patterns, etc. which the teacher believes to be desired from the study of a particular unit of work.]

4. The pupils' purposes or objectives.

    [An example of these may be the immediate things the learner wishes to accomplish. They are the answers to real and current questions which students ask.]

It is the purpose of this chapter to introduce the student to the meaning of the curriculum and ways in which it may be organized in order to provide a meaningful and effective educational program for youth.

A Few Terms

The term *curriculum,* as it is generally and broadly used today, has come to mean those experiences which the child has in school or under its jurisdiction. Thus the curriculum may include such activities as field trips, observations, and the like, and even related experiences at home. It would be ridiculous, however, to include everything the child does, for much of his activities out of school, and not infrequently some in school, might well be totally unrelated to the best educational objectives accepted for that age or grade level. Certainly, a major share of the experiences must come very largely under the direction and guidance, however indirect, of the teacher and the school.

Smith, Stanley, and Shores [2] define the curriculum as "a sequence of potential experiences set up in the school for the purpose of disciplining children and youth in group ways of thinking and acting." Sowards and Scobey [3] suggest that the "school curriculum consists of those experiences that the school consciously and purposefully provides for children and youth in light of the accepted purposes of the school, using these experi-

1 William H. Burton, *The Guidance of Learning Activities,* 3rd ed. (New York, Appleton-Century-Crofts, 1962), pp. 125–127.

2 B. Othanel Smith, William O. Stanley, and J. Harlan Shores, *Fundamentals of Curriculum Development,* rev. ed. (Yonkers, N.Y., World Book, 1957), p. 3.

3 G. Wesley Sowards and Mary-Margaret Scobey, *The Changing Curriculum and the Elementary Teacher* (San Francisco, Wadsworth, 1961), p. 41.

ences, also, as the major source of data upon which to base the evaluation of individual and group progress toward these purposes."

More recently Broudy, Smith, and Burnett [4] refer to curriculum as "a part of a total influence system directed toward the student." They further state that "curriculum consists primarily of certain *content* organized into *categories of instruction* and *modes of teaching.*" This meaning is more specific in describing its components. This chapter directs attention to each of the components as well as to practices dealing with curriculum development.

Historically, the curriculum has had a much different meaning. Generally it has been assumed to be a list of the subjects offered. This will generally rule out many things that occur outside classes, such as work experience, certain trips, and the like, whether related or not. Yet, there is much evidence that all of these activities contribute immeasurably to a pupil's understanding more about the culture of a society of which he is a part. In high schools it is still common practice to speak of a "commercial curriculum," a "college preparatory curriculum," an "industrial arts curriculum," and others, thus describing a certain set of subjects with a suggested sequence that leads to a definite end, such as college entrance or a position in industry. The trend in modern secondary school offerings is toward a single curriculum of fundamental subject areas with provision for pupils to cut across traditional curricular lines to get the courses they need.

The *program of studies* would then be the total subject-offering of the school in all of the various curricula. This terminology still finds very common use.

The *course of study* means most usually the outline of suggested subject matter, experiences, and materials for a particular subject. Thus, there would be for the secondary school a course of study in biology, or typewriting, or literature. For the elementary school it is sometimes used in connection with the entire offering, thus becoming more or less synonymous with curriculum. A course of study given to a teacher may generally be considered to be an outline of work to be followed by all the schools of a city or county or in some cases a state. Generally today it will be flexible and suggestive rather than rigid and compulsory, as has all too frequently been the case in the past.

Still another term becoming more widely used and in many instances replacing the course of study is the *teacher's guide*. A teacher's guide is an expression which suggests a "framework of reference" on the teaching of American history, algebra, music, or any other subject in the curriculum. Its purpose is to provide the teacher with an understanding of philosophy, purposes, and methods as well as some of the content of the particular course he is teaching.

[4] Harry S. Broudy, B. Othaniel Smith, and Joe R. Burnett, *Democracy and Excellence in American Secondary Education* (Chicago, Rand McNally, 1964), p. 79.

Courtesy: Pancoast, Ferendino, Grafton &
Skeels, Architects & Engineers, Miami, Fla.
Photograph by Tierney and Killingsworth, Inc., Miami, Fla.

Learning Resources Center, Miami-Dade Junior College. This center provides the various curriculum materials to aid the teacher and student.

The modern teacher looks upon the teaching guide more favorably than he does the course of study because it offers greater flexibility. The traditional course of study was specific and definite about what should be done and when it should be done in the class. The teachers' guide permits the teacher to plan activities with and for the pupils at a time when they would be of most value as a learning experience.

THE CURRICULUM OF THE ELEMENTARY SCHOOL

When the elementary schools of early America were, in the words of Cubberley, "instruments of the church ends," their curriculum was an exceedingly simple affair, as is shown in the table on page 214.

Although remote both in distance and time from Europe, the influence of the educational reformers there soon began to be felt, as did also the changing nature of education from a church function to one serving the larger purposes of society. Rousseau (1712–1778) contributed a great deal "to changing the point of view of instruction from subject matter to the child to be taught and the nature of instruction from formal religious doctrine, preparatory for life hereafter, to the study of the life and universe amid which man lives here." [5]

The work of Pestalozzi (1746–1827) brought about the introduction of new subject matter and new approaches to methods of teaching. He advocated the study of real objects, learning through sense impressions, child activity, and individual expression.

Froebel (1782–1852), toward the middle of the nineteenth century, again advocated child nature as the starting point in education. He gave further emphasis to child interest, which was one of the important influences tending to place a declining importance upon subject matter.

The emphasis of Herbart was felt in two ways: (1) through his proposal that cultural history should constitute the core of instruction, and (2) through his stress upon teaching techniques (the five formal steps).[6] The five formal steps were given as: preparation, presentation, comparison, generalization, and application.

Gradually a larger number of scientific studies were conducted on the subject of child development. The reported results of such studies provided more reliable information on what was considered *normal* or *average* ability for elementary school age children. When this information was available and scientifically applied to teaching and to the curriculum, a more effective school program evolved.

It was not until after 1910 that public school educators dealt very seriously with curriculum development. This important task was usually cared for by private schools or colleges. However, with more scientific data available upon which the curriculum is developed, there began an era of experimentation in the elementary school. This experimentation resulted in desirable changes; for example, both teachers and parents were made more alert to the emotional and social needs of the child as well as to his intellectual development. Much stress was given to the advantages of a self-contained classroom—a kind of organization whereby one teacher spent the largest part of a school day with one group of children. More recently there has been much controversy over whether or not a self-contained classroom arrangement is as effective as a program best described as a departmentalized system. Departmentalization is believed to be advantageous because it assumes that a specialist will be utilized in every area of academic study. This type of arrangement is gaining in popularity in the upper elementary grade levels, and the self-contained type of organization remains the commonly accepted practice in the primary grade levels.

[5] Elwood P. Cubberley, *Public Education in the United States* (Boston, Houghton Mifflin, 1934), p. 347.

[6] J. Wayne Wrightstone, *Appraisal of Newer Elementary School Practice* (New York, Bureau of Publications, Teachers College, Columbia University, 1938), pp. 7–8.

Changing Approaches to Subject Matter Organization

Changes in organizational plans were not all that occurred. The number of subjects taught increased many times over the number that had been taught in the early elementary school in America. This may be one reason for the shift toward departmentalization, for it was almost impossible for one teacher to have the necessary subject-matter preparation in sufficient depth to teach all of these subjects equally well. Regardless of what plan was being followed the school program of studies became more crowded as new subjects were added, but none were removed. This fact is readily shown by the table below.

List of Subjects in the Elementary Schools

Eighteenth Century	Nineteenth Century	Twentieth Century
Reading	Reading (including	Reading
Spelling	declamation)	Literature
Arithmetic	Writing	Spelling
Bible	Spelling	Arithmetic
Catechism	Arithmetic	Algebra
	Mental Arithmetic	Grammar
	Manners and Conduct	Written
	Bookkeeping	Oral
	Geography	Geography
	Physical	Location
	Locational	Human
	History—U.S.	Language
	Elementary Science	History
	Drawing	U.S.
	Music	World
	Physical Exercises	Constitution
		Science
		Nature Study
		Elementary
		Drawing
		Music
		Manual Training
		Sewing
		Cooking
		Play
		Physical Training
		Health
		Humane Education
		French
		Spanish

Many proposals were made to try to improve the situation, such as concentrating the work about a few main subjects and correlating others with them, an idea primarily advanced by Francis W. Parker, one of the great early American educational reformers. Others suggestions had to do with the elimination of "useless" subject matter and the reduction of unnecessary repetition. We shall very soon see more of the results of studies of these problems and others as changes in the organization of the curriculum have been proposed.

Some promising developments are appearing as experimental programs. All of these indicate a break in the traditional graded lock-step school organization with the emphasis on continuous pupil progress. The most common plans might be classified as (1) "nongraded school" plan, (2) self-contained unit (3) "team teaching" plan, (4) "programmed instruction" plan, and (5) departmentalization.

The *nongraded school* plan is one which encourages continuous pupil progress with less incidence of failure and nonpromotion. It is a system whereby the conventional grades one to three are included in one unit called the primary school and grades four to six in another unit called the intermediate school. A number of attainment levels are established for each group. Further research in child growth and development may well provide educators with evidence that supports their belief that the nongraded school is best for accomplishing its stated purposes. Few schools, however, indicate they are actually reorganizing according to this plan. A recent NEA Report [7] commenting on the number of schools in the United States that are operating on a nongraded plan states, "Five percent expect to have all nongraded classes by 1966."

The report [8] further suggests that there is some trend "from separate grades to some separate grades and some ungraded sequences."

The *self-contained* unit is best described as a "workshop" or a "home away from home" where the teacher and a group of children, not exceeding 25 work together all day, every day for the entire year. The one teacher is responsible for all learning experiences including the subjects of the curriculum which are commonly described as specialized, e.g. art, music, health and physical education, etc. This plan necessitates a particular type of physical facility, the "self-contained classroom" described in Chapter 12.

Many teachers who have experimented with such a plan say they favor it because it naturally places an emphasis on the specific needs of each child; the teacher gains a fuller measure of understanding of each pupil; it provides a climate for learning which is conducive to better mental hygiene. Furthermore, the plan promotes a closer harmony among

[7] Ole Sand and Richard I. Miller, *The Principals Look at the Schools* (Washington, D.C. National Education Association, 1962), pp. 39–40.

[8] *Ibid.,* p. 40.

Courtesy: Cleve O. Westby, Director of
Building Services, New Jersey State
Department of Education. Architects:
Scrimenti, Swackhamer and Perantoni.

Model of Hanover Park Regional High School, Hanover Park, New Jersey. This is a good example of the Campus Type Secondary School. Each building in the background is a center for a particular subject-matter. Buildings in the foreground house administration, library, and food services. Gymnasium and field are shown at right of picture.

children, parents, and teacher which manifests itself in providing more meaningful educational experiences. It is obvious that many strengths of this plan are similar to those in the nongraded school. In both, the concern for a greater understanding of the individual pupil is stressed. The importance of this aspect of the teaching-learning process cannot be denied; success or failure of a teacher is often related to the extent to which he understands his pupils.

A curriculum must provide experiences which are challenging to all pupils so the teacher's knowledge must go far beyond that which aids him in learning about his pupils. The teacher's area of interest, or that subject upon which he concentrates his study while in college, is considered his field or area of teaching. It may be a broad field such as elementary education, art, music, or a more academically defined area such as physics, trigonometry, or Latin. In any instance, the teacher should be assigned to teach in the field of his major or more specifically the subject about which he has most knowledge. In the secondary school this has been the practice throughout its history. Individual teachers were assigned to teach in their major area of preparation. Such was not so in the elementary school because each teacher was assigned to instruct a given class in all subjects studied. Examination of the table on page 214 makes one realize it would be impossible to have a great depth of knowledge in all the subjects offered in one grade. So long as knowledge and concepts in each of these subject areas remained quite constant or did not expand too rapidly, elementary teachers were capable of teaching almost all that the child was believed able to comprehend. He still is quite able to handle all subjects taught in the primary grades. However, with the explosion of knowledge which has occurred and the impact of television and other lines of communication into the home, the teacher of upper elementary school children must have much more preparation than he previously received. He, like his counterpart on the secondary school level, is being required to attain a concentration of knowledge in one area of interest. Elementary teachers today have 24 to 30 credits in one subject such as English or social science. This has brought about a new type of organization in terms of the curriculum. Teachers on this level, the intermediate grades, are being assigned to teach in their areas or subjects of greatest strength or background. This is commonly termed departmentalization. It suggests that one teacher teaches only mathematics, another teaches only English, etc. Whether this is a better plan than the self-contained classroom type of organization is a subject of controversy. Each plan has almost an equal number of proponents as opponents. Surveys of common practices in elementary schools today show a trend toward an increase of some type of departmentalization, yet the smaller schools are an exception.

This concept of improving the curriculum through a more effective staff utilization has contributed to the team approach. (See Chapter 16.)

Some elementary and a larger number of junior high school teachers are involved in the team-teaching arrangement. As the name implies, this plan is accomplished through subdividing the large school into smaller units of 200 to 300 pupils, each with its own team of teachers. The program of scheduling provides sufficient flexibility to provide the small group of teachers opportunity to meet at regular intervals for planning sessions. During these sessions the curricular and guidance activities can be correlated within the framework of broad as well as specific goals for the pupils with whom teachers have regular contact and to whom they are responsible for a major portion of the educational program.

A plan such as this is often effected through the traditional grade levels of 7, 8, and 9 in junior high school. The team of four or five teachers are those who teach the major required subjects. The number of team meetings varies from once a week to once a month. Where this plan is being tried, it is found that both pupils and teachers are becoming more aware of the real purposes of education and are developing more adequate, as well as more challenging, assignments and experiences.

Programmed instruction is still in the experimental stage in spite of such well-known pioneers in the field as Sydney L. Pressey, B. F. Skinner, Robert Glaser, and others. This method is usually associated with either a mechanical device known as a teaching machine or a specially written text. Each is a series of informative statements followed by questions. Each question is answered by the learner and the answer compared to the correct answer which is provided by the programmed material. In this method, the pupil is able to work as rapidly as he chooses or as slowly as is necessary to master the material which is provided in each program. Further discussion of this topic may be found in Chapter 16.

In an age when more and more emphasis is given to technology in our lives, it is likewise certain that our schools' educational goals will be influenced by the greater availability and use of programmed learning materials.

Students preparing for a career in teaching should be reminded that their work will not be taken over or necessarily made any easier by these materials. In fact, it will demand even greater skill on the part of the teacher in making worthwhile application of programmed learning and teaching machines.

OTHER COURSES AND NEW COURSES OF STUDY

In addition to developing new organizational approaches to the curricular offerings a significant number of schools are introducing additional courses. Three areas of study receiving greatest emphasis today are foreign language, mathematics, and science.

Better schools are providing science instruction from kindergarten through the 12th grade. Where nature study was once the only science stressed in the elementary grades, schools today are providing pupils with opportunity to develop the scientific method of solving and evaluating scientific phenomena in all the areas of science and technology. To insure better science education many states have initiated institutes and workshops for in-service teachers. Through the help of consultants from business, industry, and universities, teachers are kept up-to-date with new scientific achievements and improved methods of teaching science. Some financial assistance is available from the federal government for such workshops through the National Defense Education Act and the National Science Foundation.

The second area of study, thought by many to be as important as science, is that of foreign languages. An examination of curricula shows many school systems offering foreign languages in the grades; some introducing it as early as the kindergarten, and many more starting it in the early years of junior high school. Stress is on mastery of conversational ability, whether on the elementary or junior high school level. Here, too, federal funds are made available for establishing a language laboratory to increase teaching-learning effectiveness. (See Chapter 16.)

Along with increased emphasis on science and foreign language there is a veritable revolution occurring in the field of mathematics. The new or modern mathematics being taught has developed largely from the increased use of high speed computers. A totally new language as well as a new approach to problem solving is developing in mathematics. A number of experimental projects in learning mathematics concepts are in process or have been completed. Discussed further on in this chapter are new mathematics programs, most being initiated at the secondary school level, it is sufficient to mention here that if secondary school mathematics is changing, so too must the elementary school program, in order to ready the pupils for the study of more advanced mathematics.

Some notable work in mathematics for the elementary school has been done and is continuing at such universities as Illinois, Syracuse, Stanford, and Webster College, to mention a few. At Illinois the experiment sought to learn what mathematics ideas and concepts children could learn at certain stages of growth and maturity. It emphasized teaching through the discovery method and involving the student in developing an understanding of mathematics concepts which will lead him to learn more and more mathematics for himself.

Syracuse University and Webster College employed a method whereby pupils used class discussions in place of traditional teacher explanations for finding their own solutions to problems.

Stanford is directing a series of projects to learn how much mathematics can be learned by elementary school pupils. One study related to teaching Geometry to the primary grades, another sought to teach Mathematical Logic to superior pupils in the grades 5 and 6.

With the passage of the Elementary-Secondary School Act of 1965 and the Higher Education Act it seems certain that there will be increased research dealing with effective curriculum development in the subject matter fields already mentioned and perhaps others as well.

Guidance

Inherent in all work with the curriculum is a knowledge of guidance and techniques of counseling. Throughout all levels of education, teachers are devoting much more time and energy to counseling with pupils before assigning them to sections and concurrently with class instruction. Guidance is an important aspect of building a successful and practical curriculum for today's school population. Intelligent counseling is, in effect, the difference between mediocre and high quality education for our children. In any school the curriculum *per se* is meaningless if guidance is lacking. Fortunately, administrators are sensing the validity and importance of such services, and we are moving in the right direction. Much progress has already been reported, and many studies are just getting under way.

As more schools report on their efforts to meet the challenge of criticism leveled at the elementary and secondary school curriculum, we shall undoubtedly learn of other changes which will result in higher quality education on all levels.

THE EVOLVING HIGH SCHOOL CURRICULUM

Chapters 2 and 8 noted the attempts to change the purposes and nature of the secondary schools. It may be well, however, to re-emphasize that early American public high schools, which were in no sense common until near the end of the nineteenth century, were largely college preparatory in nature and taught those subjects which particularly met that need. These were, among others:

Latin	French	Botany
Greek	German	Zoology
English	Chemistry	History (General
Algebra	Physics	and U.S.)
Geometry		Literature

The Committee of Ten

The earliest large-scale attempt to evaluate secondary education was made by the Committee of Ten on Secondary School Subjects. The Committee divided into smaller groups working on the various subjects taught and issued a final report in 1893. The need of more uniform content was emphasized, as was also the amount of time devoted to each subject. Attention was also given to the standardization of college entrance requirements.

The Cardinal Principles

Undoubtedly, the next most important landmark was the previously-mentioned work of the Commission on the Reorganization of Secondary Education, which reported in 1918 and which was responsible for the setting up of the Seven Cardinal Principles. Serving to shift the emphasis from college preparation to a considerable degree, the original report was followed by others on all of the major subject-matter areas.

The work of this group has been the leaven and the stimulus for studies by a number of state groups and by many individual secondary schools.

The Educational Policies Commission's Contribution to Curriculum Making

Another study of much significance was that represented by the Report of the Educational Policies Commission in 1944 entitled, *Education for All American Youth*. Pointing particularly toward the postwar period, it envisioned an institution that would meet the needs of all the young people of a community—those who would go to college, those whose education would be terminated in the secondary school, and those who wished more specifically to prepare for vocations. Stress was put upon the development of technical institutes for this latter purpose that would extend through grades 13 and 14 and upon the establishment of public junior colleges.

Since its origin the Educational Policies Commission has developed a number of influential statements on the educational plans and purposes as they were directly related to youth. Some of the more recent reports were of sufficient importance that they have been used as authoritative guides to curriculum study. Those most often referred to are:

1. Education for All American Youth (1944)
2. Education for All American Children (1948)
3. Education for All American Youth: A Further Look (1952)
4. Essay on Quality in Public Education (1959)
5. Central Purpose of American Education (1961)
6. Universal Opportunity for Education Beyond the High School (1964)

Education for Life Adjustment

Another approach to the problem of the reorganization of secondary education and one which had a significant impact upon the curriculum came from the work of the Commission on Life Adjustment Education (1947). This group, appointed by the United States Commissioner of Education, was composed of representatives from both general and vocational education. The purpose of the Committee was to study the educational needs of the large group of students in high school who did not continue until graduation. It was the commission's intent "to promote in every manner possible ways, means, and devices for improving education of secondary school youth."

The recommendations of this commission seemed to have had far-reaching effects on the secondary school population and the large number of those pupils remaining in high school to be graduated. This influence was especially noticeable in the decade from 1955 to 1965. During these years the number of high school graduates increased from 1.2 million in

1955 to approximately 2.3 million in June of 1965. The increase results primarily from greater enrollment, but in addition the schools have made some gains in retaining students until they graduate.

In spite of a larger percentage of students graduating, there is still much to be done to decrease the large numbers who drop out. Reliable figures indicate that only two-thirds of the individuals who enter the 9th grade will be continuing on to graduate from high school. Perhaps the schools today should have a further look at the recommendations made by the Commission on Life Adjustment Education.[9] There is much good in their statements which would apply today.

According to official statements of the group, life-adjustment education has to do with the following:

> It is concerned with ethical and moral living and with physical, mental and emotional health.
>
> It recognizes the importance of fundamental skills since citizens in a democracy must be able to compute, to read, to write, to listen and to speak effectively. It emphasizes skills as tools for further achievement.
>
> It is concerned with the development of wholesome recreational interests of both an individual and social nature.
>
> It is concerned with the present problems of youth as well as with their preparation for future living.
>
> It is for all American youth and offers them learning experiences appropriate to their capacities.
>
> It recognizes the importance of personal satisfactions and achievements for each individual within the limits of his abilities.
>
> It respects the dignity of work and recognizes the educational values of responsible work experience in the life of the community.
>
> It provides both general and specialized education but, even in the former, common goals are to be attained through differentiation both as to subject matter and experience.
>
> It has many patterns. For a school, a class, or a pupil it is an individual matter. The same pattern should not be adopted in one community merely because it was effective in another. It must make sense in each community in terms of the goals which are set and the resources which are available.
>
> It emphasizes deferred as well as immediate values. For each individual it keeps an open road and stimulates the maximum achievement of which he is capable.
>
> It recognizes that many events of importance happened a long time ago but holds that the real significance of these events is in their bearing upon life today.
>
> It emphasizes active and creative achievements as well as adjustment to exist-

9 U.S. Office of Education, *Vitalizing Secondary Education*, Bulletin 1951, No. 3 (Washington, D.C.), pp. 32–33.

ing conditions; it places a high premium upon learning to make wise choices, since the very concept of American democracy demands the appropriate revising of aims and the means of attaining them.

It is education fashioned to achieve desired outcomes in terms of character and behavior. It is not education which follows convention for its own sake or holds any aspect of the school as an end in itself rather than a means to an end.

Above all, it recognizes the inherent dignity of the human personality.

Education for life adjustment seems to have caught the imagination of many leaders in secondary education. Evidence of this may be seen in the great number of articles that have been written about it in the educational periodicals. Actually, however, it takes many years, perhaps even a half-century, for such movements really to have a broad effect upon the curricula of the many thousands of existing secondary schools. What usually happens is that a certain number of progressive schools that are always alert to find better ways of meeting social needs really tackle the problem vigorously and try to do something about it. Then they are the ones who furnish the leaven for a slow and gradual changing of purposes and methods generally. In far too many high schools today, changing the curriculum is confined to adding more subjects, but very seldom removing any that now exist. Professional leadership of a high order is more necessary today than ever in the great American ideal of free secondary education for all.

Recent discoveries in science and technology coupled with achievements made by the Soviet Union and other nations of the world have made Americans even more aware of the need for re-examining their educational programs. Large sums of money have been granted to capable and interested educators for the purpose of evaluating secondary and higher education in this country. Their findings which are now being released will certainly guide school administrators, teachers, and communities in providing American youth with the best educational opportunities possible. One such study is reported in James B. Conant's *The American High School Today*.[10]

The Conant Report, taken up in some detail in Chapter 3, is influencing curriculum development on the secondary school level. Evidence of this influence is shown by a review of some of his recommendations and how schools are applying them. For example, Conant recommends an increase in number and kinds of science and mathematics courses required of pupils going on to college. High school transcripts of recent college entrants indicate this change is occurring. He recommends a greater number of years be applied in a given foreign language. School guidance officers are encouraging pupils to take a third and fourth year of one language rather than two years of each of two languages.

[10] James B. Conant, *The American High School Today* (New York, McGraw-Hill, 1959), p. 47.

He advocates schools offering a summer session for the gifted as well as those who may be required to repeat a course. There is a noticeable increase in the number of districts offering summer schools for such purposes.

In addition to these, many more examples could be cited which are applications of Conant's major recommendations and which are referred to in the following paragraphs.

One suggestion pertains to the need for a program of general education for all graduating students. Included in these required courses would be

. . . four years of English, three or four years of social studies—including two years of history (one of which should be American history) and a senior course in American problems or American government—one year of mathematics in the ninth grade (algebra or general mathematics), and at least one year of science in the ninth or tenth grade, which might well be biology or general physical science. By a year, I mean that a course is given five periods a week throughout the academic year or an equivalent amount of time. This academic program of general education involves nine or ten courses with homework to be taken in four years and occupies more than half the time of most students, whatever their elective programs.

Another recommendation which concerns the academically talented students states:

A policy in regard to the elective programs of academically talented boys and girls should be adopted by the school to serve as a guide to the counselors. In the type of school I am discussing the following program should be strongly recommended as a minimum:

Four years of mathematics, four years of one foreign language, three years of science, in addition to the required four years of English and three years of social studies; a total of eighteen courses with homework to be taken in four years. This program will require at least fifteen hours of homework each week.

Many academically talented pupils may wish to study a second foreign language or an additional course in social studies. Since such students are capable of handling twenty or more courses with homework, these additional academic courses may be added to the recommended minimum program. If the school is organized on a seven- or eight-period day, at least one additional course without homework (for example, art or music) may also be scheduled each year.

If as school policy a minimum academic program including both mathematics and a foreign language is recommended to the academically talented pupils and their parents, the counselors will have the problem of identifying as early as possible the members of the group. It may well be that, in the next lower 10 or 20 percent of the boys and girls in terms of scholastic aptitude on a national basis, there are a number who ought to be guided into similar but less rigorous programs.[11]

[11] *Ibid.,* p. 57.

In addition, Dr. Conant recommends that highly gifted students be identified in the junior high school and offered special instruction. Upon reaching the 12th grade these students could profit from entering a course or two in what is termed the Advanced Placement Program. Courses so specified constitute college level achievement, and students may be excused from similar courses in their first year of college. This is now being done in many school systems.

The study further suggests that all secondary school students take a required course in physical science or biology with sections grouped in relation to ability, with content and method modified accordingly. Two types of chemistry and physics courses are recommended—one designed for those of lesser mathematical ability and another with certain mathematical prerequisites. All science courses should be sufficiently rigorous to challenge all pupils.

Also, the report calls for a program leading to the development of marketable skills for those who will seek employment upon graduation. The value of English composition is re-emphasized, and it is suggested that all students have course work in this field.

Any important change in the senior high school grades will, in some degree, affect the program for grades 7, 8, and 9. Dr. Conant's report [12] on the junior high school sets forth many recommendations, not the least of which refers to a need for greater articulation between these commonly accepted levels of the educational system. He believes much more of educational value can be accomplished if grades 7 and 8 reflect their real purpose—transition *from* the elementary school to the secondary school and preparation *for* the secondary school. Instruction in the basic skills of reading and arithmetic should be continued in the junior high school grades as long as the pupils need it and can gain from it.

This report, as did the one on the high school, places a major emphasis on studying the academic subjects, but it does not rule out the need for the exploratory purpose of the junior high school. Dr. Conant believes instruction in art, music, and physical education should be afforded all pupils. He recommends home economics instruction for girls and industrial arts for boys.

Recognizing the importance of the social, emotional, and physical aspects of early adolescent development the report recommends the need for establishing an environment in which all these areas of growth can be cared for. A concern for group activities, self-government, ability grouping for academic subjects, block-time teaching, increased emphasis on guidance, and a need for competent teachers with imagination working in adequate facilities are some of the more positive suggestions.

Dr. Conant deplores the idea of so much emphasis being placed on

[12] James B. Conant, *Recommendations for Education in the Junior High School Years* (Princeton, N.J., Educational Testing Service, 1960).

interscholastic athletics, marching bands, and graduation ceremonies in the junior high school. His recommendations along this line cannot be passed off lightly by administrators and citizens who are nearest to the problem of paying for the best education for every child.

These are only a few of the specific recommendations found in the reports on the American junior and senior high schools. It is especially important that students refer to the primary sources for the complete story.

In addition to schools themselves implementing many of Conant's recommendations there have been a number of colleges and universities involved. These have done research in cooperation with schools to improve courses in a number of subject fields. Some of the important projects are described briefly; a few readers may recognize having studied the courses mentioned.

PSSC, BSCS, CBA, and CHEM Study. These letters represent the major curriculum studies in science for the secondary school. Most teachers, especially science teachers and school administrators, are aware of these projects sponsored by the National Science Foundation.

The Physical Science Study Committee (PSSC), organized and carried on by the assistance from Massachusetts Institute of Technology and the Educational Testing Service, developed a complete course in modern physics for high schools. The Committee produced a complete set of textbook, laboratory guides, a series of sound films, laboratory equipment and evaluative materials. These materials are now beginning to find rather wide-spread use throughout the nation. According to preliminary reports, the results attained are very encouraging.

Since the Committee believed that only the better students in high school studied physics, the course was designed for those who would be in the upper one-fourth of the class. Already there is some evidence to indicate that students below the 75th percentile could do quite well in the course.

The Chemical Bond Approach (CBA) study was similar to the PSSC Project. The project staff of college chemistry professors and a limited number of high school chemistry teachers worked with a group of selected high school chemistry teachers in developing a total course including a textbook and laboratory materials for secondary school chemistry.

The course was a different approach to the study of chemistry in that it was outlined around the theme of chemical bonds and stressed the atomic and molecular structure of matter. Likewise in this project Educational Testing Service prepared accompanying tests to evaluate the pupils' understanding and progress. Test results indicate students with high scholastic aptitude test scores made excellent progress in the revised chemistry course.

The second study dealing with chemistry was developed by the

Chemical Education Materials Study (CHEM Study). Like the two previously described projects, this study group prepared a complete kit of teaching materials including a text and laboratory manual for a high school chemistry course. The emphasis is on laboratory work wherein the pupil "discovers" for himself the theories and basic principles of chemistry.

A fourth project, The Biological Sciences Curriculum Study (BSCS), sought to develop a new high school biology program through the preparation of three distinctly different approaches. Each version was complete with textbook, laboratory guide, and manual, high schools could use any one to teach an effective course in biology.

Each approach had a different emphasis, namely, (1) ecological and evolutionary, (2) genetic and developmental, and (3) bio-chemical and physiological.

This program like the others has been directed to the secondary school level, but original plans included the preparation of materials for the elementary school as well.

SMSG, UICSM, UMMaP. As in science education, the study of mathematics curriculum in the schools has involved a number of projects devoted to the improvement of the mathematics program. SMSG, UICSM, and UMMaP indicate particular committees that worked on specific projects. These and many more dealt with research which would ultimately define the effective mathematics program for the schools. Again, most of these programs applied to secondary school.

The School Mathematics Study Group (SMSG) was supported by the National Science Foundation. It sought to study and improve the mathematics program in schools by the preparation of a total package of text materials, teachers guide, and suggestions for meaningful solutions to mathematical problems.

This group also has indicated that it was interested in developing correspondence courses and programmed text materials; it devoted considerable attention to preparation of materials for elementary school mathematics programs.

The University of Illinois Committee (UICSM) spent ten years of study in preparation of materials for college preparatory mathematics. Like the many science curriculum projects, this one stressed the importance of discovering mathematics principles and concepts. Courses were written for grades 9, 10, 11, and 12. The University of Illinois conducted an extensive teacher education program for those teaching in the project.

In Maryland, the University has conducted a project (UMMaP) to prepare materials for experimental courses in 7th and 8th grade mathematics. Learning through both inductive and deductive reasoning is emphasized. The pupils are taught the use of the language associated with mathematics.

It is not possible to describe all the research being done in improving the study of mathematics. These are examples of major importance and those which, along with many others, will influence curriculum development in the nation's schools.

Mathematics and science curriculum studies have received the greatest share of financial support. This is due mainly to our tremendously accelerated effort to succeed in technology as it becomes an ever more important influence on our daily life. It would be inaccurate to imply to the reader that all curriculum study has occurred in these two fields only. One has only to scan the professional journals for articles dealing with contemporary studies on curriculum to learn that there are research projects on nearly all subject areas in the school.

Some of the projects will be of interest to the teacher who finds his major subject included. It is for that reason that a few are mentioned here. A review of the project is often available in the journal of that specific subject.

1. The Commission on English of the College Entrance Examination Board
2. The Joint Project of the National Council for the Social Studies and the American Council of Learned Societies
3. Program for Improving the Teaching of World Affairs
4. The High School Geography Project
5. National Task Force on Economic Education
6. The FLES Program—Foreign Languages in the Elementary School

NEA Project on Instruction

In its continued interest in improving the quality of American public education, the National Education Association has sponsored a national committee and supplied a headquarters staff to make a thorough study related to instruction. The committee headed by Ole Sand is identified as The Project on Instruction. The NEA has described the function of the committee by merely stating that it will "seek to give direction on crucial curriculum decisions facing the public schools."

Several monograph reports are available on the various topics studied. The results of the study are available and provide considerable guidance to teachers and administrators contemplating curriculum improvement studies. The two publications are titled "Deciding What to Teach" and "Planning and Organizing for Teaching."

As a part of the project, a number of surveys were completed which are of considerable importance in guiding the curriculum worker or the school administrator. It is not the intent to review the committee's findings here, but a few statements of trends or present practices reported will be of assistance and interest to the person entering the profession of teaching.

The Committee [13] reports:

1. Science, mathematics, and foreign languages are expected to receive major stress. Both elementary and secondary principals believe the emphasis on these subject areas will reach a proper balance soon.
2. There will be continued emphasis on reading instruction. A number of different approaches in methodology will continue. There is a trend toward greater use of diversified reading materials for individualized reading.
3. Over half of the elementary schools surveyed indicated a trend toward organizing for teaching upon broad curriculum fields. One-third expect to organize further toward specific subject being emphasized. Secondary schools indicated continued emphasis on single subjects, but a fair share believed there will continue to be more subjects combined to form broad fields.
4. There will continue to be a movement of courses downward. This practice seemed to be indicated in both the elementary and secondary schools.
5. A greater use of audio-visual teaching aids will occur. Over eighty percent of the secondary schools surveyed indicated varied degrees of use of language laboratories.
6. Over half of the schools will use homogeneous grouping of students.
7. Approximately one-fourth of the elementary schools believe they will have non-graded programs by 1966.
8. Departmentalization seems to be on the increase in the elementary school. Only about one-third will be organized on the self-contained classroom basis.
9. A third of both elementary and secondary schools indicated that they would be using some form of team teaching by 1966.

These factors indicate to some degree the status of practices which relate to curriculum and instruction. It will be of value to the student to keep abreast of these practices and to note any important changes which may occur by the time he is in his own classroom.

CORRELATION AND INTEGRATION OF SUBJECT MATTER

Two ideas or approaches to subject-matter organization and method should be noted as helpful solutions to some of the complex problems that present themselves. The first is generally spoken of as correlation. It indicates the attempt to modify the separateness of subject matter and proposes that teachers take special pains to find common ground between subjects and to search constantly for relationships. The mathematics teacher can find many points in common with the science teacher, as can the history and geography teacher, and the English teacher and the art teacher. Brammell [14] points out: "Correlation does not eliminate the fences, but it results in a lot of over-the-fence talking and planning."

The second approach, integration, must be understood as a continu-

[13] Ole Sand and Richard I. Miller, *The Principals Look at the Schools* (Washington, D.C., National Education Association, 1962).
[14] P. Roy Brammell, *Your Schools and Mine* (New York, Ronald, 1952), p. 260.

ous process and as something which takes place in the individual. The things to be learned are so organized and presented that they will become interwoven with those understandings, skills, abilities, and attitudes which the learner already possesses. The learning experiences will effect real changes in the personality of the learner as these experiences call for the individual to react and interact with problems growing out of a topic chosen for study.

In the elementary school, for example, all classroom activities might center around the building of a train or around a farm project. All learning of many kinds—such as reading, drawing, numbering—would center around the topic chosen. Much responsibility is placed upon the teacher for selecting or directing the selection of projects that will involve the desired experiences and learnings and for giving the proper guidance day by day. It is pointed out that this method parallels real life experiences. Surely this type of program is far more easily conducted in the lower grades of the elementary school, although it is presently being attempted elsewhere, even in the colleges.

If we consider this more from the point of view of the individual, it is the learner who does the integrating. The things that are learned, when integration takes place, become a part of the individual's personality. Burton [15] suggests: "This means that he comes to understand, influence, and get along with other persons and improve the institutions within which he lives."

A study of curricular practices in use in schools across the nation can pretty well be summed up in three central patterns of organization. As Smith, Stanley, and Shores [16] suggest, these organizations of curriculum are basically:

1. The subject curriculum.
2. The core curriculum.
3. The activity or experience curriculum.

As a variation of subject curriculum, one might list the "broad-fields" curriculum as a fourth type of organization which many schools indicate as a particular pattern of curriculum.

Some of the characteristics and practices common to these four types of organization are given here for better understanding of the kinds of curricula which are most widely used.

The Subject Curriculum

This, as is surely obvious to the student, is the traditional pattern. Each subject—English, arithmetic, history, algebra—is studied sepa-

---

[15] Burton, *op. cit.*, p. 80.
[16] Smith, Stanley, and Shores, *op. cit.*, Chs. 16 to 21, pp. 372–531.

rately. Each is given a required number of minutes or hours each day or week for a semester or term depending upon the school's program. Each subject is believed to have a logical organization of its own, and it is felt that pupils should study it systematically through contact with it in succeeding years. The chief purpose of this type of curriculum is for the learner to gain an understanding of the information about that particular subject. Explanation and recitation has been the teaching method. However, some subject teachers are skilled in developing units which call upon the learner to solve problems through the laboratory method.

This curriculum pattern is still popular in school because parents understand it, having experienced it themselves. The textbook dealing with a subject represents an accumulation of the best knowledge available. The material is organized logically and systematically for teachers and pupils. A large percentage of school administrators know this pattern best because they have taught and were taught by means of it. Most instructional materials have been geared to specific subject matter rather than to other patterns of organization.

This type of curricular organization has its serious defects, as the student can see in part from what has gone before. It can too easily result in mere memorization of facts, and learning can become compartmentalized. Repetition comes about much too easily, and the student all too often fails to see any use for what he is doing. On the other hand, it is systematic, easy to handle, and can more easily provide for drill and detailed concentration. But, and very important, the curriculum through actual need, through social pressures, and legislative prescription has become so crowded that there simply are not enough hours and minutes available.

The Broad-Fields Curriculum

This pattern of organization is a modification of the subject curriculum and stresses relationships among subjects. Some authorities refer to this as a "fused" curriculum; others call it an "integrated" curriculum. The terminology does not change the idea of an attempt to blend together two or more courses or subjects with the expressed purpose of strengthening the learning experience.

A typical broad-fields curriculum, for example, might consist of the following large divisions: social studies, general science, language arts, health and physical education, general mathematics, and general arts. Through this type of curriculum it is still possible to retain the values of the subject curriculum and at the same time provide much more freedom in method.

In general science one might find pupils devoting a large part of their time to problems dealing with electricity, but concurrently developing an understanding of and an appreciation for its relations to chemistry and physics. In the language arts, reading, writing, spelling, written and oral language are studied as one large related field. Spelling, for instance, is not taken up in an isolated fashion but in connection with reading and writing. Thus, in all areas, it is believed, compartmentalized learning is reduced, and the ability to associate related ideas is acquired; the amount of time allotted to any one "field" is longer; topics studied are more general, and understanding of broad fields of knowledge is emphasized. Here is a type of organization that is finding increased use in the colleges as well as in the elementary and secondary schools. Even some graduate schools are using it to some extent on the doctoral level, particularly where instructors are being trained for working in general education in the undergraduate colleges.

The Core Curriculum

The core concept is based upon the assumption that on any particular level of education or area of living there is a common body of knowledge and experience that all must have, regardless of their special interests. In high schools it is usually that part of the total curriculum which is referred to as general education. It is not at all new in elementary schools where it has been practiced in some places under such names as, "centers of interest," "areas of living," and the like, for over 30 years. A small number of high schools, as represented partly by the "Eight Year Study," have experimented with it for about half that time.

The core curriculum at the secondary level is usually organized on the basis of units or problems. These may be on such subjects as family living, housing, our community, civil liberties, unemployment, and others. At either level of education, the core becomes the unifying center "from which all specializations stem, find their relatedness, and draw their significance."

Alberty [17] lists some of the characteristics which should be common to most core programs. These characteristics are as follows:

1. Learning activities are not restricted to conventional subject-matter lines. Two or more subjects may be combined.
2. The core class is usually scheduled for a relatively large block of time. This may include two or three usual class periods.
3. The core provides as well as encourages extensive teacher-pupil planning on the basis of needs and interests of the pupils.
4. The core encourages as well as provides for the most effective use of special aptitudes or abilities of staff personnel.

[17] Harold Alberty, *Reorganizing the High School Curriculum,* rev. ed. (New York, Macmillan, 1953), pp. 194–195.

5. The scope as well as sequence of learning activities is governed by the pupils' needs rather than the organized subject-matter of particular fields.

6. Drill periods are planned as the need develops rather than on the supposition that all pupils must have long periods of such activity.

7. The core program absorbs many of the usual homeroom responsibilities.

8. Guidance and the curriculum become more closely related.

9. The core program encourages the development of broad units of work upon which the learning activities are based.

A core program is more generally accepted and practiced in elementary and junior high schools. Ordinarily it does not comprise the entire school day. It is usually devoted to that portion of the students' program termed general education or common learnings. A group of schools surveyed by the authors indicated that time allotted to core per day varied from a maximum of five hours in 7th grades to a minimum of two hours in 9th grades. Some junior high schools organized on a core basis may eliminate 9th grade entirely. Lack of understanding about the core program and pressures upon students for high marks in academic subjects for college entrance seem to be responsible for not including 9th grade pupils. These are excellent core programs which have even more stress placed on instruction in mathematics, science, and English, but when a student's secondary school record is evaluated for college admission, marks in these specific areas are not always clearly defined. Because of this a number of schools reporting core programs really mean that a "combination of courses" are taught in a two- or three-hour block or at least a multiple-period arrangement. Providing an honest effort to correlate courses is made and properly taught, this is a fine step toward achieving a core program in the future. Good examples of correlation, fused courses, and problem-centered approaches can be found to some extent in most schools.

Grace S. Wright [18] of the U.S. Office of Education reported in a 1958 study of core and block-time programs in junior high schools that the number of block-time classes had doubled since a study made in 1950.

An example of how a junior high school might organize on the basis of a core curriculum is given in the table below. The time listed as core would refer to that portion of the pupils' program commonly referred to as required general education. The larger time-block for this part of the pupils' program will give ample opportunity to devote to field trips, library work, films, discussions of films, research, preparation, and presentation of reports of the research. These activities often require extra time. The periods of the day devoted to other activities usually do not require extra time.

[18] Grace S. Wright, *Block-Time Classes and the Core Program in the Junior High School* (Washington, D.C., U.S. Office of Education, Bulletin No. 6, 1958).

Table 9-1. Core Program—Junior High School, Daily Time Schedule (6-hour day)

Grade	Core	Additional Required Subjects	Electives
7	English, Social Science, Science, Math 4 Hours	Health & Physical Education, Foreign Language 2 Hours	0 Hours
8	Same as Above 3 Hours	Health & Physical Educ., Science Lab., Shop, Homemaking 2 Hours	Art, Foreign Languages, Science, etc. 1 Hour
9	Same as Above 2 Hours	Health & Physical Educ., Industrial Arts, Homemaking, Science Lab. 2 Hours	Added Major Subject e.g. Math, Foreign Language 2 Hours

The Experience or Activity Curriculum

The most important element of this type of curriculum is the increased emphasis upon building a learning program around the pupil. The first and classic example of a school in America to function under this curriculum pattern was the Laboratory School at the University of Chicago. Here, as early as 1896, John and Mary Dewey established a curriculum which was based on needs and interests of pupils. As pupils' needs and interests were identified, activities and experiences were planned through which these would be fulfilled. Oftentimes one activity would lead to further activities, each building more understanding and offering satisfaction in the development of the pupil at a time when he was ready for and in need of the answers to his problems.

The activity or experience curriculum has not met with wide acceptance largely because the subject organization is so well entrenched and the greater share of administrators and teachers feel more sure of themselves teaching the way they were taught, which for the most part was based on the subject-matter type of organization. Too, there has been the prevailing misconception that this curriculum pattern is weighted heavily toward mere physical activity. If children did things, were kept active, it was thought that education was taking place and the outcome was good. This idea, of course, failed to include the second part of the activity, the *intellectualizing* phase, or making use of what was learned. How the activity affected him or what it meant in terms of past and future experience are the important phases of the activity curriculum that so many teachers fail to incorporate into this type of teaching or learning experience.

There are many experiences in a learning situation that need not be first-hand or direct. Today a large share of school children come to school with a background of many first-hand experiences that need not be repeated. Experiences of a vicarious nature, such as those gained through pictures, demonstrations, recordings, or reading may well be the stimuli the individual needs to motivate his desire to solve the problems at hand. It is absurd to believe that *all* experiences must demand real materials in real life situations. This, in addition to being impractical, is psychologically unsound.

A study of recent literature concerned with curriculum, courses of study, and teaching guides indicates that more and more elementary schools and a few scattered high schools are making greater use of the activity or experience curriculum on the ground that it is fundamentally sound pedagogy and in accord with what is known about child growth and development.

Bossing and Cramer [19] writing about experience learning state:

Experience learning is based upon a recognition that learning can be effective only when the pupil has a purpose in learning. He can have such purpose, or motivation, only when he understands why, in a given situation, he should learn. It is generally accepted that genuine motivation for learning must be related to situations in which the learner has an immediate interest and finds a personal significance. The curriculum that considers vital personal and social and related societal concerns will be most likely to challenge the interest of the learner and provide effective learning situations.

In the experience or activity curriculum much use is made of such varied teaching materials and equipment as movable furniture, appropriate audio-visual aids, newspapers and magazines, living specimens, and the like. Group activities are an essential part of this type of organization.

Certainly here is a special need for teachers who have broad general education, a real understanding of pupils, a knowledge of guidance, skill in presentation of materials, and "a large measure of courage." Possibly the most important and critical task for the teacher is that of attempting to balance the intellectual needs of the learner with his social needs. If this is not done, chaos can take over, and the real goals of education are lost.

[19] Nelson R. Bossing and Roscoe V. Cramer, *The Junior High School* (Boston, Houghton Mifflin, 1965), p. 127.

Some representative problems which have been used to guide pupils and teachers in implementing the experience curriculum are listed here to give a clearer meaning of this type of organization.

1. Making a survey of a community to learn the needs for schools, churches, recreational centers and shopping facilities.
2. Organizing a student council.
3. Publishing a school newspaper.
4. Making a survey of job opportunities and training necessary for these jobs.
5. Making a survey of slum areas to determine needs for action in new housing and slum clearance.
6. Making a survey of recreational facilities and to what extent they are used and abused to determine better attitudes toward conservation of our natural resources.

On occasion the teacher may be more successful in structuring learning activities to provide answers to questions pupils ask. A few representative questions are listed for examples.

1. How can I better understand the world about me? How can I solve problems which are close to me because of the world about me?
2. How can I develop interests in the things about me, such as art, literature, nature, and appreciate them more?
3. What must I know to provide for good family relations?
4. How can I better understand politics in my community and state and work to make government operations more democratic?

A school's curriculum built around problems and questions listed above would most certainly be termed functional. It would encourage pupils to study issues which are closely related to them and to their environment.

A curriculum organized on the activity or experience approach demands that teachers are willing to experiment. For the most part, the learning experiences must be wisely selected and directed in order for the pupil to have evidence upon which to reach conclusions and make and test assumptions in his environment. This sort of learning requires action by pupils. This action almost always affects behavior, and this changing behavior is a measure of the maturity or intellectual growth of the pupils.

USING THE CURRICULUM IN TEACHING

The teacher who faces the practical task of teaching the 30 or more children who face him daily is the one who must translate the curriculum into action—put it to work, in other words. In some instances, far too many, the teacher relies entirely upon the textbook, teaching it from cover to cover. If the text is a superior one, such practice is not too bad, but it certainly is not consistent with modern educational thinking.

In other instances, the textbook is used as a guide, with supplementary material of many types, but a formal course of study or an official guide prepared by administrators, supervisors, and teachers is followed. This may include the aims, the expected outcomes, and the scope and nature of the materials studied, with suggestions as to suitable instructional aids, texts, supplementary reading, activities, teaching methods, and measurement of achievement.

Recently, however, the teacher is likely to find an outline of units to help him organize his own methods and materials. Through the years the term *unit* has been defined in terms of many different points of emphasis such as subject matter, process, experience, and source or resource. Having so many definitions served to confuse rather than make clear the best practices in organizing teaching and learning experiences. Burton [20] points out that "a unit is any combination of subject-matter content and outcomes and thought processes into learning experiences suited to the maturity and needs (personal and social) of the learners, all combined into a whole with internal integrity determined by immediate and ultimate goals." He further states:

The education of *little children,* of *beginners* on almost any level, and of all classes *in the area of general education* will proceed best via units wherein the purposes, problems, interests, and "felt needs" of the learners largely determine the amount and complexity of subject matter to be included and the degree of attention to be given to the study or thought processes; wherein direct experience predominates over the vicarious.

The education of students who have *adequate reading ability,* who have achieved sufficient maturity to be able to *learn through verbal abstractions,* and who are entering upon *areas of specialization* which involve a look to the future will proceed best via units wherein ultimate social goals and more remote personal goals, with due regard for the necessity for challenge now, will largely determine the amount and complexity of subject matter and the degree of attention to the study of processes of learning and of thought; wherein greater use will be made of vicarious experiences.

When we consider the unit in terms of what Burton suggests, it is much easier to understand how to organize the subject matter and the processes for teaching those things which will bring about the desired outcomes in the individual. These outcomes should be concerned with first— those things which we might identify as understandings, attitudes, values, and meanings, and second—with what makes for effective habits of logical thought and problem-solving.

The extent to which a teacher will use the unit depends upon the individuals in a particular class—how much information they already possess, the availability of the materials, the need and method by which a teacher can involve the group into the learning activities suggested, and,

[20] Burton, *op. cit.,* p. 329.

of course, the background, training, and ability of the teacher. There should be no hard and fast rule as to method. What is an extremely effective method in one situation may prove least effective in another. The important thing is to keep oneself reminded of methods which are proving successful in accomplishing the outcomes established for that particular group of individuals.

This brief survey of the chief types of modern curricula and the units through which they may be made effective will give the student an introduction to some important basic philosophies concerning the learning process. Much study will be given to these matters during his later years of preparation for actual teaching, and he will need to be familiar with them in considerable detail.

Some schools may use one approach to learning; others, another one; still others a combination of several. The student who gains a reasonable mastery of them during his college experiences should be able to adjust himself satisfactorily to local requirements.

ORGANIZING FOR CURRICULUM STUDY AND DEVELOPMENT

It is not difficult for the beginner to see that in light of the educational philosophy herein presented the teacher must be the key person in any process of curriculum development. Time is long since past when it was considered justifiable for a superintendent to say, "I and my assistants went into our 'sanctum sanctorum' and made a course of study for our county," and yet this is what was said at a large professional meeting where the author was in the audience. What a travesty on democracy! What an authoritarian type of set-up!

Nearly all educational literature now emphasizes the point that the development of a curriculum should be a highly co-operative process but that the teacher must be at the center of all such efforts. Actually the whole staff of the school must participate. The pupils should be taken into partnership in the task, too, and their wants and needs can be brought to the attention of the larger group by the teachers who work most closely with them.

Experimental activities carried on in the classroom and promising developments throughout the system or an entire state should be collected and brought to the attention of the directing agencies, which may be a state committee, a county committee, or one for a particular system. Here they will be evaluated and accepted or rejected.

There is a trend, especially in larger school systems and in many counties, toward establishing a "curriculum materials center." Such a center serves many purposes for teachers. First, it is a depository for display of new textbooks, teaching materials, and projects. This alone stimulates teachers to keep up to date in conducting learning experiences. Secondly, teachers are encouraged to contribute displays to the center. These may be projects or activity units which have proven successful in a particular unit of study. Also, teachers may borrow materials from the center at a time when they are most needed for a class. Further, teachers are permitted to work in the center to prepare materials peculiar to their instructional needs. The center is usually staffed and equipped to offer assistance to all personnel.

The Use of Consultants

In many cases, where funds permit, it will be highly desirable to employ experts in curriculum planning who can serve as consultants or advisers. They may serve in particular subject-matter areas, such as science, art, or music. The city of Detroit employs an anthropologist to assist in developing a program of intergroup education. Sometimes, too, an expert may be called in to direct the entire project. These individuals may come from state departments of education, college or university departments of education, or other school systems. In large cities a permanent director of curriculum planning is frequently employed.

The Community Can Help Also

All too frequently in curriculum work, little or no use is made of important individuals and resources in the community. If a new curriculum in industrial education is being developed, certainly it is highly desirable to secure all the assistance possible from agencies that employ the graduates of the school. The same technique of seeking co-operation will apply to other aspects of the curriculum. Civic and professional leaders, PTA groups, and others who may have much to contribute should be called upon for help. It is most unfortunate that greater use of local resources has not been made. At the very least, it is public relations at its best.

Workshops and Conferences

In many school systems, curriculum-construction workshops have been organized to assist those who are participating. Here ideas and experiences may be shared, and groups work on their own particular problems under the guidance of experts. Again these may be held by and in the school system or at some outside educational institution. In either event, participants work under the guidance of experts and consultants.

Better schools are making a practice of scheduling two or three in-service meeting days each semester for all teachers. These are spaced regularly on the calendar for the school year. On such occasions group conferences and workshops are planned for the staff. Leadership may come from the local system or from nearby higher education institutions. Meetings are keyed to specific curriculum problems and the improvement of instruction.

Many school systems are finding it advantageous to have a certain number of curriculum committees operating throughout the summer. The most able teachers are employed during the vacation months to revise and develop curricula.

Finally, the over-all committee will bring all the work to a point where publication is advisable. This is often printed or set up in somewhat temporary form in which it can be tried for a year or longer, after which it is revised and general publication carried out, following suggestions resulting from actual trial. It is important to remember, however, that no curriculum is ever static. It must be continually revised and adapted to new conditions. Curriculum revision, indeed, is a continuous process.

QUESTIONS AND PROJECTS

1. Study the school laws of your own state and of one or more others to see what is required to be taught. Discuss your findings with the class and note the problems involved.

2. Why is it necessary to re-evaluate a school's curriculum periodically? What ways should be used for determining what the curriculum should include?

3. Compare the four curricular patterns described and evaluate each as to its ability to fulfill the obligation of "meeting the needs of the learner."

4. List some behavior patterns that you believe should be acquired by elementary school pupils, by secondary school pupils. Which of the four types of curricula do you believe would accomplish this best? Why?

5. Secure a copy of *Schools for the Sixties* and prepare an evaluation of the various recommendations listed.

6. Suggest ways of employing the experience curriculum in the subject or grade level you wish to teach.

7. Investigate the current professional journals or look in your curriculum laboratory to find arguments for and against organizing a school on the basis of core curriculum.

8. Secure a copy of the curriculum structure from the school where you graduated. Analyze it as to type, according to what you have gained from this chapter.

9. Describe some of the ways in which the curriculum for a rural school should probably differ from that of a school in a large urban center.

10. Analyze the chart on pages 338 and 339 in William H. Burton, *The Guidance of Learning Activities,* 3rd ed. (New York, Appleton-Century-Crofts, 1962). What is the purpose and significance of this chart? What are the chief differences between teaching elementary and secondary pupils? Which suggested type of approach to teaching would provide more meaningful and more lasting learning? Why?

11. In the same book referred to in question 10 refer to the flow chart on page 282. Study this chart, and write an experience which you have had that followed the ideas presented in the chart. Relate to as many of the steps as possible. Was this experience a learning experience similar to all your past learning? Explain.

AUDIO-VISUAL AIDS

MOTION PICTURES (16 MM)

And No Bells Ring—National Association of Secondary School Principals, National Education Association, 1201 16th St. N.W., Washington, D.C., 56 min., sd., b&w. Presents a review of the "Trump Report" on reorganizing the secondary school staff. Discusses the flexibility of the program and its advantages for development of individual interest and abilities both in pupils and teachers.

Answering the Child's Why—Encyclopaedia Britannica Films, 1150 Wilmette Ave., Wilmette, Ill., 13 min., sd., b&w. Dramatizes actual situations in which youngsters meet with positive or negative attitudes toward their questions, and suggests the resulting effects on their personalities.

Biology Plus—University of Illinois, Urbana, Illinois, 38 min., sd., b&w. Presents highlights of an experimental biology class for academically talented pupils. Shows early class meeting to relate pupils to the experimental study of living things. Describes how pupil projects develop.

Broader Concepts of Curriculum—McGraw Hill Book Co., Text-Film Dept., 330 West 42nd St., N.Y., 19 min., sd., b&w. Discusses the responsibility of the school in developing competencies in four major areas: civic, vocational, family living, and health and physical fitness.

Characteristics of a Core Program—Bureau of Publications, Teachers College, Columbia University, 525 West 120th St., New York, N.Y., 20 min., sd., b&w. This film is designed to explain to prospective teachers, teachers in service, and interested laymen some distinguishing characteristics of high school levels. An interested parent visits her son's school and observes a core class at work on a unit of study.

Children Are Creative—Bailey Films, Inc., 6509 De Longpre Ave., Hollywood 28, Calif., 11 min., sd., color. Stresses the importance of the child's innate creative ability. Demonstrates that the work of the teacher is to stimulate and develop the child's creativity by providing interesting environment and introducing new techniques and stimulating ideas.

Children Learning by Experience—United World Films, 1445 Park Avenue, New York. 30 min., sd., b&w. Shows young children in everyday situations which illustrate the urge to learn practicing simple skills, understanding the world around, learning second-hand, and learning through imagination.

Developing Pupil Interest—McGraw-Hill Book Co., Text-Film Dept., 330 West 42nd St., New York, N.Y., 16 min., sd., b&w. Presents a typical conventional, teacher-dominated, lesson-hearing type of recitation, and shows effects on student attitudes, responses and learning.

Elementary Teacher: Beginning Student Teaching—Indiana University, Audio-Visual Center, Bloomington, Ind., 10 min., sd., b&w. Discusses the training and functions of the teacher in a world of rapid change. Shows Janet, a student teacher, as she acquaints herself with a classroom, the school, its program, and experiences of practice teaching. Uses flashbacks to emphasize the points being discussed by the teaching supervisor and Janet during an evaluation of the latter's progress.

Freedom to Learn—National Education Association, 1201 16th St., N.W., Washington, D.C., 27½ min., sd., b&w. and/or color. Shows that modern schools prepare our children to assume their responsibilities as good citizens. It explains that respect for facts, constant search for the truth, and knowledge of the world are essential in this preparation.

Fundamental Skills in a Unit of Work—Bailey Films, Inc., 6509 De Longpre Ave., Hollywood, Calif. 20 min., sd., b&w. Shows how a skillful teacher can arouse the interest of the class and guide them in developing and carrying out a unit of work.

Helping Children Discover Arithmetic—Wayne University, Detroit, Mich., 15 min., sd., b&w. Pictures the progress of a third-grade class from the introduction of an arithmetic process new to them—borrowing in subtraction—to the point where the pupils understand and are able to work problems relating to the process. Utilizes the "discovery" method.

How Good Are Our Schools?—NEA, Washington, D.C., 28 min., sd., b&w. Summarizes Dr. Conant's study of the American High School Today. Points out the needs and gives examples of effective educational programs.

Introduction to Student Teaching—Indiana University, Audio-Visual Center, Bloomington Ind., 20 min., sd., b&w. Shows the activities of Bill, Nancy, and Carol during the early weeks of their student teaching experiences. They get acquainted with the school personnel and policies, become accustomed to handling routine classroom matters, become familiar with a wide variety of instructional materials, and learn as much as they can about the pupils. Designed primarily for student teachers on the secondary level.

Learning Is Searching—New York University, Washington Square, New York, N.Y., 30 min., sd., b&w. Shows how a 3rd-grade class carries out its studies of a unit on "Man's Use of Tools." Defines the terms that will be used in direct experiences and field trips and describes the solutions to problems. Concludes with exhibits and presentations that are made at the end of the unit.

Learning Through Co-operative Planning—Bureau of Publications, Teachers College, Columbia University, 525 W. 120th St., New York, N.Y., 20 min., sd., b&w. Shows how elementary school children can acquire one of the most important skills of our modern times—effective participation as members of a group.

Motivating the Class—McGraw-Hill Book Co., Text-Film Dept., 330 West 42nd St., New York, N.Y., 19 min., sd., b&w. A student teacher of mathematics learns that motivation is basic to good teaching and that for the work to be meaningful to young people it must be related to their interest and experiences.

Philosophies of Education: Education for Life Adjustment—Indiana University, A-V Center, Bloomington, Indiana, 29 min., sd., b&w. States the purposes and ideas of life adjustment education, and relates these to situations which will occur in the lives of the pupils.

Philosophies of Education: Education as Intellectual Discipline—Indiana University, A-V Center, Bloomington, Ind., 29 min., sd., b&w. Comments on the importance of a disciplined mind, and gives methods of obtaining intellectual discipline in a democratic society.

Promoting Pupil Adjustment—McGraw-Hill Book Co., Text-Film Dept., 330 West 42nd St., New York, N.Y., 20 min., sd., b&w. Shows how important it is for the secondary school teacher to stress the social and emotional as well as the intellectual growth of her pupils. Points out that effective classroom learning is closely associated with the teacher's awareness of individual differences.

The Search: Accelerated Study—Young America Films, Inc., 18 East 41st St., New York 17, N.Y., 25 min., sd., b&w. This film demonstrates new understanding of language and techniques for teaching English and explains how to learn to speak our complicated language in eight weeks at the English Language Institute, University of Michigan. Suggests implications which this program holds for changes in the teaching of English at schools and colleges across the country.

Three R's Plus—McGraw-Hill Book Co., Text-film Dept., 330 West 42nd St., New York, N.Y., 27 min., sd., b&w. Offers a graphic, over-all view of the teaching program, the curriculum, materials, and techniques in the elementary school. Natural classroom scenes point up all the extra goals, subjects, methods, and special programs which have been added to the elementary curriculum in the last few years.

We Plan Together—Bureau of Publications, Teachers College, Columbia University, 525 W. 120th St., New York, N.Y., 20 min., sd., b&w. Designed to help teachers gain a better understanding of co-operative planning between teachers and students. Shows a grade 11 group planning and working together in their core class over a period of several months.

FILMSTRIPS

Core-Curriculum Class in Action—Wayne University, Detroit, Mich., 50 fr., si., b&w. Presents the work of a 9th grade class organized under the core-curriculum pattern. The filmstrip shows the class as it is organized, its activities, and its evaluation.

Deciding What to Teach—National Education Association, 1201 16th St., N.W., Washington, D.C., 107 fr., sd. (record), color. Presents a discussion of issues such as establishing priorities and balance in the curriculum, selecting and organizing content, and determining the school's role in dealing with national problems.

Directions for the Future—NEA, Washington, D.C., 115 fr., color, sd., 33⅓ r.p.m. record. Presents background ideas for planning elementary instructional programs.

Guidelines for Decision on Issue in Elementary Education—NEA, Washington, D.C., 134 fr., color, sd., 33⅓ r.p.m. record. Deals with contemporary problems in elementary education.

Planning and Organizing for Teaching—NEA, Washington, D.C., 110 fr., sd. (record), color. Analyzes three sets of related problems: organizing the curriculum; organizing the school and the classroom; and organizing personnel, space, and materials.

Making Teaching Effective—Ohio State University, University Hall, Columbus, O., 1952, 40 fr., si., b&w. Shows the curriculum atmosphere in which audio-visual materials are most effective.

FURTHER READINGS

Alberty, Harold, and Elsie J. Alberty, *Reorganizing the High School Curriculum,* 3rd ed. (New York, Macmillan, 1962).

Alcorn, Marvin D., and James M. Linley, *Issues in Curriculum Development* (Yonkers, N.Y., World Book, 1959).

Anderson, Vernon E., *Principles and Procedures in Curriculum Development,* 2nd ed. (New York, Ronald Press, 1965).

Association for Supervision and Curriculum Development, *Changing Curriculum Content,* Report of the Conference on Curriculum Content, Chicago, October 19–20, 1963. Prepared by William M. Alexander for ASCD Commission on Current Curriculum Developments (Washington, D.C., ASCD, 1964).

Association for Supervision and Curriculum Development, *Individualizing Instruction,* The ASCD 1964 Yearbook Committee (Washington, D.C., ASCD and NEA, 1964).

Association for Supervision and Curriculum Development, *One Hundred Years of Curriculum Improvement, 1857–1957* (Washington, D.C., NEA, 1957).

Association for Supervision and Curriculum Development, NEA, Washington, D.C.

1956 Yearbook, *What Shall the Schools Teach?*
1957 Yearbook, *Research for Curriculum Improvement*
1958 Yearbook, *A Look at Continuity in the School Program*
1960 Yearbook, *Leadership for Improving Instruction*
1961 Yearbook, *Balance in the Curriculum*
1963 Yearbook, *New Insights and the Curriculum*
1964 Yearbook, *Individualizing Instruction*

Bair, Medill, and Richard G. Woodward, *Team Teaching in Action* (Boston, Houghton Mifflin, 1964).

Beauchamp, George A., *Planning the Elementary School Curriculum* (Boston, Allyn and Bacon, 1956).

Bereday, George Z. F., and J. A. Lauwerys, eds., *The Secondary School Curriculum: Yearbook of Education* (Yonkers, N.Y., World Book, 1958).

Bossing, Nelson L., and Roscoe V. Cramer, *The Junior High School* (Boston, Houghton Mifflin, 1965).

Brown, B. Frank, *The Nongraded High School* (Englewood Cliffs, N.J., Prentice-Hall, 1963).

Bureau of Educational Research and Service, *Theory into Practice* (Columbus, Ohio, Ohio State University, Five issues annually).

Burton, William H., *The Guidance of Learning Activities,* 3rd ed. (New York, Appleton-Century-Crofts, 1962).

Conant, James B., *The American High School Today* (New York, McGraw-Hill, 1959).

Dull, Ronald C., *Curriculum Improvement: Decision-Making and Process,* (Boston, Allyn and Bacon, 1964).

Educational Policies Commission, *The Central Purposes of American Education,* (Washington, D.C., NEA, 1961).

Fleming, Robert, ed., *Curriculum for Today's Boys and Girls* (Columbus, Ohio, Merrill, 1963).

Hansen, Carl F., *The Four-Track Curriculum in Today's High Schools* (Englewood Cliffs, N.J., Prentice-Hall, 1964).

McNally, Harold J., A. Harry Passow, and associates, *Improving the Quality of Public School Programs* (New York, Teachers College, Columbia University, 1960).

National Education Association, The Project on the Instructional Program of the Public Schools.

Major Reports:

Goodlad, John I., *Planning and Organizing for Teaching* (Washington, D.C., NEA, 1963).

Schools for the Sixties (New York, McGraw-Hill, 1963).

Auxiliary Report:

The Scholars Look at the Schools: A Report of the Disciplines Seminar (Washington, D.C., NEA, 1962).

National Education Association, Project on Instructional Program of the Public Schools, *Deciding What to Teach*. Prepared by Dorothy M. Fraser. (Washington, D.C., NEA, 1963).

Oliver, Albert I., *Curriculum Improvement, A Guide to Problems, Principles and Procedures* (New York, Dodd, Mead and Co., 1965).

Passow, A. Harry, ed., *Nurturing Individual Potential: Papers and Reports from the ASCD Seventh Curriculum Research Institute* (Washington, D.C., ASCD and NEA, 1964).

Ragan, William B., *Modern Elementary Curriculum*, rev. ed. (New York, Holt, Rinehart and Winston, 1960).

Rasmussen, Margaret, ed., *Individualizing Education* (Washington, D.C., ACEI, 1964).

Schuster, Albert H., and Milton E. Ploghoft, *The Emerging Elementary Curriculum* (Columbus, Ohio, Merrill, 1963).

Stratemeyer, Florence B., H. L. Forkner, M. G. McKim, and A. H. Passow, *Developing a Curriculum for Modern Living* (New York, Teachers College, Columbia University, 1957).

Trump, J. Lloyd, *Images of the Future*, National Association of Secondary School Principals (Washington, D.C., NEA, 1959).

10

Cocurricular Activities

PREVIEW

▶ The term cocurricular, taking the place of extracurricular and similar usages, refers to a minimum of separation between regular classwork and such activities as the following:
1. Those pertaining to guidance and school services.
2. Those pertaining to clubs.
3. Those pertaining to music.
4. Those pertaining to athletics.
5. Those pertaining to journalism and speaking.
6. Auxiliary activities.

▶ Most schools face two major problems in connection with their cocurricular activities:
1. How to get reasonable participation by all students.
2. How to prevent certain students from participating in too many activities.

▶ Criticisms most frequently made of the cocurricular programs are:
1. They cost too much for the average student.
2. Too much money is spent on too few students and activities.
3. Activities, such as athletics, may frequently be lost to the control of the school.
4. Social life is overemphasized to the disadvantage of academic achievement.
5. Some common activities fail to contribute to the attainment of the aims of education.

▶ A basic principle to be kept in mind to help in meeting the criticisms is that those activities that are educationally worthwhile should be carried on at public expense and be freed from the pressures inherent in public spectacles for which admissions are charged.

▶ There is every indication that the gap between the curricular and the cocurricular will continue to narrow through:
1. Credit given for cocurricular participation.
2. Greater use of the activity period.
3. More financial support from tax money.
4. Greater use of student planning in classroom teaching.
5. The placing of many activities on a regular class basis.

In contrast to the school two or three decades ago wherein there operated a truly *extra* program of activities, today these activities and services have become an integral part of the total learning situation. A few years ago it was quite customary to designate any informal or pupil-inspired activities as extra-curricular. At that time they were usually considered non-academic or semi-academic, and thus they were not of sufficient importance to schedule during the regular school day. It became common and accepted practice to provide for such activities after school was dismissed or on some occasions before the formal school day began.

It should be acknowledged, though, that in spite of the general acceptance of the more modern philosophy mentioned above, the older term extra-curricular still persists in the terminology used by the great majority of high schools.

THE NEW PHILOSOPHY

This modern concept of education insists that the so-called cocurricular activities must really parallel those of the academic curriculum. A careful examination of many a good school's cocurricular program will reveal how much of it is an outgrowth or an extension of what is being studied in the formal classroom. Teachers are frequently approached by groups of pupils who seek to establish an organization, usually a club, that would permit those who have a real interest in the subject to pursue its study or investigate further some of the applications of a particular classroom exercise. For example, a lesson on electronics as it relates to sound reproduction may be the beginning of a radio and television club or a hi-fi club, which meets regularly to work on the assembly of a radio, television, or hi-fi record player, report on current developments in sound communication or develop skills in testing and repairing such equipment. Thus, an opportunity will be provided for pupils to gain greater knowledge of electronic equipment through intensive research which would not have been possible in the regular class.

Staff Responsibilities

Much is written about the importance of having students actively participating in the cocurricular program, but there are times when faculty members too, must be urged to enter into these activities as advisors. In recent years there has been more and more stress placed upon having the individual preparing to teach becoming a subject specialist. In order to do so the person has not had time and, in a few cases, has been discouraged from entering into cocurricular activities himself. Also, a large number of teachers, especially on the secondary level, are not given an opportunity in their undergraduate work to pursue courses which give them sufficient background and appreciation of what values are derived from such an activity program. Those entering teaching must recognize that the school has accepted, or has had given to it, much of the responsibility for the personal and social development of its pupils. The teacher might well view his role in these cocurricular activities as a real opportunity to commit himself to better understanding adolescents, their interests, and their needs in order to better relate the academic program in a more meaningful way to those in his class.

Today it is possible to find cocurricular programs well established on all levels of education, with each activity making a contribution to the over-all education and development of those individuals who wish to associate themselves with others who have the same general interests. A look at the modern elementary school will make one aware of how closely knit the curricular and cocurricular activities really are, and it is entirely possible that no distinction whatever will be discernible. A large majority of junior high schools and a very considerable number of senior high schools regularly provide scheduled periods during the school day for cocurricular activities. Necessity has in part been the motivating factor here, it must be admitted, because with pupil transportation becoming so common, it is obvious that participating in after-school affairs is out of the question for many, if not most, students. Finally, a few colleges do provide for extracurricular activities (they still use the term) during the regular periods of the day. In many colleges, however, and in the graduate schools in particular, many students find themselves too busy with study and investigation to take part in activities outside of their regular classes.

WHO SHOULD PARTICIPATE?

In the early history of extracurricular activities frequently only the better pupils were allowed to participate or, to put it another way,

Architects-Engineers: Caudill, Rowlett, Scott &
Associates, Bryan, Texas, and Perkins
& Will, Chicago, Illinois.
Photograph by Hedrich-Blessing, Chicago.

The student center is the "hub" of the Norman, Oklahoma High School.

scholastic eligibility was required. If it was an athletic activity, only those who were extremely skilled were permitted to take part. Today there is a trend, and a very worthwhile one, to get every member of the school population into some cocurricular activity. In one junior high school where one of the authors was a staff member, the slogan was: "An activity for every boy and girl and a boy and girl for every activity." Statistics for this program, which was in fact cocurricular, showed that the idea was a very practical one.

Secondary schools, in particular, are faced with two major problems: (1) how to get participation by every student, and (2) how to prevent too many activities for certain students.

It has long been a practice in some institutions to require that every student participate regularly in some cocurricular activity, just as he might be required to choose one subject from a group of electives. In such instances, credit toward graduation is generally given for such participation.

Other schools, and their number is fairly large, may leave it up to the student to choose or not to choose an activity, which very likely in such a situation would be classed as extracurricular and would probably be held after the regular class schedule had ended. Actually, if the school is able to secure participation of 85 percent or more of the student body, it is considered excellent. On the other hand, 70 percent or less can be a hazard to the entire program of activities.

Very often the problem of regulating the participation of those who (as a result of their abilities, the pressures of parents and friends, and the urgings of sponsors) get involved in far too many things for their own good is a very difficult matter. The method usually adopted is a point system where, for example, one point may be given to the student who is an ordinary member of an organization, whereas the president of the group may receive three or more points and other officers two. A limit is then set on the total number of points any student may obtain, thus limiting total participation to some reasonable extent. Such a system, while reasonably effective, requires careful faculty supervision. Probably one of the best solutions to the problem of unbalanced or overparticipation is found in an adequate guidance set-up where counselors are alert to the complete school program of those students whom it is their obligation and privilege to counsel.

Another factor that limits actual participation in many aspects of the cocurricular program is that of the expense involved. To many children who come from families without adequate financial resources, this is a serious matter. The expense of sending their children to high school is for many families a major problem. Clothes must be better, and they cost more for an older child. Lunches are not cheap, and the family is without the earning capacity of the youth. Then, when he must be provided with money for club dues, for activity tickets which may cost several dollars, for subscriptions to school newspapers, admissions to dances, parties, and the like, it is quite obvious that he will be left out of many things which could be of much value. A good many schools are now facing the situation squarely and saying that anything that is properly carried on by the school as a cocurricular activity and is educationally valuable should be free and supported by the tax program. Otherwise, they allege, it should not be done as a school function. Where this has been really tried it has worked well, and many of the evils inherent in such activities as athletics disappear almost overnight. This is one of the ways in which the schools can serve all the children and the democratic ideal.

PRINCIPLES AFFECTING COCURRICULAR ACTIVITIES

If a school is to provide a program of cocurricular activities which will serve to produce well-adjusted personalities, develop character

Photograph by Robert Galbraith, Jamaica, N.Y.
Courtesy: The Board of Education of the
City of New York. Architects: Katz, Waisman,
Weber, Strauss, and Joseph Blumenkranz, consultant.

Playground equipment should provide children with opportunities for proper muscular development, poise, and balance. Public School 197, Queens, New York.

and leadership ability, there are certain principles that should guide its organization:

1. The program of activities should be such that every pupil of the school would be afforded an opportunity to participate.
2. The pupil should be limited to membership in only as many activities as he is able to carry in terms of health and study requirements.
3. The program of activities should be constructive, well balanced, and the result of pupil-teacher-administrator planning.
4. The activities should contribute toward achievement of desirable social, civic, and moral values.

5. The activities should be in accordance with the basic philosophy, ideals, and practices of the school.
6. The activities should represent the co-operative efforts of pupils and teachers.
7. The activity program should be organized and conducted under democratic rules of procedure.
8. Activities should be scheduled in such a manner as to provide a definite time and place in or near the school building when and where the meetings are to take place.
9. A minimum amount of expense should be connected with membership in any activity. (Dues and expenses for club activities often limit membership and defeat the purpose of the activity.)
10. Sponsors for each activity should be selected carefully. A sponsor should have interest in the activity as well as the necessary educational and experiential background in carrying on the activity with the pupils. It is good practice to invite pupils to share in choosing a sponsor for the activity in certain cases where it is possible, for example, hobby groups, student council, and assembly programs.

TYPES OF COCURRICULAR ACTIVITIES

School administrators and teachers agree there is much value derived from a rich cocurricular program for the pupils, but it is quite difficult to get agreement on which type or kind of activity contributes to a particular type of growth for the pupil. For example, the athletic coach will be able to cite many examples to prove that being a member of an athletic team develops leadership and the spirit of co-operation. Another faculty member who sponsors the student council will list these same qualities as outcomes from membership on this governing body. Thus it is evident that classification of cocurricular activities cannot be made on the basis of purpose and function without some overlapping.

If we agree that all student activities should be participated in on the basis of interest, and that these activities will contribute to a better spirit of co-operation along with promoting the ideals of the democratic way of life, it is only for purposes of discussion that we attempt to group the various kinds of activities. Each activity may make a unique contribution as well as fulfilling a similar function and purpose of another. The groupings for a basis of discussion are activities pertaining to:

Guidance and school services
Clubs
Music
Athletics
Journalism and speaking
Auxiliary activities

Guidance and Service Activities

All of the types of cocurricular activities mentioned above will contribute to the guidance of the pupil, but most schools believe there are certain ones which are directly responsible for this function. The most common among these are homeroom and class or grade organizations.

It is not unusual either for a boy to find such real interest in a photography club, for example, that it will result in a vocational choice for him; the same may be said for certain other club activities as well. Particularly, too, do such organizations serve to develop such lifetime hobbies as swimming, hiking, chess, and many others.

Homerooms. Whether a school is large or small, it is common practice today to find pupils assigned to a room where they spend the school day, if in the elementary school, or a brief period in the morning, in the junior or senior high school.

For elementary school pupils, the room serves as a unit where they carry on most of their learning activities as well as being a home-away-from-home. Here, in the presence of an adult, the teacher, the pupils sense a feeling of security and begin sharing experiences and individual problems. The teacher in turn keeps them in touch with the over-all school program. Though it may appear to be only an administrative arrangement, it is truly an environment for learning. It is here that pupils have their first guidance in how to live with others and share responsibilities. It is most necessary that the teacher be vitally interested in the pupils as individuals and direct their activities into meaningful experiences. The welfare of each pupil is as important a consideration as the subject matter he learns.

Perhaps the term *homeroom* is more often used when discussing the junior and senior high school. In the junior high school much of the administrative routine is accomplished by the homeroom. Taking the attendance, making announcements, distributing report cards, discussing school policies and activities are a few of many things that are routine in the homeroom period. Besides these there is excellent opportunity for the teacher and pupil to become better acquainted. Individual problems can be discussed sympathetically and with an understanding on the part of the pupil that his homeroom teacher is close enough to him and his problem that a solution can be worked out.

All schools should develop a schedule which will afford the opportunity for a homeroom period of class length when the pupils and teacher can discuss problems of the group or those that might pertain to the whole school program. In many schools this homeroom period is given to guidance problems. Some schools encourage the pupils to determine, within limitations, the problems or subjects discussed. For example, all grade 7 homerooms may discuss problems which deal with orientation to their new surroundings, the junior high school. The topics for discussion may concern opportunities to participate in the music organizations, health and physical education programs, intramural sports, student government, art, and vocational offerings.

In grade 8, homeroom periods may be devoted in part to discussing problems dealing with educational guidance, such as study habits, and in grade 9 to vocational guidance. If the senior high school is a separate unit from junior high school, it is often a policy of the administration to discuss the curricula of the senior high school some time during the second semester of the 9th year. On many occasions prescheduling and registration may well be accomplished during the last few homeroom periods for 9th-grade pupils.

In many secondary schools, participation in student government is based upon homeroom representation. Furthermore, leadership training for student government can be enhanced by first acting in the capacity of a homeroom officer. This leads us to the second group of cocurricular activities.

The Student Council. One of the most important contributions our schools can make to society is that of making democracy work. The public schools of America have been severely criticized on occasions because it has been alleged that pupils in the schools are not taught enough about

Figure 10-1.   Services Performed by a Student Council

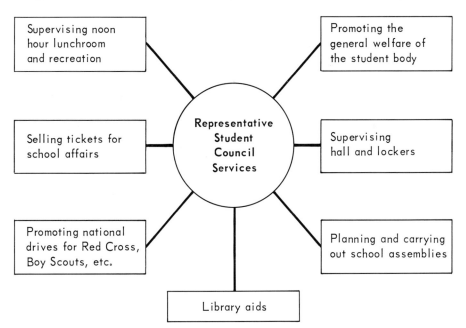

our way of governing ourselves. Besides the courses taught in American Government and Problems of Democracy, the schools are doing considerable and should do even more to encourage pupils to participate in governing themselves. One of the best ways of accomplishing an understanding of democracy in action is to provide for a self-government organization within the school, namely, the Student Council or Student Government. If properly set up, it may encourage open discussion of school problems and afford equal representation from all units within the school.

The student council should be an organization that trains individuals for co-operative living in our democratic society. It should provide the pupils with a means for practical application of subject matter taught in a course in Problems of Democracy. Besides being a parliamentary body, it is responsible for building morale within the school population. It will, by example, stimulate and promote a sense of honor and moral conduct which will effect a set of ethical values by which the students deal with one another.

In most schools today the student council is responsible for encouraging as well as regulating the over-all program of cocurricular activities. For example, many schools require that any group of students, with an interest in a particular kind of cocurricular activity, which has succeeded in selling the idea to a faculty sponsor, must submit its plan for organization to the student council for approval prior to having the activity recognized as one which contributes to the best interest of the school. If approval is granted, it may subsequently receive a charter.

It is also important to suggest here that a student council is not established in a school with the purpose of being a spy organization. It should not be controlled by the administration nor should it act as a court to try all violators of rules of good citizenship. The fewer rules and regulations a council has, the more good it can do for the student body and the administration. The one basic purpose of the council will be training citizens for living in and away from school, citizens who have respect for law and order and sense the responsibilities for participation in our form of government.

When a student council is functioning well, it necessarily senses a need to provide many services to the school's organization and administration. The services its members perform should not be the result of administrative pressures, but rather a true manifestation of a sense of duty. Any member of a governing body is a public servant, whether it be on a local or federal level. Some of the services performed by members of committees stemming from the student council are:

1. Supervision of halls and lockers.
2. Supervision of noon-hour lunchroom and recreation.
3. Library aids.

4. Selling tickets for school affairs.
5. Promoting national drives for Red Cross, Boy Scouts, etc.
6. Planning and carrying out school assemblies.
7. Promoting the general welfare of the student body.

As an example of how effective a student council could be in organizing a student body to carry out a committee's plan, the following case is cited. A student council, with the approval of the school administration, organized a committee to study the problem of vandalism occurring in and around their school. Each homeroom representative was provided with detailed information of the work of the committee. This in turn was discussed in the homeroom, and volunteers were invited to serve on sub-committee assignments. The information gathered by sub-committees was discussed by the total committee and after considerable time a "white paper" of recommendations was presented to each homeroom, to the faculty, and to the parents. The results were indeed heartening; vandalism was practically overcome. The new spirit and feeling toward the school had been accomplished by the pupils themselves, an achievement which added to their status and to the improvement of the community.

Club Activities

Almost any cocurricular activity may be considered a form of club organization. To distinguish this section on clubs from other organized cocurricular activities, one may term them *special-interest* clubs. Because they are based almost entirely on hobby ideas, their variety is nearly endless. There is no reason to believe that all schools would have the same club offerings anymore than there would be to believe the interests of pupils are always the same. It should be through pupil interest that most clubs are initiated and organized. A club should serve to promote and provide for active participation on the part of each of its members, otherwise a pupil will get little satisfaction out of belonging. For example, a school may decide there is enough real interest to establish a photography club. If this club provides an opportunity for each of its members to take, develop, and print pictures, it will satisfy the needs of most of the club members. However, if there are members of this club who have already mastered these more elementary activities and want to explore the possibilities of enlarging photos, it should also be possible for them to do some photo enlarging or their interest will wane.

When a club offers its members the satisfaction of getting something accomplished in the area of their special interests and contributes to their sense of belonging, it has served its main objectives. McKown [1] lists the following principles basic to club organization:

[1] Harry C. McKown, *Extra-Curricular Activities*, 3rd ed. (New York, Macmillan, 1952), pp. 155–161.

1. The club should be based on definite and worthy objectives.
2. The purposes and activities of the club should be those of its student members.
3. Wherever possible, club activity should grow out of curricular activities.
4. The club program should fit the local situation.
5. Provision should be made for the proper encouragement and limitation of participation.
6. Every student should belong to a club.
7. Club membership should be voluntary.
8. All students should have equal opportunities for joining clubs.
9. The club should be limited in size.
10. The club should not be considered vocational in purpose.
11. Normally, the club should be scheduled on regular school time.
12. Club meetings should usually be held on school premises.
13. Club sponsors should be carefully chosen and assigned.
14. Generally speaking, there should be no outside sponsorship.

It would be impossible to list all the club activities that might be established on the basis of pupils' wants and needs. Interest changes with time and locality. It is usually a fact, however, that, in general, one will find a close relationship between the various clubs and the curricular subjects. An example is the photography club growing out of science class, model-building out of manual arts class, or "music of the masters" out of music appreciation class.

Music Activities

It is difficult to separate curricular from cocurricular activities in the field of music because so often we see and hear organizations performing for the school or for the public. Much music instruction results from belonging to musical organizations. Many pupils, because of a real interest in music, either vocal or instrumental, belong to the organization even though a large share of work in the activity is performed beyond the regular school day.

Vocal Organizations. Chief among these music activities are the glee clubs. Usually, where enrollment is large enough, there is a separate organization for boys and for girls besides a mixed group. Further, a school may afford opportunity for choir groups. In some of the larger cities across the country, there is an all-city chorus made up of pupils from all the schools. This offers a grand opportunity for its members to get acquainted with one another and to experience working under various leaders or directors.

Instrumental Organizations. The school band is perhaps the most common and well-known of the instrumental groups. This organization is called upon for public concerts and for various school programs. In the fall, the marching band usually appears before large audiences at football games. In many states there is state-wide competition for honors in this particular activity. All of these activities as carried on in many places require a great many hours of outside-of-school-hours preparation.

It is becoming more and more common, however, to schedule the rehearsals of major musical organizations, such as the band, in regular periods during the day, sometimes two or three times a week, sometimes daily. Credit is then given toward graduation for satisfactory work, and, indeed, a great many colleges will likewise give credit for college entrance. It cannot be denied that to many of those students who are members of such organizations the values are far greater than those received from many formal academic classes. Why, then, should it not be taken seriously, given proper time on the schedule and not be merely a matter for public display? Then will it be truly cocurricular.

Most schools today will also have a symphony orchestra which will provide for those pupils who are more interested in classical and semi-classical music and who play instruments common only to the orchestra. This group also performs for many school functions. Many of its more skilled musicians will undoubtedly have opportunity to play with city symphony orchestras.

Out of these two larger instrumental organizations it is quite common to find smaller groups such as a string quartet, a trumpet trio, dance band, and symphonietta. These smaller groups are given opportunity to do some of the more advanced musical compositions and arrangements especially written for their particular instruments.

All of these activities bring together a large number of pupils having similar interests and will help them develop poise before audiences and broaden their social horizons.

Athletic Organizations

A well-organized and well-administered physical education program should provide for two types of activities: *intramural* and *interscholastic* athletics.

Intramural Athletics. The term *intramural* refers to those activities which take place within the local school. These activities emphasize participation of all pupils in the school. Rivalry runs high among the teams competing, but the emphasis is on large-scale participation rather than on always being a winner. Through this sort of competition pupils learn the rules of the game, good sportsmanship, leadership, and co-operation, as well as developing skills in their favorite sports.

Leadership training and experience is an important aspect of the intramural program. The large number of teams which can be formed for each sport offers an excellent opportunity for many students to serve as managers. For many, the responsibility of directing a team activity is very often more challenging than actual participation. Too, it provides those students less skilled in a particular sport to be closely associated with it even though they do not play.

Intramurals furnish students with much more variety than do interscholastic sports, thus a far greater number of students participate. It would be difficult to find an effective intramural organization that did not provide at least one activity for every student, regardless of ability and interest.

Junior high schools especially, should develop a comprehensive schedule of intramural offerings. For this age, student participation should be encouraged and a minimum emphasis, if any, given to interscholastic sports.

Dr. James Conant's study of the junior high school calls attention to a need for re-examination of the sports program for this age youth. He points out that far too many junior high schools overemphasize interscholastic athletics. He indicates that this defeats the established purposes for a well-rounded health and physical education program for grades 7, 8, and 9.

Interscholastic Athletics. The term *interscholastic* refers to those activities which afford competition between schools. The most common of these are football, baseball, basketball, wrestling, soccer, and track and field events. Perhaps the greatest criticism leveled at interscholastic athletics is that the major share of a school's activity fund is spent on them. When one examines the number of pupils who are talented enough to "make the team," it is often difficult to justify such a large expenditure for so few pupils.

The justification for this practice is usually stated in one or both of the following:

1. The demand is for a winning team, and that costs money.
2. The receipts from such a major sport, as football or basketball, are often sufficient to carry much of the rest of the athletic program which will not consistently draw large crowds.

The trouble all too often is that these activities, usually football, may get out of the hands of the school and be operated as a community project without any relation to the educational values involved. Large stadiums are built, games are played at night as public spectacles, some athletes are paid, postseason championship games are receiving greater and greater emphasis, and coaches who may easily become overzealous find that their tenure depends on their ability to produce winning teams.

In a recent publication, the Educational Policies Commission [2] lists eight types of bad practices in athletics:

---

[2] Educational Policies Commission, *School Athletics* (Washington, NEA, 1954), pp. 6–10.

1. Overemphasis on varsity.
2. Distortions in the program.
3. Coaches under pressure.
4. Financial woes.
5. Recruiting by colleges.
6. Involving younger children.
7. Neglecting the girls.
8. Distorting school organization.

They [3] further point out that in many schools the following may be found as false values:

1. Overemphasis on winning.
2. Glorifying star athletes.
3. Disparaging the nonathlete.
4. School games as public spectacles.

The Commission [4] is careful, on the other hand, to indicate that there are significant values in a proper interscholastic athletic program and makes the following comment:

We believe in athletics as an important part of the school physical education program. We believe that the experience of playing athletic games should be a part of the education of all children and youth who attend schools in the United States.

Participation in sound athletic programs, we believe, contributes to health and happiness, physical skill and emotional maturity, social competence and moral values.

We believe that co-operation and competition are both important components of American life. Athletic participation can help teach the values of co-operation as well as the spirit of competition. Playing hard and playing to win can help build character.

With this important statement of philosophy in mind and with the support of the athletic program coming from the school budget, many of the undesirable pressures will disappear and interscholastic sports can be run so that they will really contribute to the all-around development of young Americans. No other point of view seems justifiable.

Journalism

The major emphasis in journalism has been on the school newspaper and annual or yearbook. Other publications, such as student handbooks, magazines, and programs for student events and activities are included. More recently radio and television script-writing have been added to this group and have taken on much importance. They also may consume a great amount of time of both students and sponsors.

[3] *Ibid.*
[4] *Ibid.*, p. 3.

The School Newspaper. This type of publication is common not only in the secondary schools and colleges; more and more elementary schools are issuing a paper describing events that are of general interest to their students. Some schools mimeograph their paper at a very nominal cost and distribute it free to all school patrons. Other large institutions have their papers printed and charge subscription rates. Still others co-operate with local newspapers to provide a page or two of strictly school news. Only the larger colleges and universities attempt to publish a daily newspaper. The majority of schools publish a paper weekly, bi-monthly, or monthly.

The value of a school paper lies in the training pupils receive in the practical application of ideas and knowledge gained from courses in English or communications. The pupils learn the responsibilities of being a staff member and the importance of reporting the truth about issues which are a part of school life. Regardless of the size of the school or the magnitude of the newspaper, it is an important medium for keeping students and faculty informed about school affairs as well as for encouraging school spirit.

Such organizations as the National Scholastic Press Association, Columbia Scholastic Press Association, and the Educational Press Association have contributed a large measure of assistance in developing worthwhile school publications.

School Yearbooks. Like the school newspaper, the yearbook or annual varies in style and manner of publication. Some small schools merely collect pictures of classes and class activities and send them, along with stories of the year's events, to a printer who completes the book. Larger schools contract with photographers and printers to work with the yearbook staff throughout the year to complete the necessary work. In either event the pupils themselves are responsible for the planning and carrying out of plans to make the finished yearbook a real story of the events taking place in their school during that year. Style, proper editing, attractive art work, and the meeting of deadlines for publication all serve to give pupils valuable experience in preparing such a publication.

There is a very considerable body of feeling developing, however, that the yearbook, at least in the public high school, is not worth the money and time spent upon it—and it takes a great deal of both. The values are so few that surely it cannot be justified at public expense, and if sufficient money is spent on it to produce a good publication it is much too expensive for many students to buy. Many administrators would be very happy if it could be eliminated.

Student Handbooks. This particular handbook is usually a co-operative production of faculty and student body. It serves as a pamphlet for orienting new pupils to the school. These small booklets are inexpensive and yet are most valuable in interpreting the school to the new pupil and to the community. Many pupils from all grade levels in a school may well work on this particular project each year. Changes in regulations, curricula, activities, staff, and philosophy must be brought up-to-date annually if the handbook is to serve the purpose it should.

Magazines and Activity Publications. Many schools afford opportunities for pupils to do creative writing and art work for a magazine publication. In instances with which the writer is acquainted, these publications are limited to once a term or semester. In some larger high schools this same practice is followed. Creative art classes often prepare such a magazine devoted entirely to art done by students.

Other publications which student groups prepare are those concerned with activities in the athletic and drama departments. These may be programs for football games with pictures of the team, individual players, and stories relating to the team's standing or a success story of the coach. The same sort of program is often prepared for dramatic or music events.

Frequently the revenue from the sale of these publications is earmarked for a particular fund-raising campaign within the school, or it may go into the general activity fund.

Speaking Activities

The main divisions of activities concerned with speaking are drama and forensics. Drama is concerned with the memorization of lines and the acting or playing the role of some particular character based on the ideas brought out by the playwright. Forensic activities which are prevalent in today's schools include orations, declamations, extemporaneous speaking, choral reading, debates, forums and panel discussions, and radio and television speaking.

Dramatics. Though a certain amount of actual class time is spent on dramatics, a larger share of the time devoted to these activities is outside of the class. Only larger schools provide a curriculum which includes regular drama classes. However, the smallest as well as the largest school will produce plays during the year. In the small school, perhaps, the only two plays of the year are the junior class and senior class plays. These are often a regular part of the class work in English. The larger schools, on the other hand, will very frequently produce many plays beyond the class plays, and these are usually prepared by students in drama or little-theatre organizations which are cocurricular rather than curricular. It is quite common to find these organizations offering many experiences other than acting. Committees are often delegated to carry out the details of lighting, costuming, scenery, publicity, and other related duties. Though the activity is organized to provide experience in speaking, these related activities afford a greater participation and may develop a keener appreciation for the entire program of drama.

One of the problems involved in play production is that of getting more students to participate in the acting itself. In a good many instances the casts needed are small, and since only the very best are chosen, there is not much opportunity for many to develop whatever abilities they may have along this line. To an extent, the situation has some of the same angles as does interscholastic athletics. Are we after perfection or wide participation or both? Must the dramatic coach be judged by the brilliant performance he gets out of a few or by the stimulation that he gives to large numbers? The dilemma is a difficult one, and schools are doing different things to try to meet the problems. Possibly the most promising is the plan whereby a performance is given at two or three different times and a different cast used on each occasion. This is not without its own problems, but neither is it without promise.

Forensic Activities. The term *forensic* refers to the kind of speaking which takes place in public discussion or debates. Orations of an argumentative nature were perhaps the oldest form of forensic speaking. Declamatory speaking has its values in that it trains the individual in proper delivery of a message and, although the message is memorized, it calls upon the pupil to use good enunciation, pronunciation, and meaningful gestures.

Debates and extemporaneous speaking motivate pupils to do research on a particular problem or issue and from this research to try to make a logical presentation of the facts bearing on the topic. This sort of experience carries over into the popular forum or panel discussion of issues pertaining to all sorts of problems which grow out of the regular subject-matter classwork. Today the forum or panel discussion types of radio and television program are a very effective means of getting our political issues discussed. It provides opportunity for an individual to think logically and trains him in the ability to express his thoughts with meaning.

Auxiliary Activities

Here are included, among other things, the various social events, the parties, teas, and dances that are a part of the life of any modern high school and, within limitations, of most elementary schools. Properly carried on, these contribute to a young person's growing up and to his getting along with others. They can help develop self-confidence and the manners and courtesies that are needed by everyone.

One of the major problems of administrators is that of keeping this social program within bounds. Another is the ever-present one of getting those who need it most to participate. No one has ever come up with an easy solution to the problem of how to get the reluctant adolescent to be present at a tea, for example, when it probably could do much for him. He is bashful, and he simply won't believe that it will help him at all.

Then, also, many teachers feel that there is often too much social and not enough academic life at many secondary schools. Studies have indicated that a considerable number of students feel the same way. Teachers from other countries are quick to note that the average high school student in the United States is much further advanced socially and consider-

Architects: Howell Lewis Shay and Associates.
Photograph by Lawrence S. Williams.

This circular cafetorium is in use as auditorium. Furniture is easily adapted for use in cafeteria or as work or study tables. Stetson Junior High School, West Chester, Pennsylvania.

ably less advanced academically than their own students. May it not be well for us to seek some middle ground, through the scheduling, limitation, and proper direction of the entire social program? Fundamentally, it is to a large extent a problem of adequate guidance.

Assembly Programs

The school auditorium can be the one place where integration takes place as nowhere else. Here common purposes and problems are presented to the group, school and individual achievements noted, and the entire program tied together. A school without an auditorium is lacking in something that is vitally important.

The assembly programs of the modern school will be carefully planned for a semester or a year, will take place during a regular period of the school day (usually weekly), and will be conceived and carried out through administration, faculty, and student co-operation. They can and should involve the community too, for they may frequently be a means of tying the community and school a little more closely together. They may also be an excellent means of developing rapport between faculty and student body.

Other Activities

Through closer co-operation between the school and other agencies, a richer and more varied cocurricular program has resulted. Many activities once considered quite separate from the school are now thought of as an integral part of cocurricular offerings. Reserve Officers' Training Corps (ROTC), (HI-Y), and (Tri-Hi-Y) are typical illustrations of such activities.

Mention should be made of the growing interest in camping. Today a number of schools offer camping experience as a part of the cocurricular or curricular program. Particularly has this been true in the state of Michigan where it was developed under the stimulus of the late Lee Thurston when he was State Superintendent of Public Instruction there. A significant number of large cities are also carrying on notable programs where camping becomes a part of the experience of nearly all children. It has much to commend it.

As a summary, we may point out the signs that seem to indicate that the gap between the curricular and extracurricular is continuing to become more narrow and that our use of the term *cocurricular* is fully justified. We have suggested:

1. Credit toward graduation is now given for many activities heretofore called "extra."

2. The introduction of an activity period in the regular class schedule is now accepted.
3. The tendency to secure financial support from tax money rather than student fees and admissions is growing.
4. The adoption of student planning into regular classroom teaching is to some extent being utilized.
5. Many activities once considered "extra" are now placed on a regular class basis, as is noted in the case of music, health education, and other programs.

QUESTIONS AND PROJECTS

1. Describe an incident, activity, or personal experience which shows how cocurricular activities are helpful in developing greater interest in the curricular activities in a school.
2. Prepare a summary of the cocurricular activities in which you participated while attending high school. Why did you choose these activities, and what value did you receive from belonging to the group?
3. In what activities do you participate at the present time? What organization or activities do you hope to be associated with before graduation from college?
4. Comment on this statement: "Every individual preparing to teach should have an opportunity to explore several different cocurricular activities while taking undergraduate study."
5. Evaluate the homeroom program with which you had an experience in junior or senior high school. If it was an effective program, what made it effective? If the program was ineffective, explain why.
6. Prepare a schematic diagram of the student government in your college. Show relationships between administrators, teachers, and students.
7. Prepare a list of advantages and disadvantages for the following cocurricular activities:
   A. Intra-mural athletic program
   B. Interscholastic athletic program
   C. Interest clubs
8. Prepare a list of advantages and disadvantages for an interscholastic athletic program.
9. Prepare a three-minute speech on the topic: "Benefits that can be derived from being active in a school's cocurricular program."
10. Why should it be of value to all students preparing to teach in the elementary school to be associated with some musical activity during their pre-service education?
11. What characteristics should one possess to be a successful advisor to a cocurricular activity? How much control should the advisor exercise in a given activity? Do some activities call for more control than others? Why? Why not?
12. Analyze the list of principles suggested by McKown stated on page 258. Which is of greatest importance? Why?

AUDIO-VISUAL AIDS

MOTION PICTURES (16 MM)

Are You a Good Citizen?—Coronet Films, Coronet Building, Chicago, Ill., 11 min., sd., b&w. The film follows Mr. Heineman, an active citizen who is the leader for "Citizenship Day," and develops a checklist of characteristics of good citizenship from his actions and his instructive talk with boys. Stresses the need for organized youth activities, and shows how young people themselves can be influential in establishing such a program.

Careers in the Making—Boston Univ., Film Library, 332 Bay St. Road, Boston, Mass., 38 min., sd., color. Shows the courses, career programs and extra-curricular activities at Boston University. Intended to help pupils in upper classes of secondary schools decide on what college to attend after graduation.

Garnet and Gold Sketches—Wurtele Film Productions, P.O. Box 504, Orlando, Fla., 18½ min., sd., color. Pictures the campus and the laboratory and field work of Florida State University at Tallahassee. Includes sports and other extracurricular activities, including the all-student circus.

School Activities and You—Coronet Films, Coronet Bldg., Chicago, Ill., 11 min., sd., b&w. A high school girl is planning her school activity program. Through the advice of her older brother, she learns the importance of choosing activities for their values by considering what she can learn, what her interests are, how much time she can give, and how to balance her program.

The School—The Child's Community—Wayne University, Detroit, Mich., 16 min., sd., b&w. The many ways a school can encourage children to accept responsibilities and share in the making of decisions that concern them are pictured by showing student participation in the "community" activities of an elementary school.

The Junior High School Story—National Education Association, 1201 16th St., N.W., Washington, D.C., 28 min., color. Interesting examples of programs and activities in 50 junior high schools in California. Shows well the relationships between the curricular and cocurricular.

FILMSTRIP

Lincoln High School Organizes a Student Council—National Association of Student Councils, 1201 16th St., N.W., Washington, D.C., 50 fr., si., color. Traces the development of a student council from the time the principal and the students realize the need for it up to the time that the council is organized and functioning.

RECORDING

Improving the Services of Extra Class Activities—Educational Recording Services, 5922 Abernathy Dr., Los Angeles, Calif., 20 min., 33⅓ r.p.m. microgroove. Dr. J. Lloyd Trump, Professor of Education, University of Illinois, discusses ways and reasons for improving "extraclass" activities.

FURTHER READINGS

Austin, David V., Will French, and J. Dan Hull, *American High School Administration: Policy and Practice,* 3rd ed. (New York, Holt, Rinehart and Winston, 1963), Chapter 10.

Braham, R. V., "What Role for Student Activities in the New Emphasis on Quality in Secondary Education?" *National Association of Secondary-School Principals Bulletin,* Vol. 44 (April, 1960).

Conant, James B., *Education in the Junior High School Years* (Princeton, N.J., Educational Testing Service, 1960).

Dolen, R. A., *Special Interest Activities and Club Program* (Highland Park High School, St. Paul Minn., Bulletin, 1962).

Frederick, Robert W., *The Third Curriculum* (New York, Appleton-Century-Crofts, 1959).

Gruber, Frederick C., and Thomas B. Beatty, *Secondary School Activities* (New York, McGraw-Hill, 1954).

Johnston, Edgar G., and Ronald C. Faunce, *Student Activities in Secondary Schools* (New York, Ronald, 1954).

Miller, Franklin A., James H. Moyer, and Robert B. Patrick, *Planning Student Activities* (Englewood Cliffs, N.J., Prentice-Hall, 1956).

Trump, J. Lloyd, "Extraclass Activities and the Needs of Youth," *Adapting the Secondary School Program to the Needs of Youth,* Fifty-second Yearbook, National Society for the Study of Education (Chicago, University of Chicago Press, 1953).

11

The Child and
His Development

PREVIEW

▶ A knowledge of child growth and development is fundamental to teaching.
No two individuals follow the same pattern of growth.
Growth is a broad term which describes change in many areas of development.

▶ Both heredity and environment influence an individual's growth and development pattern.
The extent to which these factors affect growth and development is difficult to ascertain.

▶ Patterns of growth and development are distinct for various age groups.
Ages 1 to 6 are considered here as early childhood.
Ages 6 to 10 describe the period of middle childhood.
Ages 10 to 13 are termed later childhood.
The age of adolescence refers to the ages between puberty and adulthood.

▶ Mentally exceptional pupils are cared for in the modern educational program.
Gifted children are provided with opportunities for more challenging study.
Slow learners are given every opportunity to progress.

As research continues to reveal more about the growth and development of the individual, the trained teacher, too, is made more aware of the great challenge he has in working with the learners in his classes. The modern educational program includes much more than the imparting of facts and the teaching of skills. Today, the school is an environment in which the individual child is given an opportunity to develop emotionally, socially, and physically, as well as mentally. If the school is to provide for maximum development, the teacher must have a real understanding of the various characteristics that indicate child growth. He must be able to recognize an individual's needs and be ready to do something constructive toward satisfying those needs.

The well-trained teacher knows that children cannot be forced to learn. When a child reaches a particular stage in his development, he is ready to try a specific learning experience. Reaching this stage is an individual matter; one child may be younger or older than another. Nevertheless, an effective teacher will recognize when the child has reached a point of readiness to learn and provide the necessary learning activities. Normal children sieze upon the opportunities for new learning experiences providing the teacher affords them a proper learning environment. Teaching is far different from building a house. When we build a house we select the plans we wish and then secure the kinds and amounts of materials necessary to complete the house. When working with children we soon learn that they come to us with not only the pattern but with the materials as well. If we are observant and understand the characteristics of child development, we recognize that each child presents a pattern which should guide us in bringing about the changes necessary for him to grow and develop into the mature individual he should become. The materials with which we have to work are inherent. When a child is "ready" he will learn. No two children are ready at exactly the same time. One child may be able to button his sweater or tie his shoes when he enters kindergarten; another child of the same age may not be performing such tasks for another month, or even a year later. The same can be said for reading; one child may be ready to read a year before another child of the same age. Teachers today recognize this fact and are able to provide learning activities which will benefit the child most at any given stage of development.

Every individual is a changing human being, and changes occur with every passing day. What seems important at one stage in a child's development is not important a day, a month or a year later. For example, a child of preschool age uses anything which looks like a pencil to pretend he is writing. Later it is important to have a real pencil and make some real marks to satisfy a desire to write. Following this experience the child begins to make marks which resemble letters or numbers, and soon he seeks help from adults or older children to make letters, numbers, or figures which he can copy in an attempt to satisfy his need for written communication. At this particular time a child receiving praise and encouragement, plus a little help when he wants it, will show great spurts in certain abilities to create pictures of things common to his environment. As this child grows a little older he may resent any help or interference from older children—it now seems important for him to do things himself. Another child of his same age may react quite differently to being helped, he may continue to depend a great deal on older children or adults. The teacher, if he senses these differences, can provide the kind of experiences

Courtesy: H. Lockwood Frost, A.I.A. and
Rossie Moodie Frost, A.I.A., Architects.
Photograph by R. Wenkam.

A teacher and a little girl make friends outside the new Ewa Beach Elementary School on Oahu, Hawaii.

which will be challenging to each child, thus affording opportunity for maximum growth no matter in what stage a child may be found.

When a school is well organized and properly staffed with understanding teachers, it will provide the type of curriculum which cares for the individual's needs and makes possible the realization of his desires. The curriculum should include outlets and experiences that contribute to all aspects of children's growth.[1]

MEASURES OF GROWTH

When describing the growth of an individual in very general terms, we ordinarily think of only age, height, and weight. These are undoubtedly the most obvious of all measures, yet educators are interested in growth in much broader and much more complex terms. In order to describe all the ways a child grows, experts in child study have devised several other measures called ages, which help describe the development of an individual. Olson and Lewellen [2] refer to these ages in very simple and understandable terms:

weight age	(based on weight in pounds)
height age	(based on height in inches)
mental age	(arrived at through individual's tests of intelligence)
grip age	(the strength of the child's grip as measured on a special machine)
dental age	(determined by the number of permanent teeth)
carpal age	(arrived at by an x-ray showing the bones of a child's hand and wrist)
reading age	(based on knowledge of words, ability to follow printed directions, and ability to understand the meaning of a paragraph or passage)

In addition to these ages we, of course, always consider the chronological age.

Though the individual teacher does not compute all of these ages in order to arrive at the kind of learning experiences a group of pupils should have, it is quite important to have some knowledge of them to understand why individuals are different in these various respects. As indicated previously, each child is an individual, and his growth and development pattern is controlled by his heredity and environmental factors. There is a positive correlation among the various measures of growth for a given individual. If he is of average height likewise he will most likely be average weight as well as show average grip and dental

[1] Association for Childhood Education, *Modern School Practices in the U.S.A.* (Washington, D.C., 1947).

[2] Willard C. Olson and John Lewellen, *How Children Grow and Develop* (Chicago, Science Research Associates, 1953), p. 10.

growth for all boys of this same chronological age. On other occasions a child in a given group is apt to be different for each of these measures when compared to other children of the same chronological age. For example, Tom who is an average boy of 6 years of age is at an average of 6 years in all of the measures listed. A girl who is 12 years old was found to read and spell as well as a junior in high school. Her mental age was 17, her figure was robust and mature, her height and grip were equivalent to an age of an average 15-year-old. Her dental and carpal ages were equal to those of a 15-year-old. This girl was an early maturer, and her case is quite representative. If the child had been a slow maturer, all seven ages would most likely have indicated it. It is quite unusual to find a child who is high in one age measure and low in all the rest. The few exceptions occur when a child is very heavy or tall for his age and thus lags behind in some of the other age measures. Or a child may have a mental age that exceeds any of his other age measures.

Knowledge of all of these aspects of growth gives a much more accurate picture of a child's development and capacity for learning than if only his chronological age, weight, or height were known. This more scientific approach to measurement of child growth and development has led schools to provide the kind of learning activities which more nearly meet the specific needs of children. As the teacher learns more about child growth and development, the more understanding he will have in dealing with individuals in his classes. Learning activities will take on greater meaning, and the school experience will offer much more for the individuals concerned.

HEREDITY AND ENVIRONMENT INFLUENCE DEVELOPMENT

There are two basic factors which affect an individual's development. These two factors are *heredity* and *environment*. Those characteristics that a child inherits from his parents are called hereditary influences. Many of those characteristics and their development can be predicted quite accurately. An individual will tend to be very similar in size, in color of eyes and hair, and other bodily structure to his family.

Those things which we might define as behavior characteristics are somewhat different. The child may inherit certain potential traits, and what happens to those potentialities depends, to a great extent, on the kind of environment he is afforded. A number of studies have been reported which attempt to show how much influence heredity has on the individual. Likewise an even greater number of studies are concerned with determining what influence environment has on the individual. These reports give conclusive evidence that human growth and development respond to both factors; changes occur in the individual as a result of an interaction of heredity and environment.

Recent studies indicate that environment is, in part, responsible for the development of general intelligence. The amount of its influence seems to vary with extreme conditions and during periods of an individual's most rapid growth. Important to teachers is the fact that greatest development of an individual's intelligence takes place at an early age, before the child is eight years old. Referring to intelligence scales formulated by Thorndike, Thurstone, and Heinis, Bloom [3] suggests: "in terms of intelligence measured at age 17, about 50 percent of the development takes place between conception and age 4, about 30 percent between ages 4 to 8, and about 20 percent between ages 8 and 17." Bloom further states, "although there is relatively little evidence of the effects of changing the environment on the changes in intelligence, the evidence so far available suggests that marked changes in the environment in early years can produce greater changes in intelligence than equally marked changes in the environment at later periods of development."

The implications for the school are obvious. A school must seek to provide the kind of environment which challenges and stimulates as well as satisfies the developmental processes of children and youth. There must be an opportunity for the child to interact with the life around him. The school can and should provide a kind of social setting wherein the student has guidance in developing language skills. These skills in turn will open new avenues of learning through reading and speaking, as well as through interacting with his environment. A setting for learning which is concerned with both the hereditary and environmental factors will most assuredly extend the limits of what the mind can accomplish.

Environments Affecting a Child's Development

The child's first conscious environment is his home. His first teachers are his parents. The kind and amount of training he receives in the home and through his associations with other people constitute his preschool education. The home is the center for a child's first educational, emotional, physical, and social development. The degree to which this development is normal depends on the kind of home life which exists. A child who is loved by his parents and made to feel secure in his home environment will have little trouble making the necessary adjustments to school. He soon becomes an active participant in this new environment away from the sheltered care afforded him by his parents up to this time.

The kind of home and school life afforded a child will determine how well he will be able to use his innate capacities for development. Any inborn capacity for learning will be stifled if the surroundings are not conducive to its development. For example, a child who has an inborn

---

[3] Benjamin S. Bloom, *Stability and Change in Human Characteristics* (New York, John Wiley and Sons, 1964), p. 88.

capacity for learning numbers or reading words will probably never do so if opportunities for developing these capacities are not provided. A boy or girl who has the potential abilities for being a great musician and yet grows up in an environment devoid of any music, will most likely never become the musician he or she was capable of being.

The home and school are not the only environmental factors at work on the child. The community in which a child is reared is also responsible for influencing his growth and development. The large city with its crowd of people oftentimes lacks good play areas and is not always as conducive to good physical development as the suburbs or rural areas. On the other hand, a number of cultural advantages such as libraries, operas, concerts, museums, and the like are lacking in most rural areas. One could go on comparing life in the city and country and point out advantages as well as disadvantages for each. Whatever might be said for each, it is important to keep in mind the kind of environment a child is experiencing as we attempt to establish learning activities in school which will be worthwhile and significant for his further growth and development.

Significant progress is being made today in offering programs for pre-school age children who live in poor neighborhoods. Children from these areas—and the number is considerable—are given an opportunity to attend a four, six, or ten week summer program which readies them for school in the fall. Only large cities seemed concerned with this originally, but research indicates a need for similar programs throughout the nation. This program will undoubtedly develop with greater speed and regularity with the implementation of the Elementary and Secondary School Act of 1965. Title I of this federal law is specifically designed to promote effective education for culturally disadvantaged children. The program known as Headstart, referred to in greater detail in Chapter 13, will perhaps lead to a normal downward extension of elementary education.

GROWTH AND DEVELOPMENT PATTERNS

Even though we know or read about exceptional growth patterns among individuals, and we are aware that children all grow at different rates of speed, we also know that nearly all children go through the same sequences of growth and development. For example, children generally creep before they walk, walk before they run, babble before they talk, talk before they read, and read before they spell. They usually read before they write and write single words before writing phrases or sentences. The rate at which a child progresses through these stages is directly related to his readiness for each experience. When he has developed a readiness for the next level of learning, the teacher must provide him this opportunity. These stages may be reached at different times for different pupils and in different subjects or activities to be learned.

We know that teachers must recognize individual differences and offer learning experiences which consider this fact. To perceive a child's readiness for a given learning experience, the teacher must consider five different measures of maturation. Most authorities suggest the following: mental, physical, emotional, social, and educational maturity. An effective teacher understands the importance of knowing the relationship of these maturity levels to a child's readiness for learning. It is of no use to hurry a child to a new and more complex developmental stage. Until he is ready for the new experience, it will have little or no meaning and therefore be of little value to his future normal development.

Much more research is needed to fully understand children and their growth patterns inasmuch as each one is slightly different from every other. In order to gain greater insight into human growth and development, a number of interesting studies have been made with identical twins, whose growth patterns are most nearly the same. From such research it is evident that intelligence is more attributable to heredity than to environment, although a share of an individual's ability is due to the effects of environment. Extremes in environment may show as much spread as twenty points on an IQ scale when one identical twin is placed in a deprived or disadvantaged neighborhood and the other placed in an environment rich in cultural, educational, and social advantages.

Child study specialists have been able to identify certain characteristics of growth and development for the various age groups. These groups are identified here as early childhood, middle childhood, later childhood, and adolescence. (See chart on pages 280–81.) Consideration of these characteristics will help us better understand how children grow and develop and make us more aware of what to look for as we provide the learning experiences for the children in our classes.

Early Childhood

Early childhood describes the child between the ages of 1 to 6. During this period some very great changes occur in the development of the child.

He has learned to stand, to walk, to talk, and to care for many of his individual needs. He has adjusted to spending a few hours in school away from the protection of his home and parents. He desires constant activity; he wants to climb, run and jump so that he can develop his large muscles, which are growing rapidly. When he tires he usually gets cross. He enters into all kinds of activities; and because of uneven development of his motor skills, he may be very adept at one kind of skill but be very poor at another. He enjoys a lot of imagination, and laughter is oftentimes his only form of communication.

At this age a child's bones are very soft. This prevents breakage

In the kindergarten individual expression is encouraged. Upper Merion Township Public Schools, Pennsylvania.

resulting from his many tumbles. He has grown his full set of baby teeth and at age 5 or 6 begins to lose some. The 6-year molars should be appearing. These are his first permanent teeth. At the age of 5, a child has established eyedness and handedness which should not be changed. His body organs are sufficiently developed so that desirable eating, resting, and elimination habits are becoming established.

He needs companionship with other children. He must derive security from his family and other adults with whom he has regular contact. A variety of activities and toys should be available for him to develop his muscles. He should be encouraged to help parents with daily tasks even though it takes a longer time. He should sleep approximately 12 hours and an afternoon nap of one or two hours is advisable.

Table 11-1. Children All Grow Differently *

	Physically	Mentally	Socially and Emotionally
The First Year	Grows rapidly. On first birthday may weigh three times as much as at birth. First tooth may appear at 6 or 7 months. Bodily proportions change—head relatively less large than at birth. Begins to grasp things with hands, to kick, and to crawl.	Touch, taste, and smell help him get acquainted with world around him. Recognizes much of what he sees, and understands some of what he hears. Shows preference for certain toys. Tries to imitate sounds he hears.	Shows anger when hungry or uncomfortable. Shows affection for parents. Around third or fourth month, begins to respond socially to those around him, and to show interest in what is going on.
Early Childhood: 1 to 6	Learns to walk between 1 year and 18 months. Toilet, sleeping, and eating habits gradually established. From 2 to 6, large muscles develop rapidly; motor co-ordination, unevenly. Girls usually a year ahead of boys in physical development.	Begins to say "Mama" at 1, and by 2, uses short sentences. Vocabulary grows by leaps and bounds. Likes songs, nursery rhymes, cutting, pasting, coloring. Learns many games, asks lots of questions, and sees relationship between ideas.	Temper tantrums to get own way. Says "no" a lot. Plays alone at first. Interested in group activities in third year. Likes creative play. Doesn't differentiate much between boys and girls. May go through period of handling sex organs. Can carry some responsibility.
Middle Childhood: 6 to 10	Rate of growth slows down. Begins to lose baby teeth and gets first permanent tooth. Sexual organs grow at slower rate than rest of body. Muscular co-ordination still uneven	Learns to read. Is gradually acquiring other knowledges and skills. Enjoys myths, nature stories, heroic tales, comics, radio, TV, and movies.	Sexual feelings and interest very lively—masturbation may increase. In spite of sexual feelings, interest of boys and girls diverging—less play together.

280

and incomplete. Better control over large muscles than small ones. Manual dexterity and hand-eye co-ordination increase. Enjoys play that uses whole body.	Learns best when can be active while learning. Acquires some sex information—much of it outside the home. Recognizes differences in how boys and girls are expected to behave.	More independent—learning to take responsibility and control emotions. Some understanding of time and money values. Concern about right and wrong.
Later Childhood: 10 to 13 — More rapid growth—muscles expand, bones lengthen. Bodies may be ungainly and awkward because of sex changes. Voice changes in boys. Girls mature before boys, but in both sexes colorless hair appears around genitals. In girls, hips and breasts round out and menstruation may begin.	Wider range of learning and greater acquisition of skills and knowledges. Growing ability to reason and think out own problems.	May not fully accept changes in body. Grown-up one minute and irresponsible and childish the next. Great desire to be part of the group and accepted by others his own age. Awakening interest in personal appearance. Growing interest in other sex.
Adolescence — Rate of growth slows down, but still rapid. Girls reach adult height at about 16. Boys grow until 17 or 19. Increase in appetite. Co-ordination improves. Sexual maturity is reached.	Learning becomes more specialized in preparation for job or career. Interest in abstract moral and philosophical problems, and in social questions. More critical of own learning achievements.	Moody spells, rebellion, drive toward independence. Changing relationships with parents, teachers. Interested in problems of marriage and vocation. More guidance needed since this is time of many life decisions.

281

* They won't all reach the same point in growth at the same time. Keeping this in mind, you can get a pretty good idea from this chart of what to look for as children grow up.

SOURCE: Williard C. Olson and John Lewellen, *How Children Grow and Develop.* Reprinted by permission from Science Research Associates, Inc.

This is a time when a child begins to show rapid development of vocabulary and exhibits ability in using the words in meaningful sentences. He learns verses and sentences from books read to him by his parents and other children. He is curious to learn and to discover new things in his environment. Provision should be made to accommodate this desire to learn. Picture books, manipulative devices, and playthings which call for creativity all aid the child in developing personality.

The Child in Nursery School. During early childhood many children have their first introduction to school life. This new experience occurs when the child enters nursery school. The question is often asked, Why do we need nursery schools if a child has a home environment which provides him with a place to work and play? Unfortunately, many homes do not provide such space. In some homes both parents are working, and small children must not be left unattended. Even in homes where one parent is always on hand, there are times when children must necessarily be messy. Playing with clay, paints, and water is bound to take supervision. A busy parent preparing meals and carrying out the routine of maintaining a home will not always understand the little accidents such as spilling and breaking of play materials, and as a result there are many scoldings which need not be. It is easy to understand why parents who have established a home and furnished it nicely have a problem of understanding a child's accidents and activities which appear destructive but are all a part of growing up. Today, children spend hours looking at television shows. It is only natural to expect some of the activities which have looked delightful to children to be tried out by them. For example, a child watching other children performing on a trampoline will enjoy trying his skill at this same activity. Since he has no trampoline, he will use his bed. Parents are not tolerant of this activity because to them it seems most destructive of furnishings they have worked hard to acquire. Most understanding parents do set standards of behavior and at the same time make allowances for an occasional mishap. In homes where parents do not take this attitude, children are continually scolded and soon get the impression that the home is a place for adults only.

In such instances, the best answer to providing the kind of environment a child needs for good, wholesome development seems to be the nursery school. In the nursery school a child discovers a sense of belonging to a group which is interested in doing the things he likes to do. His activities are looked upon as natural ones. He learns to share his experiences with other children, and if he spills his paints the teacher will take time to show him why it happened and explain ways to overcome doing it again. There is no scolding, but rather an opportunity is made for learning responsibilities—he does have to help put away his toys and clean up the paint brushes.

Play becomes creative activity. The sand box, the large blocks, and boxes are used to build the things children imagine. Clay, finger paints, and moistened mixtures of salt and flour are wonderful media for children to experiment with. Although the finished product is not always recognizable as what a child says it is, the important thing is that it is his achievement and, since it was fun, he finished it. The children learn to talk about what they do, and the teacher has time to help them find answers to their many questions. The child learns that good behavior has its rewards; the pattern of his life takes on more meaning.

In summary, the nursery school helps the child *physically*. He gains *socially* through his contacts with other children. There is an opportunity for *emotional* growth. He learns through actual experience the time and ways of responding emotionally in a manner acceptable to his group. His *mental* growth is apparent through his ability to participate in an organized learning environment. The way he solves simple problems of working and playing with the materials he is provided gives evidence of some of his thought processes.

It would seem educationally sound to predict that the nursery school will increasingly become a recognized division of school organization and more will be established. Most nursery schools will be private schools for some time to come mainly because their effectiveness depends on limiting class size to a number less than many public schools can afford and because the public is not yet convinced of their value.

The Child in Kindergarten. For many children the kindergarten is their first experience with organized school activities. The child who has been in nursery school will have been introduced to some experiences in group living that kindergarten offers, but now his activities will have greater direction toward readiness for reading.

Thus it can be said that the kindergarten provides an opportunity for the extension of home and nursery school life. The kindergarten had its beginning during Froebel's time when he advocated a type of school where children would carry on constructive play activities in an environment of toys, sand boxes, pets, and growing flowers. The kindergarten teacher is understanding and skillful in giving a child the kind and amount of help he needs when he should have it.

At this age the child becomes aware of his surroundings. He knows the names for most objects in his everyday life. He takes more interest in going shopping, singing the songs he hears, playing on the playground or in the park. He begins to sense an orderliness to events; he looks forward to his birthdays, to parties with his friends, to certain programs on holidays and to summer vacation.

The play activities for kindergarten children involve more plot and realism. Observe children on a playground or in the schoolroom and you will note how quickly they get to work on some project, perhaps building a fort, playing house, or dramatizing cowboys and Indians. The child of this age continues to love working with paints or tools, but he shows greater interest in building a boat or painting a box, something that is more real.

The kindergarten child will develop many interests in the world about him and the teacher can use field trips to the schoolground or around the block to arouse interests to the point of having projects grow out of these experiences. For example, a story about buildings or pets, plus a walk around the schoolyard with the teacher pointing out the things described in a story, can generate ideas for many pictures done with crayons or paints. The child is thus developing ways of communicating. He uses his picture and talks about his experience.

The regular routine of the days in kindergarten helps children establish certain patterns of living. Going to the toilet, washing hands, and getting drinks all help in establishing habits of orderly living. All of these things are part of a maturity schedule which prepare a child for his next stage of growth.

Middle Childhood

Middle childhood describes the child between the ages of 6 to 10. During this period growth is continuous but slowed down in comparison to earlier years. At the age of 6 a child has grown to about 40–42 percent of his adult size. His heart is growing rapidly. During these ages the body is highly susceptible to respiratory infections. Rheumatic fever is a disease most often contracted during this period, and overexertion should be avoided. Muscular co-ordination is developing, but complete control is still not achieved. The loss of baby teeth continues, and the "toothless grin" is a familiar sight in the first-grade room. Posture habits tend to become lax, the long spindly body is likely to droop. In some instances this may indicate a chronic infection or fatigue or similar condition which calls for medical attention. Eye defects such as nearsightedness may become apparent during these ages.

Some children may be entering the puberty cycle at the age of 10. Girls usually experience a spurt of skeletal growth at that time. They attain skeletal maturity before boys do.

The child between 6 and 10 is still very energetic. He has a wider range of interests and longer attention span. He is becoming more interested in group or team games and co-operates better than at an earlier age. He seems to have a greater sense of rhythm. He is becoming more interested in eating and refuses fewer foods. He assumes greater responsibility for household tasks.

At these ages he needs to participate in planning of family affairs. He needs social approval from his companions. Membership in the community "gang" is a must as far as he is concerned. He should be afforded all kinds of activities that will develop body control and strength. He should be encouraged to participate in activities which use the whole body, such as throwing, running, and stunts. The child still needs about 11 hours of sleep.

The Child in the Primary Grades. Although many children entering first grade will have had experience in nursery school or kindergarten, there will be many more who have not. For many a child, the first grade is his first introduction to school. If the teacher senses the growth and development of the primary school child as an integral part of his total growth pattern, his understanding of the elementary school child will be more complete.

The teacher must recognize that the child entering the first grade looks upon himself as grown-up. It is an exciting new world the 6-year-old is about to experience. He is suddenly aware of many new people in his environment, and he is no longer able to rely solely upon his parents to help him with his problems.

Since the primary school child is extremely active, sitting still for any length of time is difficult. It is normal for him to be busily engaged in some activity which is satisfying and purposeful. It is an age for collecting things. A boy's or girl's room at home or desk at school will give evidence of this. For the most part, their possessions are important because of the purpose they serve or of the interest there is in having them, rather than their monetary value. These curious possessions can be of inestimable value to the teacher in his plan for learning activities. Real lessons in nature study or understandings dealing with the community can grow out of exhibits, scrapbooks, or play-acting based upon interest drawn from possessions which children of this age feel are important.

Because the primary school child is being taught to read with more and more understanding, through the years he gradually senses the need to do some of his reading for information about the things that are interesting to him. His vocabulary grows, and he is beginning to write the words he knows into meaningful sentences.

His attitudes toward adults change markedly. Since he is growing and developing both physically and mentally, he tends to lean more on his own abilities than to depend on adults for protection and direction. He doesn't question authority when it is fair but he dislikes, and rightfully so, any unjust authority coming from adults. The teacher recognizes the importance of handling the child's problems with prudence and fairness so as to encourage competitive activities and yet sees to it that all members of the group achieve some measure of success in the eyes of their classmates.

During the latter part of middle childhood, when the individual is in grades 4 and 5, we observe some very marked social and emotional changes occurring. The child suddenly becomes more aware of his own sex. Play among mixed groups tends to disappear. Small arguments still occur regularly but, we note, the child exercises greater control over his emotions. Each child is becoming more independent. Forgetting little tasks around home and at school is quite natural. This is not hard to understand if we recognize what a world of new things is constantly appearing on the horizon of a healthy, active, 3rd, 4th, or 5th grade pupil.

Later Childhood

Growth is rapid in later childhood. The sex organs, muscles, bones, and teeth are all developing at a rate beyond the child's powers of complete adjustment. Both boys and girls at this age are awkward. At age 11, girls are usually larger than boys. For some children, this is the age of puberty. Secondary sex characteristics begin to appear. Girls' breasts and hips begin to develop. Boys' voices change and pubic hair begins to appear.

During this period the child is keenly interested in competitive activities. The more highly organized team activities he can enter, the better he likes it. There is sometimes a danger of entering too many—thus causing fatigue. At this age the child leaves the "gang," and an interest in one or two best friends is developed.

This child between 10 and 13 or 14 has a tremendous appetite. He has more mature interests which need to be met. Interest is great in club programs, "Y" and church activities, and scouting. He is more interested in his personal appearance, and he is self-conscious in the company of the opposite sex. He still needs about 10 or 11 hours of sleep.

Adolescence

The adolescent age usually extends from 12 to 21. This is the period so often spoken of as "teen-age." It is a period of growth when there seems to occur a rebirth of the individual. Most boys and girls become physically mature, yet lack the experience of adult life.

This age is recognized as one of conflict or turmoil. The individual is progressing from his childhood life of dependence to an independent adult life. He should be capable of doing independent thinking, making decisions and taking on responsibility—yet he finds himself in situations both in and out of school where he attempts to act grown-up and be accepted by adults as an adult before he is adequately equipped physically, mentally, or emotionally. This change to greater maturity is slow and gradual. Only through careful guidance can the individual proceed from childhood to adulthood. This is a time when the individual needs a teacher who is understanding and willing to help him make the necessary

Courtesy: Dr. J. Maurice Strattan, Superintendent,
Paoli Area High School System. Architects:
Chappelle and Crothers. Photograph by
Thompson Studio of Photography, Paoli, Pa.

Print Shop, Valley Forge Junior High School. Junior high school boys are offered an opportunity to explore a wide variety of vocational opportunities. Here they are being introduced to the operation of the printing press.

adjustments to a new life of independent thought and action. To deal effectively with adolescents, it is necessary to start with an understanding of the biological changes which occur and know how they affect the behavior of the individual as he attempts to adjust to the demands of his environment. The physical growth and the physiological changes which are common to this age make the individual very conscious of himself and his associations with others.

Physical growth is rapid during this period. Boys continue to grow in height until about 19 or 20 years but continue to increase in weight after this age. Girls reach a mature height a year or two before the boys. The thin girl often gains weight, and those who are overweight tend to lose some weight.

Physiological growth is marked in the adolescent period. This is a period in the lives of most boys and girls when they reach puberty, defined as the earliest age of achieving sexual maturity. Girls usually gain this level of maturity a year before boys. It has been known that some reach puberty at the age of 9 years, whereas others are as old as 17 or 18.

During this age boys and girls achieve mental maturity within the limits of their ability and experience. Some become interested in a vocation and begin at once to prepare for it; others show little interest and cannot decide on any one thing they would like to do as an adult. This is a time when a teacher should offer help in guiding the individual in the right kind of approach to vocations. Many pupils will drop out of school during this period at they reach an age when they are permitted to work.

Most adolescents wish to explore many more activities than they can possibly participate in and maintain good health. However, one of the basic concepts underlying the junior high school organization is to provide as wide a variety of activities as is possible in order to satisfy this exploratory desire. The senior high school then follows up with a program which permits greater specialization in the areas this individual has chosen to pursue.

The age of adolescence is an interesting but a difficult one, both for the individual and the teacher who works with him. Burton [4] suggests that "the adolescent is an odd, awkward, graceful, respectful, impudent, selfish, altruistic, idealistic, narrow-minded, sympathetic, cruel individual."

The foregoing discussion of the various age groups is not meant to be entirely complete. An entire book can be written on any one of the age classifications.

This general pattern of growth and development including a few specific characteristics about each age group of children will prove helpful in understanding more about the kind of activities which should be a part of the school experience for the child. These are considered characteristics for the normal growing child.

MENTALLY EXCEPTIONAL CHILDREN

All children do not fit within the range of mental ability which is considered normal. On the basis of intelligence quotients, a ratio determined by dividing the mental age by the chronological age, we find a wide range of mental ability. However, intelligence quotients (IQ) are but one measure of ability, and too much significance should not be at-

[4] William H. Burton, *Introduction to Education* (New York, Appleton-Century-Crofts, 1934), p. 501.

tached to them. They do help us to identify children who possess varying degrees of abstract intelligence, such as the ability to generalize and to show a high degree of skill in nonmechanical, verbal thinking. They, therefore, are, to some extent, indicators of possible future accomplishment, and as such they are helpful. The tendency today is to think in terms of broad groups, such as *trainable* or *educable,* at the same time keeping constantly in mind that many aspects of personality, drive, environment, and culture are highly determining factors in accomplishment.

It is dangerous if not impossible to set up dividing lines that will be more than slightly useful in classifying children. However, a classification that has some value and which finds considerable use is suggested at this point:

LEVEL	IQ INTERVAL
Idiot	0– 25
Imbecile	25– 50
Moron	50– 70
Borderline	70– 80
Low normal	80– 90
Normal	90–110
Superior	110–120
Very superior	120–140
Near genius	140 and over

Gifted Children

Much is known about the behavior characteristics of the child generally described as normal or average in academic ability, and for the most part the curriculum in the typical school is geared to his learning ability or capacity. This has been natural because there are more children in this group than any other.

More than a few individuals, however, have long pointed out that we have been neglecting those who belong to the superior or gifted group—those who can make significant contributions to our society. This neglect, which is real and not imagined, can be attributed to several factors: (1) teachers have not known how to meet the needs of the superior child, (2) in crowded classrooms there has been little opportunity to individualize instruction, (3) the superior child may not cause any discipline problems even though he isn't intellectually challenged in the classroom, and (4) there has been a general apathy toward the problem on the part of the public. It should be pointed out that these are very general factors and certainly do not apply to all situations. More and more schools today are initiating programs to care for these very able pupils.

With the development of the new age of science and the pressure of international events there has come a new awareness of the problem. The continuing manpower shortage, in the scientific fields especially, has made it imperative that we seek out and develop to the fullest the intellectual and creative power of our youth if we are to survive as a nation.

We have come to accept the idea that there are many kinds of giftedness and that it is widespread, existing in villages, on farms, and in cities. We know too that so-called "ordinary" families produce most of the gifted children.[5]

It is recognized also that giftedness exists in many aspects, science, literature, art, music, social relations, mechanical skills, and others. A rather good definition is that the gifted or talented child is one who shows remarkable performance in any worthwhile line of endeavor.

How shall we identify and stimulate these superior abilities that we now realize we have been neglecting? How can we encourage the creativeness that is so vital to human progress? Far-sighted individuals and forward-looking school systems have sought some of the answers during recent years. It is only very lately though that genuine public concern, greater understanding about a suitable curriculum for these pupils, and the availability of more funds from business and government sources have influenced a growing number of schools to experiment with programs for these pupils. Many issues remain unresolved.

The problem of identifying the gifted child is in itself not easy. Terman [6] and others have pretty well established that initial recognition of the academically talented can generally be accomplished by certain types of mental tests administered as early as 6–10 years. Intelligence tests will, of course, not identify all gifted children. In certain fields, as creative writing, social leadership and the like, identification must result from the observation of performance. The need for alert, sympathetic teachers here is obvious.

Schools are experimenting with a variety of plans to provide a better education for the gifted child, among these, two which seem to have greatest expectations are some form of accelerated and some form of enrichment program. Both of these may mean changes in administrative practices. Chief among these are: providing for nongraded organization, varying in time blocks for scheduling, team teaching, cross grouping, meeting of special groups before or after the regular school day and increased working of faculty committees with these pupils.

Variations of acceleration would include: an earlier age of entrance to school, skipping grades, rapid promotion of various types, a lengthened school year providing for earlier graduation. Probably the strongest argument for acceleration lies in the fact that when the lives of our really

---

[5] *Education for the Gifted,* Fifty-seventh Yearbook of the National Society for the Study of Education (Chicago, University of Chicago Press, 1958), p. 19.

[6] Lewis M. Terman, "The Discovery and Encouragement of Exceptional Talent," *The American Psychologist,* Vol. 9, No. 6, (1954).

gifted are studied it is found that their most creative work had been done before they were forty years old. Society loses, therefore, by their delayed entrance into productive life.

Judging from what is being done, it seems that most school people and probably the public are inclined to the idea of enrichment rather than acceleration. Space will permit little more than a listing of some of the more promising methods of approach.

Enrichment may be carried on in the regular classroom, as in the Portland, Oregon, elementary grades where provision is made for students to follow special interests, to apply creative ideas, and generally to develop a broader program of activities.[7] Enrichment in the elementary grades may also be carried on in certain classes for high ability children who are taught with the rest of children at other times. Such is the plan in the Colfax School in Pittsburgh. An outstanding illustration of a special elementary school where initial selectivity is used is that at Hunter College where the school is an integral part of the New York City School system.

In the secondary schools there has been a similar variation in the approach to the problem. Special schools for the talented have existed for some time in the large cities, particularly Philadelphia, Chicago, New York, Boston, and others. New York has for a number of years operated special high schools of music and art, of science, and of the performing arts. Philadelphia has its Central High School for superior academic students. These are but illustrations of what may be found in other cities. In Cleveland the so-called Major Work Classes serve as a successful example of special grouping.

Elsewhere many high schools are offering special classes in certain subjects, most frequently the various sciences or mathematics, for pupils of high ability. In many such cases students may enter college with advanced standing after having passed examinations. Other minor illustrations of caring for the gifted in regular high schools may be represented by Saturday classes, extra course load, summer sessions, and late afternoon or early morning classes. One thing is certain—no one plan will fit all situations.

Then, of course, there have always been scholarships of various kinds for students of superior ability. Recently these opportunities have been increasing. An outstanding example is the National Merit Scholarships with which nearly every secondary school teacher is familiar.

Where cost studies have been made, the results indicate that while education of the gifted student is more expensive than the average-per-pupil cost, it is considerably less than that for the retarded child. In view of the results that are likely to accrue to society certainly the good education of talented children is a sound investment.

[7] National Society for the Study of Education, *op. cit.,* p. 246.

In teacher education programs much more attention must be given to the matter than is now current practice. A few institutions offer special courses in the education of the gifted, still fewer offer a sequence of courses, more include it as an area in other courses. Many school systems have found their best method to be in-service programs, frequently carried on in co-operation with colleges and universities. Here again there is no one answer. Rather, what we need is a more practical and inspired approach to the problem of how we may help each child realize his fullest potential. As novelist John Hersey suggests, no "crash program" can be the ultimate or even the immediate answer.

Slow Learners

Until quite recently, the slow learner has been given far more attention in the school than has the gifted child. This group includes those pupils whose IQ is between 70 and 90. These slow learners are quite often found in regular classes with pupils of normal IQ. In some instances this has proven to be the best practice, especially if the pupil is not at the extreme low point on the scale.

There seems to be divided opinion as to whether or not children identified as slow learners make greater achievement if they are separated from those having higher IQ's. There are a number of studies to support both practices. A few common understandings should guide the teacher who teaches these children.

Classes need to be small for slow learners to receive the attention they need. They must be taught differently than children with normal IQ's because they have fewer interests, limited vocabulary, and little imagination. Most have difficulty with reading which in turn effects their achievement in other subjects. Many of these pupils are able to learn simple arithmetic functions that deal with everyday life problems, such as making change with money or measuring with common measuring tools. Remedial drill, audio-visual techniques and a great variety of teaching aids and special methods will fill a very particular type of need for the slow learner.

Stressing success and deemphasizing failure is good practice in teaching; it is especially important with slow learners. Assignments should be such that pupils can always accomplish them. The results should be tangible.

MENTALLY RETARDED CHILDREN

Some children fall below those classified as slow learners; they are defined as mentally retarded. This group of children may be of at least two distinct levels: the *educable* and the *trainable*. Public schools

*Courtesy: Department of Institutions and
Agencies, State of New Jersey. Architect:
Vincent G. Kling, Philadelphia, Pa.
Associates: Diehl and Stein, Princeton, N.J.
Photograph by Lawrence S. Williams, Inc., Upper Darby, Pa.*

Model of the Woodbridge, New Jersey State School for Retarded Children.
A number of smaller units provide more of a home atmosphere than
would one large structure.

may have to provide for the educable; the other group should be assigned
to an institution which deals specifically with this group of individuals.

Educable children are those whose IQ's are between 50 and 70. In
some instances these may be in regular classes, but more often a school
will provide special classes for them. The level of work assigned is very
low, but it should be of such nature that he can accomplish it. He learns
best when audio-visual techniques and materials are part of the lesson.
He can learn to do simple tasks and often is capable of being a self-
sufficient individual in society.

The trainable child is more often in an institution other than the public school. If he is able to attend school, he will need much individual attention. He can be trained to learn simple operations on a machine or by hand. Most of the work a child of this mentality will be assigned in school will be manual. Authorities differ in their views as to whether or not these children should be in a public school with average children. They are not a good influence on other children, yet it is hoped that the affected child would learn some good attitudes and patterns of proper behavior from the normal children. In this way he may be able to care for himself throughout life.

EMOTIONALLY MALADJUSTED CHILDREN

On occasion an emotionally maladjusted child may be in the regular class. These children are not necessarily slow learners, but because of this emotional condition they do not adjust to the routine of school. Hence, they often become discipline problems or become so mentally ill that they will need psychiatric treatment. The trained teacher will be able to identify this child by observing symptoms of maladjustment as the child reacts to his environment. When a child is identified as an emotionally disturbed individual, he should be referred to the school psychologist. The psychologist may suggest treatment which can correct his condition; if it is a serious case he will recommend that he be referred to a psychiatrist and the family doctor. Children who have serious emotional problems would profit most from regular treatment at a mental health clinic or in an institution. Some children can carry on a minimal educational program while receiving psychological treatment.

In conclusion, it is well to remember that each individual has certain developmental characteristics that must be recognized and understood by those who plan his school experiences. These experiences must be of the variety and type which lead the individual, whatever his capabilities are, to achieve the necessary mental, physical, emotional, and social growth and development which will make him able to accept the responsibilities of a well-adjusted member of society.

QUESTIONS AND PROJECTS

1. Why is a knowledge of psychology so necessary for a teacher? To what extent does psychology enter into dealing with problems of child development?
2. If it is possible for you to do so, select four or five children in a primary school (Grades 1, 2, and 3) and secure as many of the age measurements referred to in the previous question as possible. Write a report on your findings.
3. What characteristics of children are determined by heredity? By environment?
4. How does a young child learn so much before the time he is able to read? Why is this age often spoken of as an age for molding basic moral and spiritual values?
5. Is a good home environment with understanding parents equal to a nursery school environment? Why or why not?
6. Visit a nursery school or a kindergarten class and observe the various activities of the children. Write an evaluation of what you have observed.
7. Tests for determining IQ are often given to children in the elementary grades. What IQ range or limits are related to an individual described as "normal," "dull," "gifted"?
8. What is the age span for adolescents? Why is this often spoken of as an "age of conflict"?
9. What are some difficulties you recall having had in making social adjustments during your period of early adolescence? Do you recognize now that any teacher helped you overcome these difficulties? How was this accomplished?
10. Why is it important to provide special educational programs for those pupils who fall in the extremes of mental ability?

AUDIO-VISUAL AIDS

MOTION PICTURES (16 MM)

By Experience I Learn—Wisconsin State Board of Health, 20 min., 2 reels, si., b&w. Shows the development of Judy from the age of 9 to 18 months. She learns to walk, climb, feed herself, and play by herself and with others.

Child Care and Development—McGraw-Hill Book Co., Text-Film Dept., 330 West 42nd St., New York, N.Y., 20 min., sd., b&w. Considers the habits of daily physical care that insure a happy, healthy child. Eating, sleeping, bathing, proper clothing, and outdoor exercise are discussed.

Child Development Series, Set II (4 films), McGraw-Hill Book Co., Text-Film Dept., 330 West 42nd St., New York, N.Y.:

Children's Play—27 min., sd., b&w. Shows how play differs at each age level and describes some different forms of play such as free spontaneous play, make-believe play, and constructive play. It emphasizes the need for play time, ample space for play both indoors and out-of-doors, proper equipment, and companions.

Children's Fantasies—21 min., sd., b&w. This film explores the reasons for a child's fantasies and explains how they develop as well as how the child can be affected by them. Deals with common problems such as how should Santa Claus be presented; what to do about imaginary friends; why some children imagine that they are adopted; how to combat fear of the dark. The film points out how fantasy, properly channeled, can be an impetus to artistic, creative living.

Sibling Relations and Personality—22 min., sd., b&w. Through a series of case studies, this film demonstrates the relationships a child has with his brothers and sisters throughout developmental years. The film explores personality influences on the oldest child of a large family, the middle child, the girl who has been reared to be a model child, the girl who feels that her parents would have preferred a boy. It also presents studies of differences in siblings—the boy whose brother is more talented, the girl whose sister is prettier and more popular, and the boy who feels his grandparents prefer his sister.

Sibling Rivalries and Parents—11 min., sd., b&w. The film shows that friction is a normal trait and that with proper understanding and guidance a family can move through the years of childhood with a minimum of quarreling. It describes the reasons for rivalry and the varied manifestations of it. It answers a number of questions which grow out of rivalries among brothers and sisters.

Children's Emotions—McGraw-Hill Book Co., 21 min., sd., b&w. Discusses, through short dramatic illustrations, the development and guidance of children's emotions at various age levels up to 10 years. The commentator explains that the very young child's emotions, while intense, are changeable and harmless because they are completely expressed. Shows how parents can deal with fear, anger, and curiosity, thus making happiness the most frequent and dominant emotion to influence the child's personality development. Designed to be used with a child development text.

Developing Responsibility—Coronet Films, Coronet Bldg., Chicago, Ill., 10 min., sd., b&w. Students learn that although responsibilities often entail hard work, difficult decisions, and missing some fun, the rewards, both material and spiritual, more than compensate.

Early Adolescence: Age of Turmoil—McGraw-Hill Book Co., Text-Film Dept., 330 West 42nd St., New York, N.Y., 20 min., sd., b&w. Presents problems of young people from 13–15 years of age. Discusses behavior that reflects the emotional turmoil of this age, such as giggling, destructive criticism of school, and unrealistic ideas of their own future.

Elementary School Children—McGraw-Hill Book Co., Text-Film Dept., 330 West 42nd St., New York, N.Y. (series of films with accompanying filmstrips). *Developmental Characteristics of Pre-Adolescents*—18 min., sd., b&w. Discusses the patterns of development common to 8- and 9-year-old children of both sexes. Portrays children as they relate to each other, to their parents, and to others in groups, and identifies their patterns of behavior as generally intolerant, self-centered, prone toward identification and imitation of adults, intensely interested in group and personal relations, and revealing a definite preference for their own sexes.

Elementary School Children, Part I, Each Child Is Different—16 min., sd., b&w. Pictures a 5th grade class on the first day of school, and selects five pupils to show the nature of their home life and the differences in their backgrounds, abilities, interests, and needs. Indicates that a teacher is most effective when she knows her pupils as individuals and is familiar with the influences that shape their behavior.

Elementary School Children, Part II, Discovering Individual Differences—25 min., sd., b&w. Uses individual cases to show how an elementary school teacher systematically investigates the differences in backgrounds, activities, and needs of the pupils in her class. Outlines steps in investigation including casual and controlled observations, consulting records, conferences with teachers, parent-teacher interviews, and staff conferences. Illustrates the need for resourcefulness and understanding in improving the educational and social adjustments of pupils.

Farewell to Childhood—International Film Bureau, 57 East Jackson Blvd., Chicago, Ill., 24 min., sd., b&w. Dramatizes the emotional conflicts within a teenage girl and her parents' bewilderment. When her mother consults the school counselor, in whom the girl has complete confidence, everyone concerned gains new insight into the problems of growing up.

Feeling of Hostility—McGraw-Hill Book Co., Text-Film Dept., 330 West 42nd St., New York, N.Y., sd., b&w. Dramatization of the factors producing resentment and hostility in personal relationships. The case history of a girl from early childhood through early adulthood. An attached trailer sums up the factors that have contributed to the girl's personality, her emotional inadequacy, and the feeling of hostility in personal relationships.

The Gifted Ones—National Film Board of Canada, Room 658, 630 Fifth Ave., New York, N.Y., 22 min., sd., b&w. This film shows a classroom where a gifted group is being taught. In addition, it presents a discussion by two prominent Canadian educators, each giving his views on the importance of challenging these students in terms of present day needs.

He Acts His Age—McGraw-Hill Book Co., Text-Film Dept., 330 West 42nd St., New York, N.Y., 15 min., sd., b&w. Shows play activities of a group of children at a picnic, pointing out typical behavior of each age group from 1–15 years of age. Emphasizes the importance of recognizing and understanding these stages of growth.

Individual Differences—McGraw-Hill Book Co., Text-Film Dept., 330 West 42nd St., New York, N.Y., 23 min., sd., b&w. Case study of a shy, slow child who is different from his classmates and from his older, socially adept brother. Points out that it is the job of the teacher to know her pupils and to work toward meeting each child's needs.

Into the Known—Richard Lyford, Prod., Sterling Movies, 27 min., sd., color. Stresses the importance of books in stimulating the imagination of children and enlarging their thinking. Illustrates the needs filled by books through the mind pictures of children as they read. Reflects the delight experienced by a child as he learns to read and comes "into the known." Points out that the ability to read in order to gain knowledge is power.

Learning and Growth—EBF, Arnold Gesell, 11 min., sd., b&w. Clarifies some of the principles which govern the learning process. Describes the possibilities and limitations of training infants from twenty-four to forty-eight weeks old. Relationships between age, growth, and learning are indicated. Several learning problems are analyzed with reference to the effect of maturity. Points out laws which determine learning in older children.

Life with Baby—MOT, 19 min., sd., b&w. Shows the findings of Dr. Arnold Gesell, at the Yale University Clinic, concerning the mental and physical growth of children. Consists of candid-camera shots photographed through a one-way vision dome.

Life with Junior—MOT, 19 min., sd., b&w. Outlines a typical day in the life of a 10-year-old boy, stressing the need for the development of his individual aptitudes, abilities, and personality pattern. Pictures the anxieties of parents over the proper guidance of their children and shows the ways in which these parents obtain scientific help. Also touches upon some major problems of child behavior.

Preface to a Life—United World Government Films, 1445 Park Ave., New York, N.Y., 29 min., sd., b&w. A son, Michael, is born to the Thompsons. Shows the possible effects on his growth and development of his father's aspirations for him and contrasts these with the possible effects of his mother's aspirations. Also shows what he would become if his parents help him to develop according to his own capabilities.

Principles of Development—McGraw-Hill Book Co., Text-Film Dept., 330 West 42nd St., New York, N.Y., 17 min., sd., b&w. Outlines the fundamentals of child growth and development from early infancy, considers factors which make each child different from every other child.

Sex Adjustment During Adolescence—McGraw-Hill Book Co., Text-Film Dept., 330 West 42nd St., New York, N.Y., 22 min., sd., b&w. Presents the importance of the understanding of sex in teen-agers. A boy and girl are taken through their entire adolescent experience which culminates in their marriage.

Problem Children—Div. of Mental Hygiene, Ohio, 22 min., sd., b&w. Presents the problems of an aggressive, trouble-making boy who tries to compensate for being babied by his mother and ignored by his father, and those of a shy, quiet boy who becomes a complete introvert when the divorce of his parents makes him feel insecure. Adjustment in their educational program and improved home conditions help the two boys to take their proper places in society.

Psychology I: Human Abilities and Mental Growth—NET, Indiana University A-V Center, 30 min., sd., b&w. Discusses the testing of human abilities and mental growth and explains how to calculate the IQ. Contrasts the two-factor and multi-factor theories of intelligence. Describes the various kinds of tests available for testing the primary abilities. Features Dr. Edwin G. Boring of Harvard University.

Teacher as Observer and Guide—Metropolitan School Study Council, 22 min., sd., b&w. Six school situations illustrate the following concepts: guiding pupils to better ways of solving their problems, developing artistic talent, promoting the growth of character and citizenship, and providing needed assistance for slow learners.

Social Development—McGraw-Hill Book Co., Text-Film Dept., 330 West 42nd St., New York, N.Y., 16 min., sd., b&w. Analysis of children's social behavior at different age levels; gives reasons underlying the changes in behavior patterns as the child develops.

FURTHER READINGS

Almy, Millie, *Child Development* (New York, Holt, Rinehart and Winston, 1955).

Barr, John A., *The Elementary Teacher and Guidance* (New York, Holt, Rinehart and Winston, 1958) .

Bossard, James H. S., *The Sociology of Child Development,* rev. ed. (New York, Harper & Row, 1953).

Burton, William H., *The Guidance of Learning Activities,* 3rd ed. (New York, Appleton-Century-Crofts, 1962).

Ebel, Robert L., *Measuring Educational Achievement* (Englewood Cliffs, N.J., Prentice-Hall, 1965).

Egg, Maria, *When a Child is Different: A Basic Guide for Parents and Friends of Mentally Retarded Children* (New York, John Day, 1964).

Fusco, Gene C., *School-Home Partnership in Depressed Urban Neighborhoods,* OE-31008, Bull. 1964, No. 20, U.S. Department of Health, Education, and Welfare (Washington, D.C., Office of Education, 1964).

Hymes, James L., *A Child Development Point of View* (Englewood Cliffs, N.J., Prentice-Hall, 1955).

Jersild, Arthur T., *Child Psychology,* 5th ed. (Englewood Cliffs, N.J., Prentice-Hall, 1960).

Lane, Howard, and Mary Beauchamp, *Understanding Human Development* (Englewood Cliffs, N.J., Prentice-Hall, 1959).

Lee, J. M., and Doris May Lee, *The Child and His Development* (New York, Appleton-Century-Crofts, 1958).

Martin, W. E., and C. B. Stendler, *Child Behavior and Development* (New York, Harcourt, Brace, 1959).

Millard, Cecil V., *Child Growth and Development* (Boston, Heath, 1958).

National Society for the Study of Education, *Child Psychology,* Sixty-second Yearbook, Part I (Chicago, University of Chicago Press, 1963).

National Society for the Study of Education, *The Impact and Improvement of School Testing Programs,* Sixty-second Yearbook, Part II (Chicago, University of Chicago Press, 1963).

National Society for the Study of Education, *Theories of Learning,* Sixty-third Yearbook, Part I (Chicago, University of Chicago Press, 1964).

Ritchie, Oscar W., and Marvin R. Koller, *Sociology of Childhood* (New York, Appleton-Century-Crofts, 1964).

Staats, Arthur W., and Carolyn K. Staats, *Complex Human Behavior: A Systematic Extension of Learning Principles* (New York, Holt, Rinehart and Winston, 1963).

12

Necessary and Desirable
Physical Provisions
for Education

PREVIEW

▶ The school plant is an integral part of the educational program.
Planning the school plant should be a concern of many persons.
Some guiding principles are helpful in determining adequacy.

▶ The design of school buildings has changed markedly in recent years.
More thought is given to the instructional program as well as to the
safety and attractiveness of buildings.

▶ A school building must have an adequate number of classrooms and
auxiliary rooms.
The classroom, both in the elementary and secondary school, determines, to a large extent, the quality of the instructional program.
An important part of the total school experience depends on a
school building having auxiliary rooms.
The "self-contained" classroom is planned to promote the best instructional methods.

▶ Modern methods of teaching depend upon a variety of equipment
and supplies.
The practices for textbook selection vary from state to state.
Necessary equipment and facilities for use of audio-visual materials
should be a part of every classroom.
Good selection of supplies enhances the learning process.

Public school buildings and related facilities represent one of the largest investments made by local communities. School administrators and other authorities on public school finance indicate that almost twenty percent of each year's school budget is spent for the school plant and other equipment. Today, as never before, the quality of an educational program is dependent upon facilities made available to the teachers. If a teacher is prepared to utilize all the modern instructional tools and techniques, and the school where he is employed is not such that he can apply those new methods, his instruction is bound to be less effective than he would like.

In a recent report on school facilities, the U.S. Office of Education makes this statement:

Classrooms and facilities can affect quality of the educational processes favorably by providing an efficient and effective environment. Conversely education suffers when (1) the educational program of pupils is limited by insufficient areas; (2) the spaces provided are unsafe; or (3) the teaching-learning functions are inhibited by inadequate facilities.[1]

There is evidence of considerable progress being made toward getting the type of buildings and equipment necessary to accomplish the most effective methods of teaching, but much more needs to be done. New designs for buildings, more attractive decorating, and more functional

*Courtesy: Sargent-Webster-Crenshaw
& Folley, Architects, A.I.A.*

Architect's Model, Longbranch Elementary School, Liverpool, New York.

[1] George J. Collins, *National Inventory of School Facilities and Personnel*, Misc. No. 44 (Washington, D.C., 1964), p. 1.

equipment within the building will gradually augment the kind of instructional program educators believe is most practical for today's youth.

THE SCHOOL PLANT

For the purpose of definition, the school plant includes the school site, the school building, and equipment. The total school plant is a long-term project. In most cases when a building is erected and equipped it will be used for the next 75 or more years. Careful planning is most important before the plant becomes a reality, and that planning must project into the future. The physical layout based on present-day needs is all too often inadequate before it is completed. Today's population is a mobile one. It is most difficult to predict what a school's enrollment will be from one year to another. There are countless factors, too numerous to elaborate here, which make small communities large in a very short period of time. It would seem that to accommodate this changing population, a community should make certain to acquire school sites and plan buildings which would allow for expansion and modification as such needs arise.

It is most unusual today to find any school buildings with empty classrooms. Many schools are overcrowded and a large number are entirely inadequate from the standpoint of facilities which are both safe and modern. It has been pointed out earlier in this volume that the shortage of adequate classrooms approximated 127,000 in 1961–62, using studies from the United States Office of Education and the Rockefeller Report. The figures have been disputed by the United States Chamber of Commerce, but it appears that discrepancies exist mostly because of different definitions of adequacy.

If the current birthrates continue, an annual increase of approximately one million pupils is certain for five to ten years ahead. Obviously, this increase calls for more classrooms. How many are built each year is something that the American people must decide. It is clear, however, that the pressure for federal aid for school construction will increase until some reasonably adequate program is adopted.

CHOOSING A SCHOOL SITE

A well-chosen site for a school building is the first step toward providing adequate educational facilities. The choice of land for a school building should be a co-operative venture. The board of education, the administration, the city planning authority, and state department of education should have a part in determining the best possible location for a school. It is becoming very common for the local school board to employ specialists from universities to conduct surveys of possible population growth in order to avoid choosing a site which will not meet future needs. This problem of site selection must be based on long-term planning.

A suitable site for a school should meet the following criteria: (1) *Location*. It should be situated in an area where the population warrants it and where it will serve future population growth resulting from residential development. It should be accessible by the modes of transportation available. (2) *Size*. It should be large enough to allow for additional building, provide adequate play areas and, if it is a secondary school site, it should provide enough space for the health and physical education program. The site should provide adequate parking areas for autos and separated from this an area for bicycles.

The suggested standard today is a site of at least 5 and preferably 10 usable acres plus an additional acre for each 100 pupils of ultimate enrollment for elementary schools; for secondary schools, a minimum of 20 usable acres plus an additional acre for each 100 pupils of ultimate enrollment. In densely populated cities one would believe this to be almost impossible, yet in one of our largest cities at the present time there are sites chosen for schools which vary in size from 16 acres to 60 acres. (3) The third factor to be considered is the *soil and topography*. It should be suitable for the type of structure planned. It should be favorable for planting and grass growth. The cost of excavation required should not be prohibitive. The site should have natural drainage, if possible. Some sites may be impractical due to excessive costs for installing drainage systems.

With careful thought and planning, the site will become a functional part of the school plant. As the Yearbook on American School Buildings [2] suggests, "Site beautification must be subordinated to recreational use but the less utilitarian features of the school site—grassy places, flowers, shrubs, and trees—will provide enjoyment for the pupils and will give opportunity for developing appreciation of beauty and pride in their school."

THE SCHOOL BUILDING

The design and construction of the school building are of major importance. Preliminary planning for a school building should be a co-operative project entered into with teachers, administrators, pupils, office staff, board members, and specialists from the universities and the state department of education. Before hiring an architect it is a good policy to visit some buildings which are representative of his work.

Guiding Principles for Planning School Buildings

Two basic space units should be considered in planning school buildings. They are *instructional rooms* and *auxiliary rooms*. The first refers to classrooms, laboratories, shops, music rooms, and gymnasiums where regularly scheduled classes are held. The auxiliary rooms include

[2] American Association of School Administrators, *American School Buildings*, Twenty-seventh Yearbook (Washington, NEA, 1949), p. 83.

the more general purpose rooms such as libraries, auditoriums, lunch rooms, faculty rooms, toilet rooms, and offices.

In planning the building to achieve the purpose it is to serve there are certain essential qualities to keep in mind. The qualities most often referred to are:

1. Safety	5. Utility
2. Healthfulness	6. Adequacy
3. Flexibility	7. Beauty
4. Economy	8. Expansibility

Some architects use the term *fluidity*, which relates to large open areas which permit an easy flow of students. This is of considerable importance in halls, auditoriums, and entry ways.

If more attention had been given in the past to such a list of essential qualities for good school buildings, there would not be as many obsolete structures as we have today. A large share of what might be described as old school buildings are educationally inadequate for present-day curricula and teaching methods. This fact lends further support to those who would build a school which would accommodate the educational program in contrast to building a school and then attempting to fit the curriculum to it.

Once the educational program has been determined, it is much easier to go to the architects and point out the basic building needs for facilitating that program. In turn, the architects will be able to plan a building with the necessary rooms of the right size in the best location for maximum utilization. This should avoid what often has resulted—a good building architecturally, but one that actually interfered with good educational practices.

Important Changes That Have Occurred in School Buildings

School buildings have changed greatly in the past 25 years and almost radically since World War II. There is now more concern over orientation of the building to the site. Greater window or glass-brick areas have been incorporated into the building to allow entrance of more natural light. The trend is toward one-story buildings rather than multistory. This provides for greater safety through the elimination of stairs and the provision of an increased number of exits. Many elementary schools and some of the secondary schools built on the one-story plan have a door to the outside from each room. Halls have been made wider; lockers and drinking fountains have been recessed into the walls, and in most elementary schools placed in the classroom rather than in halls, thus easing the traffic problem through the halls. Noise level has been reduced by

*Courtesy: Dr. Calvin E. Gross, Superintendent,
and Morris Ketchum, Jr. and Associates, Architects.*

Public School 45, Brooklyn, New York. This "Inner World" school, will face away from the street and have all its windows on interior courts. Designed as an experimental school, it is planned to keep glass breakage at a minimum, to reduce noise from the street, and to test a number of innovations in classroom and corridor design.

acoustical treatment of ceilings and walls. Room temperature conducive to efficient work habits is maintained through the use of unit ventilators controlled by a master control panel.

Modern artificial lighting is more efficient. Control of the amount of natural light entering a room is made possible through proper installation of blinds or drapes. A variety of new color schemes adds to the beauty and vitality of halls and rooms. School buildings are safer, more flexible, and more easily adapted to a changing curriculum. The over-all pattern of school building design is aimed toward providing a healthful environment for learning.

Modern Secondary School Design

More students in school for a greater number of years have caused many changes to occur in the secondary school's educational program. These changes in program along with the philosophy of what constitutes the best climate for learning have influenced the design of school buildings.

Courtesy: Senior High School, Oneonta, N.Y.
Architect: Warren H. Ashley, West Hartford, Conn.

Band uniforms are neatly stored in easily accessible area behind folding door.

Campus Plan

As the name implies, this type of school was a break from the traditional E-shaped, multistory building which was commonplace 50 years ago. The campus school might be called a decentralized school. It is usually a one-story structure which is simple in design and very flexible in terms of usability. Although the subject-matter content areas are present, rather than being a series of rooms devoted to social studies, English or science, they are separate buildings. Each building is so designed to serve its particular function in the overall educative process. This kind of building has brought about the necessity for administrative planning in terms of what interrelationships exist between the separate subject matter buildings.

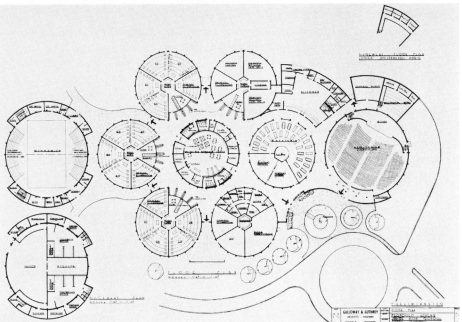

Courtesy: W. F. Whitaker, Supt. of Schools,
Athens, Tennessee. Architects: Galloway
and Guthrey, Knoxville, Tenn.
Photograph by Harry L. Whittington, Knoxville, Tenn.

Athens Junior High School, Athens, Tennessee. This modern design incorporates the type of facility for the school-within-a-school concept. Note that classroom buildings surround instructional materials center and library.

307

Many significant developments have grown out of such a building plan. The more important are better site utilization, larger and more efficiently lighted rooms, and being one-story in structure the supporting beams and walls could be of lighter steel or wood.

The cost per square foot of constructing such a building is about the same as one of a more traditional type, but the maintenance and repair costs are much less.

Schools Within the School

Another building design which accomplishes some of the same educational advantages as the campus-type school is commonly referred to as a school within a school. In such a plan the building is usually constructed of one-story wings and each wing is assigned to a certain group of 300 to 500 students. These students have all their major subjects in this wing. By comparison to the campus-type school, this school might be more student-centered than subject-centered.

Each wing might contain a grade level; for example, there might be a 7th grade, an 8th grade and a 9th grade in each of three wings. The students do, however, use certain common facilities together such as the library, cafeteria, and gymnasium.

Schools with large enrollments are finding this type of building plan superior in many ways. The possibilities for closer pupil-teacher relationships for guidance purposes is one of the more important advantages of such a building plan. The team-teaching approach to curriculum planning is a natural outgrowth of this type building and administrative organization.

SIZE REQUIREMENTS FOR SCHOOL ROOMS

The size of all classrooms should be determined by the use that is to be made of them. They must be of such dimensions as will provide adequate space for the pupils to work as well as accommodate the necessary educational equipment.

The modern school building is designed to facilitate many and varied activities which grow from a functional curriculum. Therefore, classrooms as well as multipurpose rooms and gymnasiums are designed as large areas which can be converted into two or more smaller areas by moveable soundproof walls or doors. In the discussion of the various spaces which are common to most school buildings, the sizes are given on the basis of that particular space being used to house a traditional size class of 25 to 30 pupils. Modern instructional practices which call for large group instruction, small group instruction or individualized study necessitate increasing the sizes of some of these spaces to the extent that they can

Courtesy: Dr. J. Maurice Strattan, Superintendent.
Architects: Chappelle and Crothers.
Photograph by Thompson Studio, Paoli, Pa.

Valley Forge Junior High School, Paoli Area High School System, Paoli, Pa. This facility is constructed to house grades 7, 8, and 9—each in a separate wing. This accommodates team teaching and the concept of school-within-a-school. The fourth wing houses administration offices, library, gymnasium, and other facilities common to all classes.

accommodate up to 90 to 120 pupils. In such cases the size would have to be doubled or tripled. In all school buildings there should be a few classroom spaces of traditional size. They could be utilized for the small or traditional size group of pupils when class discussions are needed.

Elementary School Classrooms

Most specialists in elementary education suggest a minimum of 30 square feet of floor space per pupil. This would require that a classroom for 30 pupils be 30′ x 30′, or perhaps 24′ x 38′. A room to house the

Courtesy: St. Helens Junior High School,
St. Helens, Oregon. Architects—Engineers:
Edmundson, Kochendoerfer, &
Kennedy, Portland, Oregon.

Flexible spaces facilitate both small and large group instruction. This photograph shows how one large area can be formed by moving the large flexible walls on each of four rooms. This kind of facility accommodates team teaching very well.

kindergarten should contain approximately 1,000 square feet. This amount of space will permit the kind of activities common to children of this age; it will accommodate the building of a playhouse, a store, a post office, or other structures. It will also provide adequate space for rest periods when each child may lie down on the floor. There should be ample cupboard space where the children can store their toys, blocks, picture books, and their blankets or rugs for rest periods.

Since one of the keywords descriptive of the elementary grades and kindergarten is "activity," the size of all elementary classrooms must be such that the children have room to move about freely. The room should accommodate small groups working on projects at the same time that others in the class are engaged in working with the teacher.

*Courtesy: Gerald G. Hottenstein, Supervising
Principal, and Dunlap and Rienzi, Architects.*

Plymouth Elementary School, Plymouth Township, Pa., is an interesting example of a modern suburban elementary school.

Secondary School Classrooms

In the traditional recitation rooms where the policy was to have fixed desks, an adequate amount of space per pupil was considered to be about 20 square feet. The trend today is away from fixed seating. There is more need for tables to facilitate small group discussions and activities, supervised study, and panel discussions. More instructional materials such as reference books, recorders, record players, projectors, and models are provided within the classroom. These all require more space. The recommended floor area per pupil is about 30 square feet, a standard requiring a building considerably larger than heretofore.

Laboratories

A science laboratory should provide a minimum of 30 square feet per pupil plus a minimum of 125–150 square feet for storage space. The laboratory should be planned to meet the requirements for the particular science being taught, for each science course has requirements peculiar to itself. For example, a general science laboratory may require only one demonstration table in the front of the room. This table should be equipped with running water, a sink, and sources of gas and electricity. The pupils may have individual chairs with arms to permit writing or they may be seated at tables all facing in such a direction that they can

Courtesy: Senior High School, Oneonta, N.Y.
Architect: Warren H. Ashley, West Hartford, Conn.

Well-equipped laboratories and skilled teachers motivate pupils to employ the scientific method of solving problems and to develop an interest in science.

see demonstrations as well as hear any comments from the teacher or other class members.

There are certain requirements in common for all of the science laboratories. Careful and thoughtful planning will determine the needs for the chemistry, physics, biology courses and work in photography.

Homemaking Rooms

The most common arrangement found in homemaking departments requires a minimum of two rooms. One room is usually devoted to the study of foods where stoves, cupboards, sinks, refrigerators, and work tables are necessary equipment. The other room is equipped for the study of clothing. This room is also used for the study of home furnishing, child care and development, and nursing.

The amount of floor space per pupil should be no less than 40 square

Courtesy: Armstrong, Schlichting, Torseth
and Skold, Inc., Architects.
Photograph by C. N. Dean Paris.

Penn Junior High School, Bloomington, Minnesota. A large mirror mounted above the teacher's desk enables all pupils to see the demonstration.

feet. A minimum floor area of 1200 square feet is desirable to provide storage space, free work areas, and sufficient space for pupils at their regular laboratory stations.

Business Education Rooms

The area to be used for this training should be incorporated into a suite of rooms. The typing room should adjoin the stenography or office-practice room or both. The bookkeeping room should adjoin the business machines room or distributive-education room or both. Most school building planners recommend that the business-education suite be on the first floor with easy access from the administrative offices. This is especially desirable if business-education pupils perform duties or use equipment associated with the work of the central offices.

The per pupil space requirements recommended by business educators are 20 to 25 square feet for typing, 25 square feet for bookkeeping and shorthand, 30 square feet for office practice, and 32 square feet for business machines.

Shops

The school shop should provide a minimum of 75 square feet of floor space per pupil. This larger space requirement is due to the need for the power machinery, workbenches, and storage space for tools. An adjoining room for storage of lumber, sheet metal, and other supplies is also advisable. The main shop area should contribute to the safety of the pupil by allowing ample space for free movement around power equipment.

Art Rooms

The art room should be another laboratory-type area. Each pupil should have about 35 square feet of floor space, and over and beyond this there should be storage space for supplies. Large amounts of cabinet and shelf space are also necessary for storing projects which are incomplete and are worked on during class meetings. Also there is a need to provide work centers which deal with a specific problem such as working with clay, metal, wood, and textiles. The supplies for each of these should be housed in cabinets adjacent to the work area.

SOME BASIC REQUIREMENTS FOR AUXILIARY ROOMS

Much of the space in the modern school building is allotted to rooms other than what we might call instruction rooms. This does not mean that such rooms are less valuable. On the contrary, they provide pupils with training in certain skills, appreciations, and attitudes that are of utmost importance in the development of the whole personality.

Libraries

The library within a school should serve as a center for educational materials. The changing concept of the school library is away from the thought that it is merely a storage place for books and a reading room.

Courtesy: Howard D. Brooks, Superintendent,
Amity Regional Senior High School,
Woodbridge, Conn. Photograph by
Jack Stock Studio, Derby, Conn.

New library areas are equipped with proper lighting, comfortable furniture and adequate space to facilitate study and research.

The modern library should function as a workshop. In a bulletin issued by the New Jersey Department of Education [3] it is suggested:

Since there must be interplay of stimulation between the classroom and the library, the library should be functional. Adequate space, books and equipment should be provided in an attractive environment for:

1. The selection and preparation of materials by the librarians.
2. Instruction in the use of these materials.
3. The use of these materials by pupils and teachers.

If a library is to serve its real purpose in the educational program as suggested above it should be centrally located and accessible to the school

[3] School Building Services Bureau, *A Guide for Planning Facilities for the High School Library* (Trenton, N.J., Department of Education, 1955), mimeographed.

Courtesy: Aston Elementary School, Penn-Delco
Union School District, Pennsylvania. Architects:
H. A. Kuljian & Company, Philadelphia, Pa.
Photograph by Standard Photo Service, Philadelphia, Pa.

This library in an elementary school is carpeted to provide a more pleasing and quiet environment for study. Carpeted classrooms are no longer a luxury; they are considered economically sound for they provide greater safety than other surfaces.

population. Engelhardt, Engelhardt, and Leggett [4] say that "An outstanding objective in American education should be the placement of a well-planned library in every public school of two hundred pupil enrollment and above."

Many school libraries are poorly located and inadequate for their function. Because no provision was made for libraries at the time some buildings were built, regular classroom space was converted to library areas. This, at best, can serve a school only temporarily. The library should be one of the larger room areas in a school building.

4 N. L. Engelhardt, N. L. Engelhardt, Jr., and Stanton Leggett, *Planning Elementary School Buildings* (New York, F. W. Dodge, 1953), p. 82.

*Courtesy: Raymond F. Howes, Assistant
to the Chancellor—Public Affairs*

New Library Building, University of California at Riverside.

In a national survey [5] it is reported that "about seven out of ten pupils in elementary, secondary, and combined school plants have access to a centralized school library." Fewer elementary than secondary schools have a central library.

The Health Suite

In all modern school planning, the health services area should be a suite of rooms including a waiting room, examination area, treatment room, or first-aid area and a space for resting.

Since there should not be any great number of students assigned to or using this area at any one time, the over-all space requirements are approximately 1,200 square feet. One-half of this could be divided into a waiting room and a resting room with two small cots. The remaining half, or 600 square feet, would be divided into the necessary cubicles for examination and first-aid treatment.

[5] Collins, *op. cit.*, p. 22.

The health suite should include office space for nurse and doctor and for records. These office areas should adjoin the treatment and waiting room areas.

The location of the health service suite should be near the administrative office and not too far from the gymnasium, since there should be a close relationship among all three.

Auditoriums

The auditorium should be so planned that its maximum use will not result in too many scheduling conflicts. It is primarily designed

Consultants: The Blankfort Group
Architects: Carmichael-Kemp, A.I.A.

View from central patio of William T. Newland School of Fountain Valley, California, shows indoor-outdoor stage area (which doubles as a music room) and two kindergarten rooms with pinboard wall opened to form one large meeting space. There are floodlights suspended from cantilevered roof structure and from ceiling of rooms for good stage lighting, as well as daylight fluorescent lighting in rooms.

*Courtesy: Architects and Engineers—Commonwealth
Associates, Inc., Jackson, Michigan;
Associate Architects, Caudill, Rowlett
& Scott, Houston, Texas.*

Parkside High School, Jackson, Michigan. This round structure provides a maximum useable area for physical education activities and athletic events. Proper lighting and no structural uprights offer excellent playing and spectator facilities.

to accommodate assembly programs and dramatics. Because of overcrowding in schools, the auditorium has been used for many other purposes such as study hall, lunchroom, social room, and even classroom. It was never meant to function as any of these, and at best this has proven unsatisfactory.

Fixed seating is advisable in the true auditorium set-up. In instances where the auditorium is combined with the gymnasium there will be found both fixed and movable seating. The size of the auditorium is related to the maximum enrollment of the school. It should be large enough to seat half the total enrollment at one time.

The walls and ceilings should be acoustically designed and treated to keep the level of noise low. Under ordinary conditions, with proper voice reinforcement equipment, people on the stage should be heard in all parts of the auditorium. Seating should be so arranged that the stage can be seen from any point in the room. The stage should be large enough to permit the staging of dramatic productions, band and orchestra concerts, and vocal music programs. The increased use of projected materials in assembly programs requires well-placed electrical outlets and sound-system installations. The projection booth in the back of the auditorium is a regular part of most plans. The school auditorium should be accessible to community groups for their use without opening the entire school building.

The Gymnasium

The gymnasium is essential in all school buildings. It may be a separate structure adjoining the school proper or it may be a wing of the main building. It should be large enough to permit team games. It should be well ventilated and well lighted. Locker rooms with showers should be provided. An elementary school gymnasium should be 50′ x 80′. A secondary school gymnasium should provide a floor space large enough to permit the regulation size basketball court with ample space for safety zones and folding bleachers if they are to be installed. This calls for a space of 76′ x 96′.

The gymnasium should be equipped with sliding doors to divide the area into two rooms for physical education classes. One gymnasium should serve the needs of both boys and girls in the average-sized school. Greater use of the gymnasium by community organizations also makes it desirable to provide access to it without opening the entire building.

Lunchrooms

The school hot-lunch program is an important adjunct to the regular school experience. It serves more than just the purpose of feeding children. The social aspects are tremendous. The lunchroom provides experience in group living, acquisition of good manners, and an opportunity for pupils to get acquainted.

The lunchroom should be on the first floor where delivery of food and disposal of kitchen wastes can be cared for easily. It is becoming more and more common to provide access to the lunchroom for community use during evenings and vacation periods without opening the rest of the school. Many adult groups can use this area for meetings and conferences because it lends itself to such activities as well as affording food service for the group. This, of course, is not a school function and should in no way involve school personnel unless the school board and administration consent to it.

The amount of space needed for the lunchroom depends on the size of the school. Most people agree to the figure of approximately 10 square feet per person in the dining area. The school lunchroom should be used for other functions beyond food service. Many school administrators are finding it useful for study hall. School parties and dances can be held in the lunchroom. Afternoon and evening conferences can be scheduled for the area, providing time is allowed for cleaning up. Through adapting the lunchroom to other uses, there is greater justification for it. It leaves little opportunity for those who would tend to criticize having such a room for use only during lunch periods which may be but a third of the school day.

The Self-Contained Classroom

In an effort to effect a change in classroom design, educators, architects, and industry have co-operated in working out the plans for a multi-purpose classroom. (See cut of plans.) It is so planned that all the learning experiences can be provided within the "home" classroom. The room area of 1,200 square feet provides the necessary work areas, conference rooms, exhibit, display, and storage space, a stage for dramatizations, and ample stationary and movable shelving for library books. The lighting and temperature control are the best engineers can suggest. Provision is made for light control to insure the best conditions for the use of projected materials. Both boys' and girls' lavatories are provided, and work areas contain sinks with running water.

Modern design of furniture permits stacking in a small area if the room is to be used for activities calling for large free floor areas. The decorating scheme is attractive and adds to the over-all pleasant atmosphere of the room environment.

The advantages of this room over the traditional classroom make it worthy of consideration when plans for new school buildings are being formulated. It provides greater flexibility than any other room design. It promotes and provides space for greater pupil participation in activities based on the curriculum. For example, pupils have facilities available within the classroom for experimentation which calls for work area, running water, sink, and electricity. These facilities would usually be available only in a science laboratory. Projected materials can be used when pupils would benefit most from the experience. This overcomes the need for scheduling the audio-visual room for a particular period on a given day as is often true in many of our school buildings. Further, it would eliminate the need for a special audio-visual room. For the cost of building, equipping, and maintaining a special room for the use of all pro-

Figure 12-1.   Suggested Floor Plan for a Self-Contained Secondary
               School Classroom

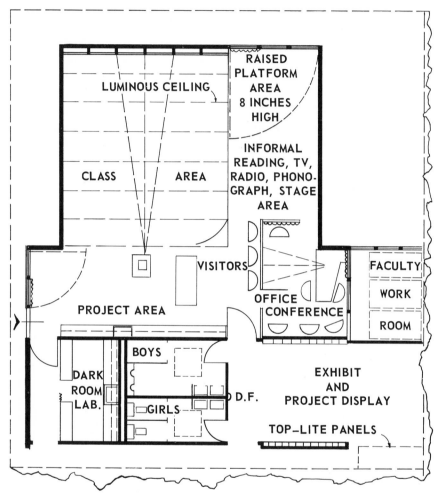

SOURCE: Department of Audio-Visual Instruction of the NEA.

jected materials, it is possible to have all the rooms in a building equipped
for light control. According to the best estimates available, the average
cost of constructing a classroom, which might be used for audio-visual
aids, is between $25,000 and $30,000. Facilities for the best light control
in *all* classrooms in a building of 25 classrooms would not exceed this sum
of money. This enables teachers and pupils to use projection equipment
in the regular classroom in a more effective setting for learning as compared to a special room for "seeing a movie."

The self-contained room gives opportunity for more individualized instruction and study. The conference room provides for such instruction and could also be used by small groups preparing reports, and working on projects, at the same time eliminating any disturbance to others in the class working on the regular assignments.

These advantages and others lead one to believe that the school building of the future will make more use of this type of classroom. The cost of constructing this room compares favorably with that of the more traditional classroom.

Actual practice indicates this type of room is found more acceptable to elementary school teachers. Secondary schools other than those organized on the plan of the core curriculum prefer a room more suited to strict departmentalization.

The foregoing discussion of the school plant is not meant to be complete. It is presented here to acquaint the student with some of the more general aspects of school plant planning. Some of the minimum requirements are listed to stimulate thought and offer some guidance to those teachers who will be involved in this tremendous problem of planning school buildings to house the growing enrollments mentioned earlier in the chapter. For a more complete account of any one phase of school building requirements, consult the references in the bibliography of this chapter.

TEXTBOOKS

Textbooks are classified as equipment because they usually serve the instructional program for a period of several years. In the more than 300 years since the first printing press began to operate in the United States, millions of books have been published. A vast number of these books have been written to serve as textbooks for all subject fields and levels of learning. They constitute the tools most frequently used in education.

The textbook today is a far superior tool for learning than it was even 50 years ago. The quality of paper, the style of type, the use of pertinent illustrative material, and improved format have all contributed to the usefulness of books in the teaching-learning process. Even though teachers employ a variety of other tools in developing interest, skills, understanding, and attitudes, the textbook is most often the basic outline to guide both teacher and pupil in organizing the material for assimilation.

However, it is well to remember that modern methods of teaching do not restrict the teacher to the use of one textbook. It is common practice to select one book as a basic text and supply an adequate number of two or more other textbooks for the reference shelf within the classroom. The pupils use the basic textbook for study and the others as supplementary reading materials. The teacher refers to the supplementary textbooks as often as the need arises. This gives the pupils opportunity to read the opinions and judgments of other authors as well as to become acquainted with different styles of writing.

Selection of Textbooks

The state law defines the responsibility for selection. At present about half of the states have statutes which require the use of uniform textbooks throughout the state or for special grades within the schools. In the remaining half of the states, the local district has jurisdiction over textbook selection. There are no set practices even in states where state-wide adoption is required. As Moehlman [6] has pointed out:

The California, New Mexico, Oklahoma, and Virginia constitutions require uniform texts within the state; Colorado and Wyoming constitutions prohibit state authorities from prescribing textbooks; Texas makes constitutional provision for textbooks at public expense; the constitutions of Illinois, Mississippi, South Dakota and West Virginia demand that teachers or other school officials shall have no interest in the sale of textbooks in the school with which they are associated. In many other states the relations between teachers and textbook publishers are controlled by statute.

Many states provide an approved list of textbooks from which the local district must choose. In some states the state boards of education, or commissions other than the state board, select the textbooks. In only one state does the state superintendent act solely as the selecting authority.

The usual method of selecting textbooks and other instructional materials is by committees appointed by the superintendent. This committee should be made up of teachers, supervisors, curriculum co-ordinators, and administrators. Selection should be based on content, format, and suitability for the course and the pupils. Some committees rely on a guide or check-list. Such check-lists usually contain the following items: authorship, date of publication, content, vocabulary, organization, pupil activities, suggested teaching aids, illustrative material, format, physical makeup, and durability.

Whatever method of selection is employed, the committee charged with the responsibility must always keep curriculum needs in mind. A particular book may rate very high on all check-list items and yet not meet the needs of pupils pursuing a given curriculum.

Purchase of Textbooks

Following the selection of textbooks they must be purchased and distributed to the pupils. The policy governing distribution varies

[6] Arthur B. Moehlman, *School Administration: Its Development, Principles and Functions in the United States,* 2nd ed. (Boston, Houghton Mifflin, 1951), p. 195.

among states and among schools. There are three general procedures: (1) the school owns the book and permits the pupil to use it free of charge; (2) the school owns the book, but rents it to the pupil; or (3) pupils are required to purchase the book. One-third of the states provide free textbooks to the pupils. In some cases this applies only to elementary schools. The tendency is toward providing textbooks at public expense. It would seem that in a democracy such as ours where free public education is provided for all this should be the practice.

AUDIO-VISUAL MATERIALS

A school's audio-visual education program depends on three factors.

1. The equipment available.
2. The facilities for using the equipment.
3. The use teachers make of the materials.

Since this chapter deals with the physical needs for education it might appear that item 3 should not be included. It is placed here because items 1 and 2 are justified in terms of item 3. This third factor is developed here, rather than in connection with equipment for special rooms, because audio-visual materials are tools which are used in all subject fields and for all levels of education. These materials when used correctly will be a part of teaching and learning in all rooms.

Meaning of Audio-Visual Materials

A definition of audio-visual materials is all those materials which appeal directly to the senses of sight and hearing. It includes the following: chalkboards, bulletin boards, feltboards, posters, field trips, maps and globes, charts, graphs and diagrams, illustrations and flat pictures, cartoons and comics, murals, museum exhibits and displays, mockups, models and specimens, dioramas, dramatizations, demonstrations, stereographs, flash cards, slides, filmstrips, motion pictures, radio, records and transcriptions, tape recordings, and television.

Most of the teaching materials listed suggest activities which should take place within the school. Some require specific equipment and facilities. The facilities and equipment should be available at any time a teacher needs them for his class.

Room Facilities and Equipment

All classrooms should provide facilities for the effective use of good teaching materials and techniques. The two words *effective use* are the keywords to all teaching with audio-visual materials. For effective use

Courtesy: Norwich City Schools, Norwich, N.Y.
Photograph by William Bergan, Syracuse, N.Y.

Large group instruction. Today's school facilities must include large spaces for instruction. Note that room is without windows for effective use of projected visual aids. Teacher makes use of overhead projector to enable all students to see. Desks on raised floor space and acoustically treated walls and ceiling facilitate effective communication.

of these materials, they must be a part of the regular teaching situation. They should be used within the regular classroom. Then when a class is ready to use a film, it will be at hand, not in the room down the hall which is designated as the audio-visual projection room. When a class is studying the works of Shakespeare and a recording of one of his plays is available, it should be used in the natural setting of the regular classroom. It should not be necessary to move the class to another room where a record player is available. What then are some requirements for room facilities?

All classrooms should be equipped with light-control shades or drapes. Electrical current (110 volt) should be available at the front, rear, and sides of the room. Work areas and tables are desirable for individual or group activities. Cupboards, cabinets, and shelving may be used to divide work areas from the larger area which may be termed the class area. Adequate chalkboard and bulletin board areas must be available. The modern classroom makes use of chalkboards which, when reversed in a sliding track, become bulletin boards or display areas. This flexibility is desirable in meeting the needs of a changing curriculum and a changing school population. For example, a room may be used for literature one semester when a greater amount of bulletin board area is needed. The next semester mathematics classes are scheduled for this room. The need is for more chalkboard space. The bulletin boards can be reversed to provide it. One of these reversible sections can be a projection screen surface to be used for viewing projected materials. Since many activities and projects call for use of water, it is desirable to have a sink with hot and cold running water in the classroom. The furniture—desks or tables and chairs—should be designed for flexibility in room arrangement. The lighting should be such that all areas where pupils read and work will receive 50–70 foot candles, a foot candle being the amount of light produced by a standard candle at a distance of one foot. Construction and materials of walls should eliminate outside noises and reduce reverberation within the room. The heating and ventilation system should provide an even temperature free from drafts and without noise. When classrooms have the features described above, the teacher will be able to use the variety of materials which make learning real and meaningful.

Then there is a further need for the different pieces of equipment which are the tools of the profession. Some of these are 16 mm motion-picture projectors, opaque projectors, filmstrip and slide projectors, overhead projectors, screens, tape recorders, disc and transcription players, radios and television.

This vast amount of material and equipment might cause one to think that the teacher and the textbook are being replaced with automation. This is not the least bit true. Teachers are the very heart of all learning activities. The textbook is still the fundamental guide for organizing thought and understanding as well as being a storehouse of knowledge.

Teachers' Use of Audio-Visual Materials

How teachers use these aids determines how effectively pupils learn. The mere fact that a teacher has a globe, chart, or map in the classroom is no assurance that pupils learn from it. The showing of a film about Mexico may do very little in teaching about Mexican people. If the same film is used with a class which has been prepared for seeing it, the results will be entirely different. The class, through help from the teacher and from reading and study, will see and understand much more in the film. Any audio-visual experience should be followed up by the teacher with the pupils. A short discussion can serve as a summary of the experience or it may identify new problems which call for pupils to do more reading, go on a field trip, or prepare projects about these related areas of study.

No matter what the aid or material, the teacher must prepare to use it. It has been said about films, "A film needs a teacher as much as a teacher needs a film." This is true of all teaching materials. It is important that the teacher knows about films, filmstrips, illustrations, pictures, and radio and television programs which pertain to the subject matter or units of work he teaches. He should do a great deal of reviewing and evaluating of these materials. He should read the journals of his profession to learn what new materials are available. When new equipment is available in the school he should learn to use it.

The teacher must have the spirit of adventure, he should not reject these aids until he has explored the ways he might make use of them to increase his effectiveness in the classroom. There are too many teachers who do not know the value of these aids in the teaching-learning process because they have never tried them.

There was a time only 15 or 20 years ago when schools did not have the equipment for showing pictures or recording sound; it may have been possible then to be a traditional teacher. Now the methods of teaching are dependent on these aids, and most schools have some equipment.

EDUCATIONAL TELEVISION

Educational television still is classified in the framework of experimentation. Indicative of the interest of educators to learn more of the possible uses of this relatively new teaching medium is shown in the following rundown on the number of places using television in varying amounts. At the beginning of the 1965–66 school year there were on record 105 educational T.V. stations, many of which were closed-circuit T.V. installations, and many large cities have two educational television stations. Some states have educational television networks in operation and a few more are rapidly moving toward establishing statewide networks; several have programs in the planning stage.

Because material is useful to more schools than exist within state boundaries, there is a concerted effort to work toward establishing *regional* networks. Three such plans now being explored are in New England, Southern and Midwestern areas. These regional plans will eventually link more than a dozen states.

A new development, airborne television, began operations in 1961.

Courtesy: *Northern Illinois University, DeKalb, Ill.*
Architects: Gilbert A. Johnson, Kile, Seehausen
& Associates, Rockford, Illinois.

Television room. Large rooms are provided for television teaching. Here one can see the location of television receivers properly placed so all can view the lesson which is being taught in another part of the building or in a T.V. studio miles away from the school.

This experiment will employ the use of an aircraft flying at more than 20,000 feet which will transmit signals (programs) to an estimated 5 million students in 13,000 schools in six midwestern states. The programs will be both live and prerecorded, originating from a university studio and retelecast from the plane. In this way, transmission is not limited to the areas ordinarily served from a surface-located station.

Some of the most representative experimental programs in operation are: Hagerstown, Maryland, where 37 of the schools in Washington County are engaged in a five-year program to study ways of improving the quality of education. The experiment includes grades 1 through 12. The extent of television programing ranges from less than one hour to a maximum of three periods per day for each grade.

In Galveston, Texas a two-way closed-circuit installation is being tried. The schools plan to employ television for direct teaching, staff communications, in-service education, and as a resource tool.

For several years there have been a number of large city school systems carrying on in-school programs. Notable among these are Philadelphia, New York City, Los Angeles, Pittsburgh, Birmingham, Seattle, Detroit, Atlanta, Oklahoma City and St. Louis.

Complete answers as to how teachers can best use television in the classroom are not available at the present time. There are, however, certain values that seem to be inherent in use of this relatively new teaching tool. Most important among these are: master teachers can be made available to large groups, students are better able to observe demonstrations involving the use of specimens and equipment in science experiments, and a better redeployment of the teacher's time and ability can be accomplished.

SUPPLIES

The teacher will be issued a great number of supplies when he begins to teach. Many of these will deal with pupil accounting for a particular school system, others will be such staple items as pencils, paper, notebooks, class books, plan books, paper clips, and rulers, to mention just a few.

Some of the larger items which may be termed supplies are important for the role they play in the educational process. These are usually requested by the teacher, since they may fill a specific need for a specific teacher.

Workbooks

The interest in and demand for workbooks seems to be growing. Careful selection of a workbook as a study help for pupils is important. Some workbooks may be mere busy work. The better workbook will contain thought-provoking questions and challenging activities. A well-trained teacher will not rely on workbooks for pupil activities, but certain drill materials in workbooks can be a time-saver for teachers.

Newspapers and Magazines

These publications are justified in terms of value for social studies classes alone. Science, guidance, shop, homemaking, health, art, spelling, English, and mathematics classes could get a great deal of material from studying a newspaper or magazine. They are good for encouraging leisure-time reading. The material included in a newspaper covers such a wide variety of interests that it reaches all pupils.

Entire classes sometimes subscribe to educational magazines or newspapers. Two examples of these are *My Weekly Reader* and *Junior Scholastic.*

Tests

More and more teachers are using standardized tests to evaluate their own teaching effectiveness as well as determining the progress of the pupils. Schools usually purchase a battery of tests designed to get a picture of a pupil's total educational growth. Guidance directors often use diagnostic, aptitude, social adjustment, IQ (intelligence), and other tests to help them identify areas where guidance is necessary. After the results of the tests are known, the scores or profile charts (charts which portray graphically a pupil's standing on tests as compared to a norm or common scale) should be made available to all the teachers who can make use of them.

More recently, as a result of our increased technological development, teaching machines have begun to appear on the scene. Many of these may be classified as devices for testing and drill. In the future they will very likely find increased use in the evaluation of pupils' educational growth. Much more research is needed, however, before any wide use will be made of them in school.

Effective evaluation must not rule out the use of essay-type questions. All students should be expected to use learned facts in solving problems and be able to state what they believe to be a logical answer for searching questions. This kind of test is difficult to score and is very time-consuming. Nevertheless, teachers must use the kind of testing or assignments which will teach students proper skills in written communication.

Catalogs of Source Materials

There are many published lists of sources of free and inexpensive materials which are valuable for teachers. Some of the material is excellent. These catalogs are very helpful to beginning teachers who have not had an opportunity to build a file of supplementary pictures, pamphlets, charts, and bulletins.

QUESTIONS AND PROJECTS

1. Which part or parts of the school plant should teachers have a voice in planning?
2. In a new residential development, there is estimated to be an ultimate enrollment of 3,000 children. The community must build an elementary school to care for this school population. What size plot of ground should be set aside for the school site?
3. Should state laws govern the minimum-size plot of ground for an elementary school building? for a secondary school building? Should the size requirement for a plot of ground for a city elementary school building be different than for a rural elementary building?
4. List some of the factors which should be considered in choosing a school site. What changing conditions affect the school needs of the community?
5. What are the advantages for the self-contained classroom? Are there any disadvantages? Discuss them.
6. Go to the library and select books of five, ten, twenty, thirty, and fifty years ago. Compare them for style, format, illustrative materials, size of print, quality of paper, and vocabulary. Prepare a summary of your findings.
7. What are your reactions to some of the established policies and statutes concerning textbook selection? Search current educational journals and periodicals for recent articles on textbook selection and adoption. Can any significant trends be identified?
8. What physical requirements are necessary in the school to facilitate better use of audio-visual teaching materials? Why are the audio-visual materials important in modern education?
9. Visit a new school building in your community. Compare its design with the school you attended. Are the changes improvements? How do you think they contribute to making a better learning situation?
10. If you used any workbooks in high school what were your reactions to them? List some of the ways they were helpful. List any disadvantages you can remember. Bring samples of workbooks you used to class. Display them in your classroom.

AUDIO-VISUAL AIDS

MOTION PICTURES (16 MM)

Carpet under Every Classroom—Marion Hoch, 17 min., sd., b&w. Shows ways the library and librarians can help to realize objectives of a secondary school. Presents the library as a resource center for students and teachers, and demonstrates teacher-librarian cooperation. Gives examples of reading guidance, work of pupil assistants, exhibit planning, and guiding and developing interests of students.

Climate for Learning—Minneapolis-Honeywell Co., Minneapolis 8, Minn., 15 min., sd., color. This film describes the importance of proper thermal environment for children in classrooms. The point is stressed that the comfort standard for the children differs from that of adults. It calls attention to the importance of proper visual and acoustical conditions.

Design for Learning—Photo and Sound, and Franklin and Kump Architects, 18 min., sd., color. Shows the building of a modern school, and explains new methods of planning construction. The completed building is shown in detail with emphasis given to reasons for using new departures in architecture. Develops the idea that building a school is a community project.

Elementary School, Part I: School Environment and Healthful Living—Va. State Board of Ed., 24 min., sd., color. Scenes in many schools in Virginia emphasize aspects of good school environment, such as the adaptation of plant and equipment, pupil and teacher welfare, knowledge of children as individuals, and the human relationships which exist in the school.

The Search: Inadequate School Facilities—McGraw-Hill, 26 min., sd., b&w. This film deals with the planning of school buildings. It shows how one community used citizen's advisory committees, school personnel, an architect, and a school building consultant to help plan their schools.

The Search:Inadequate School Facilities—McGraw-Hill, 26 min., sd., b&w. Portrays the "shadow technique" used by Harvard University's Center of Field Studies in discussing the problem of inadequate school facilities. Shows how researchers follow the children through their school day in a Massachusetts community in order to determine the needs from the children's point of view. Depicts interviews with parents and teachers, and follows the analysis of the data through to recommendations for improvement.

Tomorrow's School Is Here Today—Chemstrand Co., 15 min., sd., color. The film points out the advantages of carpeting in schools and contends that the use of carpeting effects a substantial saving both in floor covering and maintenance costs.

FILMSTRIPS

Contemporary School Design—School Executive, 470 Fourth Ave., New York 16, N.Y., 50 fr., si., with captions. Series of five. Materials developed from the 1952 Annual Competition for Better School Design, sponsored by School Executive Magazine. Photographs, plans, section, and sketches are included. Titles are: *Sites and Building Exteriors, Interiors and Instructional Spaces, Interiors and Large Group Spaces, Technical Features of Buildings, Outstanding Design Solutions.*

Co-operative School Plant Planning—Indiana University, Audio-Visual Center, Bloomington, Ind., 100 fr., si., color. Presents a functional approach to dynamic group action as applied to the community planning of school buildings. Outlines the roles of the board of education, the superintendent of schools, the educational consultant, the architect, the engineer, other experts, children, teachers, and citizens of the community as they take part in a co-operative school plant planning procedure. Many details of administration are covered, as well as ways in which co-operating groups and individuals can benefit.

More Take Home Learning—National Education Association, 1201 16th St.,

N.W., Washington, D.C., 60 fr., si., color. This filmstrip brings out the need for creating a physical environment for learning. It dwells especially on temperature control. It points out that one factor, proper control of heat, can affect the amount of learning children acquire in the classroom.

School Buildings—National Education Association, 1201 16th St., N.W., Washington, D.C., si., b&w. A series of three filmstrips of varying number of frames showing external and interior views of school buildings which represent the best in school planning.

School Buildings and Equipment—American Council on Education, 744 Jackson Place, Washington 6, D.C., si., b&w, series of two. Shows current trends in school buildings and equipment, and indicates how these support the educational programs of the modern elementary and secondary schools. Part I: 66 frames. Deals with the elementary school. Part II: 58 frames. Deals with the comprehensive high school.

FURTHER READINGS

American Association of School Administrators, *American School Buildings,* Twenty-seventh Yearbook (Washington, D.C., NEA, 1949).

American Association of School Administrators, *Planning America's School Buildings* (Washington, D.C., NEA, 1960).

Association for Supervision and Curriculum Development, *Creating a Good Environment for Learning* (Washington, D.C., NEA, 1954).

Bursch, Charles, and Helen Hefferman, *Curriculum and the Elementary School Plant* (Washington, D.C., NEA, Association for Supervision and Curriculum Development, 1958).

Bursch, C. W. and J. L. Reid, *High Schools Today and Tomorrow* (New York, Reinhold, 1957).

Caudill, William W., *Toward Better School Design* (New York, F. W. Dodge, 1954).

Darling, Richard L., *Survey of School Library Standards,* OE-15048, Circular No. 740. (Washington, D.C., U.S. Department of Health, Education, and Welfare, Office of Education, 1964).

Department of Audio-Visual Instruction, *Planning Schools for Use of Audio-Visual Materials* (Washington, D.C., NEA), No. 1, Classrooms (1952) No. 2, Auditoriums (1953) No. 3, The Audio-Visual Instructional Materials Center (1954).

Educational Facilities Laboratories, *Design for Educational Television,* Planning for Schools with Television (New York, 1960).

Educational Facilities Laboratories, Publications Series (New York, EFL).
Case Studies:
No. 8. *The Schools and Urban Renewal: A case study from New Haven* (1964).
No. 9. *Air Structures for School Sports* (1964).
Reports:
New Buildings on Campus: Six Designs for a College Communications Center (1963).
Relocatable School Facilities (1964).

Engelhardt, N. L., Jr. and Stanton Leggett, *School Planning and Building Handbook* (New York, F. W. Dodge, 1956).

Frye, R. A., *Graphic Tools for Teachers,* 2nd ed. (Austin, Texas, E. & I. Printing Co., 1963).

Herrick, J. H., and others, *From School Program to School Plant* (New York, Holt, Rinehart and Winston, 1956).

Katz, William A., and Roderick G. Swartz, eds., *Problems in Planning Library Facilities: Consultants, Architects, Plans, and Critiques,* Proceedings of the American Library Buildings Institute, 1963 (Chicago, ALA, 1964).

National Society for the Study of Education, *Audio-Visual Materials of Instruction,* Forty-eighth Yearbook, Part I (Chicago, University of Chicago Press, 1949).

Perkins, Lawrence B., *Work Places for Learning* (New York, Reinhold, 1957).

Sumption, M. R., and J. L. Landes, *Planning Functional School Buildings* (New York, Harper & Row, 1957).

Trump, J. Lloyd, *Images of the Future,* National Association of Secondary School Principals (Washington, D.C., NEA, 1959).

IV

EDUCATION AND SOCIETY

13

Nonschool Educational Agencies in the Community

PREVIEW

▶ Millions of individuals out of school need further education.
The community agencies, beyond the schools, share in the responsibilities for providing education for these out-of-school youth and adults.

▶ A variety of national, state, and local organizations and agencies are concerned with education for out-of-school youth.
The school should implement ways of keeping more youth in school.
The agencies within a community provide educational programs for out-of-school youth.
Religious organizations have always felt a need to provide educational programs for children and youth.
Recreational needs of youth are cared for by scores of community agencies.
Cultural programs are sponsored by libraries, museums, and civic associations in the community.
Camping education is becoming more popular.

▶ Business and industry co-operate in a large number of educational and recreational programs.

▶ The adult education movement has grown tremendously in recent years.
A number of communities have well-established adult education programs.
The Institute of Lifetime Learning is an active new school for adults.

The Americanization program must expand beyond its original
objectives.

Education for our aging citizens is becoming more and more important.

▸ Mass media of communication play an important role in the education of adults.

Throughout the world nations are attempting to place a greater
emphasis on learning. Nearly every nation recognized as a leader in world
affairs has gained this stature through education. The United States still
is the leader among nations in offering more years of schooling to the
greatest number of its people. This ideal is basic to a democracy such as
ours. It stems from the faith that most Americans have in education:
a belief that education will provide the necessary knowledge to keep men
free and that at some future time there truly will be equal opportunity for
all. Obviously this goal has not been reached, for there are millions in
America wanting and needing more education. Not all of these millions
are youth; a significant number are adults. This fact poses a real problem
for educators and laymen alike. The educator is concerned, inasmuch as
schools should provide the kind of program which would hold the youth
and prepare him for the future whether it be for education in college or
for becoming a young citizen in the community. The layman is concerned,
because he must be associated with the individual either at the shop, in
the office, on the street, or at home. The NEA has indicated the serious-
ness of this problem in its research on instruction.[1]

Most out-of-school youth are in need of some type of guidance and
education in order that they may be gainfully employed. Many of those
employed are on seasonal or part-time jobs which do not afford them
the security for which all people strive.

This group termed *out-of-school* includes many more than those who
have dropped out of school. Thousands may well be high school graduates
who for one reason or another are not employed or not able to go to
college and are merely waiting until they are adults when, they believe,
the course of things will change for them. However, becoming an adult
does not solve the problem, for many adults, too, are in need of more
education. There are thousands more "senior" citizens today than ever
before. The expectancy tables reveal that people are living one to two
years longer now than ten years ago. A significant number of these older
persons seek more education.

[1] *Schools for the Sixties*, A Report of the NEA Project on Instruction (New York,
McGraw-Hill, 1963), pp. 35–40.

Another problem concerns those who enter America from foreign countries. Thousands of these—many who are adults—need education for citizenship as well as vocational training to qualify for jobs entirely different from those held in their homeland.

All of these existing conditions grow more complex and urgent as the number of persons in each of the categories continues to get larger. Some of the implications that have grown out of these problems, as well as what is being done about them, are the concern of everyone in the teaching profession. Even though it is a matter of national concern, the local communities ultimately must find ways of providing the kinds of programs that deal specifically with their needs. In the following pages, a few of the efforts made by various nonschool agencies toward meeting this problem are discussed with attention to what schools might attempt to do to reduce the number of dropouts.

EDUCATIONAL PROGRAMS FOR OUT-OF-SCHOOL YOUTH

Federal Government Programs

America has always been concerned about its youth. The pioneers of this country established schools and colleges which would help youth learn those things which would make the best possible future for themselves. The history of our country is filled with a record of events which have dealt specifically with the handling of problems affecting youth. A few examples are called to your attention here.

Massachusetts passed the first child-labor laws as early as 1842. Ten years later legislation in the same state made school attendance compulsory. In 1899 Chicago established a juvenile court to deal sympathetically with youthful delinquents. In 1933 the federal government passed legislation which provided emergency aid for youths. The Civilian Conservation Corps (CCC) was a program which provided employment for thousands of young men. Many state and national parks and forest preserves were cleaned, bridges and cabins were built and restored as a result of the CCC. In 1935 the National Youth Administration (NYA) was established to provide employment for youth between the ages of sixteen and twenty-four.

During World War II, the GI Bill was enacted. This provided, along with other benefits, financial assistance for returning service personnel to complete an interrupted education. Thousands of service men and women were able to get further education as a result of this financial help. It served to put many out-of-school youth back in school.

Then, too, several federal government agencies are concerned with activities to promote the welfare of youth. Chief among these agencies are the United States Department of Health, Education, and Welfare,

United States Department of Labor, United States Department of Agriculture, and the United States Department of Defense. The White House Conferences on Youth held in Washington have also been a demonstration of federal leadership in considering the problems of young people.

The armed services, under the Defense Department, have continually stressed the importance of education. Thousands attend school and college during off-duty hours. The services maintain schools which deal with specific training programs for electricians, carpenters, machinists, cooks, and a score of other trades and vocations. The United States Armed Forces Institute (USAFI), started during World War II, offers correspondence courses on hundreds of different subjects.

In the last few years a number of important programs of an educational and social reform nature have been initiated by federal legislation. Most important of these which are now underway are Peace Corps Volunteers, Job Corps, VISTA, and Headstart.

Peace Corps Volunteers

The Peace Corps originated as a federally supported program during the term of the late President John F. Kennedy. It was established for the purpose of sending assistance to nations through an educational program. Peace Corps Volunteers are sent throughout the world to those nations known to need help in developing their resources which enable them to have a better life. The volunteers, from various backgrounds and vocations, are carefully selected and given an intensive training program for preparation for a given assignment in some underdeveloped country. The men and women are provided a clothing allowance and a subsistance allowance while they are out of this country, and each corpsman will receive a sum amounting to fifty dollars per month of service at the time of his discharge from the Corps.

Many of the personnel accepted as volunteers are teachers or have been teachers. This type of background is valuable because so much of the program centers on assisting other nations in education. Volunteers are expected to become a part of the community life where they are assigned to duty. This entails living, playing, teaching, learning, and worshiping with the natives. Some assignments are not easy and may call for much sacrifice, but through this sacrifice and assistance there is hope of helping men earn greater freedom, a better life, and a new sense of values both for the country visited and for our country.

Reports about the work and accomplishments of the Peace Corps are most encouraging. Many of the countries are requesting our government to assign further groups of Corpsmen to their countries, and a good share of them are asking that we send larger numbers.

Anti-Poverty Programs

President Lyndon Johnson has set forth a number of social reform programs which had been encouraged by John F. Kennedy. In his Great Society movement he has introduced and sought passage of much legislation which would alleviate the injustices forced upon families who live in poverty. The Economic Opportunity Act of 1964 authorized funds to establish new programs to combat poverty in the United States. This legislation was responsible for initiating the Job Corps—a sort of on-the-job training and study program; Volunteers in Service to America

Courtesy: National Education Association.
Photograph by Carl Purcell.

Thousands of preschool age children all over America are offered experiences during the summer through Project Headstart. After a few weeks of this summer experience every child will have a better opportunity to succeed in school.

(VISTA)—commonly called a domestic Peace Corps, and Headstart—a program for pre-school age children who live in deprived neighborhoods and lack all or most of the early experiences children should have prior to entering school; it is a summer program to ready children for school in the fall. A few communities are organizing such programs which will offer more children these benefits inasmuch as it will be conducted the year around. Through this program children are provided a variety of experiences and training so vital to success in school. By affording these culturally deprived children this opportunity they are believed to be nearer like other children who have had the advantage of these experiences in their normal home life.

As the "War on Poverty" continues, it is hoped that these programs and perhaps many more will be successful in breaking the poverty cycle which has heretofore shackled an ever increasing percentage of our population.

Other National Programs

In addition to federal government programs a number of national organizations sponsor numerous youth activities. The National Congress of Parents and Teachers plays an active role in promoting the welfare of youth through providing leisure-time activities, working with community officials to curb juvenile delinquency, and co-operating with other national agencies to find ways to meet the needs of youth. The NEA, through its affiliated agencies, publishes bulletins, yearbooks, and articles which deal with current youth problems. A recent yearbook of the American Association of School Administrators is titled, *Youth Education Today. Education for All American Youth* and *Education for All American Youth—A Further Look* are illustrative of publications by the Educational Policies Commission.

State and Local Programs

A variety of interested individuals and groups at state and local levels have sensed the need for an action program to cope with out-of-school youth problems. Every means of communication is being employed to focus attention on the problem. Seldom is a newspaper printed without a story about the "teen-ager." Radio and television time has been given to programs which awaken the public to the needs of youth. "The College Bowl," "Exploring and Discovery" are good examples of programs which serve children and youth with inspiring and interesting leisure time activities which are educational. Other programs discuss specific problems dealing with youth, such as work opportunities, teen-age drivers, juvenile delinquency, camp programs, educational opportunities, and recreational programs. Being alerted to youth problems is only the beginning of a program to meet their needs. One approach in a solution of the problem would be to keep them in school, the other is to establish programs for out-of-school youth which will help them come to a realization of their own needs and provide the opportunities to meet them.

Many states have sensed the importance of adult education programs and employed personnel in the Departments of Education to provide leadership and guidance where it is needed. Along with this practice these states are also giving financial aid to public schools offering programs for education of adults.

WHAT THE SCHOOL CAN DO

The school itself needs to evaluate the kind of educational program it offers. The formal academic character of the school must be replaced with a more dynamic approach to learning. The individual's needs must be met through broader curricular offerings. As the NEA Project on Instruction [2] points out:

The schools can help to combat such serious national problems as youth unemployment and juvenile delinquency by: (a) evaluating the intellectual and creative potential of all children and youth in the schools; (b) identifying early the potential dropout and delinquent; (c) developing positive programs to challenge these young people to educational endeavor; (d) participating in cooperative programs with parents and with community groups and organizations—business and industry, labor, service groups, government agencies, and the many youth-serving agencies.

The ever-increasing demand for men and women to work in business, industry, and the professions must certainly be reflected in curriculum patterns in the secondary school. What kind of high school program will fulfill this demand? Most educators agree that a major share of every young person's high school experience should be devoted to "general education." Some schools refer to this as a "core of common learnings." Regardless of the name, it refers to the development of the basic attitudes and abilities which are needed for effective citizenship. The school and community agencies must share in the responsibilities of helping young people reach their greatest potential.

More secondary schools should implement a work experience program to supplement regular classroom instruction. Much more than learning a skill, trade, or business is derived from this type of experience. Character building and personality development are associated with these responsibilities. In addition to contributing to the individual's general development, the program can become a powerful public relations device between the school and the community.

[2] *Ibid.*, p. 27.

Much greater emphasis must be placed on guidance. Both teachers and guidance specialists should assist pupils in planning the kind of educational program which will best meet individual needs.

The suggestions advanced here for what schools can do should not imply that all school needs are the same. The better schools already have incorporated into their program these and other good practices.

HOW OTHER COMMUNITY AGENCIES HELP

In the more progressive communities one can find a number of nonschool agencies that furnish programs and activities of an educational nature for youth. A few of these may be entirely divorced from the educational program of the schools; others may supplement school programs. Some long-established organizations in the community have always recognized their responsibility to youth and have had ongoing programs to care for these needs. With society changing and becoming more complex, owing partly to the age of automation and atomic energy and partly to a socioeconomic conflict which prevails, many more public and private agencies are offering assistance. A brief discussion of these agencies will serve to make us more aware of the important part community agencies have in caring for out-of-school youth.

Religious Agencies

Inasmuch as the issue of religion and education is discussed in more detail in Chapter 17, only a few activities which religious organizations sponsor are dealt with here.

Vacation Bible School. Most religious organizations provide sessions of varying lengths of time from one week to four weeks during regular school vacation periods for children and youth to attend. During the three to five hours the pupils are in school they are taught more about the values and importance of spiritual guidance. This affords more time for religious educators to develop beliefs and concepts related to a particular religion. For many young people who attend public schools, the vacation Bible school is the only real religious teaching they receive. Much more understanding about religion can be taught in an organized school such as this is than in a one-hour period spent in church school on the Sabbath day. Also, the use of youths as teachers for younger children affords a real opportunity for building leadership among church members.

Youth Fellowship Organizations. Most of the religious denominations provide youth fellowship activities which are conducted by youths with the help of some adult as a sponsor. The programs deal with a variety of activities and topics vital to problems of youth. Some of the most promising and effective educational programs on preparation for marriage and home and family living are carried on by church fellowship organizations. A number of denominations provide building space for wholesome recreational as well as educational programs. All of the activities are conducted in an atmosphere of religious training which advances the moral and spiritual values of life.

Recreational Agencies

In most communities, regardless of size, there is a significant number of organizations which offer a variety of recreational activities. A cardinal principle of education is "worthy use of leisure time." The school, through its cocurricular program, offers quite specific leisure-time programs, but during the hours school is not in session and during vacation periods, the community must take some of the responsibility for providing such activities.

In recent years, communities have made provision for an increasing number of supervised playground programs. School grounds, parks, community centers, and vacant lots are the setting for organized recreation as well as instruction in a variety of arts and crafts. These furnish an opportunity for wholesome leisure-time activities for younger children and in turn give older youth experience in leadership, for in most instances older boys and girls and young adults are employed to supervise and lead the activities.

Communities are becoming more and more aware of the need for recreational facilities and consequently are providing swimming pools, golf courses, tennis courts, outdoor little theatres, and many other similar facilities. A good example of the outdoor theatre is one on the Antioch College campus, Yellow Springs, Ohio. There, students from the college and youth from the village co-operate in producing plays which are presented for residents of the surrounding area. This is an excellent means of giving those youths interested in drama, but who are not in school, the kind of experience they seek.

Libraries, museums, and music groups offer a variety of educational activities. These groups sponsor programs throughout the year. Civic leaders in many cities and towns have formed associations which have been instrumental in scheduling a series of lectures, forums and discussion groups for the youth and adults of the community. Statistics indicate more and more that individuals are interested in this kind of program.

The YMCA, YWCA, YMHA, YWHA, and CYO have very complete programs of which out-of-school youth can take advantage at very little cost. In some of the larger cities the "Y" program covers every kind of leisure-time activity that one can imagine. All of these are under the direction of skilled recreational and educational leaders.

Local Rotary, Kiwanis, and Lions clubs and numerous other men's and women's organizations co-operate in promoting recreational programs for youth. Other ways of helping range from the purchase of glasses for school children who cannot afford them to the awarding of college scholarships to worthy high school graduates.

Youth Centers. As an outgrowth of World War II, there has been more interest in providing youth centers. The program is usually recreational. The centers are operated by young people, with adults helping by acting as leaders or giving financial aid. The problem in furthering this type of organization is a financial one. In New York, money is appropriated by the government to support such programs.

Camping Activities. Camping education is becoming an important phase of recreational and educational programs. Some states provide summer camps for youths. In other instances, local community organizations sponsor camping activities. Camping programs are really a kind of laboratory experience with nature. The variety of experience which camp life affords goes far beyond the acquaintance with works and beauty of nature; it provides ample opportunity for character-building as well as fostering an awareness for conservation of our natural resources.

Some schools are now offering course credit in camping activities, but for the most part this is an activity sponsored by charitable associations and private individuals. In most localities the Boy Scout and Girl Scout camps are provided by civic-minded individuals or groups who realize the young person's needs for outdoor activities. The Boy Scouts, Girl Scouts, Campfire Girls, 4-H Clubs, and Hi-Y Clubs are a few examples of organizations which are nationally recognized for their character-building and citizenship-training programs for young people. These are usually sponsored by local community organizations, but are responsible to state and national leadership for some of their larger projects.

Business and Industrial Organizations

The impact of educational programs sponsored by business and industry reaches children and youth in every community of America. It would be impossible to describe here the vast number of educational programs with which business and industry are connected. The best that can be done is to call attention to some as examples.

In most every community there is a Little League or Sandlot League for boys who aspire to become good baseball players. Most every team is sponsored by a business place in the local area. The boys are outfitted with uniforms and regulation equipment as well as provided with a field for practice and games—all of which is financed by the sponsor. The same is true for such other team sports as basketball, football, bowling, and tennis. A year-around program is thus provided for youth who are not able to participate in team sports in school.

Business also provides educational programs for their employees. Many firms provide time and financial aid for employees to attend workshops aimed at promoting greater efficiency. On occasions a group of similar businesses will employ consultants to come to their city and meet with employees to discuss better merchandising practices, improved accounting procedures, or effective sales and service programs.

It is not uncommon to find large department stores offering educational programs for people in the community through a series of lectures, demonstrations, or formal classes. This type of activity may be concerned with home decorating, art, sewing, or cooking, as well as baby care and home and family living.

Industry supports any number of nation-wide programs of an educational nature. An example of one which young boys enter into with great interest is the popular Soap-Box Derby sponsored by Chevrolet, a division of General Motors. Thousands of boys across the country enter this event to attempt to build a soap-box car that will win over all others in a national contest. This contest not only offers a college scholarship and a host of other prizes for the winners, but it gives young boys in every community an opportunity to incorporate the best kind of engineering they can think of into design and construction of the car. Usually a number of local agencies co-operate in this annual event.

The Ford Motor Company has always carried on a training program for mechanics and engineers who are connected with the vast number of Ford sales and service establishments all over the United States. Perhaps more publicized is the Museum in Dearborn, Michigan, which Ford Motor Company maintains. The auto industry is not alone in this project of education. Large manufacturers of electrical equipment, chemicals, motor fuels, and food products are but a few more whose educational programs have tremendous impact on our society. Through the medium of television programs, sponsored by large industrial and business concerns, millions of people have an opportunity to view performances of some of the all-time "greats" in the fields of art, drama, music, science, and sports. In spite of the fact that there is still much to be desired in TV programming, one cannot overlook the millions who have much more understanding about our society and culture because of it.

ADULT EDUCATION

"To be an effective member of society today requires a life-long commitment to learning. This has been evidenced by growing attention to programs of adult education."[3] Members of a society have always learned from one another on an informal basis, and such was the case for adults for most of the early years of education in this country. Only recently, during the last fifty years, has there been evidence of a more or less organized adult education program. In 1926 the American Association of Adult Education was organized. Through its leadership and guidance hundreds of community agencies offer courses in fields of study of particular interest to adults. Although the school is an important force, there is no one agency in a community which is solely responsible for education of its adults. Just as school pupils are affected by all the forces in a community, so are adults.

As Sheats, Jayne, and Spence [4] point out:

The process goes on *through* the media of radio, motion pictures, press, and classroom; *for* farmers, parents, businessmen, workers, and housewives; *in* schools, libraries, museums, settlement houses and public auditoriums; *with* programs ranging from social dancing to Sanskrit and services ranging from child-care training to old-age counseling.

A program of adult education should grow out of the needs of the people concerned. If there is a need on the part of adults for greater understanding in the process of democratic living, this should be the objective for the program. If our senior citizens need further education or re-education to adjust to a new kind of life, this need should be met. The number of adults participating in adult education activities has been growing steadily year after year. A recent survey estimates that over 40 million adults want more education and approximately 30 million are receiving it. The kind and amount of this education varies from a one-week course to a semester of training on everything from atomic energy to vocabulary building.

In 1963 the NEA Research division survey on adult education [5] indicated that a large number, 78.9 percent of the school superintendents polled, believed that public schools should be responsible for adult education programs. This same survey indicated that over half of the superintendents believed that the program should offer adults instruction in vocational education. Also, over half of them believed that there should be some federal support for adult education programs.

There is ample evidence to support the fact that public school superintendents are anxious to support adult education because more and more schools are providing the facilities and staffs for the purpose. In a few states, California, for example, the schools provide "continuing edu-

3 National Education Association, "Superintendents and Adult Education," NEA Research Bulletin, Vol. 42, No. 1, Feb., 1964 (Washington, D.C.), p. 8.

4 Paul H. Sheats, Clarence D. Jayne, and Ralph B. Spence, *Adult Education* (New York, Holt, Rinehart and Winston, 1953), p. 2.

5 "Superintendents and Adult Education," *op. cit.*, pp. 8–11.

cation" free to those who wish it. However, a greater number of states require the student to pay tuition. Courses are offered one or two nights each week for periods of time, varying from five to fifteen weeks. The areas of study cover a broad field of interests and needs. Some courses are strictly concerned with recreational activities, such as golf, bridge and dancing; some, vocational; and others deal strictly with general education.

These programs give no credit, but help the individual in self-improvement and in developing new interests. In many cases teachers are not certified, but are highly skilled in their particular field; therefore, they are quite effective in teaching others this particular skill.

In some cities, the library—in cooperation with other organizations —provides adults with an opportunity to learn new ideas through book review sessions and lecture series. These activities give young adults and older people the chance to associate with one another on a high intellectual level and gives them a common topic of discussion. This is valuable for both younger and older adults.

Other adult education programs than those mentioned are doing equally as well in meeting the needs of their local communities, but space does not permit a discussion of each of them. There may be differences in the organization, financing, staffing, and administration, but for the most part the basic philosophies do not vary a great deal.

Americanization Programs

For years this country has afforded immigrants who have taken residence here the necessary education to qualify for American citizenship. For the most part, this education has been concerned only with teaching adult aliens the rudiments of the English language and an elementary knowledge of the United States Constitution. Today, the educational program for immigrants is expanding to include the kind of training which will better fit the individual into his new environment. It should include the kind of education which will make them active participants in the social, cultural, spiritual, political, and economic life of America. This process of assimilation calls for a concerted effort on the part of all community organizations; each has an educational role to play. American Legion, the National Council of Jewish Women, Settlement House, business and industrial organizations, religious organizations, and civic associations, to name a few, are agencies already engaged in programs which will bring about the assimilation as well as the citizenship education of the foreign born. Even greater efforts are needed if these newcomers to our land are expected to become truly Americanized. This assimilation is a slow process, but since the time required for an alien to become a citizen is from two to seven years, there is ample time for community agencies to provide a thorough Americanization and integration program.

Education for Our "Senior" Citizens

During the last 50 years there has been a startling change in the age composition of our population. The greatest increases have occurred in the older age groups. While the percentages of the U.S. population between the ages of 5 and 24 have remained about the same or possibly declined, the percentage of persons between age 45 and 64, and 65 and over has shown a marked increase. In 1920 only 4.7 percent of the population was 65 and over; by 1970, projected growth figures indicate that this same age group will comprise 8 percent of the total population, or roughly, 17 million persons.

It becomes apparent that more attention should be directed toward an entirely different kind of education for an increasingly large segment of the population. With increased numbers of senior or aging citizens comes a larger number of new problems. Owing to the advances made in medical science, the shorter work week, and further mechanization of one-time manual tasks, people are retiring in much better physical and mental health than ever before. So much so, in fact, that it is difficult for many to adjust to the more sedentary life of retirement.

The kind of education needed by these older adults is not different in terms of fundamental needs; they still have a need for an income, for adequate shelter and clothing, and for physical and mental health. Existing adult-education programs attempt to care for these needs.

Beyond these, however, are a number of more intangible needs. Mary Hollis Little [6] lists some and suggests that these must be met through adult education programs:

1. The need for companionship and affection (the need to give and get in terms of human relationships; the need to belong; the need to love and be loved).
2. The need to be useful (the need to feel constructive significance in one's actions; the need to work towards a purposeful goal).
3. The need to have status (to be recognized, appreciated, regarded as worth while).
4. The need for self-reorientation (which may be the need to believe in something, to discover the elements in one's life which are common to others).
5. The need for fun, for play, for the appreciation of life's lighter moments.

Institute for Lifetime Learning

In 1963 a new type of school, the Institute for Lifetime Learning, began in Washington, D.C. Two associations, namely, the National

[6] Mary Hollis Little, "How Gray Is Gray?" *Adult Leadership,* Vol. 3, No. 1 (May, 1954), pp. 14–16.

Courtesy: Doris Robinson Fitch, Dean,
Institute of Lifetime Learning.

Adult education: a class in painting helps to make life richer. This is part of the work of the Institute for Lifetime Learning, Washington, D.C. The Institute is an affiliate of the National Retired Teachers' Association and the American Association of Retired Persons.

Retired Teachers Association (NRTA) and the American Association of Retired Persons (AARP), operate the school. Dr. Ethel Percy Andrus, founder and president of the NRTA, was the inspiration for the Institute's beginning.

The Institute seeks to provide continuing education for persons of 55 years old and older. It operates on a year-round in four separate ten week sessions. Classes are offered in the following areas of study: art, creative writing, music, sewing, world affairs, and personal development. All classes meet once, and some twice each week; tuition averages about $12.50 per course. Although attendance is a personal matter, Certificates of Social Maturity are awarded to those whose attendance is regular and who complete sixteen units of study.

Figure 13-1. Poster of the Institute of Lifetime Learning

PLAN YOUR DAY

... enroll today for Summer Session of Classes!

Registration Accepted Through June 28

MONDAY	Oil Painting	Mon. and Thurs.	10:00-12:00 Noon
	Sketching	Mon. and Thurs.	1:00- 3:00 p.m.
	Basic Sewing	Monday	10:00-12:00 Noon
	Basic Sewing	Monday	1:00- 3:00 p.m.
	Looking Behind the Headlines	Mon. and Wed.	1:30- 3:00 p.m.
	Music Appreciation	Mon. and Thurs.	1:30- 3:00 p.m.
TUESDAY	Oil Painting	Tues. and Fri.	10:00-12:00 Noon
	Oil Painting	Tues. and Fri.	1:00- 3:00 p.m.
	Advanced Sewing	Tuesday	10:00-12:00 Noon
	Advanced Sewing	Tuesday	1:00- 3:00 p.m.
	Reading for Enjoyment	Tuesday	10:00-11:30 a.m.
	Shorthand Refresher	Tues. and Thurs.	10:00-11:00 a.m.
	Personal Typing (Beginners)	Tues. and Thurs.	11:15-12:15 p.m.
	Typing Refresher	Tues. and Thurs.	1:00- 2:00 p.m.
	Modern Office Procedures	Tues. and Thurs.	2:00- 3:00 p.m.
	Ceramics (Advanced)	Tues. and Fri.	10:00-12:00 Noon
WEDNESDAY	**The Every Wednesday Morning Summer Film Series**		10:00-11:00 a.m.
	Looking Behind the Headlines	Mon. and Wed.	1:30- 3:00 p.m.
	Creative Writing	Wednesday	1:30- 3:00 p.m.
THURSDAY	Oil Painting	Mon. and Thurs.	10:00-12:00 Noon
	Oil Painting	Mon. and Thurs.	1:00- 3:00 p.m.
	General Sewing	Thursday	10:00-12:00 Noon
	General Sewing	Thursday	1:00- 3:00 p.m.
	Shorthand Refresher	Tues. and Thurs.	10:00-11:00 a.m.
	Personal Typing	Tues. and Thurs.	11:15-12:15 p.m.
	Typing Refresher	Tues. and Thurs.	1:00- 2:00 p.m.
	Modern Office Procedures	Tues. and Thurs.	2:00- 3:00 p.m.
	Ceramics (Beginners)	Thursday	10:00-12:00 Noon
	Music Appreciation	Mon. and Thurs.	1:30- 3:00 p.m.
FRIDAY	Oil Painting	Tues. and Fri.	10:00-12:00 Noon
	Sketching	Tues. and Fri.	1:00- 3:00 p.m.
	General Sewing	Friday	10:00-12:00 Noon
	General Sewing	Friday	1:00- 3:00 p.m.
	Ceramics (Advanced)	Tues. and Fri.	10:00-12:00 Noon
	Rhythmic Exercise	Friday	10:00-11:00 a.m.
			11:15-12:15 p.m.
	Conference on "Every Wednesday Morning" Lecture		3:30 p.m.

START OF CLASSES

The Summer Session of five weeks will begin June 28 and end July 31. The July 5 classes will meet August 2, because of the holiday. **All classes held on the 6th floor, Dupont Circle Building.**

INSTITUTE OF LIFETIME LEARNING

NATIONAL RETIRED TEACHERS ASSOCIATION AMERICAN ASSOCIATION OF RETIRED PERSONS
1346 Connecticut Avenue, N.W., Washington, D.C. 20036   **Phone: DEcatur 2-7843**

SOURCE: The Institute of Lifetime Learning, Washington, D.C.

The tremendous interest shown in this Institute may well be an inspiration to other localities. It is a fine example of what retired persons can do for themselves in providing lifetime learning possibilities.

There are hundreds of nonschool agencies in the community which are at work attempting to find ways to satisfy some of these needs. Some are doing such good work they are worthy of mention here.

Bryant Industries in Florida employs handicapped and older workers to make replicas of early American furniture. The workers come when they please and work at their own speed. The League of Arts and Crafts in New Hampshire has over 3,000 older people at work creating jewelry, weavings, etchings, pottery, metal ware, and numerous other items. Most of these people at work learned these skills in the second half of life. In Haverhill, Massachusetts, Sunset Industries was formed by local business-men to provide employment of the 65-plus groups. The Citizens Commit-tee has started businesses and manned them with these older citizens. They have all proven successful.

A variety of responsibilities have been assigned to older people, and for the most part the benefits to both the organization and to the indi-vidual have been most satisfactory. A few examples will serve to show the possibilities for making older people feel useful. Some are engaged in managing drives for the collection of food and clothing to be sent over-seas. Others are regular visitors to the housebound. A large number of older people do campaign work by telephone, mail, or personal calls. Many religious and fraternal organizations assign responsibilities to their older members because they have the time and the interest to carry them out.

Mass Media of Communication—A Tool for Adult Education

Through the media of radio, television, and motion pictures, millions of adults are becoming better informed on local, state, national, and international affairs. Though most radio and television stations are affiliated with national networks, almost all devote a certain amount of time to problems of a local or state interest. Local agencies sponsor the programs and bring news, entertainment, and informative discussions of local issues. In many instances the local station will provide, free of charge, a small amount of air time for purely educational programs. The radio, especially, has always been a source of information for the Midwest farmer. For example, local stations carry reports on markets, weather, and improved methods for growing animals and crops. The farmer's wife also gets a vast amount of information from radio. It is quite common for the county home-demonstration agent to use the local radio station to de-scribe improved methods for preparing foods for canning or for the food freezer. Baby care, child's clothing, home improvement, family care, and budgeting are only samples of the numerous adult-education programs made available through radio. Since the advent of television, these same services are brought to some farm families with a greater understanding than was possible through the spoken word alone.

Colleges and universities all across the United States have found large numbers of adults interested in furthering their education when TV brings the opportunity right into the living room. A number of agencies, for example, The National Science Foundation, and the Fund for the Advancement of Education have become interested in providing funds to produce nation-wide network educational programs. Perhaps most popular of these is "Continental Classroom." This program has done much to motivate an interest in science for hundreds of thousands of adults and youth across the country. Many colleges are offering credit for this course providing students register, view the program regularly, complete assignments and successfully pass the tests which are provided by the television instructor and administered at the local level.

Greater interest and concern for adult education on the part of colleges and universities is indicated by reports of an increasing number of them offering courses via television. Western Reserve University was one of the pioneers in this venture. In 1951 it offered a series of programs on social problems and current issues. Some 70,000 persons viewed the programs regularly, and over 60 students registered for credit.

Since 1957 New York University has offered literature courses and others. The Chicago public school system, through facilities of the Chicago Teachers College, offer a wide variety of courses for credit. Students can earn an Associate Arts degree upon completion of courses offered on television. In a recent report by the Chicago Public Schools [7] appears the statement: "When the course titled 'Overview of Human Relations Problems' was last offered on WTTW, it was estimated that approximately sixty-five thousand individuals viewed the program."

Many more colleges offering an even wider variety of courses over television could be listed. Space does not permit a complete story of all of these educational opportunities available to adults. This comparatively new communication medium will surely reach thousands who otherwise would never be served by other community agencies.

With the many nonschool agencies in the community working as they are to provide educational as well as recreational activities for children, youth, and adults, it is clearly shown that citizens are recognizing that the school's resources and capacities are limited. Too often in the past there has been a tendency to assume that the school should be responsible for all the education an individual received. It is a good sign of progress toward greater understanding between school and community.

[7] Board of Education of the City of Chicago, "Adult Education," Study Report No. 11, 1964 Series (Chicago, Illinois), p. 39.

As the agency in a community and the school learn that each has a responsibility and a contribution to make toward the total educational pattern for the citizens of that community, we will find less criticism being leveled at the school because there will be fewer children and youth with problems.

QUESTIONS AND PROJECTS

1. Make a list of reasons you have heard for high school pupils quitting before they have graduated. To what extent was school responsible in each of the reasons given? What other forces were responsible?
2. Should states raise the age limits for compulsory school attendance? Discuss.
3. Look up more information about the Civilian Conservation Corps and the National Youth Administration. Would such programs as these be of value today?
4. Speak with a returned Peace Corps Volunteer and ascertain from his experiences whether or not this type of service would be of interest to you. Write a paper evaluating the Peace Corps in terms of what you learned from the Volunteer. Compare this with the stated purposes for the Peace Corps.
5. Do you think colleges for teacher education should provide a work-study kind of program so that a student could work in a school with a master teacher for a semester before he enters the junior year of college? Discuss.
6. Why should community agencies be responsible for certain kinds of educational programs? List some areas of education where these agencies could be most helpful.
7. In your community what organizations and agencies sponsor educational activities? List them.
8. Visit a class conducted for adults in your community. Describe the class, the teacher, and the activities you observed.
9. Visit a lecture or demonstration conducted in a large department store in your community. Report your reactions to this type of educational program.
10. Look through the television and radio program listings for one week. List those you find to be of an educational nature. Look at or listen to some of them and report your reactions as to their value as educational programs.
11. Interview a retired person to learn how he spends his days. Is he attending a class? Does he have hobbies? Is he active in community organizations? What does he indicate to be his greatest need? Could an adult education fill this need?
12. See if you can find information on adult education programs which are new in the last two years. List them and give a brief description of each.

AUDIO-VISUAL AIDS

MOTION PICTURES (16 MM)

Campus Comes to the Steelworker—Pennsylvania State University, University Park, Pa., 18 min., sd., b&w. A record of co-operative effort in workers' education pioneered by the Pennsylvania State College and the United Steelworkers of America. Follows a group of workers from their jobs in the steel mills to the campus. Shows them studying in the classroom and playing during the recreational periods after classes. Philip Murray appears in the film to state the purposes of the program.

The Community and the Exceptional Child—Syracuse University Kinescope, available from Indiana University, Bloomington, Ind., 29 min., sd., b&w. Examines the role of the community in helping the exceptional child achieve the maximum of his potentiality. Specialists discuss the many agencies in the community that contribute to the growth and development of the exceptional child. The common problems faced by parents, school, and the community are presented in relation to their responsibility to the exceptional child.

Golden Age—McGraw-Hill Book Co., Text-Film Dept., 330 West 42nd St., New York, N.Y., 27 min., sd., b&w. Problems faced during the retirement age are reviewed through the experiences of three men. Each man has a different approach to retirement years.

It Can Be Done—NEA, National Association for Public School Adult Education, 15 min., sd., b&w. A filmograph presentation which focuses on today's critical social problems and the ways in which many communities are solving them through adult education programs.

Learning for Life—NEA, 28 min., sd., color. Gives overview of adult education as a new force in public schools through which people can learn to live for themselves and their communities. Explains the reasons for having adult education programs, and shows how critically they are needed to meet the future challenges facing society. A brief historical treatment is given emphasizing the social changes in our country. The dividends of further education are highlighted by actual personal endorsements. Shows what such a program can offer the community, state, and nation. Closes with a question directed to the viewing audience to urge them to start an adult education program, and offers help through the National Association of Public School Adult Educators.

School and the Community—McGraw-Hill, 13 min., sd., b&w. Animation shows a school which is isolated from the community, neither benefiting its community nor benefiting from it. Points out advantages of cooperation between the school and the community. Shows how the school can be used for adult activities.

FILMSTRIPS

Know Your School—Stanley Bowmar Co., 513 West 166th St., New York, 32, N.Y., 36 fr., si. Presents the multitude of educational opportunities for adults in a public school program—classes, workshops, discussion groups, hobby clubs, etc. Pictures, cartoons, and titles are intended to provide information and stimulate discussion.

Learning Goes On—American Council on Education, 744 Jackson Place, Washington, D.C., si., b&w. Suggests the importance of one aspect of adult education in the United States—participation in group learning activities to satisfy individually recognized needs. Part I, 48 fr. Deals with noncredit courses offered by a community evening school. Part II, 54 fr. Deals with noncredit courses and activities offered by a university and variety of community organizations.

Learning Theory and Classroom Practice in Adult Education—University of

Michigan, Ann Arbor, Mich., 28 min., color, 81 frames with tape recording. The learning theory filmstrip is of real value to instructors of adults. It provides an overview of several psychological theories with implications for classroom practice.

Working Man's University—British Information Services, 30 Rockefeller Plaza, New York, 20, N.Y., 24 fr., si., b&w. Illustrates the courses offered and other activities for daytime and evening school students at the Regent Street Polytechnic in London. University degrees are offered in professional fields. Training is also provided in tailoring, hairdressing, motor body engineering, photography, and domestic science.

FURTHER READINGS

Bergevin, Paul, and others, *Adult Education Procedures* (Greenwich, Conn., Seabury Press, 1963).

Holden, John G., *Adult Education Services of State Departments of Education* (Washington, D.C., U.S. Department of Health, Education, and Welfare, 1959).

Knowles, Malcolm, *Handbook of Adult Education in the United States* (Chicago, Adult Education Association of U.S.A., 1960).

National Association of Public School Adult Educators, *Counseling and Interviewing Adult Students* (Washington, D.C., 1960, 1963).

National Association of Public School Adult Educators, *The Case for Adult Education* (Washington, D.C., 1959).

National Association of Public School Adult Educators, *When You're Teaching Adults* (Washington, D.C., 1959).

14

Education
and International Relations

PREVIEW

▶ Present-day conditions demand that civilized people learn to co-operate with one another.

▶ Our hopes for better international understanding are through the United Nations organization.
The Preamble to the United Nations Charter clearly states the principles upon which peace must be based.

▶ Each of the six organs of the United Nations has a responsibility for achieving peace in the world.
Much of the real work of an international organization such as the United Nations must be accomplished through the activities of specialized agencies.

▶ UNESCO—United Nations Educational, Scientific and Cultural Organization—is dedicated to world understanding through education.
Some of the ideas for furthering world understanding can be traced to educational, scientific, and cultural activities already established.
The American school can do much in furthering an understanding of UNESCO.
Some schools have already discovered ways of introducing its study into the curriculum.

▶ The characteristics of some common problems in the world are identified with specialized agencies.

There is much evidence today to prove we are living in a period when science and technical ability are bringing the peoples of the world ever closer together. Improved methods of communication through the media of radio and television have made it possible to send messages around the world in seconds. Telephone service from one continent to another is becoming almost as commonplace as is service from city to city within the United States. Events happening in one part of the world are known by the whole world in a matter of minutes or, at the most, a few hours.

Improved methods of transportation, increased speed, and the discovery of new air routes are forcing man to discard the concept of distance which has in the past been responsible for keeping peoples separated.

What, then, are the ultimate results of all this technical knowledge? One nation can no longer feel isolated from another nation because of its location. What one nation is doing is no longer a secret to another. What one nation does affects all others; how one nation acts becomes the concern of all the others. All of these facts would force us to one conclusion. For peace, economic security, and prosperity we are no longer solely dependent upon our own nation's actions, but we must enter into a new phase of co-operation with the peoples of other nations of the world. It becomes more and more obvious that nations must learn and practice ways of coming to closer understanding of one another. As is heard spoken quite generally among thoughtful political, service, and community groups, we are living in an age when we must have "one world or none."

This premise would lead us quite naturally to a consideration of the one organization in the world which is concerned with the future of all civilization, namely, the United Nations Organization.

THE UNITED NATIONS ORGANIZATION

The United Nations is no longer an experiment. Since this important world organization became officially recognized on October 24, 1945, the member nations have worked diligently to accomplish its purposes as stated in the Charter.

Too few people are aware of the work being done by the various organs of this great world body. Much more knowledge and understanding of its operations, functions and services must be made available if its stated goals are to be achieved. It would seem that everyone preparing to teach should have some basic understandings about the UN, and it is with that belief that a brief discussion of its structure, functions, and work are presented here.

The following information was taken from *Everyman's United Nations:* [1]

Preamble of the United Nations Charter

The preamble states the needs and intentions which were responsible for founding the UN. It says:

We the Peoples of the United Nations, Determined to save succeeding generations from the scourge of war, which twice in our lifetime has brought untold sorrow to mankind, and to reaffirm faith in fundamental human rights, in the dignity and worth of the human person, in the equal rights of men and women and of nations large and small, and

to establish conditions under which justice and respect for the obligations arising from treaties and other sources of international law can be maintained, and to promote social progress and better standards of life in larger freedom,

and For These Ends

to practice tolerance and live together in peace with one another as good neighbors, and

to unite our strength to maintain international peace and security, and

to ensure, by the acceptance of principles and the institution of methods, that armed force shall not be used, save in the common interest and

to employ international machinery for the promotion of the economic and social advancement of all peoples.

Have Resolved to Combine Our Efforts to Accomplish These Aims

Accordingly, our respective Governments, through representatives assembled in the city of San Francisco, who have exhibited their full powers found to be in good and due form, have agreed to the present Charter of the United Nations and do hereby establish an international organization to be known as the United Nations.

PURPOSES

The four purposes of the United Nations are:

1. to maintain international peace and security;
2. to develop friendly relations among nations based on respect for the equal rights and self-determination of peoples;
3. to co-operate in solving international problems of an economic, social, cultural, or humanitarian character, and in promoting respect for human rights and fundamental freedoms for all, and
4. to be a center for harmonizing the actions of nations in attaining these common ends.

PRINCIPLES

To fulfill these purposes, the United Nations acts in accordance with these principles:

[1] United Nations, Department of Information, *Everyman's United Nations,* 4th ed. (New York, 1953).

1. the organization is based on the principle of the sovereign equality of all its Members;
2. Members are to fulfill in good faith the obligations they have assumed under the Charter;
3. they are to settle their international disputes by peaceful means;
4. they are to refrain in their international relations from the threat or use of force in any manner inconsistent with the purposes of the United Nations;
5. they are to give the United Nations every assistance in any action it takes in accordance with the Charter, and to refrain from giving assistance to any state against which the Organization is taking preventative or enforcement action;
6. the United Nations is to ensure that non-Members act in accordance with these principles so far as is necessary for maintaining international peace and security;
7. the Organization is not to intervene in matters essentially within the domestic jurisdiction of any state. This provision does not apply, however, when enforcement action is taken with respect to threats to the peace, breaches of peace, and acts of aggression.

PRINCIPAL ORGANS OF THE UNITED NATIONS

The United Nations is made up of six principal organs:

1. The General Assembly
2. The Security Council
3. The Economic and Social Council
4. The Trusteeship Council
5. The International Court of Justice
6. The Secretariat

The General Assembly

The General Assembly is the one organ which is made up of representatives (not more than five) from each Member State. The United Nations started with 51 Member States and by the end of 1965 this number had risen to 117.

The main functions of the General Assembly are:

1. Maintenance of international peace and security.
2. Responsibility for international economic and social co-operation.
3. Exercise of UN functions with regard to the international trusteeship system.
4. Consideration of all matters concerned with information on non-self-governing territories.
5. Control of the finances of the UN. It considers and approves the budget and apportions the expenses among the Members.

The UN's operating budget has grown from $19,390,000 in 1946 to over $80,000,000 today. The number and scope of services has grown accordingly. Voting is by two-thirds majority on important questions and a simple majority on other questions.

Figure 14-1.   The United Nations and Related Agencies

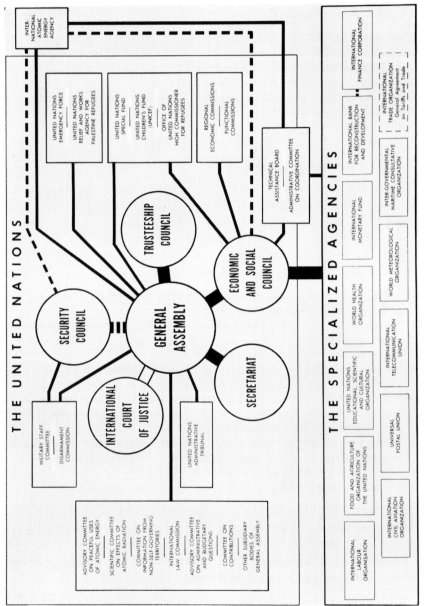

SOURCE: United Nations.

This body meets once a year in regular session. It commences on the third Tuesday in September. Special and emergency sessions can be called. The General Assembly conducts its work through seven main committees on which all members have a right to be represented.

The Committees are:

First Committee (Political and Security, including the regulation of armaments).
Special Political Committee (to share the work of the First Committee).
Second Committee (Economic and Financial).
Third Committee (Social, Humanitarian and Cultural).
Fourth Committee (Trusteeship, including non-self-governing territories).
Fifth Committee (Administrative and Budgetary).
Sixth Committee (Legal).

The Security Council

The Security Council is composed of 11 members, five of which are permanent and six elected by the General Assembly for two year terms. The five permanent members are Nationalist China, France, United Kingdom, United States, and Russia. Each member acts as the Council's president for one month.

The functions of the Security Council are:

1. To maintain international peace and security in accordance with the purposes and principles of the UN.
2. To investigate any dispute or situation which might endanger international peace and security.
3. To recommend ways for settling disputes.
4. To be responsible for formulating plans for regulating armaments.
5. To determine preventive or enforcement action in case of threats to the peace, breach of the peace or act of aggression.
6. To call on members to apply economic sanctions and other measures short of war in order to prevent or stop aggression.
7. To recommend the admission of new members and the terms on which states may become parties to the Statute of the International Court of Justice.
8. To exercise the trusteeship functions of the UN.
9. To provide annual and special reports to the General Assembly.

The Security Council functions continuously and a representative of each of its members must be present at UN Headquarters at all times. Subsidiary organs which report to the Council are the Military Staff Committee, the Disarmament Commission and various standing Committees, *ad hoc* committees, and commissions.

The Economic and Social Council

The Economic and Social Council is composed of 18 members elected by the General Assembly, one-third of which are elected each year for a three-year term. The Council holds two regular sessions a year, and may call special sessions.

The important functions of this organ are:

1. To promote higher standards of living, full employment and conditions of economic and social progress and development.
2. To help solve international economic, social, health, and related problems.
3. To promote international cultural and educational co-operation.
4. To promote universal respect for, and observance of, human rights and fundamental freedoms for all regardless of race, language, sex or creed.
5. To make or initiate studies and reports on international economic, social, cultural, educational, health, and related matters; and to make recommendations on such matters to the General Assembly, to the UN, its Members and to other specialized agencies concerned.
6. To call international conferences on matters within its competence.

It is within the jurisdictional framework of the Council to form commissions for specialized functions or for studies of a regional nature. Four such regional commissions have been formed:

Economic Commission for Europe (ECE), 29 members.
Economic Commission for Asia and the Far East, 23 members; 2 associate members.
Economic Commission for Latin America (ECLA), 24 members.
Economic Commission for Africa (ECA), 15 members; 7 associate members.

Other functional commissions through which the Economic and Social Council works are:

1. Commission on the Status of Women, 18 members.
2. Commission on Human Rights, 18 members.
3. Commission on Narcotic Drugs, 18 members.
4. Transport and Communications Commission, 15 members.
5. Fiscal Commission, 15 members.
6. Statistical Commission, 15 members.
7. Social Commission, 18 members.
8. Population Commission, 15 members.
9. Commission on International Commodity Trade, 18 members.

Besides these regional and functional commissions, the Council works with many special bodies, agencies, and standing committees. Various nongovernmental organizations may be consulted on questions with which the Council is concerned. These are divided into two categories, *A* and *B*. Those in Category *A* are those which have a basic interest in most activities of the Council and are closely linked with the economic or social life of the areas they represent. Examples of these are International Chamber of Commerce, International Confederation of Free Trade Unions, and World Federation of Trade Unions. Representative of Category *B*, or those with a special competence in a limited area of the Council's operations, are the following: Inter-American Federation of

Automobile Clubs, International Federation of University Women, International League for the Rights of Man, World Confederation of Organizations of the Teaching Profession. In this category there were 114 organizations by the end of 1965.

Trusteeship and Non-Self-Governing Territories

The United Nations Charter contains a "Declaration on Non-Self-Governing Territories." This provides that the United Nations has accepted as "a sacred trust" to promote the well-being of the inhabitants of those territories. There are 47 countries or a population of over 100 million people, who do not govern themselves. These people are governed by other countries through a "sacred trust" agreement. The governing countries have declared they will promote their well-being and help them become self-governing. Over 25 nations have become either independent or autonomous since the United Nations was created. Most of these have become full-fledged members of the UN. The objectives of the trusteeship system are as follows:

1. To further international peace and security.
2. To promote the political, economic, social and educational advancement of the inhabitants of the Trust Territories, and their own government and independence.
3. To encourage respect for human rights and fundamental freedoms for all.
4. To insure equal treatment in social, economic, and commercial matters for all Members of the United Nations and their nationals and equal treatment for the latter in the administration of justice, provided it does not conflict with the attainment of the other objectives of the Trusteeship System.

The Trusteeship Council

This body is composed of:

1. Those Members administering trust territories;
2. Permanent Members of the Security Council; and
3. As many other Members elected for three-year terms by the General Assembly to ensure an equal division between countries which administer trust territories and countries which do not.

Functions and Powers. The functions and powers of the Trusteeship Council are:

1. To consider reports from administering authorities.
2. To accept and examine petitions with the administering authority.
3. To make periodic visits to the trust territories.
4. To formulate a questionnaire to check the political, economic, social and educational advancement of the inhabitants of Trust Territories.

The Trusteeship Council usually meets twice a year in regular session.

The International Court of Justice

This body is the principal judicial organ of the United Nations. It deals with legal questions only and has nothing to do with political questions. The membership (judges) of the court number 15 and are elected by the General Assembly and Security Council. Judges serve for nine-year terms, and no two judges may be from the same country.

The jurisdiction of the Court comprises all cases which the parties consent to referring to it. Those states which are parties to the Statute may at any time recognize as compulsory the jurisdiction of the court in all legal disputes concerned with:

1. The interpretation of a treaty.
2. Any question of international law.
3. The existence of any fact which, if established, would constitute a breach of an international obligation.
4. The nature or extent of the reparation to be made for the breach of an international obligation.

One example of cases tried concerned two small islands, Minquiers and Ecrehos, near the coast of France which were claimed by both France and England. They were of value for fishing rights. The court decided in favor of England.

The Secretariat

The Secretary General is appointed by the General Assembly upon recommendation of the Security Council and has "such staff as the organization may require." The Secretary General is the chief administrative officer of the United Nations. As secretary he meets with all other organs of the UN and is required to submit an annual report to the General Assembly on the work of the total organization. He is authorized to bring to the attention of the Security Council any matter which in his opinion threatens peace and security.

The Secretary General's term of office is five years. U Thant of Burma, the third to hold this high office, was appointed November 3, 1961.

The brief summary of the six principal organs of the United Nations organization is presented here as an introduction to this whole problem of international understanding. A look at the purposes and functions of each of the organs will serve to remind us that there is in existence an organization whose chief concern is dedicated to international peace and security.

Like any other organization whose function and scope are as far-reaching as this, it was found necessary to establish agencies to study problems of a specialized nature. It is within the framework of a number of these specialized agencies that we find implications for education and better international relations.

Specialized Agencies

It is through the work of specialized agencies that much of the work is done in achieving the aims of the UN Charter which relate to economic, social, cultural, educational, health, and related fields. The one agency and its functions with which teachers should be especially

Courtesy: United Nations.

Participants in an Institute of Science course in Marine Biology, a program sponsored and organized by UNESCO. This particular course was held in Bombay, India.

concerned is the United Nations Educational, Scientific, and Cultural Organization (UNESCO). This agency was proposed in 1945 and came into being in November of 1946. Its Constitution defines its purpose which is to "contribute to peace and security by promoting collaboration among the nations through education, science and culture in order to further universal respect for justice, for the rule of law, and for the human rights and fundamental freedoms for all." [2]

Those representatives of 43 nations who first met to discuss UNESCO's work had a firm belief that despite prejudices and a wide variety of ideologies, it was possible to identify common grounds for co-operation among peoples of the world. These men were convinced that ignorance and lack of understanding among the nations of the world had contributed to past wars. Since today's weapons of mass destruction have threatened to annihilate all of civilization, we are the first generation to be faced with such a challenge and necessity of keeping peace. The one possible way is through reaching the minds of men with ideas that will provide us with the answer to the important question—What is the way to live together? As UNESCO implies, there is a threefold approach through education, science, and culture.

Membership in UNESCO has grown to include 82 countries plus six associate members. This phenomenal growth indicates the importance nations place on creating favorable conditions for increasing international understanding.

EDUCATION'S RESPONSIBILITY

In the preamble of UNESCO's Constitution we read: "Since wars begin in the minds of men, it is in the minds of men that the defences of peace must be constructed." Herein lies a challenge for everyone and more especially those who have chosen teaching as a profession.

Education is concerned with the spreading of knowledge which will help men live better and more efficient lives. It is logical to assume that educators should be charged with the responsibility of promoting UNESCO's principles and finding ways of making these principles effective. The educator can see that schools, universities, libraries, the press, films, radio, and television can be used to help people better understand one another. Prejudice, suspicion, and hate can be combated by spreading truth about all peoples. Illiteracy can be overcome, and a higher standard of living can be brought to those who never had such an opportunity before.

Teachers from one nation can exchange with another for a year's work with a faculty and students to nurture a better understanding among neighbors. The International Federation of Secondary School

2 *Ibid.*, p. 366.

Teachers had been playing an important role in bringing teachers together for an exchange of experiences long before UNESCO, but since their budgets were small, this was a somewhat limited effort. Today the UN offers some financial aid to further this kind of activity.

SCIENCE AND ITS RESPONSIBILITIES

The great scientists of the world can stimulate the free exchange of research results. They can readily co-operate on disease control methods. Just recently through the World Health Organization (WHO), data on the Salk polio vaccine was made available to all those nations who were members. This again makes it clear that no one group or organization is responsible for all spreading of knowledge—it must be a co-operative effort.

Science specialists can help promote better use of natural resources. Herein lies a tremendous opportunity to build good relations among nations. There are millions of the world's people who work with the soil to earn a livelihood, and it becomes a natural point of discussion, for it is a subject about which a large portion of the world's population is interested and has some understanding.

With population figures growing so rapidly, it is even more important that unproductive land areas be studied with the view of making them productive. Along this line UNESCO has set up advisory committees composed of scientists from all parts of the world to study the problem of the available underground water. This study includes desert areas where, if water sources can be tapped, it would mean an entirely new life for thousands of people who live on and around the desert. Similar research has been done on plant growth to learn what species would thrive in arid regions and would stop the erosion caused by wind.

Other scientific research is being carried on in social science in an effort to determine what kind of problems contribute to tensions among peoples and nations. A specific problem now under study deals with the effects of industrialization upon the lives of people, especially in places where modern industry is being introduced and established for the first time.

UNESCO has also given its assistance to introduce the teaching of science in several countries. The first of this help has been in the Middle East, South Asia, and in some Latin American nations. In some of these areas, science has never been taught at the elementary school level. Realizing the critical shortage of science teachers, textbooks, and equipment, UNESCO has prepared handbooks to help the untrained teacher, prepared and published catalogues describing necessary equipment and how to develop it, prepared sets of drawings and pictures to aid the teacher, provided a means through sales coupons and gift coupons for purchas-

Courtesy: United Nations.

UNESCO's pilot project in Haiti's Marbial Valley. UNESCO's team started a campaign to educate thousands of inhabitants who previously could not attend schools.

ing scientific equipment, and prepared scientific exhibits which tour the member states.

CULTURE—ITS CONTRIBUTIONS

UNESCO has had a difficult time attempting to overcome the belief that culture is limited only to those who might be classified as intellectuals and that culture cannot be made a part of the daily lives of great masses of people. Gradually this barrier is breaking down, and as a result there is evidence of much progress being made toward the exchange of ideas in the arts. Through art, people are finding out more about themselves and about the customs and habits of life in other parts of the world.

Some examples of projects being carried on by UNESCO are the following: The establishment of the International Centre for the Preservation and Restoration of Cultural Property. This center with headquarters in Rome has the task of preparing documents concerning cultural property and contributing to the training of research workers and technicians. At present, this group is concerned with preserving the famous historical monuments of Nubia in Egypt and Sudan which are in danger of being submerged by waters of the Aswan High Dam when it is completed.

The International Music Council, established through UNESCO's initiative, collects and distributes recordings of music of various nations of the world.

Also, masterpieces of the world's best literature are translated and disseminated to all member nations.

The International Science Council has developed a number of courses to train teachers and lecturers in areas of the subject matter where research is needed.

In recent years UNESCO has sent nearly a thousand teachers into low income countries to prepare more teachers, work on curriculum, and help establish schools, even to the extent of building them. The UN has established over forty education missions all over the world to help countries plan better educational programs.

Through the United Nations Special Fund it has been possible for countries to support a large number of projects dealing with advanced training for teachers, engineers, and technicians who in turn can help develop the resources of each country concerned.

These programs are a part of UNESCO's long-range plan for improving living standards and for developing a greater appreciation for man's contributions to society.

The discussion of the six main organs of the United Nations and the one specialized agency (UNESCO) which is concerned mostly with our problem of education indicates the many efforts being made to improve international relations. The more each of us understands about this most important issue and the ways in which to implement a program to promote better world understanding, the more we realize how vital this whole problem is. A world whose nations and people are so close physically cannot afford to overlook the efforts being made by an organization through which we can better understand one another's actions.

Besides these above-mentioned projects, UNESCO has worked very hard on the problem of bringing a program of fundamental education to the rural peoples of the world. One of these fundamental education centers is located in Patzcuaro, Mexico. This center is discussed more in detail in the section on Mexico, Chapter 15. Other projects for which UNESCO is directly responsible are the extension of free and compulsory education, including education for women, and a program for workers' education which is reaching the grass roots of our civilization. Through these projects there is being made possible the necessary exchange of experiences which will eventually, it is hoped, bring men and their ideas closer together.

This discussion brings us face to face with the question: How do we implement a study of UNESCO, and how can we strengthen it? The Association of American Colleges [3] has prepared the following statement which describes the thinking of that group of educators:

The substantive program of UNESCO will afford opportunities for American educators to participate in international projects both as individuals, through their professional organizations, and through the colleges themselves. We now ask what steps can be taken by an individual college to promote UNESCO's purpose "to advance the intellectual and moral solidarity of mankind." Among the Objectives to which the individual college should direct its efforts are:

A. To prepare itself by appropriate administrative action to participate as an institution, and through its faculty members, in the international program of UNESCO.

B. To consider whether its curriculum can be improved so as to further the basic purposes of UNESCO.

C. To promote student activities which will contribute to a better understanding of the peoples of the world and of their cultures, and activities which best support UNESCO in its efforts to promote this better understanding.

D. To render services to its community in order to develop within the local and regional areas that sense of participation and dedication and that habit of co-operation without regard for race, class, or creed that must ultimately prevail throughout the world.

The above statement of policy for implementing a program of education on the college level represents the kind of effort American colleges can make to further the aims of UNESCO.

There are those who believe that learning about international problems should be confined to adult education, and they would stop after providing a workable program on this level. As examples of the pressure brought against schools to prohibit the teaching about UNESCO or the UN, in Los Angeles, California, and Houston, Texas, the schools were not permitted to allow pupils to participate in the annual essay contest because it became such a controversial issue.

In Pawtucket, Rhode Island, a club of students who called themselves the "UNESCO Thinkers" were forced to disband because it was charged that "UNESCO itself had atheistic and communistic leanings." [4]

Surely the job of promoting international understanding is so gigantic and so important that we cannot wait until we are adults to build understandings which are necessary for the maintenance of world peace. In the authors' judgment, every level of American education should contribute to this great task. The elementary and secondary school should play an important part.

THE AMERICAN SCHOOL'S ROLE

There are so many ways in which children acquire international understanding that it would be impossible to relate all of them here. A few examples of what some classes have done will serve to show that worldmindedness and a concern for world problems can be integrated into the school curriculum. Many individual school systems and a few states are requiring students to take courses in World Cultures. On many occasions these courses introduce students to materials about the UN. Some high schools are implementing a direct approach to a study of UNESCO, much as State Teachers College, Moorhead, Minnesota, did in the training school.[5]

Their outline of the unit for 11th and 12th grade social studies classes was:

1. History of UNESCO
2. Aims
3. Who may be members
4. Organization
5. How UNESCO might execute a project
6. Possible field of action for UNESCO
7. Suggested teaching activities for students
8. Materials.

This same reference [6] describes how a high school class in Deming, New Mexico, prepared exhibits for display in the public library and in the school. Beyond this they formed a radio committee and a press committee to publicize their work.

In Douglass High School, Baltimore, Maryland, a class prepared a "Junior Town Meeting" radio broadcast and discussed the question: "What Chance Has UNESCO to Make a Peaceful World?" [7] Through a

---

[4] Association for Supervision and Curriculum Development, *Forces Affecting American Education*, 1953 Yearbook (Washington, NEA, 1953), p. 204.

[5] Committee on International Relations, *Education for International Understanding in American Schools* (Washington, D.C., NEA, 1948), p. 145.

[6] *Ibid.*

[7] *Ibid.*, pp. 145–146.

broadcast of this type, citizens have an opportunity to learn what the school is doing to promote understanding of UNESCO and to acquaint themselves with some of the main objectives of this world-wide agency.

In 1947 the Northampton, Pennsylvania, Senior High School fashioned its commencement program on a dramatized interpretation of UNESCO.[8] In this activity the students played the roles of various representatives from member nations.

The elementary school can develop ideas for dramatizations, simulated radio broadcasts, assembly programs, and the like with UNESCO as the central theme. The United Nations has prepared a very elementary filmstrip titled, "A Garden We Planted Together," which can be used with primary children to present how nations can form such an organization as the UN. This in turn will begin to develop thinking about international co-operation and understanding. The use of this filmstrip will lead quite naturally to a study of peoples of other parts of the world.

The story of the Boulder, Colorado, Public Schools' study of UNESCO is an example of the magnitude of such a study.[9] The teachers and pupils worked closely with the community to initiate a series of programs and activities which would promote a better understanding of UNESCO's functions. The activity met with such approval that the Board of Education appropriated $3,000 for the project. The faculty and student body raised funds to supplement the board's appropriation. With these funds it was possible to bring internationally known speakers into the community for conferences and lectures. Students and teachers attended UNESCO's conferences in Mexico City in 1947 and in San Francisco in 1948. This program became so much a part of the schools and community of Boulder that they established a city-wide organization for UNESCO.

The possibilities for ways of implementing a study of UNESCO within a school and the community are limited only by the imagination of skilled teachers and an administration and community which senses the value of knowing more about international relations.

INTERNATIONAL UNDERSTANDING THROUGH OTHER AGENCIES

Governmental and Related Agencies

Besides co-operating in the furtherance of the functions of UNESCO, our nation has many established agencies which promote better international relations through the work they do. The United States Office of Education has a special Division of International Education Re-

[8] *Ibid.*, p. 146.
[9] *Ibid.*, p. 148.

lations. Each year this division arranges for foreign students to attend colleges and universities in this country. While the students are here they are permitted to visit other campuses, state departments of education, industrial plants, and farms. They are encouraged to participate in state and national conferences as well as tour our cities and towns to learn from firsthand experience the way of American life. We believe these visiting students can do much to interpret the United States to their native countries when they return.

Such organizations as the Pan-American Union and the Office of Inter-American Affairs have dealt specifically with problems of education as they concerned both the United States and our neighbors to the south. A joint Canada-United States Committee on Education was appointed in 1944 to discuss problems common to both nations. This committee has served to weld the spirit of friendship and understanding that has always existed between the two lands.

Another real way to promote international relations is through the teacher-exchange program. The enactment of federal legislation, the Fulbright Act of 1946, has provided funds for teachers in the United States to teach for a year in a school in a foreign country. Many graduate students and teachers in foreign countries are brought to this country to spend a year in one of our schools. These exchange teachers teach their regular subject or grade level in the school visited. Through this experience, the individual teacher learns more about education in the land he visits, and the pupils he has in his class have a real opportunity to learn about the teacher's homeland and people. Those interested in learning more about the teacher-exchange program should write to the United States Office of Education, Washington, D.C.

In addition to the provisions of the Fulbright Act there are other agencies which assist in promoting this exchange for teachers. Recently the Educational Development Association of Great Britain, an association comparable to the National Education Association, arranged for teachers to visit the campus of an American college. These teachers are provided with a series of lectures about our educational system and our form of government. A number of field trips to places of historic interest plus visits in American homes help to bring about a better understanding of each other's land, people, and traditions.

The American Association for Colleges for Teacher Education through its Committee on International Relations provides for groups of teachers to visit foreign countries to study their educational programs and report on their observations. The U.S. State Department has sent the Association's representative official to discuss international teacher exchange. The Association is co-operating with Phi Delta Kappa in preparing study tour guidelines. These tours have been and should continue to be beneficial in creating a better understanding of education as it is related to

Courtesy: West Chester State College.
Photograph by Mark Mock.

Visiting teachers from Great Britain. A group of teachers visit an American college to learn about its teacher preparation program.

the over-all problems and operations of the governments and the people of those nations.

Such organizations as the World Confederation of Organizations of the Teaching Profession, the International Council on Education for Teaching, the Commission on International Education of Phi Delta Kappa, the Committee on International Education of the American Association for Colleges of Teacher Education are all engaged in activities which will help nations to better understand and work with each other through the medium of education.

Many of our nation's best educators have traveled to foreign countries to study, to act in consultative capacity, and to enjoy vacations. During these periods of living with the citizens of other countries, it has been possible to exchange ideas which promote a better understanding of each other.

The Contributions of Noneducational International Agencies

Not included in UNESCO or other agencies which are fundamentally educational in nature are a number of other agencies which must be considered as counterparts to the manifestation of international co-operation. Too, some of the nations do not belong to UNESCO, yet are members of these other agencies. For example, Iceland, Ireland, Portugal, and Union of South Africa are not members of UNESCO. It is important, then, that these nations be encouraged to co-operate through the work of other agencies.

The names of some of these agencies are descriptive of the work and problems with which they are concerned: International Bank for Reconstruction and Development, International Labor Organizations, International Monetary Fund, International Telecommunication Union, International Trade Organization, International Civil Aviation Organization, Universal Postal Union, World Health Organization, and the United Nations International Children's Emergency Fund (UNICEF). Through the work of these agencies, common problems can be defined and a solution can be found which may satisfy all concerned. If, through these agencies, enough common problems can be solved and co-operation among the nations involved becomes sincere, there still is a ray of hope that a better understanding of international affairs will be reached. There is the possibility that nations who have not joined these agencies will eventually see the importance of becoming members and that war, which has formerly been the method used to settle international problems and disputes, will be replaced by discussion and peaceful negotiation.

Man has become so advanced in scientific and technological skill that he has in his possession now the weapons which could destroy all of civilization. It is time that we develop ways of understanding each other and through a spirit of co-operation, control or outlaw all weapons of war in order that this generation and all future generations can enjoy peace in every nation on the earth.

The challenge seems to be directed toward education. New and greater responsibilities face the American school. It is a prime requisite that we explore these responsibilities with pupils in our classrooms and in our communities and prepare them for life in a society that is internationally minded as well as nationally minded.

QUESTIONS AND PROJECTS

1. To what extent do better international relations depend on education?
2. What are the six principal organs of the United Nations, and how is each concerned with better international understanding?
3. Find out as much as you can about exchange teachers. Interview one or more in your community to learn how the program of exchange teachers is set up. Learn how they were chosen.
4. List some of the specialized agencies of the United Nations and explain how each would contribute to a better understanding among nations.
5. In some cities teachers have been criticized for teaching anything about the United Nations. Explain how you could justify teaching a unit of work based on the organization and functions of the United Nations.
6. How would the outlawing of all weapons of war effect world understanding?
7. Look up some of the projects of UNESCO and report some of its accomplishments.

AUDIO-VISUAL AIDS

MOTION PICTURES (16 MM)

A Report to the American People on Technical Cooperation—International Cooperation Administration, 14 min., sd., b&w. Explains and documents the functions, objectives, and activities of the International Cooperation Administration in technical assistance, programs of health, education, and community development. Stresses the concept that these programs are set up at the request of the host country. Shows programs in Latin America and Asia and teachers and leaders of these areas who come from various countries to America for study. Revised version.

Our Shrinking World—Young America Films, Inc., 18 E. 41st St., New York 17, N.Y., 10 min., sd., b&w. This film deals with the way in which developments in transportation, communication, and technology have brought peoples of the world together. Many man-made barriers and the difficult natural barriers of ocean, forests, mountains, and deserts, which so long have separated peoples, have slowly been overcome. The film attempts to bring out the need for co-operation among nations if we are to have a better life.

That All May Learn—United Nations Films, United Nations, New York, N.Y., 19 min., sd., b&w. The human story of a Mexican farmer and his family who are exploited because they cannot read or write is used as a case to stress the need for education of all the peoples all over the world. UNESCO's part in correcting these conditions is portrayed.

The Task Ahead—United Nations Films, United Nations, New York, N.Y., 20 min., sd., b&w. This film describes the mission of UNESCO. It tells of its first director, Julian Huxley, and of Jaime Torres Bodet, his successor. It describes some of the annual conferences and the work carried out through some of its projects.

Tomorrow Begins Today—United Nations Films, United Nations, New York, N.Y., 12 min., sd., b&w. By the questions of a group of young people of several nations, the films tells about the United Nations' work in health, agriculture, and education. It points out how political disagreement in the UN hinders its beneficial work. Two UN representatives give their impressions on the organization's work and its success.

Town Meeting of the World—United World, 14 min., sd., b&w. Illustrates how the UN meets the need of men and groups everywhere for a forum in which men can speak to each other and discuss their problems. Shows briefly the forming of the UN, the interrelationships of its component bodies, the part played by the General Assembly regarding the Korean war, and the role of the Communist powers in that conflict. Refers to the peace treaty with Japan, expresses hope for the membership of Japan in the UN, previous to her entry.

United States Responsibilities to the Rest of the World—Indiana University, Bloomington, Ind., (WOI-TV Kinescope), 29 min., sd., b&w. Discusses the responsibility of the United States to other countries of the world. States that the wealth of our country conveys a responsibility to help less fortunate nations by exporting both goods and technological discoveries. Describes the state of technological development in Asiatic countries and other less fortunate countries, and suggests ways in which our country can help them advance.

World Affairs Are Your Affairs—Encyclopaedia Britannica Films, 1150 Wilmette Ave., Wilmette, Ill., 26 min., sd., b&w. The film points out that decisions made by one group of people will influence other groups. Shows the work of the Cleveland Council on World Affairs, with radio forums, community services, and leadership training available. Stresses the importance for being well informed on world affairs.

World Without End—UNESCO, United Nations, New York, N.Y., 45 min., sd., b&w. This film shows the work of UNESCO and other UN agencies in sharing and applying knowledge through education for the peoples of Mexico and Thailand.

Youth and the United Nations—University of Minnesota, St. Paul, Minn., 26 min., sd., b&w. A group of high school students shown on a pilgrimage to the United Nations. The film concludes with students describing what the trip meant to them and how they are eager to share their experiences at home.

FILMSTRIPS

Ten Years of UNESCO—United Nations Films, United Nations, N.Y., 42 fr., si., b&w. Illustrations and examples of UNESCO's work over the last ten years.

We're All in the Same Boat—United Nations Films, United Nations, New York, N.Y., 92 frames, si., color. A story about UNESCO's Fundamental Education Center at Patzcuaro, Mexico. It describes the development of the center through the co-operation of UNESCO and other specialized agencies and explains how it operates.

FURTHER READINGS

Association for Supervision and Curriculum Development, *Forces Affecting American Education,* 1953 Yearbook (Washington, NEA, 1953).

Bereday, George Z. F., and Joseph A. Lauwerys, eds., *Education and International Life: The Yearbook of Education, 1964* (New York, Harcourt, Brace and World, 1964).

Flack, Michael J., *International Educational Activities* (Washington, D.C., American Council on Education, 1958).

Harley, J. Eugene, *Documentary Textbook on the United Nations* (Los Angeles, Center for International Understanding, 1950).

Hill, Norman, *International Organization* (New York, Harper & Row, 1953).

Hoselitz, Bert, ed., *The Progress of Underdeveloped Areas* (Chicago, University of Chicago Press, 1952).

Kenworthy, Leonard S., *Introducing Children to the World* (New York, Harper & Row, 1956).

Laubach, Frank C., and Robert S. Laubach, *Toward World Literacy* (Syracuse, N.Y., Syracuse University Press, 1960).

Laves, Walter, and Charles Thomson, *UNESCO: Purpose, Progress, Prospects* (Bloomington, Indiana, Indiana University Press, 1957).

Nicholas, H. G., *The United Nations as a Political Institution* (New York, Oxford University Press, 1959).

United Nations, *The United Nations and How it Works* (New York, Mentor Books, 1965).

United Nations Association of the U.S.A., *Mind Your World: A Citizen's Guide to International Understanding* (New York, UN Publications Service, 1965).

UNESCO, *Teaching About the United Nations and Specialized Agencies* (New York, United Nations, 1958).

UNESCO, *Youth and Peace: Some Ways of Promoting Among Young People the Ideals of Peace and International Understanding* (Paris, UNESCO, 1964).

Washburne, Carleton W., *The World's Good: Education for World-Mindedness* (New York, John Day, 1954).

15

Education
Among Our Neighbors
to the North and South

PREVIEW

▸ Since knowledge is a prelude to friendship, an understanding of educational matters among our nearest neighbors is essential.

▸ Canadian education is organized largely on a provincial rather than a national basis.
Differences in traditions have in some areas resulted in two systems of schools.
Elementary education resembles greatly the patterns in the States, and with few exceptions the high school organization is also similar.
Many fine colleges and universities exist throughout the nation.
Much interesting work is being done in such areas as Indian and adult education.
Professional teachers' associations are active and highly organized.

▸ The development of education in Mexico has been retarded by topography and language difficulties, but great progress has been made since the revolution of 1910–20.
A federal system of elementary and secondary schools has been developed, supplementing those supported by the states, municipalities, and religious groups.
The community-centered rural schools represent Mexico's outstanding contribution to education in the last 50 years.
About one-half of the secondary schools are public and one-half private, the total number being greatly inadequate.
The distinguished University of Mexico heads a system of higher education accommodating over 70,000 students.

384

▶ The fundamental education center under sponsorship of UNESCO has attracted world-wide attention as a venture in education for underdeveloped areas.

We cannot, if we would, escape the facts that bear down upon us as a result of the shrinking nature of the globe on which we live. The people of the free world realize as never before the commonness of their interests and their problems. Certainly human interaction among people of different nationalities is the rule rather than the exception. We cross national boundaries today more frequently than our ancestors crossed state lines. It is more important than ever that we understand each other better, and particularly is this true of our neighbors to the north of us and those to the south. Through knowledge and friendly associations, misunderstandings and prejudices diminish, and we can devote our efforts to the solution of our common problems. It is toward the furtherance of this objective that this chapter is aimed. The need for teachers with a broad outlook toward other peoples is surely greater than ever.

EDUCATION IN CANADA

The Land and the People

Covering an area of 3,845,774 square miles, Canada is third in size among the nations of the world, being exceeded only by China and the U.S.S.R. It is a land of regions varying widely in climatic conditions, in soil fertility, and in natural resources. From the maritime provinces on the east, across the land of lakes and the great Canadian Shield, through the broad and fertile prairies to the forests and mountains of the west, it is a country of widely varied potentialities and problems. All of these regional differences, except one, exist in the United States and can be understood there. Progression from the south to the north, however, is quite another matter. Northward from the United States border for many hundreds of miles, all the way to the North Pole in one small area, much of this far north country is uninhabited except by scattered groups of Indians and Eskimos. North from the tree line, over the muskeg to the ice fields, no population growth can be anticipated. Similar things may be said, however, of our own desert area in certain sections of the Southwest.

As a consequence of these varying conditions, Canada, with a population of nearly 19 million, has a population density of approximately four persons per square mile. Even this relatively small population is very unevenly distributed, since 500,000 people are found in a rather narrow band along the southern border.

There are, to be sure, many other regions that could support a much larger population than now exists, and consequently Canada has been concerned with encouraging the immigration of those who would contribute to her citizenry.

With the recent discovery and utilization of important deposits of iron ore, such as that at Burnt River, and of uranium, aluminum, and oil in the western and northern sections, the need for more population grows increasingly urgent. Canada is, indeed, not only an awakening industrial giant, but one that needs people and capital. It is the latter that is being found to a very satisfactory extent.

Politically, Canada's territory, 236,357 square miles larger than the United States and Alaska, is divided into ten provinces and two territories. These provinces vary in size from Prince Edward Island, only 120 miles long and with an average width of 20 miles, lying between New Brunswick and Nova Scotia, to Quebec, the largest province, occupying 594,860 square miles east of Hudson Bay.

To some extent, Canada, like the United States, is a land of many nationalities. Quebec, which is considered the home of the French-speaking Canadians, adjoins Ontario, made up more particularly of English, Irish, Scotch, and Scotch-Irish ancestry. Other groups are represented by the native Indians, the Eskimos, and by the increasing number of recent immigrants very largely of North European origin.

These are a few of the facts about our northern neighbor which have a bearing upon the educational system that has developed and which will continue to have a bearing upon the educational problems that will be a challenge in the years ahead.

The Organization of Education

Public education in Canada is a function not of the national government but of the provinces. The single exception is that of the education provided for the Indians, which is generally under central government support and control. The system, although subject to local variations, is generally the same for all provinces except Quebec. In reality two systems exist there—one for Roman Catholics, developed in the French tradition, and the other, for Protestants, in the English tradition. The public school systems of Ontario, Saskatchewan, and Alberta include a number of separate schools, mostly Roman Catholic. In Newfoundland the schools are mostly denominational—Anglican, Roman Catholic, United Church, Salvation Army and Seventh Day Adventist—with a few nondenominational.[1]

[1] Dominion Bureau of Statistics, *Canada, 1964* (Ottawa, Canada, 1964), p. 58.

It is interesting to note that approximately 95 percent of the children of school age attend schools operated by the municipalities. The remaining 5 percent attend either private schools with tuition or schools operated by departments of the Federal government.

In most provinces the schools are under the direction of a Minister of Education who is an elected member of the provincial legislature and has a seat in the provincial cabinet. In Quebec education is directed by the Provincial Secretary.

The Minister and his department have charge of the enforcement of all laws and regulations, including the training and licensing of teachers, provision of courses of study, authorization of textbooks, enforcement of attendance laws and the apportionment of provincial grants to schools. Local school boards, which are generally elected by the taxpayers except in some instances when they are appointed by the municipal council, have charge of the administration of the schools locally. This involves the hiring of teachers and the general local operation of the school.

Sources of revenue for education are generally from two areas: (1) local taxation; (2) grants from the Provincial governments. The federal government does, however, contribute through the provinces some funds for vocational and technical education (Act of 1919) which are based on a matching provision. Similar federal aid is also given for scholarship, research, and youth training.

In general, education is free through the secondary level. In some provinces nominal fees may exist. In Quebec there may, on occasion, be fees for elementary education.[2]

The following data indicate the amount and source of funds allocated for formal education for the most recent year available:

Table 15-1.   Financial Support of Formal Education in Canada, 1962 (In thousands of dollars)

Local Taxation	757,643
Provincial Governments	1,010,202
Federal Government	350,444
Fees	119,304
Other sources	86,827
Total	2,324,420

Elementary Education

In the schools that follow the English tradition, the elementary divisions are organized on a pattern similar to ours, that is, covering

[2] S. H. Steinberg, ed., *Statesmen's Yearbook* (Toronto, Macmillan and St. Martins Press, 1954), p. 359.

grades 1–8, with attendance beginning when the child is between 6 and 8 years of age. Subjects of study are very similar to those pursued in the United States. In Quebec the Roman Catholic elementary schools are organized on a seven-year basis which is called the primary division. This is followed by a sort of multiple-track system which may be properly considered the secondary level.

Secondary Education

Work in the secondary school in Canada generally covers four years and grades 9–12. In Ontario and British Columbia grade 13 is included in the secondary school. In some of the provinces junior high schools are found, covering the same grades as in the United States, 7–9 inclusive. Generally, the same curricula are found in Canadian high schools as in our own, with the usual adaptations to local conditions.

In Quebec the Roman Catholic schools provide that a boy may enter a classical college preparing for the university or pass through any of the

*Courtesy: H. C. Sweet, Assistant Chief
Superintendent of Schools. Alberta
Government photograph, Department of the
Provincial Secretary, Edmonton, Alberta.*

A modern representation of Canada's new schools. The John Russell School, Camrose, Alberta.

five divisions preparing for further educational experiences. These divisions are: general, scientific, industrial, commercial, and agricultural. The latter three are terminal courses, whereas the others lead to the professional schools.

At the end of the primary division in Quebec, the girl, too, has a number of choices: (1) a general five-year course leading to normal school; (2) a three-year household science course; (3) a four-year commercial course; (4) a two-year domestic arts course, or (5) a classical college course leading to study in a university.

Much attention is being given throughout the Dominion to the development of larger high schools mainly of the composite or comprehensive types. These are generally organized on a "regional" basis and are made feasible as a result of the enlargement of districts either by stimulation, as in Alberta, or by legislation, as in Saskatchewan. In fact, all provinces except Quebec and Newfoundland are moving in this direction. These two seem to be adhering to the more traditional idea of separate high schools for separate curricula.

Canada, as the United States, is finding a continually higher proportion of its youth in the secondary schools. In 1962–63 the percent of youth enrolled in these institutions reached 68.9 percent whereas in 1951–52 it was but 41.6.[3]

Higher Education

Enrollments in institutions of higher education in Canada are increasing at a rapid rate, comparable to the same situation in the United States and many other parts of the world. In 1962–63 in the Dominion there were 141,388 full time students enrolled in the various colleges and universities, representing a 9.7 percent increase over the previous year. A total of 312,000 is predicted for 1970.[4]

To meet growing needs, colleges and universities nearly everywhere are being enlarged, and new institutions are being founded in many areas.

Enrollment in the graduate schools is also undergoing a comparable growth.

Latest figures available on the proportionate distributions of support for higher education indicate the following:

Endowments	5	percent
Federal government	24	"
Provincial government	31	"
Students' fees	28	"
Other sources	12	" [5]

[3] Dominion Bureau of Statistics, op. cit., p. 58.
[4] Dominion Bureau of Statistics, op. cit., p. 59.
[5] R. D. Mitchener, Canadian Universities and Colleges, Reference Paper No. 106 (Ottawa, Canada, Department of External Affairs, 1960).

Vocational and Technical Education

It is highly probable that in no other areas of public education has Canada made as intensive an effort to improve existing conditions as in the broad areas of vocational and technical education.

It was in the post "Sputnik era" that every province began to reassess its entire field of general education.[6] Several provincial commissions gave careful study to changed conditions and needs, and one of the most significant results was the passage of the Technical and Vocational Education Act of 1960 which broadly provided financial assistance to the provinces to develop technical and vocational services within the provincial systems. The legislation, in brief, provided:

1. 75 percent of the cost of new buildings and equipment would be paid by the federal government, and then 50 percent after a specified population had

Courtesy: Toronto Board of Education.
Photograph by Metropolitan Photos, Willowdale, Ont.

Parkway Vocational School, Toronto, Canada. Canada's stress on vocational education is shown in part by the facilities provided.

[6] Dean H. Goard, *Current Development in Canada of Technical and Vocational Education, Phi Delta Kappan,* Vol. 46 (April, 1965), pp. 395–400.

been reached (until 1967). Progress in providing new facilities under the Act has been quite satisfactory.

2. Operating costs are shared with the provinces on a 50–50 basis.[7]

The specific fields that have benefited and are benefiting from the Act are:

Existing vocational programs in high schools
Trade and occupational training in adult centers
Cooperative industry-school programs
Training the unemployed
Training the handicapped
Training vocational teachers
Training for federal services
Student assistance
Apprenticeship training

Goard [8] suggests that, while the progress is still underway, "its full impact will probably not be felt until 1968–1969 when all of these new services come into full operation. . . . The goal of all this federal activity, then, is providing well-trained individuals to function in the work force of the nation." Certainly the ways and means appear to be readily available for the attainment of this objective.

Other Educational Activities

Indian Education. As has been previously stated, education for the Indians, which includes by law the Eskimos, is carried on by the federal government's Indian Affairs Branch of the Department of Citizenship and Immigration. Both day and residential schools are operated, again, very similarly to present practices in the United States. Enrollment in the Indian Schools has increased steadily in recent years, attributable partly to greater accessibility and partly to the greater recognition of the value of education.

Adult Education. Not only because of the sparsity of population, which in itself stresses the great need for modern programs of adult education, but because of the more or less world-wide recognition of its value, this form of activity has greatly increased throughout Canada. Much use is being made of the radio and motion pictures. Excellent films, documentary and otherwise, have been produced by the National Film Board, and radio forums of various types are also widely used.

Correspondence courses for adults are common, and many formal classes are being offered by existing institutions or are established as extension services in many areas. Particularly is this true in agriculture and

[7] *Ibid.*, p. 396.
[8] *Ibid.*, p. 399.

home economics. Probably the most recent large-scale project in the extension field is that conducted by the University of Newfoundland, initiated in 1955.

Canada, as the United States, has been giving its educational problems much serious study. Numerous surveys have been made and reports issued. Some of the more significant have been:

The Report of the Royal Commission on National Development in the Arts, Letters and Sciences.
The Report of the Royal Commission on Education in Ontario.
The Canadian Research Committee on Practical Education's Reports including:
  1. *Your Child Leaves Home* (1950)
  2. *Two Years After School* (1951)
  3. *Better Schooling for Canadian Youth*

These reports have suggested standards of good educational practice that are now widely accepted on both sides of the border and are likely to be of great significance as we both move forward toward the goal of a more adequate education for all children and youth.

Canada has quite naturally had a fairly large proportion of small one-teacher schools, but much effort is presently being made toward the consolidation and the development of larger units of administration. New modern schools of the finest type are appearing in Canada on every level.

Teacher Education. The qualifications for teaching and therefore the requirements for the issuances of licenses vary among the provinces. Generally, more education has been required for teaching in the secondary than in the elementary schools. MacDougall [9] has pointed out that "Canada's traditional approach to the preparation of teachers merited the name of teacher training rather than 'teacher education.'" The pattern of preparation for elementary school teaching was generally for the candidate to enter the normal school from senior matriculation and then to receive one year of intensive professional preparation. For secondary school teaching, the one year of professional work, usually in a university, came after the attainment of a bachelor's degree. So it was that universally the "training year was a thing apart."

However, with the desire to improve the preparation of teachers on all levels and the general status of the profession as well, a great deal of concern has been shown for making teacher education a regular part of the work of the university. Experimental work in the western Provinces seems to indicate the desirability of this move. It is very likely that this will be the future direction of the preparation of teachers.

Professional Associations. The majority of Canadian Provinces, excluding only Nova Scotia and Prince Edward Island, have laws on their

[9] J. Innes MacDougall, "Teacher Education in Western Canada," *Phi Delta Kappan,* Vol. 36, No. 4 (January, 1955), p. 150.

statute books known as Teaching Profession Acts.[10] This legislation provides for the legal status of Teacher Associations, giving them legal corporate powers and defining their aims and objectives. Compulsory membership is a common feature, with membership in most provinces being optional for those serving outside the regular school system. Membership and discipline are left to the associations themselves, subject to the approval of the Minister of Education or corresponding authority. No such legal status as described is found in the States.

The various Provincial Associations are now bound together into a national organization known as the Canadian Teachers' Federation with a central office and staff in Ottawa. The Federation is generally carrying on the same activities as is the NEA in the United States—crusading for the improvement of conditions for teachers and for the advancement of the cause of education. So much are we and our neighbors alike.

The Canadian Federation is a member of the World Confederation of Organizations of the Teaching Profession and works actively for the promotion of international understanding.

EDUCATION IN MEXICO

Mexico, our neighboring republic to the south, has experienced some very trying times in developing a pattern of education. As late in the history of its people as 1911, at the end of Dictator Porfiria Díaz's rule, there were only about 3 million of the 15 million population who were literate. Today, under a democratic form of government the percentage of persons not able to read nor write is still high, but much progress has been and still is being made in reducing this number. Even though Mexico can boast of having the oldest established university on the North American continent, the University of Mexico, Mexico City, 1553, there still remains the problem of providing an educational program which will reach all the people. One is able to understand, to some degree, why education has had a difficult growth when the history of the country is studied.

The Land and Its People

The republic of Mexico has an area of nearly 760,000 square miles with a population of over 35 million, nearly twice that of Canada. The density of population per square mile is 50. Compared to the state of Texas, Mexico is three times as large in area with a population of over three times as many people. The mestizo * makes up approximately 55

---

[10] H. E. Smith, "Teaching Profession Acts in Canada," *Phi Delta Kappan,* Vol. 33, No. 1 (September, 1951), pp. 54–55.

* *Mestizo*—the product of intermarriage of Indians and Spaniards.

percent of the population, Indians 30 percent, and white 15 percent. Spanish is the dominant language. Eighty-six percent of the people use this language, and the remainder use the Indian language. However, these data are based on a very general classification terminology. Redfield,[11] writing about "the Indian in Mexico," refers to as many as 54 different languages listed by census classification. He points out that in parts of Mexico where Indians meet in local markets they "speak languages as different from one another as are English, Chinese and Hebrew." Cline,[12] writing in *The United States and Mexico,* reports that in the early history of Mexico "at least two hundred and perhaps as many as four hundred languages and dialects reflected the distinct usages and ways of thought of as many tribes." This matter of language barrier is mentioned here to give insight into the problems facing education when we consider communication as being basic to furthering understanding among peoples.

Though we are most acquainted with the Aztec empire in Mexico, it is known that at least two civilized races—the Mayas and the Toltecs— preceded them in the early periods of history.[13] All of these people must be recognized as contributing in one way or another to the Mexican culture and society of today.

Following the fall of the Aztec empire, Mexico was ruled by Spain for 300 years until 1821. During the years of Mexico's independence, the administration of the government has changed so frequently that education had received little or no backing on a national scale until 1920.

Today, the people elect a president for a period of six years and, like many of our states' governors, he cannot succeed himself. He governs with a cabinet of 16 members. The legislative congress is composed of two houses. The Chamber of Deputies, elected for three years, is made up of 162 members, and the Senate, elected for six years, has 60 members. Both men and women of the required age of 18 or 21 years are eligible to vote. (Married male citizens may vote at age 18; single male citizens must be 21.)

Each of the 29 states within the nation is governed by a popularly elected governor and legislature. Mexico's recent presidents including the incumbent, Gustavo Diaz Ordaz, have maintained friendly relations with the United States government.

It is easily recognized how there once existed a feeling of disunity among the peoples of Mexico when one studies its geography. Nearly every extreme in topography, vegetation, and climate is present in Mexico. The heart of Mexico is a great plateau, surrounded on three sides by high mountains, the only open side being toward the north. Two-thirds

[11] Robert Redfield, "Mexico Today," *The Annals of the American Academy of Political and Social Science,* Vol. 208 (March, 1940), p. 135.

[12] Howard F. Cline, *The United States and Mexico* (Cambridge, Harvard University Press, 1953), p. 28.

[13] *Information Please Almanac* (New York, Macmillan, 1965), p. 667.

of Mexico is mountainous, and the remaining one-third is described as "rolling." About 8 percent of this "rolling" land area is relatively level. On the eastern seaward slopes, the land is drenched with as much as 120 inches of rainfall yearly. Here the vegetation is so dense that it is almost impenetrable. Moving westward to the Pacific side, where the high mountains receive the rainfall and moisture, we find the slopes of a desert land. With the many mountain ranges receiving the greatest share of the rainfall, proper amounts of moisture, coupled with favorable temperatures necessary to produce food crops, is limited to less than 15 percent of the total land area. Irrigation is needed badly and to some extent is being provided.

Those people who were fortunate enough to be born in an area where nature supplied the conditions favorable to growing crops for food were found to spend their entire lives there, without being aware of other villages a few miles up, down, or on the other side of the mountains.

Natural Resources. The natural resources of Mexico include various minerals, oil, coal, and forests. Recently there has been an upward trend in exporting graphite, zinc, iron ore, and sulphur. Gold and silver, formerly the leading exports, have declined. Mexico supplies the world market with large supplies of copper, tin, mercury, lead, tungsten, antimony, and cadmium. New petroleum fields are discovered each week. At present over 2,600 operating wells produce over 300,000 barrels of crude oil daily.

Transportation and Communication. Since 1925 the national government has built about 50,000 miles of new highways. Of these about half are paved; the others are graveled or hard-surfaced. With financial help from the national government, the states have added many miles of secondary and market roads. A total of nearly 117,000 miles of highways and roads are now completed.

To this must be added the nearly 15,000 miles of railroads which connect most of the larger cities and the United States. Slowly but surely, Mexico is breaking down the natural geographic barriers which have kept her a nation of rural inhabitants. A network of telephone and telegraph lines which is being constructed and the radio, television, and the airplane make possible a communication system which will promote the progress of education.

Religion

The dominant religion in Mexico is Roman Catholic. There has been conflict between church and state in Mexico because the Mexican Catholic Church was patterned after the medieval church, the Colonial Church, which was both church and state. The many indictments made against the Mexican clergy cannot be construed as indictments against the Catholic Church or the spiritual beliefs of Catholics. No one can deny that the church has made a real contribution to Mexico's people through its educational activities.

During the Revolution of 1910–20 the improvement of education was made a crucial issue. In fact, the cry of the Revolution itself for the improvement of the masses was *"Educar es reimir"* (to educate is to redeem). Largely as a result of this urgently felt need, one of the major outcomes was the authorization for the development of a national school system. Article 3 of the constitution of 1917 was recently revised to reflect broadened present needs. Where it formerly concerned only the federal government's authority to participate in educational matters, today it prescribes additional objectives of the educational program. The revised law prescribes that education must concern itself with the total child, encourage a patriotic spirit and an awareness of international cooperation. It was to be more democratic, free of religious doctrine and give more emphasis to the individual's personal dignity, family integrity, social good and fraternity, and to stress the equality of citizens before the law.[14] Early in 1921 the Department of Education was created, and José Vasconcelos became its first secretary.

As director of the University of Mexico, Vasconcelos had strong convictions about educating the masses. He believed it was necessary to educate those in the university, but this was not enough—the abandoned and neglected children left to roam the streets were to be educated too. Education was thus to be for all—a worthy goal indeed.

The schools then in existence, whether supported publicly or privately, were allowed to continue, and beyond these more were to be supported by federal funds. Libraries were established; books were translated into languages of the various Indian tongues and dialects. Itinerant or "ambulatory" teachers were sent out to the rural areas where communities lacked the necessary funds to hire a teacher or establish a school. The program grew faster than the supply of teachers. Teachers from the cities were not able to understand many of the problems of rural Mexicans. The noble experiment bogged down, and political leadership changed.

The next President to face up to the problems of education was Ávila Comacho, who was in office during World War II. He accepted as his one important task that of removing education from politics. Earlier during Cárdenas' term as President the highly "socialistic" educational program developed, and many Communists had influenced this growing program. It was necessary for the Comacho administration to shift the program to stress "democracy." Even during the war years, when defense was receiving the greatest share of the government's budget, Comacho was able to launch a federal program directed toward school construction and reac-

[14] Howard F. Cline, *Mexico* (New York, Oxford University Press, 1962), pp. 195–196.

tivation of "cultural missions" to educate the rural population. A cultural mission is composed of a "team" of about a dozen persons who have a thorough knowledge of working with people living in rural areas. The team always includes teachers, a social worker, and a nurse.

In 1955 there were 73 such missions. More were to be established and financed out of the 1960 budget for education. Adolfo López Mateos, president from 1958–64 and a former educator, did much to further education for his people. He was not only successful in attaining greater governmental support but in addition influenced private enterprise to give financial aid.

The Ministry of Public Education was allocated $150,766,000 (1 billion 800 million pesos), or over 18 percent of the total national budget for 1960. The pattern of increasing education's budget annually seems most likely to continue under President Ordaz's administration.

Dr. Jaimé Torres Bodet, Ministry of Public Education, allocated a large part of the budget to construct 3,000 new classrooms and employ more than 3,000 additional teachers. This still was almost 500 classrooms short of the number needed in 1960. An estimated 4,500 additional classrooms were needed by 1965. Besides this considerably large outlay needed for facilities and teachers, there is a continually rising budget which provides for some rudimentary education to Mexico's Indian tribes.

Administration of Education

Schools in Mexico are for the most part classified as municipal, state, or federal. Private schools are permitted and do appear in all parts of the nation. Regardless of type, all schools are under some restricted limitations by the government. For example, even private schools are subject to supervisory control, and the instructional program must correspond in every way to the plans, curriculum, and methods established by the official federal government schools. If the government wishes, it may, at any time, revoke authorization granted to a private school, and such action is final.

The highest authority in education is the Secretary of Public Education. He is appointed by the President and is a member of his cabinet. In addition, each state is assigned a Director of Federal Education, who maintains an office in the capital of each state. The Director represents the Secretary of Public Education and with the help of his staff, coordinates federal, state, and local educational programs. He is in complete control of all federal schools in the state. The number of employees in the Ministry of Education on the federal level is reported to be 78,000 which approximates the total number of teachers in a state the size of Texas. This number includes all the teachers and related personnel in all federal schools.

Figure 15-1. The National Education System of Mexico

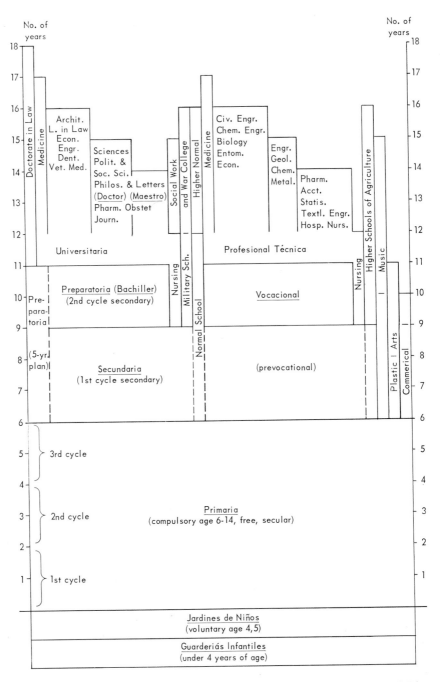

SOURCE: Marjorie C. Johnston, *Education in Mexico* (Washington, U.S. Office of Education, 1956).

State and municipal schools are the responsibility of the Director General of Schools who is appointed by the Governor. State authorities appoint and supervise teachers in all schools in the state, even those established and maintained by municipalities. State legislatures determine the amount of state income to be used for education, since most states have no special school tax. In recent years this has varied from 10 percent of the total budget in some states to as much as nearly 50 percent in others. The federal government has aided local state educational systems by building schools in all the states where they are most needed.

It is obvious that all levels of government are dedicated to providing educational opportunity for more and more of the children and youth in Mexico. The diagram above will give a pretty complete picture of Mexico's educational system. Further insight can be gathered from the description of the various levels of the total school program.

Pre-Elementary Education

As is true in the United States, development at this level of education has shown slow progress. With the great need for schools and teachers to care for educational needs of compulsory school-age children only a small number of nursery schools and kindergartens have been established. However, there are a growing number of large government offices, business, and industries which maintain day nurseries. Here, the children receive educational supervision and medical attention. Children under four years of age may attend the nursery school.

As early as 1904 a few kindergartens were started, but little progress was noted until 1942 when the kindergarten was made an integral part of the national education program. Today there are more than 1,300 kindergartens with an enrollment of more than 200,000 children between the ages of four and six years.

The curriculum in kindergarten emphasizes activities associated with the home and community. An attempt is made to build civic responsibility and patriotism through music and dramatizations appropriate for celebration of national holidays. In addition to this, the children are taught good health habits and social and emotional adjustment.

Elementary Education

Mexico emphasizes elementary education more than any other school level. This stems from the fact that facilities are still lacking for approximately half of the school-age population and it is imperative that the younger children are cared for first. The minimal standard of 6th grade education for all is far from being reached.

Because so large a percentage of children leave school before completing the 6th grade, the elementary school curriculum is taught in each cycle of two years. It is then repeated the next two years but on a more intensified basis. The philosophy for such a plan is that those students who drop out before completing all six grades will have received as comprehensive a preparation as possible in all the basic skills.

The Secretary of Public Education prescribes what is to be taught as well as giving guidance or instructions as to what rate of progress the students should be making at a given time. However, teachers are ex-

This building is a typical example of modern architecture of the new Mexican schools.

pected to use a variety of techniques or methods according to the children's needs and abilities. Stated objectives for elementary education are almost identical to goals set for schools in the United States. Likewise, all subjects taught would be found in our elementary schools.

Undoubtedly, the most important achievement in elementary education has been the increased emphasis upon the establishment of rural schools which were virtually nonexistent before 1920. Most of these (70 percent) today are federally supported. The remainder are state and municipal or supported jointly by both private and government sources.

Since all schools in Mexico are supposed to adapt the common curriculum to local needs, a great variety of programs designed to improve rural life has resulted. In one community emphasis may be put upon the improvement of farming; in others, upon recreation, local crafts, and adult education.

Many localities are still without elementary schools; where schools are established it is not uncommon that instruction is offered only in the first two or three grades. Moehlman and Roucek [15] point out that this situation, along with the inadequacy of the urban programs, "explains why more than two million children of school age are not in school." Thus illiteracy remains at a remarkably high level. Recent figures estimate the number of illiterates as high as 24 percent of the total population. This indicates some improvement over 1950 when this percentage was close to 40 percent of all persons over 25 years old.

As is usual in many other countries, secondary education begins at the end of the six-year elementary program. Actually the usual Mexican secondary school is a three-year institution generally followed by two years of separate vocational or preprofessional schools. These may, in reality, be considered a part of higher education, although for purposes of comparison with institutions in the United States it is common to think of the secondary school as a five-year unit. The curricula in these schools are similar to those in our own high schools.

Mexican secondary schools are approximately half public and half private. Secondary education in the country is really only in its infancy and is in urgent need of expansion if the educational needs of the people are to be met in the near future.

One significant change has occurred in recent years in devising a new public secondary school program. This new type school is an extension of the curriculum offered in the primary and elementary school. It more nearly meets the needs of all students rather than only those preparing for college. Youths completing this school's program are much better equipped to play an important role in the work which still must be accomplished for Mexico to flourish as a leading nation in Latin-American affairs.

Higher Education

Reference has been made earlier to the fact that the University of Mexico was established at Mexico City in 1553, which is about 100

15 George I. Sanchez, writing in Arthur H. Moehlman and Joseph Roucek, *Comparative Education* (New York, Holt, Rinehart and Winston, 1952).

years prior to Harvard. Before 1553, however, a college had been established for Indians in 1536, and the lower college of the University of Michoacan came into existence in 1540. Seven colleges were established in Mexico City before the end of the sixteenth century. These facts together with many others come as a considerable surprise to most residents in the United States. They indicate a strong and early interest in higher education that even well-informed people here did not know existed.

After higher education had been at a rather low ebb, especially during the nineteenth century, owing to lack of money particularly, a reform movement set in which, in spite of interruptions of the Revolution, has brought higher education to a modern form in which science has tended to balance the old humanism and important professional schools have been established.

The University of Mexico has been entirely rebuilt; the last of its very modern facilities were completed and in use in 1955. These facilities provide for nearly half of the 70,000 students enrolled in Mexico's colleges and technical institutes. It is encouraging, too, that a larger number of students from the United States are attending the University of Mexico each year. Increasing numbers of students and professors from Mexico study and teach in colleges and universities in the United States as well. This exchange should serve to weld a closer friendship between the two nations.

Teacher Education

The Superior Normal School in Mexico City, enrolling approximately 1,000 students, is comparable to teachers colleges in the states. A number, about a score, of rural normal schools are federally controlled. These enroll approximately 4,000 students, mostly men, and emphasize the activities that are important to the improvement of rural life. All of these are boarding schools, and students generally receive federal aid. Normal schools in urban centers enroll a slightly larger number of students. Many of the universities, too, offer professional courses. The lack of sufficient trained teachers has long been and probably will continue to be a serious problem in Mexico, but in this respect indeed they are not alone.

In spite of the many unsolved problems of education in Mexico, one cannot help but be impressed with the progress made in the past 25 to 30 years. During these years each succeeding President's report on the state of the nation has stressed educational needs. Thousands of elementary schools have been built, and tens of thousands of teachers recruited. Teachers' salaries have improved steadily, and fringe benefits have increased. Facilities have been made available for more students to take technical and scientific training either in postgraduate high school programs or in colleges or universities.

From the time of the founding of the United Nations, Mexico has exhibited a real interest in its problems and has served on most of the important councils and committees. The one council with which we particularly identify Mexico's fine work is that of the UNESCO. Until his resignation in November, 1952, Jaimé Torres Bodet, a distinguished Mexican leader, was chairman of this important body.

Since education is one of the major concerns of UNESCO, it was fitting that Mexico, because of the results she attained in combating illiteracy among her people, was chosen for the establishment of the first of six Regional Fundamental Education Centers.[16] The purpose of these centers is to train teachers and prepare instructional materials for all underdeveloped areas. Rural teachers and other social and welfare workers assemble at these centers to exchange ideas and plan materials which have proven to be effective in raising the intellectual and economic levels of rural populations. The UNESCO provides fellowships for the people chosen to attend the center.

The Center's first director was Lucas Ortiz Benitez who possessed a wealth of experience as an educator working with rural schools of Mexico. Through his fine leadership the Center's program has continued to set the pace for similar establishments in other parts of the world. Each year new teams of students gather at the Center for intensive training in fundamental education pertaining to all aspects of furthering improved health, home life, recreation and economics. The entire training program takes 19 months which includes actual experience working in rural communities. Upon completion of the program the trainees are awarded a diploma of Specialized Teacher of Fundamental Education.

All of Mexico's school problems will not be solved at once; during recent years there is evidence of a much greater concern for urgency in meeting the country's educational needs. Some hopeful signs for further progress in an attempt to provide better public education in Mexico are these: the goal of free and compulsory education for ages 6 to 14 has been accepted; the separation of church and state is gradually becoming a reality; more federal funds for education are made available each year.

In 1958 there were over 29,000 elementary schools with an enrollment of nearly 5,000,000 pupils. Over 193,000 pupils enrolled in secondary school the same year. A great increase in numbers being encouraged to prepare for teaching is noted, and their services are urgently needed. Mexico's 21 universities and institutes have an enrollment of approximately 65,000 students.

The success Mexico has had in bringing fundamental education to so many millions of her own people is phenomenal. It would seem that her experience in teaching the rural peoples will serve as a pattern for other countries faced with problems similar to hers.

[16] This first center was set up in Patzcuaro, Mexico. Other centers already operating or to be established are in Africa, the Far East, and Oceania.

On the other hand, like many another land, educational progress in Mexico continues to be hampered by the persistence of ideas and practices from the nineteenth century and earlier. There is, for example, still too much conflict between the church and the state; this will have to be resolved if progress is to continue at a desired pace.

Sanchez points out that "another type of inheritance is the resistance to the professionalization of secondary and university-level teachers." He further suggests that as a result of the failure to develop a real educational profession, "nonprofessional forces have had an undue influence in educational matters." This indictment sounds strangely familiar to those who are acquainted with educational history in the United States.

QUESTIONS AND PROJECTS

CANADA

1. If possible, interview a Canadian exchange teacher or an American teacher who has been teaching in Canada for a year. It will be especially interesting to secure comparable reactions and opinions on the schools of the two countries.
2. Write to the Ministry of Education in several Provinces asking for specific information relative to the schools of each.
3. Write to the Canadian Film Board at Ottawa asking for a list of films made and circulated by them. Prepare a selection of films from there and from other sources that might be used in schools in the United States to develop better understanding between the two countries.
4. Try to arrange to exchange an American history textbook used in the seventh and eighth grades for a Canadian history book used in comparable grades there. Possibly one of the Ministers of Education will be able to help you in this matter. Compare the treatment of the same topic in the two texts.
5. Secure catalogs from such universities as Queens and McGill and discuss with the class the offerings and opportunities available.

MEXICO

1. What was and still is the biggest problem for Mexico's educators? Explain why it is more a problem in Mexico than it might be in another country of similar size.
2. How is the health of Mexico's people likely to be affected through educating the people of rural areas?
3. Look in United Nations publications for details on UNESCO's educational projects. Summarize one project which is interesting and appealing to you.
4. Describe the purposes and plans for UNESCO's Regional Fundamental Educational Centers. Write to the United Nations for help here.
5. How has topography, climate, and a variety of cultures helped deter education for Mexico's people?
6. Look up more information about Mexico's Revolution of 1910, and list ways that this revolution proved beneficial to the educational program in Mexico.
7. Investigate the movement of many Mexican citizens into the States and some implications of this for our own public schools.

AUDIO-VISUAL AIDS

CANADA

MOTION PICTURES (16 MM)

French Canadians—United World Government Films, 1445 Park Ave., New York, N.Y., 20 min., sd., b&w. Introduces a farm family on Ile d'Orléans, near

Quebec. Shows their daily and weekly activities, their school, their religion, and their co-operative enterprises.

Peoples of Canada—International Film Bureau, 57 East Jackson Blvd., Chicago, Ill., 21 min., sd., b&w. Canada is first presented as the early explorers saw it. Then came the first settlers, with the family of a French habitant portrayed. The natural resources of the new country are developed by Scots in Nova Scotia raising fine apples, fishermen from Normandy and Brittany securing harvests from the Grand Banks. Lumbermen are in the woods; miners in the coal fields. An industrial Canada is built upon the enterprise of all these people that have come from all parts of Europe.

Sight and Sound—National Film Board of Canada, Room 658, 630 Fifth Ave., New York, N.Y., 11 min., sd., b&w. Shows the use of audio-visual aids and stresses their value in education. The examples given illustrate how (by means of a film) a class of children "jump a continent" to visit Mexico, how a film-strip on cut-outs stimulates creative activity, and the use of a radio broadcast in a history class.

Tomorrow's Citizens—National Film Board of Canada, Room 658, 630 Fifth Ave., New York, N.Y., 10 min., sd., b&w. An examination of the question, "Is the school child's sense of social responsibility keeping pace with his technical knowledge?" The changes following a global war, the release of atomic energy and setting up of the United Nations body, are an inheritance awaiting young citizens as they approach adulthood. The film illustrates the significance of the new inheritance and seeks in the classroom for evidence that children are being prepared to administer it.

Canada's History: Colony to Commonwealth—Coronet Films, 15 min., sd., color. Blends motion picture footage scenes of Canadian historic sites, state papers, and official edicts and authentic models and paintings of historic incidents to trace the history of Canada. Stresses the major events that brought Canada from the status of frontier colony to a full-fledged member of the British Commonwealth. Considers Canada's exploration, conflicting territorial claims, population make-up, culture, industry, and government. Shows how the history of the U.S. and Canada have intermingled and touches on the highlights of Canada's growth in the nineteenth and twentieth centuries.

FILMSTRIP

Teaching as a Career—National Film Board of Canada, Room 658, 630 Fifth Ave., New York, N.Y., 47 fr., si., b&w. Examines the pros and cons of teaching as a career with special reference to educational requirements, personal aptitudes, specialized training, remuneration, and opportunities for advancement.

MEXICO

MOTION PICTURES (16 MM)

Forgotten Village—Brandon Films Inc., 200 West 57th St., New York, N.Y., 60 min., sd., b&w. A Mexican village, its life geared to the tempo existing since it was founded, takes its first hesitant steps toward educational and medical progress. The village elders gradually change their customs and beliefs and give way to youth and the urge for a better life. The film is helpful to depict the customs of a primitive society; to show the religious and sociological problems of changing a primitive culture. Based on a story by John Steinbeck.

Mexican Agricultural Program—Rockefeller Foundation, 49 W. 49th St., New York, N.Y., 21 min., sd., color. Pictures the agricultural experiment carried on by the Mexican government and the Rockefeller Foundation to improve crops by developing better seed and better soil-conservation practices. Shows the research involved, the various experiments, and the ultimate effects on the standard of living in rural Mexico.

Mexican Village Family No. 2—Paul Hoefler Productions, 7934 Santa Monica Blvd., Los Angeles, Calif., 17 min., sd., color. Shows the way of life in the agricultural village of Tlacotepec near the market town of Toluca in central Mexico. Depicts kinds of crops and methods of cultivation, harvesting, and marketing; use of wild products such as cactus, mustard, and wood; water resources and the way in which the village solves its water problem. It shows children's activities at school and at play; and the influence of the church.

Mexico at Work—Paul Hoefler, Walt Disney, 16 min., sd., color. Pictures the coastal zone, the middle or subtropic zone, and the central plateau of Mexico to show how the climate and distribution of natural resources influence the occupation of a great number of the people. Also surveys Mexico's trend toward mechanization and growth in technology by depicting modern cities where modern factories, oil refineries, assembly plants, stores, and office buildings employ thousands of skilled and unskilled workers.

Mexico Builds a Democracy—United World Government Films, 1445 Park Ave., New York, N.Y., 20 min., sd., b&w. Shows the Mexican Government's efforts to bring modern education to a Tarascan Indian Group who had no written language and felt no incentive to learn Spanish, the national language. The importance of the subject—Mexico's campaign to wipe out illiteracy—must be balanced against the film's poor photography and failure to establish clearly that the educational work shown in the film is part of a nation-wide program.

Portrait of Mexico—University of Arizona, Tucson, Ariz., 33 min., sd., color. Describes present day Mexico in terms of its history, geography, religion, culture, and people. Shows some famous historical sites and architecture.

Schools of Mexico—Coronet Films, Coronet Bldg., Chicago, Ill., 10 min., sd., b&w. A comprehensive view of educational institutions, from the ultra-modern Ministry of Education in Mexico City to remote one-room adobe schools far in the interior. It includes normal schools, vocational and agricultural institutions, and kindergarten.

The Unfinished Revolution—Indiana University, Bloomington, Ind., 53 min., sd., b&w. Describes Mexico, the country of the Unfinished Revolution. Depicts the 1910 revolution against economic and political oppression. Shows the great advances which have been made in crucial areas of national life, such as agriculture, industry, and education.

Tomorrow's Mexico—MOT, 17 min., sd., b&w. Covers 36 years in Mexico, from the revolution of 1910 to its modern industrial expansion. Shows the growing determination of the Mexicans to overcome ignorance and raise their stand-ards of living.

FURTHER READINGS

CANADA

"A Salute to Canada," *The Instructor,* Vol. 64 (April, 1965).

Dominion Bureau of Statistics, *Canada, 1965* (Ottawa, Department of Trade and Commerce).

Information Services Division, Dominion Bureau of Statistics, *The Organiza-tion and Administration of Public Schools in Canada,* 3rd ed. (Ottawa, Canada, 1965).

Kandel, I. L., ed., *Educational Yearbook of the International Institute of Teachers College, Columbia University* (New York, Bureau of Publications, Teachers College, Columbia University, 1935, 1936, 1938, 1940, 1941, 1943).

Katz, Joseph, ed., *Canadian Education Today* (New York, McGraw-Hill, 1956).

MacDougall, J. Innes, "Teacher Education in Western Canada," *Phi Delta Kappan,* Vol. 36, No. 4 (January, 1955), pp. 150–154.

Moehlman, Arthur H., and Joseph S. Roucek, eds., *Comparative Education* (New York, Holt, Rinehart and Winston, 1952).

Phillips, Charles E., "District Reorganization in Canada," *Phi Delta Kappan,* Vol. 32, No. 7 (March, 1951), p. 308.

Putnam, Donald F., ed., *Canadian Regions: A Geography of Canada* (New York, Crowell, 1952).

Smith, H. E., "Teaching Profession Acts in Canada," *Phi Delta Kappan,* Vol. 31, No. 1 (September, 1951), pp. 54–55.

Twitty, Tom, and Mason Wade, *Canada, A Great Small Power,* Headline Series, No. 103 (New York, Foreign Policy Association, 1954).

MEXICO

Cline, Howard F., *Mexico, Revolution to Evolution, 1940–1960* (New York, Oxford University Press, 1962).

Ferguson, Erna, *Mexico Revisited* (New York, Knopf, 1955).

Fisher, Glen H., *Directed Culture Change in Nayarit, Mexico: Analysis of a Pilot Project in Basic Education* (New Orleans, Middle American Research Institute, Tulane University of Louisiana, 1953).

Johnston, Marjorie C., *Education in Mexico* (Washington, D.C., U.S. Office of Education, 1956).

Logan, Lillian M., "Kindergarten Education in Mexico" (Doctoral Dissertation, University of Wisconsin, 1953).

Sanchez, George I., *Mexico, A Revolution by Education* (New York, Viking, 1936).

Wilson, Irma, *Mexico, A Century of Educational Thought* (New York, Hispanic Institute in the United States, 1941).

V

PROMISES AND PROBLEMS

16

Some Innovations
and Promising Practices

PREVIEW

▶ At present there are a number of innovations and practices in American education that seem to hold considerable promise for the future.

▶ In order to bring about a more flexible school organization, experimentation with the elimination of the traditional grades is occurring on both elementary and secondary levels.

▶ Vocational and technical education is receiving greatly increased emphasis in the schools of both the United States and Canada.

▶ Recent developments in the teaching of modern foreign languages chiefly involve emphasizing the attainment of a speaking knowledge and extending instruction in the languages into the elementary schools.

▶ An age of technology demands that teachers make greater use of automation, which results in the widespread adoption of teaching machines and programmed books.

▶ Continued emphasis on world leadership calls for an educational program to fully develop the capabilities of gifted pupils.

▶ Teaching teams more fully utilize a teacher's knowledge of his field of preparation.

Progress is made in the industrial world through research, experimentation, and testing. To a somewhat lesser extent the same may be said of most professions. There are obvious differences, however. In industry and manufacturing we are concerned mostly with material things, but in many professions we are working chiefly with people. This emphasizes the significance of conducting our research with unusual care. No injury nor harm may come to our children. It is their welfare and their lives that are important.

This, of course, does not mean that experimentation should not be attempted and that no innovations may be carried out. Indeed, quite the opposite is true, for the alternative to experimentation may be stagnation. That may be as unfortunate for children as the other extreme.

In speaking to the 1965 White House Conference on Education, John W. Gardner, United States Secretary of Health, Education, and Welfare, stated, "The toughest question facing us now, in my judgment, is whether we have the courage and flexibility and imagination to innovate as the times require. . . . The old ways of doing things are not good enough. . . . We are a flexible and inventive people. We are at an intensely creative moment in American education. And we care a great deal about the outcome."

It is in the spirit of this declaration that we consider in this chapter six major practices that hold considerable promise, although other creative attempts to improve education are being carried out also. Those chosen for presentation here, however, may be described as being far enough advanced that they appear to have much to offer.

THE NONGRADED SCHOOL

The idea of nongraded schools in America is not particularly new. The earliest one-teacher elementary schools were ungraded, and it was not until around the middle of the last century that the European (largely German) idea of grades or "forms," as they are commonly called in Europe, came to be introduced into the United States. Roughly by 1870 most American schools were organized on grade-to-a-year basis, and curricula were developed with this organization in mind. Even one-teacher schools were similarly organized, and promotion or nonpromotion became the order of the day in this type of school as elsewhere.

After World War I we became somewhat more conscious of the type of organization that had come to be so common. The effects of failure and nonpromotion were studied, and methods were sought by which children might move through the school at their own best rate of speed—the slower ones more slowly, but without failing an entire grade; the faster ones at a speed and with a curriculum that might better challenge their abilities. Many attempts were made to improve the situation that then existed. Probably the most outstanding effort was that in Winnetka, Illinois. There, Washburne, as superintendent, evolved a system in the elementary schools and partially in the junior high school whereby children were able to move at their own rate of speed. Generally it was highly successful. Curricula were revamped; goals were set up with very little regard for old grade levels, and teacher re-education became a significant part of the Winnetka program. Winnetka was visited by a host of interested educators, and parts of the program were adopted or adapted for use by many schools where the need for change was seriously felt. Winnetka became a good leaven for American educators, but it was only here and there throughout the nation that extensive changes were made.

Probably the greatest stimulus for reorganization came as a result of the post-Sputnik feeling that today's schools were not responding nearly as well as they should to the increase of knowledge and the pressure of a new age of science. It was clear too that not as many students were moving as rapidly through the schools as they were able and that their potentials for creativity were not being utilized.

As is usually the case, the movement for reorganization was first felt in the elementary schools. Here the nongraded unit was most frequently found in the grades of 1 to 3 where subject matter lines had always been more indistinct and curricular reorganization was no great problem. Grades came to be called groups, and flexibility was more easily possible. It was not difficult to conceive of a primary group as consisting of former grades 1, 2, and 3, and it was not difficult either (although there were greater subject matter problems) to see as unit two the former grades of 4, 5, and 6.

Nongrading "implies a focus on the individual and his mental maturity rather than on grade level material that must be mastered at a particular year."[1] It is also planned to emphasize nongraded, continuous progress or growth and to eliminate non-promotion. The child progresses as fast as his abilities permit.

Of course, this sort of program necessitates the complete revision of the curriculum, the frequent use of reliable measures of growth and attainment, and the *stimulation* of growth by a rich variety of teaching aids. Most of all, it requires teachers who are sympathetic to the fundamental ideas and principles involved and who are willing to venture into pioneering fields.

The physical facilities should be designed with consideration of the non-graded principles and beliefs. Generally such a building will be constructed with two major divisions—one for the primary section or group, and one for the intermediate section. The building should emphasize flexibility as far as partitions, which should be movable, are concerned,

[1] From brochure prepared for parents and others at the Garden Springs Elementary School, Lexington, Kentucky; Dan Purdom, principal.

and should be readily adapted to team teaching which is further described later in this chapter. It has become customary in the nongraded schools to use carpet as a floor covering, primarily for noise reduction. Of course, a good library and a materials center are imperative.

The nongraded elementary school is attracting considerable attention throughout the country, but it is difficult at any time to know how many schools are actually operating on this plan either in whole or in part. Probably there are over 500 but less than 1,000 of them presently functioning.

Not all of the nongraded plans are found in the elementary schools. They are appearing occasionally in junior high schools and less frequently in senior high schools. The best opportunity for beginning the new plan is presented when a new junior or intermediate school is organized or when a new senior high school is formed. A new junior high school, for example, may come into existence with only the equivalent of grade 7 and then add the equivalent of grade 8 the second year and the grade 9 equivalent the following year. In that manner dislocations are reduced to a minimum, and both students and teachers more easily see the entire school as a unit. Such a new nongraded junior high school is presently in formation in Lexington, Kentucky—the Beaumont Junior High School. This will serve as an excellent follow-up for the nongraded elementary school previously mentioned there.

A few senior and four-year high schools are becoming nationally known because of the success they appear to be having with the adoption of the nongraded plan. The first high school to abolish grades and to call itself nongraded was that at Melbourne, Florida. Established in 1958, it has since been a focal point for those who are seeking to eliminate some of the weaknesses of the formal grading system that has long been practiced. The Brigham Young University Laboratory School is given credit for being the second nongraded high school in the country, followed by the Middleton High School at Newport, Rhode Island and the Hamilton Junior High School at Newton, Massachusetts. Others may be found in Borrego, California, and, as previously mentioned, in Lexington, Kentucky. Another recent and promising one is the Nova High School in Broward County, Florida. The same general principles apply to the nongraded secondary school as have been described as underlying the elementary school.

The subjects at Melbourne are designed in five phases as follows;

Phase 1   Subjects are designed for students who need special assistance in small classes.

Phase 2   Subjects are designed for students who need more emphasis on the basic skills.

Phase 3   Material is designed for students with average ability in subject matter.

Phase 4   Subject matter is designed for capable students desiring education in depth.

Phase 5   Challenging courses are available to students with exceptional ability who are willing to assume responsibility for their own learning and go far beyond the normal high school level.[2]

Changes in course content toward a greater variety of material have been effected; students are accelerated on a continuing rather than a yearly basis; study halls have been abolished, and class sizes have been altered to fit the needs of the particular learning field. Basic subjects are stressed first, and when students require special help, it is provided.

Probably one of the most outstanding aspects at Melbourne is the Quest Phase. This is "designed to foster and expand traits of curiosity and imagination, which will lead to the development of inquiring minds." [3] Obviously this phase is set up to accommodate students with unusual abilities and talents. The student will find it highly worthwhile to delve further into the details of the plan discussed here briefly and will find abundant material in the reference cited as well as in a number of periodicals.

The Nova High School classifies itself as a "Space Age School." [4] It opened in 1963, and its "philosophy is based on a concept described as scientific learning for a scientific age." Despite a seeming rigidity in its curriculum there is considerable flexibility in its operation. The main feature of the institution is its nongrading. The emphasis is continually upon individual differences and individual progress, and it is hoped that large numbers of capable students will be able to complete in high school a number of courses currently offered in college. Again there is much use made of team teaching, closed-circuit television, other visual aids, laboratories of many types, and large, medium, and small group instruction.

Certainly the nongraded school is not a panacea for all the ills of today's education, but it does seem to answer some of the problems that are prohibiting many schools from doing as much for their students, their citizens, and their country as they know they should be doing.

THE EXTENSION OF VOCATIONAL AND TECHNICAL SCHOOLS

One of the earliest concerns for the development of vocational efficiency as a fundamental aim of secondary education is evidenced in its inclusion in the Cardinal Principles of Secondary Education in 1918. It has continued to be so accepted for many years and has been given

---

[2] B. Frank Brown, *The Nongraded High School* (Englewood Cliffs, N.J., Prentice-Hall, 1964), p. 50.

[3] *Ibid.*, p. 57.

[4] Burt Kaufman and Paul Bethune, "Nova High Space Age School" *Phi Delta Kappan,* Vol. 46 (September, 1964), pp. 9–11.

emphasis in the objectives of the Educational Policies Commission and the Imperative Needs of Youth report. Actually every set of educational objectives has recognized that a major function of the secondary school is to prepare young people, as much as is reasonably possible, for the task of earning a living through the development of salable skills.

A great deal of controversy has existed over whether the type of vocational education needed could be best provided in the comprehensive high school or in the vocational and technical schools. Actually both can be used, although Dr. Conant has given his support to the comprehensive high school. It is in the large cities that the separate vocational or technical school has been more easily possible and successful.

In much of the task of vocational education, industry has cooperated to a considerable extent, frequently contributing large sums for the equipment of a shop of a certain kind, such as metalworking where there is great need for skilled graduates. In some cases the pattern of industry in a community has changed, and the emphasis upon certain types of training in the schools has shifted. A community which has long been a vital railroad center has greatly reduced its emphasis upon metalwork because of the coming of the diesel locomotive, and the consequent need for less frequent shop work. In another city where a major furniture manufacturing industry closed, woodworking was largely deemphasized and work in electrical courses and highly technical electronics greatly strengthened. Thus does a school change its program to meet changing community needs.

It is, indeed, significant that when a large national magazine, the *Atlantic*,[5] decided to do a series of feature articles upon "Our Six Best High Schools," two of those chosen were vocational schools. In each case reference was made to the background of general education that is given to those enrolled in order to strengthen the basic skills in English, mathematics, science, and social science. This is as it should be.

For some time it has been clear that the future worker must be "conditioned to adaptability," and a school that fails to attempt to develop this and to *condition itself* in the same manner is doomed to failure.

In the immediate future many workers will be faced with the necessity of changing jobs, due largely to automation, innovation, and increased productivity. Thus the vocational school will need to change and improve its equipment in order to reach farther into adult fields and to provide new year-around opportunities for training and retraining.

There are a number of individuals who insist that education for employment is not a legitimate aim or objective of the modern secondary

[5] John T. Schuman, "Allentown's Vocational Program," *Atlantic,* Vol. 214 (December, 1964), pp 90–94, and Benjamin C. Willis, "The Dunbar School of Chicago," *Atlantic,* Vol. 215 (January, 1965), pp. 83–86.

school.[6] The authors hold strongly that it is, indeed, a desirable and proper function.

The recent rapid growth of the technical institute can be justified by the magnitude of the task of educating for employment; opportunities must be extended beyond the secondary school level. In a few states, such as New York, these have been developed as part of a planned program of higher education. They may be partly publicly supported and partly maintained by student fees. They will tend to deal more thoroughly with such highly technical fields as electronics and computorization. In not a few cases students will have found their interest aroused in science and will continue to study engineering and specialized scientific fields in the usual four-year colleges.

In a great many of the community colleges being formed throughout the country, it is certain that the most prominent courses will be those in the technical fields. These institutions encouraged by state and federal financial assistance are being established at a rapid rate and usually with state-wide planning.[7] Much of the same sort of thing is happening in Canada as in the United States and was discussed in Chapter 15.

Much encouragement in the furtherance of vocational-technical education has resulted from the Vocational Education Act of 1963 as passed by the Congress of the United States and signed by the President.

In the words of the Vocational Education Act, its purpose is:

To authorize Federal grants to States to assist them to maintain, extend, and improve existing programs of vocational education, to develop new programs of vocational education, and to provide part-time employment for youths who need the earnings from such employment to continue their vocational training on a full-time basis, so that persons of all ages in all communities of the State—those in high school, those who have completed or discontinued their formal education and are preparing to enter the labor market, those who have already entered the labor market but need to upgrade their skills or learn new ones, and those with special educational handicaps—will have ready access to vocational training or retraining which is of high quality, which is realistic in the light of actual or anticipated opportunities for gainful employment, and which is suited to their needs, interests, and ability to benefit from such training.

The programs are designed "to develop the occupational abilities of all Americans." They are to benefit:

Students in high schools
Those who have dropped out of school and are unemployed

---

[6] Gart L. Magnum, "The Vocational-Technical Education Debate Flourishes," *Phi Delta Kappan,* Vol. 46 (September, 1964), pp. 30–31.

[7] John Corey, "North Carolina's New System of Vocational and Technical Education," *Phi Delta Kappan,* Vol. 46 (April, 1965), pp. 383–387.

Those who have completed high school but seek specialized training
Those who suffer from cultural and economic handicaps
Employed adults who want to upgrade their skills and technical knowledge
People of all ages who must learn new skills to earn their living

These opportunities will be established in public school systems, vocational departments of high schools, nonprofit agencies and institutions, specialized vocational high schools, vocational-technical schools, junior and community colleges, and four-year colleges and universities, both public and private.

For any occupation exclusive of the professions, skilled, semi-skilled, or technical training that is realistic in terms of present and future employment opportunities will be given. There will be close cooperation with business, labor, and public employment services at all levels.

It is important to note that the Act authorizes grants of Federal funds to help the states maintain, extend, and improve vocational education, to develop new programs, to promote research and experimentation, to provide teacher training and the development of up-to-date instructional materials and curriculums. The Act also authorizes pilot programs for experimentation with residential vocational schools and for work-study programs for youth who need money to stay in school full time. Former vocational acts are continued and amended.

As assurance that the training programs are geared as closely as possible to current needs and conditions, the Act contains special provisions for the following advisory and review bodies to be made up of persons who are familiar with the vocational education needs of management and labor or who have special knowledge and experience of vocational education:

- —State advisory councils, in States where State boards for vocational education do not have sufficiently broad representation.
- —A 16-member National Advisory Committee (to include the U.S. Commissioner of Education, representatives of the Departments of Commerce, Agriculture, and Labor, and 12 nongovernmental members, not more than 6 of whom shall be educators) to advise on policy and administrative procedures under the Act.
- —A 12-member National Advisory Council on Vocational Education, to review and evaluate all publicly supported programs of vocational education, starting in 1966 and reporting its findings by January 1, 1968. Similar reviews are to be made periodically thereafter.

Complete details of the Act as signed may be secured from Part A of Public Law 88–210.

Whatever else is happening in American education, it is certain that the whole field of vocational-technical education is in the midst of widespread expansion. It is an expansion designed to meet the needs of a growing population and a changing economy—one that will be affected by automation and the development of new occupational needs and patterns.

It is a gigantic task to which the schools and the government are committed.

DEVELOPMENTS IN THE TEACHING OF MODERN LANGUAGES

For many years it has been felt that reform in the teaching of foreign languages was long overdue. Many questions had been raised relative to the values of the ancient and modern languages, and since this discussion has gone on for so many years it will scarcely be considered at this point. It should be noted here, however, that the values claimed for the so-called classical languages did not generally include the fluent use of them orally. What value would there be, for example, in developing in the majority of students a good speaking knowledge of Latin? With whom would one be likely to converse in Latin? The same questions might also

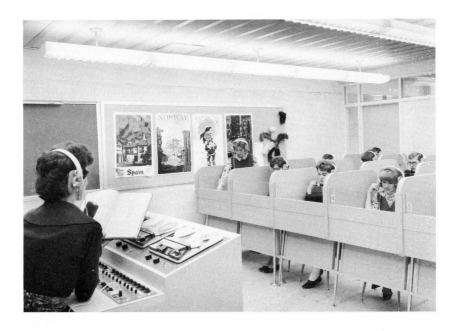

Courtesy: Louis C. Kingscott & Associates, Inc.,
Architects-Engineers; and The Starmont
Community School District, senior high
school of Strawberry Point, Arlington and
Lamont, Clayton County, Iowa

New audio equipment makes possible more effective teaching in the foreign languages. Adequate teacher preparation programs should involve instruction and practice in the use of such aids.

be asked relative to classic Greek. Even French and German were taught with very little effort to develop a speaking knowledge. The emphasis was almost wholly upon translation.

Of course, it has been the shrinking world that has been largely responsible for our changing outlook. Two world wars, the coming of the space age, and the improvement of communications of all sorts, and the large scale extension of American business overseas have made necessary: (1) The emphasis upon developing oral and written fluency in at least one foreign language, and (2) The broadening of the languages taught in the public schools to include languages other than the more usual French, German, and Spanish, sometimes including others, such as Russian and Chinese.

Our attention here will be directed rather exclusively to the first of the above situations. As long as 25 or more years ago there began to be some evidence of an increasing emphasis upon the development of a speaking knowledge of French and Spanish. It was not so true of German, because German was omitted from the high school curriculum at the time of World War I and never came back to any extent.

Actually, the development of a speaking knowledge of any modern language never gained total support. Two chief reasons for this were: (1) teachers in the secondary schools were not trained to be really accomplished linguists themselves, and (2) very few high school students took a language for a long enough time to acquire any oral fluency in it.

In reference to the improvement of the preparation, several things should be noted.

In the first place, there has been a general raising of the amount of language work required for certification—something which is true for practically all of the academic fields. The requirements differ from state to state, but the trend is general.

Secondly, many colleges and universities maintain houses where those who are majors in a particular language may live with others who have the same interest. This facilitates oral fluency. The idea is not new, but it appears to be spreading rapidly.

Thirdly, increased preparation may be secured through summer institutes at universities. These, in many cases, are being aided by the National Defense Education Act (NDEA). In a number of institutions, special assistance is available for those students who wish to specialize in seldom-taught foreign languages. For this purpose alone, awards have been granted through the NDEA to eighteen students for post-doctoral study at eight universities. The grants total $220,000 and were for work during the 1965–66 academic year and the summer of 1966. Studies are to be carried on in the following languages: Japanese, Chinese, Arabic, and Hindi-Irdu.

In the fourth place, a good many institutions of higher education are requiring undergraduate students in certain curricula to spend a year abroad in study—involving some travel—at a selected university. This, of course, should result in more teachers who are able to speak a language. Of course, such a program becomes prohibitive to many students because of the expense involved.

The major development in the language field in the public schools over the last 10 years or less has been the extension of the teaching of certain languages downward into the elementary grades. This is not new in many of the parochial schools of the Catholic church where Spanish has been taught in the elementary grades for years.

The emphasis, of course, in this new program in the public schools has been to develop a speaking knowledge. The program has been introduced in nearly every grade of the elementary school, mostly limited to studies of Spanish or French. The movement seems to be still growing, but it is meeting with varying degrees of success and enthusiasm.

In a good many schools the languages, particularly Spanish, have been introduced through television. This method has seemed to offer considerable promise, but a major difficulty has been that of augmenting the television presentation with capable persons.

The improvement in language teaching has also been greatly stimulated by the introduction of new audio equipment and the development of language laboratories. Possibly this may be listed as the greatest stimulation to improved language teaching in a number of years.

In concluding our brief discussion of the problems involved, we venture to suggest that the following appear to be the most important: (1) The shortage of qualified teachers especially for the elementary schools is a major problem. Reference has been made earlier to attempts to improve this situation. (2) No program in better language teaching beginning in the elementary schools can possibly be successful unless it is accompanied by a drastic revision of the language content and methods in the secondary schools. For those who start a language, their work should be a continuous, unbroken progression. This presents a very large problem to the secondary schools, and current information indicates that not very much progress has been made toward this end.

Certainly the ferment and experimentation in this field cannot help but contribute toward the alleviation of some of the evils and weaknesses now existing.

TEACHING MACHINES AND PROGRAMMED LEARNING

Technology, the explosion of knowledge, and greater understanding of how individuals can best learn, are all responsible to some degree for the appearance of a new dimension in teaching and learning. The new approach may be classified under the heading of programmed instruction. For, even though a machine is used, the material placed in the machine must be programmed. A theory upon which we base the value of programmed material and teaching machines has long been accepted by teachers. It concerns the nature of learning and pertains to three fundamental conditions, namely: (1) active participation by pupils, (2) logical sequence of the material to be learned, and (3) immediate evaluation of the response to a question. A number of educational psychologists believe programmed materials and teaching machines fulfill the three conditions as well as, or even better than, a large number of teachers.

Teaching Machines

Teaching machines range from very simple devices—with only a knob to turn the material to be taught through the machine—to the most elaborate electrically controlled and operated mechanisms. These machines are ordinarily used by one individual at a time.

The machine contains a series of statements to give the learner sufficient facts upon which to base his reasoning in order to arrive at conclusions or to give correct answers to questions. After reading the facts and observing a series of applications of those facts, the pupil is confronted by a question. He reacts to this question and gives an answer. The next step indicates if he has made a correct or incorrect response. If it is correct, he moves on to the next question or concept. Each correct response gives the learner the necessary motivation to continue. Each succeeding response is more difficult. If an incorrect response is given, the learner is immediately returned to review material which will be followed by subsequent questions. On the way through a programmed lesson there will be opportunity to review so the learner reinforces what he has previously learned.

The simpler machines make use of a number of lessons prepared on long strips or sheets of paper which are fed through the machine. The machine has two openings—one through which the learner reads the material, the other, where he writes a response. A more elaborate machine, electrically operated, provides buttons or levers to be used for responses. If responses are correct a light may flash, and the machine automatically moves to the next question or sequence of activities. Some machines total the correct responses so the learner will know how well he performs on the lesson or assignment as a whole.

A few machines are so elaborate that they provide for a number of individuals to use them at one time. On some, the lessons are on different subjects and at different levels of achievement. A few highly complicated machines are being "fed" programs which may be used by means of telephone, radio, and television by merely "tuning in" the machine which could be located in a central location and serve an entire college, university, state, or nation. The possibilities for educational programs through these devices are endless. It will be interesting to see future developments as they occur in this rather new media of education.

Programmed Books

A programmed book is used in a simpler approach to programmed learning, where a book is featured with a program similar to that used by a teaching machine. The reader reads and reacts to questions as he would if using a machine. As he makes correct responses he moves on to more difficult questions. If he is in error, he rereads the material and checks his reply against the correct answer. Throughout the book self-evaluations and review tests are given. The pupil can keep a record of his achievement on each test and refer to them for review; at the end of the book is a final test. Here again, the student has a means of evaluating his work.

Scrambled Books

A scrambled book is a form of program, but it does not require the learner to read all its pages. The reader begins on the first page, and after a few pages of facts and other information about a specific topic he answers a question. If he answers correctly, he may move to a page in the book ahead of where he stopped reading. Thus, if he continues to read and respond correctly, he is permitted to move through the entire book by reading only the very important pages. When the learner gives an incorrect response he may have to go back a number of pages; he studies the material and tries a different response. If correct, he is permitted to move only to the next page. If he does well on the next series of questions, makes correct responses, he is told to skip some pages to a new topic or series of statements of facts.

Summary

Apparently, this approach does fulfill the nature of learning as described by psychologists. The learner is kept working and active; he must apply what he learns all along the way, and he is informed of his progress at each step of the lesson. There are other advantages and limitations which should be considered. A few are listed here and should be evaluated before accepting or rejecting the idea entirely.

A few advantages are: (1) pupils can move at their own speed; (2) such devices could be used to enrich the curriculum, and (3) they provide a written record of achievement which indicates trouble spots in the learner's achievement as soon as they occur. In a conference the teacher can correct this weakness immediately. (4) Programs and machines are flexible; they can implement drill or call for thought processes leading to logical conclusions, (5) They are impersonal; no "teachers pet" situation occurs.

Similarly one can find limitations to their use, for example: (1) they provide little opportunity to develop a facility for oral communication; (2) since they are impersonal, the child who needs to develop his personality receives little opportunity; (3) they are noisy if everyone is using them at once in a classroom, and (4) they can become very expensive if new programs are required. Also, the maintenance of the machine may be considerably expensive; (5) they control learning too rigidly—pupils should be given opportunities to reach solutions to problems in various ways, and (6) education should include character and personality development; these are not easily cared for by a machine.

We cannot predict what proportions the application of these teaching machines or programs will reach. It is suffice to say that modern education will certainly call for their use in some learning-teaching situations.

EDUCATION OF THE GIFTED

A significant number of pupils in elementary and secondary schools are known to be very able or gifted. Often these pupils move along through the school with little opportunity really to stretch their intellectual abilities. Since the number of these students in each school is small, they ordinarily remain in a regular class which can best be described as average in intelligence. Hence, it is a rare occurrence for him to get an assignment which challenges his power to think or reason. Since our society is greatly in need of persons with high intellect, it is imperative that schools provide the kinds of programs which encourage these gifted pupils.

One of the first requirements is to identify pupils having this intellectual superiority. This is done by the aid of standardized tests and by observing pupils in various situations. Included in the tests would be those for mental ability (IQ), achievement, fine arts ability, interest inventories, and personality inventories. Observations by the teacher are concerned with matching or comparing the characteristics of the person observed with those which have been found in children who were known to be gifted. Often a school will provide teachers with guides to use in observing children. Also, parents' knowledge of the behavior characteristics of their child is useful. Teachers can best procure this information through conferences.

Gifted children may manifest this ability in many areas. For example, Chicago schools identify childrens' giftedness in the "areas of intellectual, scientific, mathematical, English and foreign language, social science, leadership, artistic, musical, dramatic, dancing, mechanical, and physical abilities." [8] If schools use screening devices to identify talent in all of the above listed areas it cannot be said that pupils with talent are being by-passed. It would appear that if a pupil has a high level of intelligence it would surely be demonstrated in one or more of these areas.

After schools identify these gifted individuals, they must be placed in a learning environment which provides: challenging assignments, a variety of projects and problem solving activities, intelligent teachers who are skilled in keeping this type of pupil highly motivated, and an excellent library. It is important to maintain this high-quality program in all the areas of study, for if it lacks excellence, the bright pupil frequently loses interest, develops poor attitudes, and eventually leaves school. If they do remain to graduate, they often take on employment which anyone with much less intellectual ability could do, and as a result creative ability is lost which may have carried the individual to greater achievements and personal satisfactions.

To provide these pupils with the kind of program referred to above, there has been experimentation with a number of organizational patterns and types of plans.

Planned Programs for Gifted Pupils

Chief among these plans for programs are: total and modified ability grouping, talent grouping, acceleration, nongraded or continuous development plans, enrichment programs, and advance placement plans.

Grouping

There are several plans for grouping pupils so that they will progress according to their ability at all times. Some schools have placed gifted pupils in one group, and this group remains together all day. In large school systems it is possible to have a sufficiently large number to group by this method. Large cities have designated schools for these better pupils. The Bronx High School of Science, New York, Central High School, Philadelphia, and the Colfax School, Pittsburgh are good examples of such schools. This type of grouping is often referred to as total grouping.

A second form is called modified or cross grouping. This plan calls for placing the gifted pupils together for their academic subjects and with ordinary ability pupils for other classes. This has merit because the stu-

[8] Board of Education of Chicago Schools, *Program of Education for the Gifted,* Study Report No. 12, Chicago Public Schools (Chicago, Illinois, 1964), p. 5.

dents should have some time for social relationships with others than those of their high intelligence group.

Still another type of grouping places the talented in mathematics together, the talented in science together, and so on throughout the required and elective subject areas. Although a large number of schools practice this plan of grouping, some authorities on the education of the gifted suggest that it is weak in that it merely emphasizes the one talent and places that in improper balance with other abilities which should be developed.

Acceleration

Because the typical public school in the United States has been small, the number of gifted pupils in its student body was also small. These few pupils stood out and were easily identified as being superior to their peers. The work to be done in their classes seemed too easy, and yet they could not be taught entirely by themselves in every case. Hence the idea of moving them into the next higher grade seemed to be the answer. There they were challenged by work that was more advanced and yet within their ability to accomplish. A few schools permitted these pupils to move from one grade to the next highest for the second half or second semester of the year. Thus they would complete two school grades in one year. When this would occur they were able to move through the school in less than the usual number of years required; therefore, they were referred to as accelerated pupils.

Some types of acceleration permit students to skip a grade entirely. A large number of schools are experimenting with advanced placement. This indicates that gifted pupils are permitted to take some college courses while still in high school and enter college with some of the first year (freshman) courses completed. This is occurring in other levels too; for example, some junior high school pupils take a few senior high school courses prior to leaving junior high school. This permits them to take more courses in high school than are ordinarily required. A plan such as this offers pupils an opportunity to have a broader and deeper background of knowledge when they enter college. They are frequently able to pass some college courses by taking only an examination.

Nongraded School

The nongraded school offers the gifted pupil an opportunity to advance at his own rate and possibly to spend only two years completing what a pupil of normal ability is capable of doing in three years. This would permit him to gain one year, or a half year at least, every two years. Thus we could speak of him as an accelerated pupil.

Enrichment

The term enrichment is best defined as: the providing of pupils with challenging learning experiences. These should include a wide range of activities which will encourage the pupil to work to his maximum ability. The activities should be such that they cause the individual to seek more information and make more unique applications of that which is learned.

Enrichment is often said to be a condition whereby we expose the learner to a large number of reference materials and permit him to explore these materials to gain greater depth and breadth of knowledge on a given subject. This is the enrichment program in many schools, but it should be a kind of thing that teachers attempt in all learning situations.

Summary

In plans described there are advantages and limitations. A plan is no better than the teacher assigned to put it into operation. Some teachers are skilled at applying one plan, and therefore, it becomes the best for their pupils. Others can be more effective in the execution of other plans. Schools will undoubtedly attempt to offer in-service workshops for teachers to learn how to function best in the plan that a certain school uses. The important aspect of any program for educating gifted children is to make every attempt to motivate those children to do their best and to provide sufficient materials and avenues for making discoveries of their own. While we know how important it is to develop the intellect we must not overlook our responsibility in offering the student the kind of educational program that will cause him to be physically and emotionally strong as well.

TEAM TEACHING

Team teaching has been referred to in previous chapters as an effective approach to improved staff assignment and as a type of educational procedure which calls for slightly different room facilities. Here we shall describe, in greater detail, what it is, how schools organize for its implementation, and what are a few of its advantages and disadvantages.

What Is a Teaching Team?

A teaching team is a group of teachers, usually between four to six in number, which are assigned to a group of 120 to 150 pupils. In an elementary school these may be on one grade level or may include some students from the preceding or following grade. Those from the

Courtesy: Fountain Valley School District.
Architects: Carmichael-Kemp, A.I.A.

Today's teachers may be challenged to work with some of the newer plans of school organization. Here is shown the interior of a class set-up as seen through the core-cluster in the Fountain Valley School District, California. The layout enables the teacher to supervise and work with the various groups easily.

grade ahead would be included for two reasons—for enrichment of the pupils from a preceding class, and for remediation for the pupils in an advanced grade.

A teaching team would consist of teachers with specialized areas of interest. For instance, one may be a specialist in the language arts; another, in social sciences; another, in the natural sciences, and a fourth, in the fine arts. In addition to these, the health and physical education teacher and the guidance counselor—or a school psychologist—may be assigned to the team for consultative functions.

On the secondary level—junior and senior high school—the team may be composed of one specialist in each of the required subjects. Most often these would be majors in English, science, mathematics, and social

Courtesy: Dr. J. Maurice Strattan, Superintendent,
Paoli Area High School System. Architects:
Chappelle and Crothers. Photograph by
Thompson Studio of Photography, Paoli, Pa.

Team teaching meeting. These Social Science teachers meet daily to plan lessons for succeeding days as well as to discuss and evaluate past lessons.

sciences. These still may operate on a structure which is departmentalized.

A second form of organization is on a subject area basis and extends vertically. For example, a team of science teachers may handle all the science instruction in the senior high school grades, or a team of English teachers may be assigned to teach all the English in the grades of 10, 11, and 12 in the college preparatory curriculum.

This team usually has a master teacher, one who is experienced and strong, to serve as coordinator or leader for the group. These team members teach a full schedule of classes and have a minimum of one period and as many as five periods per week for team meetings. In these meetings the plans for teaching are outlined and discussed. These may be concerned with very specific topics and teaching techniques to be utilized, or they may be more general, thus permitting greater initiative and creativity in class procedures. Also, the team will allot a certain number of group meetings to a discussion of the pupils for whom they are responsible. At meetings of this sort the guidance counselor and school psycholo-

Consultants: The Blankfort Group
Architects: Carmichael-Kemp, A.I.A.

A typical situation in the unique "core cluster" schools of the Fountain Valley School District, Orange County, California. Developed to expedite the individualized teaching philosophy of the district, the arrangement permits small groups to work together while being supervised by the teacher working with other groups. Seen here in a central core room, heart of a six-classroom unit, students working on a pre-taped reading lesson are viewed by the teacher in the background working with a 5–6 grade group on mathematics. Windows are readily closed with sliding chalk boards. Special white paint on hanging cabinets makes them ideal for film projection.

gist are regularly invited. This provides an excellent opportunity for teachers to learn more about the pupils, and consequently they are able to plan lessons and associated activities to meet the needs of these particular pupils. Since they have a limited number of students to teach, it is possible to get to know them well.

Some schools operate on the basis of the "small school within a school" theory. For instance, a junior high school may have a group of 7th grade teams, 8th grade teams, and 9th grade teams. Certainly, this type of organization is best handled with a building which can be separated into these small schools, each grade being assigned to a separate wing for all required subjects and homeroom assignments. This is referred to in Chapter 12.

At present there are nearly two hundred districts in the United States which have pretty well established one form or another of team teaching; many more are experimenting with it. Many new school buildings being built today are planned to accommodate team teaching. These buildings provide for flexibility in spaces assigned to instruction. (See Chapter 12.)

Representative schools which have been involved in team teaching for a period of time are often referred to in the periodical literature. Notable examples are Evanston, Illinois; Lexington, Massachusetts; Norwalk, Connecticut; Pittsburgh, Pennsylvania; Claremont, California. Before embarking on a team-teaching type of organization it would be helpful to review the evaluation of the experiments carried out in the schools listed above.

Advantages of Team Teaching

1. It provides for more effective staff utilization.
2. Pupils receive more hours of instruction per week.
3. It facilitates greater communication among teachers and hence an opportunity to help one another.
4. There is a greater use of audio-visual and other modern aids to instruction.
5. Evaluation of student achievement is more accurate, since it is based on the combined judgments of a team.
6. The teacher is kept alert because he wants to be a credit to the team.
7. The beginning teacher has supervision and help.
8. It contributes to continuous curriculum development.
9. Teachers get to know their pupils well since the number is not excessive. This promotes more effective guidance.

Disadvantages of Team Teaching

1. Opportunities for pupil leadership roles are diminished because of large group instruction being used so often.

2. Pupils cannot ask questions in a large group so they are often postponed and go unanswered.
3. It entails more scheduling problems.
4. Instruction may tend to become more formal through the use of lecture method.
5. Frequent team meetings can cause serious problems of human relations.
6. It is often difficult to find teachers of proper qualifications to serve as team leaders.
7. It has been said to cost more due to the need for a larger staff, more secretarial help, and a different type of building.

Whether or not the advantages outweigh the disadvantages cannot be fully answered at this time. One could assume that some creative teaching ideas should result, and it would be learned how much more a child may be helped by the constant availability of a master teacher who has specialized in a certain subject. If all achievement tests indicate that students have learned more subject matter and facts, but still lack ability to think and reason, or if the pupil cannot live with proper values in a society such as ours, then we have accomplished little in terms of real education. A well-prepared teacher will observe further developments and use the best of what is found effective through this type of organization.

QUESTIONS AND PROJECTS

THE NONGRADED SCHOOL

1. If possible, appoint a small committee to visit a nongraded elementary school and report in detail to the class.
2. Make a careful, critical, and detailed report on a nongraded school as described in your bibliography, and submit it to your instructor for comment.
3. What practical problems do you envisage that must be solved if a district is contemplating the establishment of a nongraded elementary school; a nongraded high school?
4. What physical features are most important for a building that is to house a nongraded elementary school?
5. What pupil enrollment do you consider as the minimum necessary for the establishment and operation of a nongraded high school? What do you consider an optimum enrollment?

VOCATIONAL AND TECHNICAL EDUCATION

1. Interview the Director of the State Employment Office in your area. Invite him to speak to the class on specific local employment problems and needs.
2. Study industrial and occupational changes that have taken place in your own community or in some other specific area of your choice. Ascertain how these changes have and should affect vocational and technical training problems in the schools.
3. Interview a prominent local employer to ascertain his views on the strong and weak points of the vocational program in the schools. What suggestions does he have for changes?
4. Conduct a panel discussion or possibly a debate on the question of the inclusion of vocational education as a legitimate objective of public education.
5. Discuss the topic: There will be a position for every individual with salable skills.
6. How do you react to this statement: "The inclusion of a broad program of vocational and technical education will inevitably dilute the entire program of cultural education provided by the comprehensive high school."
7. Debate the question: Resolved that the needs of all youth will be better served by having the vocational and technical education in schools separate from the academic high schools.

DEVELOPMENTS IN THE TEACHING OF MODERN LANGUAGES

1. Visit a school where a modern language is being taught in the elementary grades, and report your observations and reactions to the class.
2. Find out what changes are being made in the secondary schools in order to provide continuity in the language when it is begun in the elementary grades.
3. What does research say in regard to the effectiveness of the television teaching of foreign languages?

4. How can motivation be provided for further study when language teaching has begun in the elementary grades?
5. Explain the nature of regional influences upon the language program in the schools.
6. Suggest ways in which *real* opportunities for the oral use of foreign languages may be provided.
7. What problems do recent trends in the teaching of foreign languages present for teacher education?

QUESTIONS AND PROJECTS

EDUCATION OF THE GIFTED

1. Schools are often much more concerned with the average and below average pupils rather than providing for the gifted child. Why do you think this occurs? Can you think of ways a school might overcome this situation?
2. The text indicates a number of plans for providing an effective program for education of gifted pupils. Choose two of these plans, and prepare a bibliography of recent articles written about them.

TEACHING MACHINES AND PROGRAMMED LEARNING

1. List the advantages and disadvantages of use of teaching machines in a classroom setting.
2. Prepare a simple program to show how one step leads to the next, ultimately reaching an understanding of a concept which the program develops.
3. What is the difference between teaching values of a teaching machine and a programmed book?

TEAM TEACHING

1. What are the advantages for the student, the teacher, and the students' parents in a team teaching organization?
2. What are some of the major problems that are associated with team teaching?
3. How can team teaching work toward self-improvement of the teacher? Do you believe this would occur more readily when one is involved in a team approach or when one is an individual departmental teacher? Why?

AUDIO-VISUAL AIDS

MOTION PICTURES (16 MM)

TEACHING MACHINES AND PROGRAMMED LEARNING

Learning and Behavior—What Makes Us Human—Michale Sklor for CBS, Carousel, 26 min., sd., b&w. Pictures the work of Dr. B. F. Skinner and his associates at Harvard University Psychology Laboratories in studying animal behavior, and indicates the application of learned principles to the design of teaching machines for use in increasing human learning efficiency.

Teaching Machines and Programmed Learning—Norwood Films, NEA, 28 min., sd., b&w. A film dealing with the theory of programmed learning, highlighting three main features as characteristic of teaching machines. A variety of machines and materials are shown.

EDUCATION OF THE GIFTED

The Exceptional Child: The Gifted Child—NET, Indiana University, A-V Center, 29 min., sd., b&w. Discusses the special problems of the gifted child; explains how these children differ in intellectual, emotional, and physical development, and stresses the importance of wholesome home and school activities in meeting the needs and interests of the gifted. Uses filmed sequences to show negative influences in the home and school, and follows a day in the life of a well-adjusted child. Features Dr. Louis A. Fliegler of Syracuse University.

TEAM TEACHING

And No Bells Ring—NEA, Sterling Films, 56 min., sd., b&w. Presents an overview of the "Trump Report" on reorganizing the educational program in the secondary school. Shows large and small group instruction as well as individualized study. Indicates good practices in caring for individual differences.

FURTHER READINGS

THE NONGRADED SCHOOL

Carbone, R. F., "A Comparison of Graded and Nongraded Elementary Schools," *Elementary School Journal,* Vol. LXII (November, 1961), pp. 82–88.

Goodlad, John I. and Anderson, Robert H., *The Nongraded Elementary School* (New York, Harcourt, Brace, and World, 1963).

Goodlad, John I., "Ungrading the Elementary School," NEA Journal, Vol. 44 (March, 1955), pp. 170–171.

Goodlad, John I., "What About Nongrading Our Schools?" from *Change and Innovation in Elementary School Organization, Selected Readings* (New York, Holt, Rinehart and Winston, 1965), pp. 378–381.

Goodlad, J. L., "Individual Differences and Vertical Organization of the School," *Sixty-first Yearbook,* National Society for the Study of Education (Chicago, University of Chicago Press, 1962).

Hillson, Maurie, *Change and Innovation in Elementary School Organization,* Part VI-Nongrading (New York, Holt, Rinehart and Winston, 1965), pp. 293–297.

THE EXTENSION OF VOCATIONAL AND TECHNICAL SCHOOLS

Barlow, Mervin, ed., *Vocational Education,* Sixty-fourth yearbook of the National Society for the Study of Education (Chicago, University of Chicago Press, 1965).

Conant, James B., *Slums and Suburbs* (New York, McGraw-Hill, 1961).

Goard, Dean H., "Current Developments in Canadian Technical and Vocational Education," *Phi Delta Kappan,* Vol. 46 (April, 1965), pp. 395–400. See this issue for many other articles on vocational-technical education.

Graney, Maurice, *The Technical Institute* (New York, Center for Applied Research, 1964).

Harbison, Frederick and Myers, Charles A., *Education, Manpower, and Economic Growth* (New York, McGraw-Hill, 1964).

Johnson, B. Lamar, "Guide Lines and Trends in Post-Secondary Vocational-Technical Education," *Phi Delta Kappan,* Vol. 46 (April, 1965), pp. 376–380.

President's Committee on Youth Employment, *The Challenge of Jobless Youth* Washington, D.C., 1963).

Venn, Grant, *Man, Education and Work* (Washington, D.C., American Council on Education, 1964).

DEVELOPMENTS IN THE TEACHING OF MODERN LANGUAGES

Research in Language Teaching—An Annotated International Bibliography for 1945–61 (Seattle, University of Washington Press, 1962). This contains an excellent list of books and articles published that cover the teaching of languages during the years in question. Pages 182–191 are particularly concerned with the extension of languages into the elementary schools.

RECENT AND PERTINENT

Newmark, George, "Foreign Language in the Elementary Schools and the Implications for Teacher Education," *Journal of Teacher Education,* Vol. 14 (December, 1963), pp. 449–455.

Pillet, R. A., "Selected References on Elementary Instruction for Foreign Language," *Elementary School Journal,* Vol. 65 (November, 1964), pp. 101–103.

Starr, W., "Teaching of Foreign Languages: Current Issues and the Future." *School Life,* Vol. 46 (November, 1963), pp. 7–10.

Stern, H., "Current Research and the Introduction of a Foreign Language into the Primary School," Bibliography. *Educational Research,* Vol. 6 (February, 1964), pp. 86–103.

Walner, D., "Goals for Elementary Foreign Language Instruction," Vol. 45 (November, 1963), pp. 77–80.

TEACHING MACHINES AND PROGRAMMED LEARNING

Cram, David, *Explaining Teaching Machines and Programming* (San Francisco, Fearon Publishers, 1961).

DeGrazia, Alfred, and David A. Sohn, eds., *Revolution in Teaching: New Theory, Technology, and Curricula* (New York, Bantam, 1964).

Fry, Edward, *Teaching Machines and Programmed Instruction* (New York, McGraw-Hill, 1963).

Fry, Edward B., Glenn L. Bryan, and Joseph W. Rigney, *Teaching Machines:*

An Annotated Bibliography (Washington, D.C., Dept. of Audio-Visual Instruction, NEA, 1960).

Galanter, Eugene, ed., *Automatic Teaching: The State of the Art* (New York, Wiley and Sons, 1959).

Glaser, R., ed., *Teaching Machines and Programed Learning, II: Data and Directions* (Washington, D.C., NEA, 1965).

Lumsdaine, A. A. and R. Glaser, eds., *Teaching Machines and Programed Learning: A Source Book* (Washington, D.C., NEA, 1960).

Markle, S. M., L. D. Eigen, and P. K. Komiski, *A Programed Primer on Programing,* Vols. I and II (New York, The Center for Programed Instruction, 1961).

Smith, Wendell I., and J. William Moore, eds., *Programmed Learning* (New York, Van Nostrand, 1962).

Trow, William C., *Teacher and Technology* (New York, Appleton-Century-Crofts, 1963).

EDUCATION OF THE GIFTED

Abraham, Willard, *Common Sense About Gifted Children* (New York, Harper & Row, 1958).

Bereday, George, and Joseph Lauwerys, eds., *The Gifted Child: Yearbook of Education* (New York, Harcourt, Brace & World, 1962).

Bryan, J. Ned, ed., *Talent, A State's Resource, A State's Responsibility* (Washington, D.C., Department of Health, Education, and Welfare, Office of Education, 1963).

Crow, L. D., and A. Crow, *Educating the Academically Able* (New York, McKay, Inc., 1963).

Education for the Gifted, Fifty-seventh Yearbook of the National Society for the Study of Education (Chicago, University of Chicago Press, 1958).

Fine, Benjamin, *Stretching Their Minds* (New York, Dutton, 1964).

Fliegler, Louis A., *Curriculum Planning for the Gifted* (Englewood Cliffs, N.J., Prentice-Hall, 1961).

Goodlad, John I., *Planning and Organizing for Teaching,* The Project on the Instructional Program of the Public Schools (Washington, D.C., NEA, 1963).

Goodlad, John I., and Robert H. Anderson, *The Nongraded Elementary School* (New York, Harcourt, Brace & World, 1959).

Torrance, E. Paul, *Guiding Creative Talent* (Englewood Cliffs, N.J., Prentice-Hall, 1962).

Zirbes, Laura, *Spurs to Creative Teaching* (New York, Putnam, 1959).

TEAM TEACHING

Hillson, Maurie, ed., *Change and Innovation in Elementary School Organization* (New York, Holt, Rinehart and Winston, 1965).

Shaplin, Judson T., and Henry F. Olds, Jr., eds., *Team Teaching* (New York, Harper & Row, 1963).

Trump, J. Lloyd, *Images of the Future* (Urbana, Illinois, Commission on the Experimental Study of the Utilization of the Staff in the Secondary School, NASSP, 1959).

17

Further Problems of Education for Today and Tomorrow

PREVIEW

▶ Education is faced with challenging issues and problems.

▶ Five major areas merit careful attention:
  1. Problems of state-church relationships
  2. Professional negotiations and collective bargaining
  3. School desegregation
  4. Education of the culturally disadvantaged
  5. Dropouts

▶ Other problems, somewhat minor in nature and probably less crucial, also call for careful consideration.

With our rapidly increasing population and the growing complexity of our civilization, it is inevitable that new problems should constantly arise in an enterprise as important as education. Even problems inherited from the past take on new intricacy and urgency. They await help from tomorrow's teachers and citizens.

A number of these problems have been discussed in considerable detail earlier in this volume, and they will not be studied further at this point. Rather, it is our purpose to present here, for careful consideration, four of the issues that seem to be of the greatest urgency. A number of others will then be listed, and the attention of the student invited.

THE SEPARATION OF CHURCH AND STATE

Without question, the basic influence that has led to the deep-rooted American belief that the church and state must be separate was the determination of the founders to make their homes in a land where they could worship as they pleased. This belief found expression in the First Amendment to the Constitution, and it has come down through the years in this brief but eloquent and far-reaching form: "Congress shall make no law respecting an establishment of religion, or prohibiting the free exercise thereof: . . ."

It has been the problem of the courts to interpret this brief statement and apply it to cases that have arisen as our democracy and its problems have become more complex. In a ruling on a case involving the right of a school board to pay the transportation of children to a parochial school the Supreme Court observed:

The "establishment of religion" clause of the First Amendment means at least this: Neither a state nor the federal government can set up a church. Neither can pass laws which aid one religion, aid all religions, or prefer one religion over another. Neither can force nor influence a person to go to or remain away from church against his will or force him to profess a belief or disbelief in any religion. No person can be punished for entertaining or professing religious beliefs or disbeliefs, for church attendance or nonattendance. No tax in any amount, large or small, can be levied to support any religious activities or institutions, whatever they may be called, or whatever form they may adopt to teach or practice religion. Neither a state nor the federal government can, openly or secretly, participate in the affairs of any religious organizations or groups and vice versa. . . .[1]

Much difference of opinion, however, exists as to whether or not a tax is being used "to support" a religious activity or whether it is merely being used for the general welfare when it is used for such a function as pupil transportation to a parochial school. Even the Court divided 5–4 in the case cited.

In certain other cases which have been appealed to the United States Supreme Court the decision has pointed out what may not be done. In the now famous McCollum case the Court ruled that the "released time program" as practiced in Champaign, Illinois, violated the principle of separation of church and state. Mr. Justice Black held that tax-supported buildings were being used for religious purposes and thus gave the religious groups invaluable assistance through the use of their compulsory attendance machinery.[2]

---

[1] Hugo L. Black, majority (5–4) opinion, Everson v. Board of Education, 330 U.S. 1 (1946).

[2] R. R. Hamilton, and P. R. Mort, *The Law and Public Education*, Second edition (Brooklyn, The Foundation Press, 1959), pp. 30–31.

In a New York case [3] which reached the Court in 1948 covering a "released time" set-up with the limitations of the McCollum case in mind, the Court sustained the practice as it existed involving substantially less participation than in the Champaign case. The critical issue appears to be how much *cooperation* there is between the schools and the churches.

While compulsory attendance has long been held to be a right of the states, whether children are attending public or nonpublic schools, it must operate within the framework of state laws and the provisions of the United States Constitution. In an historic decision the Supreme Court of the United States denied the State of Oregon the right to compel *all* children to attend the *public schools*.[4]

A New Frontier

In the last several years two decisions of the Supreme Court have radically changed several practices that have long been in use in the public schools. For many years a number of states have required the reading of a certain portion of the Holy Bible daily; others have permitted it, and still others have forbidden it. Similar situations have existed relative to the use of the Lord's Prayer at opening exercises and at other times.

It was in the appeal of a New York case where a specially prepared Regent's Prayer was in use that the first shock came. Here in Engel v. Vitale, known as the "Regents' Prayer" case, it appeared that the court was merely outlawing a *state-composed* prayer.

The decision, however, was followed by one more far-reaching. In the case of Abington (Pa.) School District v. Schempp (1962) the Court not only ruled out prayer of any background but also devotional Bible reading.[5]

It appears also from the decision that many practices long a part of the school program must now be considered unconstitutional. The more important conclusions are:

1. Religious exercises required by state law must be so considered even if the students are excused from them. "Establishment" occurs when the machinery of the school administration is manipulated for a religious purpose.
2. Religion can be studied objectively in public schools and the Bible used as a reference work, Justice Clark commented.
3. The school may schedule a period of silent meditation.
4. Baccalaureate services sponsored by the school are unconstitutional. Celebrations of Christmas and Easter are questionable, and schools may not participate in the religious aspects of them.

3 Zorach v. Clauson, 343 U.S. 306, 72 S. Ct. 679 (1952).

4 Pierce v. Society of the Sisters of the Holy Names of Jesus and Mary, 268 U.S. 510, 45 S. Ct. 571 69 L. Ed. 1070, 39 A.L.R. 468 (1925).

5 George R. LaNoue, "The Supreme Court's New Frontier Between Religion and the Public Schools," *Phi Delta Kappan,* Vol. 45 (December, 1963), pp. 123–127.

5. The "establishment" clause does not require the schools to be blind to religious ideals; it does require them to be neutral. It may be under this interpretation of the decision that schools may find it possible to offer a course in comparative religious, for example, although the problem of finding a qualified teacher may be a very difficult task.

LaNoue [6] suggests that at the beginning of the year a school district might find it desirable to make a statement similar to the following:

This public school, according to the decisions of the United States Supreme Court on the First and Fourteenth Amendments of the Federal Constitution, engages in no religious exercises. These decisions and our compliance with them are in no way motivated by a hostility towards religion but are instead based on the belief that true religion and good government are served by a separation of church and state. This principle in no way inhibits students' asking questions concerning religion or carrying on religious discussion. It does mean, however, that this school cannot offer courses in religious history or beliefs according to any particular tradition. This policy in no way implies that such study is unimportant, but it is rather a simple reflection of the constitutional limitations on the functions of a state agency and recognition of the pluralism of American society. As an educational institution, however, this school affirms that religious and ethical questions are at the center of a liberal education, and we urge students interested in intensive study of such questions to pursue them with their families and the institutions of their separate traditions.

A possible solution to some of the problems involved may be that of "shared time." This is an arrangement by which students enrolled in a nonpublic (probably religious) school may take some courses in the public schools, and the public school students may take some work in the parochial schools. This program has met with success in some areas, but it is questionable just how widespread the practice may become; this is a partial, not a complete, solution.

It would be highly unwise to end our discussion of these important problems without making reference to the action of the 89th Congress in passing the Elementary and Secondary Education Act of 1965. This legislation described by President Johnson as "The First Work of These Times . . ." is notable for many reasons, and its impact will undoubtedly be tremendous.

At the moment we are concerned with how it has met the questions involved in the separation of church and state issues. Two features seem to stand out:

1. In all cases the moneys are granted to some approved state agency and distributed by them according to state laws and according to *need* as specified in the Act. In most cases need seems to be the determining factor, and in some situations, as in Title II of the Act, special mention is made of provid-

[6] *Ibid.*, p. 127.

ing materials for nonpublic schools. The materials, however, are issued by the states *on loan*.

Throughout the Act emphasis is put upon need in both public and nonpublic schools. Improved educational facilities for all students is the guiding principle.

2. It would seem to one who examines the Act and contemplates its future operation that the "child-benefit" theory is basic.

Certainly it is the outstanding instance when we have tried to bypass the ancient church-state controversy in recent times.

COLLECTIVE BARGAINING AND PROFESSIONAL NEGOTIATIONS

One of the major problems affecting teachers and their welfare has long been kept somewhat under cover. It has been widely assumed that it is the right of the state, through legislation, to set minimum salaries and salary schedules, thus to a large extent forcing reluctant and often unsympathetic school boards to pay higher salaries, to carry out better provisions for sick leave, retirement, and the like.

On the other hand, many school districts have found it highly desirable to go beyond minimal legislation. Enlightened leadership on the part of boards of education and by the local administrators has made this possible. The competition for better teachers naturally has had much to do with the matter. More recently, pressure has been put upon superintendents and thus upon school boards for the development of salary schedules and benefits as a result of the work of committees representing the teachers. Cooperative programs have frequently emerged that were productive of general satisfaction. Gone to a considerable extent is the master-servant pattern that has been representative of the teacher-school board or teacher-superintendent relationship. This is meant in no way to depreciate the leadership role of the superintendent of schools. Leadership through developing co-operation need not mean abdication.

It must be admitted that the co-operative process described above has long been the exception rather than the rule. As a result today we see emerging throughout the country the pattern of teacher leadership. It has been suggested that this may be accounted for largely by the following factors:

1. The reduction of the number of school districts from 120,000 in 1941 to less than 40,000 today has destroyed the unequal bargaining power between teachers and board or superintendent.
2. The teacher shortage has placed the teacher in a better bargaining position.
3. More young men with families to support are entering the profession.
4. The influence of the more militant American Federation of Teachers has been serving as an irritant to professional groups.

The result of these and other factors has been the widespread demand for a more formal pattern of negotiation between teachers and their employers—boards of education. Lieberman [7] points out that in most states school boards are not specifically mandated or authorized to enter into collective agreements. He suggests that while seven states authorize such agreements between public employers and organizations of public employees only Wisconsin requires it. He insists that "there is a world of difference . . . between negotiating in good faith and discussions" and possibly following or not following such discussions with agreements.

Types of Negotiations

It should be pointed out at this time that there are two types of collective bargaining: (1) professional negotiations and (2) negotiations of the type advocated by the AFT, similar to the procedures authorized by the National Labor Relations Board (NLRB). Since the NLRB does not regulate state and municipal employment, it is up to each state to establish its own methods and standards. Few states have recognized a major responsibility in this area.

On the other hand, the National Education Association, goaded to some degree by AFT competition, is now backing the professional negotiation standard, and revised guide lines have been prepared for use by local school systems (see *Further Readings*). In mid-1965 it was reported that 364 written professional negotiation agreements were on file with the NEA and that many more were in preparation.

It must be obvious to the reader that there is currently vigorous competition over which organization—the NEA or the AFT—shall represent the teachers in a school district as their recognized bargaining agent. Usually the answer is found through an election by the teachers themselves, sometimes after intense competition as in Philadelphia in 1965 where the AFT was the victor.

An important issue is whether administrators should be permitted to vote since they are not accepted as AFT members, although considered so by the NEA. Lieberman [8] points out that "Only persons designated by the teachers themselves should be regarded as their representatives." In the Alberta Teachers Association which has become the general pattern for the organization of Canadian teachers, senior administrators may not hold membership.[9]

In any discussion of collective bargaining or professional negotiations one cannot escape the problems of the failure to find agreement and of the

[7] Myron Lieberman, "Who Speaks for Teachers?" *Saturday Review*, Vol. 48 (June 19, 1965), pp. 64–66.

[8] *Ibid.*, p. 74.

[9] Arthur Kratzmann, "The Alberta Teachers Association, a Vision Vindicated," *Phi Delta Kappan*, Vol. 45 (March, 1964), pp. 288–292.

ultimate necessity to enforce negotiations which have been agreed upon in good faith. The AFT sees the strike as the most effective weapon while, up to present, the NEA has held to the use of *sanctions*. One must balance the frequent ineffectiveness of sanctions against the possible unfavorable public reaction to the strike. The right to strike against bad conditions does not now seem as relevant to the maintenance of professional status as it once was.

It may be pointed out that in Alberta the attainment by a group of a master contract covering salaries, working conditions and other factors brought about the abolition of the individual form of contract and substituted acceptance by letter.[10]

Recent elections in the United States where bargaining agents have been chosen indicate that the NEA has won more elections when districts are considered, but the AFT has won the right to represent more teachers, primarily because of victories in New York and Philadelphia.

Are we to assume that: (1) The struggle "to the death" to become the sole bargaining agent will continue as each organization tries to destroy the other? (2) Eventually the two organizations will merge as was suggested unofficially and promptly rejected unofficially at the 1965 Convention of the NEA? (3) From the struggle a new type of organization will emerge that will represent all teachers and that will be neither NEA nor AFT as has been the case in Alberta?

The consideration of these possibilities and questions related to them will undoubtedly continue to grow, and agreements must be reached before long for the good of the nation to which we profess allegiance.

SCHOOL DESEGREGATION

More than a decade has passed since the Supreme Court ruled on desegregation of schools, and progress toward accomplishing integrated schools has been slow. There still remains too large a number of school systems that have not complied with the high Court's decision.

The problem of desegrating schools was most serious in the South where a dual system of education has existed since colonial days. The problem is present in other sections because the attitude toward the *neighborhood* school has been firmly imbedded and accepted as fundamentally sound. However, this very fact can and often does produce a segregated school because neighborhoods too are separate. To maintain neighborhood schools which are desegregated often demands that children are transported from one area to another. This condition has caused unrest and, in many cases, violence.

There have been all kinds of maneuvering in order to avoid integration of the schools. Some districts have drawn boundary lines to channel

10 *Ibid.*, p. 290.

attendance to specific schools, which, in fact, facilitates segregation. Some states abolished compulsory attendance laws, thereby permitting children to stay away from schools without their parents being persecuted by law. A number of states threatened to abolish all public schools; a few counties actually did this and opened private schools. Of course, no such action is legal, and it only delays what must eventually be accomplished—complete desegregation of schools.

In a democracy no large segment of its population can be denied full opportunity for an education. It *must* be education which will eventually produce the society wherein every individual will have an opportunity to reach the greatest height of his aspirations. When schools are separated on the basis of race, and one school is given strong and the other weak financial support, there is sure to be inequality. We, as educators, cannot sit back and permit this problem of educational deprivation to continue to grow. We must support total integration in the schools inasmuch as we have a moral obligation and a meaningful commitment through the code of ethics to which we subscribe. This code clearly states that a teacher will deal fairly and impartially with pupils regardless of their race, religion, and their economic and social characteristics. It is also accepted that a teacher will recognize the differences among children and meet their individual needs.

It appears now that a sufficient number of court cases have been decided in favor of desegregation so that school districts will move ahead on integration with all due "deliberate speed." The National Education Association has begun to face up to its obligation of giving greater support to accomplishing full integration of schools. One of the measures taken is the adoption of a strong and well-defined resolution calling for a merger of state and local associations which had previously been separated on the basis of race. Also, it has called for a study to indicate the need for a human relations commission as an aid to solution of problems stemming from human relations.

Further action should be noted in the establishing of two special NEA projects related to integration of schools. One, the Department of Classroom Teachers, seeks to look into problems facing the schools as a result of the civil rights movement. This study is to concern an area of Northeast United States. Another project will direct its efforts to the expanding of opportunities for continuing education of the Negro teachers in the Southern states. An interesting provision in this project relates to helping displaced teachers relocate. This project is being sponsored by the National Commission on Teacher Education and Professional Standards.

To stimulate progress in desegregation, Title IV of the Civil Rights Act of 1964 authorizes the United States Office of Education to make grants to school boards and to colleges and universities. These funds may be used to train school employees in the development of integration programs. School boards may use the funds to hire expert advisers if they so desire.

It should further be noted that under the new legislation the Commissioner of Education may withhold federal funds from districts that are failing to comply with the provisions of the Civil Rights Act.

A change is taking place, and with teachers gaining a greater understanding of the problem, their efforts will be noticeable in directing educational programs to future citizens. In turn, this will effect necessary changes to give each individual the opportunity for as much education as he needs to be a productive American citizen.

THE DISADVANTAGED CHILD

One of the great tenets of the American way of life is "equal access to equal opportunity." Most assuredly teachers subscribe to this, but realize that a considerable number of children do not have equal access. Because of a child's environment he is described as being "deprived" in one or a number of ways in that he is a member of a subculture different from what is described as a normal set of societal conditions. He may be deprived of social, economic, psychological, and educational experiences during his pre-school years which in turn will limit his readiness for learning when he enters school.

Ordinarily a child identified as being deprived has been considered so because of a lower socioeconomic status or because of being from a racial minority. Today deprivation may be found in the higher socioeconomic classes—the Puerto Ricans, Mexican-Americans and other ethnic groups which constitute subcultures in the United States. Recent studies indicate that deprivation may result from a variety of causes, namely: economic values, segregation, language barriers, religious differences, and lack of motivation.

Reissman [11] states that one in every three urban children in America is deprived. The number is steadily increasing, and according to the NEA Project on Instruction [12] "by 1970 there will be a deprived child for every two." Any number of symptoms may be identified with a deprived child. Most studies indicate that the major causes are: (1) he has been denied the social experiences which a school's curriculum assumes every child has had; (2) he may be lacking in language ability; this may be due to a foreign background, or it could be deprived from limited symbolic experiences; (3) his values and expectations may be in opposition to those set by the school; (4) he lacks the motivation necessary for achievement

[11] Frank Reissman, *The Culturally Deprived Child* (New York, Harper & Row, 1961), p. 1.

[12] *Schools for the Sixties*, A Report of the NEA Project on Instruction (New York, McGraw-Hill, 1963), p. 37.

in school, and (5) he has been denied the opportunities for development offered through books, magazines, etc., in the home.

The child with one or more of these deficiencies cannot make the necessary adjustment to his peers, and his achievement will not equal those whose backgrounds include social and cultural experiences. Such a child usually drops out of school as soon as the law permits or he becomes involved in some infraction of the law which will be cause for dismissal. In many instances, this individual will have difficulty in finding employment, and he becomes assocated with a "gang" of youth of similar background and will oftentimes become a juvenile delinquent.

It seems necessary, therefore, that schools and society in general explore ways of improving the conditions which contribute to this widespread deprivation. Some programs are being organized to combat it. For example, the Headstart program referred to in Chapter 13 has been quite successful, experimenting in a large number of areas. These programs will undoubtedly grow and become more effective because federal funds are being provided to help finance them. This provision of funds is being made possible through the Economic Opportunity Act of 1965. Also, a number of social and welfare agencies on the state and local level have cooperated with the school in providing child care centers. In these centers pre-school age children are provided with opportunities for experiences which will help develop a readiness for school which is equal to that of children from a better cultural background.

Schools and teachers are providing better facilities and curricula to offer the deprived child an access to experiences needed to make satisfactory progress in the early years of school when it is necessary to gain a command of the fundamental processes. The skilled teacher is challenged to develop a program of learning experiences geared to the needs of the children; as many as a third or more students may have deficiencies which have to be, at least, partially compensated for if their work is to be satisfactory.

In some programs, the city and school cooperate in providing a summer experience for these children. It consists of a half-day of school for pre-kindergarten children. These children are given psychological tests, and the parents are interviewed and made a part of the program inasmuch as it is possible. The teachers visit the homes and attempt to establish a kind of rapport between the home and school which will be instrumental in keeping the child's experiences in school continued in the home. The children are taught to play together, get along with one another, and share and appreciate each others' experiences. Many stories are read to the children; motion pictures and slides are shown, and there are a number of field trips. All of these experiences form the basis for communication. The children learn to be more observant, give greater attention to directions, and respond to problems related to their daily life.

From experiences such as these it has been possible to observe a marked change in the child's readiness for school in the fall. Standard test results have indicated that a child's IQ is improved after a period of four weeks of such planned activities. If this kind of program can be continued for the child when he enters school, we should see an improvement in the child's achievement, his attitude toward school, and most of all in his desire to remain in school. It is a known fact that many deprived children have a high intellectual and creative capacity, and we need to devise better means or instruments for accurate evaluation of their abilities. Intelligence and achievement tests that are commonly used are not accurate for these children.

DROPOUTS

Since the beginning of free public education for secondary school age youth, a certain number from each class leave school before graduation. In earlier years this did not seem to be a problem. Those who quit school, especially the boys, were able to find work and usually did not fare too badly. In many instances the dropout would help on his father's farm or shop or undertake an independent venture. Girls who left school before graduation usually married and managed a home.

A study reported by the U.S. Department of Health, Education, and Welfare [13] indicated that out of 1000 pupils in the 5th grade in 1952, only 904 started the 9th grade in 1956; from this number only 621 graduated from the 12th grade in 1960. There are, of course, a variety of reasons why boys and girls drop out of school. Those listed most frequently are: low academic aptitude, lack of reading ability, insufficient finances, job opportunities, lack of participation in school activities, and needs at home. Often an understanding teacher could help a pupil by giving him the proper guidance at a time when he is contemplating leaving school for one or more of these reasons. For example, a pupil could be referred to a reading specialist, encouraged to join a school activity, or be given remedial assistance until he learns how to improve his study habits.

School dropouts are not limited to the low socioeconomic class; a large number are from well-to-do families. Many are from broken homes; in some there is a divorce, a separation, or a deceased parent. When this occurs, the one parent with whom the children live usually works, and as a result there is little time for him to offer the proper guidance and understanding encouragement a child needs during his attendance in school.

What happens to school dropouts? Studies indicate that pupils who drop out before graduating from high school make less money, change jobs more often, and fill jobs of lower status than graduates. Most dropouts work as farm laborers or other day laborers and operatives; those who

[13] "Health, Education, and Welfare Trends," (Washington, D.C., 1963), p. 46.

graduated from high school were able to find employment more readily and worked at jobs with a higher status.

What Schools Can Do

The total number of school dropouts each year represents a shameful waste of our greatest human resources. The schools must do something to encourage a large percentage of these students to stay in school. A curriculum must be developed which provides promise as well as challenge. A functional guidance program that reaches every pupil on an individual basis is imperative. Many times a dropout has complained that nobody knew him at school. Schools can and should provide ways for pupils to receive financial assistance when they are deserving and indicate a need for this type of help. Work-study programs should be established when possible. Through these a number of pupils could earn sufficient funds to remain in school.

OTHER PROBLEMS

Although these problems that have been discussed at some length seem to the authors to represent those of the greatest urgency, there are others, surely, and some of them are quite important. In an introductory text all of those areas in which people differ cannot be presented in detail. Many have been treated elsewhere in the context and will not be mentioned again; others must be left for further study or are so nearly matters of agreement that they are purposely not given extensive consideration. Such, for example, is so-called progressive education. So many of the proposals of this movement, such as movable furniture, stimulation of interest, and the like have been so generally adopted as to be no longer controversial. Some proposals of the lunatic fringe or, better, the extreme left, such as too-free-discipline, have been rejected or are about to be.

We shall, therefore, but list a number of the other interesting and challenging areas in education which are waiting urgently for contributions from tomorrow's educational leaders—*you*. Some of these problems are:

1. What is the role of the private institutions in the national program of education?
2. How can the administration of schools be more truly democratized?
3. To what extent shall public education be broadened and extended upward and downward?
4. How can the holding power of the high schools and colleges be increased?
5. Shall secondary education be organized for only those who can profit by it?
6. What is the place of general education in the high school program?

7. To what extent is Education for Life Adjustment the answer to the problems of secondary education of today and tomorrow?
8. What is the place of intellectualism in higher education?
9. Should all who wish to attend college go?
10. How can the integration of races best be accomplished in light of the decision of the United States Supreme Court?
11. Shall sex education and preparation for marriage be taught in our schools?
12. How can the role of athletics in the public schools be improved?
13. What is the best utilization of television in the schools?
14. Who shall really make the curriculum?
15. How can the school plant be more completely utilized?
16. How can we better evaluate pupil progress?
17. How can the educational program be better adapted to individual needs?
18. How can the size of the unit of school administration be increased without making it too large?

QUESTIONS AND PROJECTS

THE SEPARATION OF CHURCH AND STATE

1. Conduct a panel discussion on questions relating to the topic: Religion should be taught in the public schools.
2. Debate the topic: Resolved, that school boards should pay for the transportation of children to parochial schools.
3. Visit a church-supported or church-related school and make a report to your class concerning the trip.
4. Investigate an actual program of released-time religious education, and be prepared to discuss the advantages and disadvantages of it.
5. Report on some outstanding illustrations of community co-operation in the development of moral and spiritual values.
6. Have a group of five or six students discuss the Report of the Educational Policies Commission on Moral and Spiritual Values in the Public Schools.
7. Investigate an actual case where "shared time" is practical, and report to the class.
8. To what extent do you think the present and recent circumventions of the church-state issues will tend to solve the long-standing conflict on the issues involved?

COLLECTIVE BARGAINING AND PROFESSIONAL NEGOTIATIONS

1. Draw up clearly the differences between professional negotiations and collective bargaining as they might apply to a specific school system.
2. Conduct a debate or discussion on the topic: Resolved that the strike is just as professional a device for settling differences as the application of sanctions.
3. Review how sanctions have been used to bring about the enforcement of demands or in bringing about needed changes in a specific state or school district.
4. What are the weaknesses and strengths of eliminating administrators from membership on professional membership or action committees?
5. Cite specific evidence to show that the strike *has* been used as a weapon among professional groups. Has it or has it not lowered the professional status of its members?
6. Discuss the Guidelines for Professional Negotiations as stated in the 1965 publication by that name as noted in the *Further Readings*.

QUESTIONS AND PROJECTS

SCHOOL DESEGREGATION

1. Look in current periodicals and journals for articles dealing with the status of desegregated schools. Is progress being made toward reaching integrated

schools? Which states are still lagging behind or troubled with the problem? List what you believe the major problems to be in connection with desegregation of schools.

2. Find out some of the ways in which the National Education Association has attempted to help schools progress toward integration. What role do teachers play in this problem?

3. To what extent will the federal government effect change toward desegregation of schools? Write a paper on material you can find on this topic.

CULTURALLY DISADVANTAGED

1. Read current articles in professional journals and government publications to collect information on how the Elementary-Secondary School Act of 1965 is providing ways of improving educational opportunities for the culturally disadvantaged child. List some of the most important developments. Be able to describe them in class.

2. Find out how the project Headstart is helping children in your town or in a community nearby. What are its strengths and weaknesses?

3. Study any material you can locate that deals with the project known as "Domestic Teachers Corps." How will this be of help in the education of the culturally disadvantaged?

DROPOUTS

1. Read articles which deal with juvenile delinquency and ascertain to what extent those involved are school dropouts. What measures do you believe should be taken by society to correct this problem?

2. How would you organize a school's curriculum to reduce the number of dropouts? Why is curriculum related to this problem? Are cocurricular activities helpful or ineffective in reducing the number of dropouts? Why?

3. Find data on school enrollments in the public schools of the United States. (Look in the World Almanac or U.S. Office of Education Publications.) See if you can detect any change in the percentage of dropouts in the past ten years. During what school years do most dropouts occur? What are the basic reasons for this?

AUDIO-VISUAL AIDS

TAPE RECORDINGS

CHURCH-STATE RELATIONSHIPS

What shall be the Relation of Religion to Public Education? Two tapes each 20 minutes long. Two speakers, with opposing points of view, each make 20 minute presentations. The speakers are, Dr. Henry P. VanDusen and Professor John K. Norton. On your own tape from Tape Recordings Depository, University of Colorado, Boulder, Col.

SCHOOL DESEGREGATION

How Can We Best Implement the Decision of the Supreme Court on School Integration—Recorded on your tape. Send tape to National Tape Repository, University of Colorado, Boulder, Colorado. The prize-winning college Forensic Society discussion program for 1956. Five students report on the research they did to reach a satisfactory manner of solving this social problem.

The Negro and the Public Schools—Recorded on your tape. Send tape to National Tape Repository, University of Colorado, Boulder, Colo. The recording concerns the struggle for integration in the public schools. Narrator: Jack Benson for ABC Radio.

MOTION PICTURES

THE CULTURALLY DISADVANTAGED CHILD

Children Must Learn—N.Y.U. & U. of Kentucky, 14 min., sd., b&w. Shows a poor family in the Southern mountain region trying to subsist on worn-out soil. Suggests how schools and education can play a part in improving conditions in such areas.

SCHOOL DROPOUTS

Problem of Pupil Adjustment, Part I: The Drop-Out—McGraw-Hill, 20 min., sd., b&w. In an employment office Steve Martin, on the day he should be graduating from high school, sits reminiscing about things gone awry at school and his succession of mediocre jobs held after his dropout. Shows Steve's eagerness as a freshman, then the withering effect of repetitious drill over textbook material that seems pointless. Even physical education and industrial arts classes seem regimented. Truancy is easy, and finally, becomes his escape. Designed to be used with a text on educational psychology.

When I'm Old Enough—Good-Bye!—Louis De Rochemont Assoc., 28 min., sd., b&w. Depicts the problems of the school dropout, explores some of the reasons why students leave school, and emphasizes the need for young people to complete high school.

FURTHER READINGS

THE SEPARATION OF CHURCH AND STATE

American Council on Education, *The Function of Public Schools in Dealing with Religion* (Washington, D.C., NEA, 1953).

Butts, R. Freeman, *The American Tradition in Religion and Education* (Boston, Beacon, 1950).

Committee on Religion and Education, *The Relation of Religion to Public Education* (Washington, D.C., American Council on Education, 1947).

Conant, James B., *Education and Liberty* (Cambridge, Mass., Harvard University Press, 1953).

"Dual Enrollment and How It Works," A carefully documented study by the staff of the U.S. Office of Education, American Education, Vol. 1 (March, 1965), pp. 24–25.

Educational Policies Commission, *Moral and Spiritual Values in the Public Schools* (Washington, D.C., 1951).

Hartford, E. E., *Moral Values in Public Education* (bibliography) (New York, Harper & Row, 1958).

Nolte, M. Chester, and John P. Linn, *School Law for Teachers* (Danville, Ill., Interstate Printers and Publishers, 1963).

Oaks, Dallin H., ed., *The Wall Between Church and State* (Chicago, University of Chicago Press, 1963).

Stokes, Anson P., and Leo Pfeffer, *Church and State in the United States* (New York, Harper & Row, 1964).

COLLECTIVE BARGAINING AND PROFESSIONAL NEGOTIATIONS

American Association of School Administrators, *Roles, Responsibilities, Relationships of the School Board, Superintendent, and Staff* (Washington, D.C., 1963).

Kratzman, Arthur, "The Alberta Teachers' Association: A Prototype for the American Scene?" Administrators Notebook, Vol. 12, pp. 1–4.

National Education Association, *Guidelines for Professional Negotiation,* rev. ed. (Washington, D.C., 1965).

National Education Association, *Guidelines for Professional Sanctions,* (Washington, D.C., 1963).

National Commission on Teacher Education and Professional Standards and the Commission on Professional Rights and Responsibilities *Professional Practices Regulations, a Plan for Action* (Washington, D.C., 1965).

"Negotiations in Education," *Theory into Practice* (Columbus, Ohio State University, 1965). An excellent series of articles on professional negotiations and collective bargaining by six authorities.

Steffensen, James P., *Teachers Negotiate with their School Boards* (Washington, D.C., U.S. Office of Education, 1964).

Stinnett, T. M., "Professional Negotiations, Collective Bargaining, Sanctions, and Strikes," *National Association Secondary School Principals,* Vol. 48 (April, 1964).

SCHOOL DESEGREGRATION

Ashmore, Harry S., *The Negro and the Schools* (Chapel Hill, N.C., University of North Carolina Press, 1954).

Conant, James B., *Slums and Suburbs* (New York, McGraw-Hill, 1961).

Humphrey, Hubert H., ed., *School Desegregation: Documents and Commentaries* (New York, Crowell, 1964).

THE CULTURALLY DISADVANTAGED CHILD

Passow, Harry, ed., *Education in Depressed Areas* (New York, Teachers College, Bureau of Publications, Columbia University, 1963).

Reisman, David, *The Lonely Crowd* (New York, Doubleday, 1953).

Reisman, David, *The Culturally Deprived Child* (New York, Harper & Row, 1962).

Chandler, B. J., Lindley J. Stiles, and John I. Kitsuse, eds., *Education in Urban Society* (New York, Dodd, Mead, 1962).

DROPOUTS

Kelley, E. D., "Seeds of Drop-Outs," *Childhood Education,* Vol. 39 (May, 1963), pp. 420–422.

Schreiber, Daniel, ed., *The School Dropout* (Washington, D.C., NEA, 1964).

Schreiber, Daniel, ed., *Guidance and the School Dropout* (Washington, D.C., NEA & American Personnel and Guidance Association, 1964).

APPENDICES

Appendix A

Universal Declaration of Human Rights*

Preamble

Whereas recognition of the inherent dignity and of the equal and inalienable rights of all members of the human family is the foundation of freedom, justice, and peace in the world,

Whereas disregard and contempt for human rights have resulted in barbarous acts which have outraged the conscience of mankind, and the advent of a world in which human beings shall enjoy freedom of speech and belief and freedom from fear and want has been proclaimed as the highest aspiration of the common people,

Whereas it is essential, if man is not to be compelled to have recourse, as a last resort, to rebellion against tyranny and oppression, that human rights should be protected by the rule of law,

Whereas it is essential to promote the development of friendly relations between nations,

Whereas the peoples of the United Nations have in the Charter reaffirmed their faith in fundamental human rights, in the dignity and worth of the human person and in the equal rights of men and women and have determined to promote social progress and better standards of life in larger freedom,

Whereas Member States have pledged themselves to achieve, in co-operation with the United Nations, the promotion of universal respect for and observance of human rights and fundamental freedoms,

Whereas a common understanding of these rights and freedoms is of the greatest importance for the full realization of this pledge,

Now therefore

The General Assembly,

Proclaims this Universal Declaration of Human Rights as a common standard of achievement for all peoples and all nations, to the end that every

* This Declaration was approved by the United Nations General Assembly in Paris December 10, 1948, by a vote of 48 to 0. Eight countries abstained—the U.S.S.R., the Ukraine, Byelorussia, Poland, Czechoslovakia, Yugoslavia, Saudi Arabia, and the Union of South Africa.

individual and every organ of society, keeping this Declaration constantly in mind, shall strive by teaching and education to promote respect for these rights and freedoms and by progressive measures, national and international, to secure their universal and effective recognition and observance, both among the peoples of Member States themselves and among the peoples of territories under their jurisdiction.

Article 1

All human beings are born free and equal in dignity and rights. They are endowed with reason and conscience and should act toward one another in a spirit of brotherhood.

Article 2

Everyone is entitled to all the rights and freedoms set forth in this Declaration, without distinction of any kind, such as race, color, sex, language, religion, political or other opinion, national or social origin, property, birth or other status.

Furthermore, no distinction shall be made on the basis of the political, jurisdictional, or international status of the country or territory to which a person belongs, whether it be independent, trust, non-self-governing, or under any other limitation of sovereignty.

Article 3

Everyone has the right to life, liberty, and the security of person.

Article 4

No one shall be held in slavery or servitude; slavery and the slave trade shall be prohibited in all their forms.

Article 5

No one shall be subjected to torture or to cruel, inhuman, or degrading treatment or punishment.

Article 6

Everyone has the right to recognition everywhere as a person before the law.

Article 7

All are equal before the law and are entitled without any discrimination to equal protection of the law. All are entitled to equal protection against any discrimination in violation of this Declaration and against any incitement to such discrimination.

Article 8

Everyone has the right to an effective remedy by the competent national tribunals for acts violating the fundamental rights granted him by the constitution or by law.

Article 9

No one shall be subjected to arbitrary arrest, detention, or exile.

Article 10

Everyone is entitled in full equality to a fair and public hearing by an independent and impartial tribunal, in the determination of his rights and obligations and of any criminal charge against him.

Article 11

1. Everyone charged with a penal offense has the right to be presumed innocent until proved guilty according to law in a public trial at which he has had all the guarantees necessary for his defense.

2. No one shall be held guilty of any penal offense on account of any act or omission which did not constitute a penal offense, under national or international law, at the time when it was committed. Nor shall a heavier penalty be imposed than the one that was applicable at the time the penal offense was committed.

Article 12

No one shall be subjected to arbitrary interference with his privacy, family, home, or correspondence, nor to attacks upon his honor and reputation. Everyone has the right to the protection of the law against such interference or attacks.

Article 13

1. Everyone has the right to freedom of movement and residence within the borders of each state.

2. Everyone has the right to leave any country, including his own, and to return to his country.

Article 14

1. Everyone has the right to seek and to enjoy in other countries asylum from persecution.

2. This right may not be invoked in the case of prosecutions genuinely arising from non-political crimes or from acts contrary to the purposes and principles of the United Nations.

Article 15

1. Everyone has the right to a nationality.

2. No one shall be arbitrarily deprived of his nationality or denied the right to change his nationality.

Article 16

1. Men and women of full age, without any limitation due to race, nationality, or religion, have the right to marry and to found a family. They are entitled to equal rights as to marriage, during marriage, and at its dissolution.

2. Marriage shall be entered into only with the free and full consent of the intending spouses.

3. The family is the natural and fundamental group unit of society and is entitled to protection by society and the State.

Article 17

1. Everyone has the right to own property alone as well as in association with others.

2. No one shall be arbitrarily deprived of his property.

Article 18

Everyone has the right to freedom of thought, conscience, and religion; this right includes freedom to change his religion or belief, and freedom, either alone or in community with others and in public or private, to manifest his religion or belief in teaching, practice, worship, and observance.

Article 19

Everyone has the right to freedom of opinion and expression; this right includes freedom to hold opinions without interference and to seek, receive and impart information and ideas through any media and regardless of frontiers.

Article 20

1. Everyone has the right to freedom of peaceful assembly and association.

2. No one may be compelled to belong to an association.

Article 21

1. Everyone has the right to take part in the Government of his country, directly or through freely chosen representatives.

2. Everyone has the right to equal access to public service in his country.

3. The will of the people shall be the basis of the authority of government; this will shall be expressed in periodic and genuine elections which shall be by universal and equal suffrage and shall be held by secret vote or by equivalent free voting procedures.

Article 22

Everyone, as a member of society, has the right to social security and is entitled to realization, through national effort and international co-operation and in accordance with the organization and resources of each State, of the economic, social, and cultural rights indispensable for his dignity and the free development of his personality.

Article 23

1. Everyone has the right to work, to free choice of employment, to just and favorable conditions of work and to protection against unemployment.

2. Everyone, without any discrimination, has the right to equal pay for equal work.

3. Everyone who works has the right to just and favorable remuneration insuring for himself and his family an existence worthy of human dignity, and supplemented, if necessary, by other means of social protection.

4. Everyone has the right to form and to join trade unions for the protection of his interests.

Article 24

Everyone has the right to rest and leisure, including reasonable limitation of working hours and periodic holidays with pay.

Article 25

1. Everyone has the right to a standard of living adequate for the health and well-being of himself and of his family, including food, clothing, housing and medical care and necessary social services, and the right to security in the event of unemployment, sickness, disability, widowhood, old age, or other lack of livelihood in circumstances beyond his control.

2. Motherhood and childhood are entitled to special care and assistance. All children, whether born in or out of wedlock, shall enjoy the same social protection.

Article 26

1. Everyone has the right to education. Education shall be free, at least in the elementary and fundamental stages. Elementary education shall be compulsory. Technical and professional education shall be made generally available and higher education shall be equally accessible to all on the basis of merit.

2. Education shall be directed to the full development of the human personality and to the strengthening of respect for human rights and fundamental freedoms. It shall promote understanding, tolerance, and friendship among all nations, racial or religious groups, and shall further the activities of the United Nations for the maintenance of peace.

3. Parents have a prior right to choose the kind of education that shall be given to their children.

Article 27

1. Everyone has the right freely to participate in the cultural life of the community, to enjoy the arts, and to share in scientific advancement and its benefits.

2. Everyone has the right to the protection of the moral and material interests resulting from any scientific, literary, or artistic production of which he is the author.

Article 28

Everyone is entitled to a social and international order in which the rights and freedoms set forth in this Declaration can be fully realized.

Article 29

1. Everyone has duties to the community in which alone the free and full development of his personality is possible.

2. In the exercise of his rights and freedoms, everyone shall be subject only to such limitations as are determined by law solely for the purpose of securing due recognition and respect for the rights and freedoms of others and of meeting the just requirements of morality, public order and the general welfare in a democratic society.

3. These rights and freedoms may in no case be exercised contrary to the purposes and principles of the United Nations.

Article 30

Nothing in this Declaration may be interpreted as implying for any State, group, or person any right to engage in any activity or to perform any act aimed at the destruction of any of the rights and freedoms set forth herein.

The Bill of Rights
of the
United States
of
America

Amendment 1

Congress shall make no law respecting an establishment of religion, or prohibiting the free exercise thereof; or abridging the freedom of speech, or of the press; or the right of the people peaceably to assemble, and to petition the government for a redress of grievances.

Amendment 2

A well-regulated militia being necessary to the security of a free State, the right of the people to keep and bear arms shall not be infringed.

Amendment 3

No soldier shall, in time of peace, be quartered in any house without the consent of the owner; nor in time of war but in a manner to be prescribed by law.

Amendment 4

The right of the people to be secure in their persons, houses, papers and effects, against unreasonable searches and seizures, shall not be violated, and no warrants shall issue but upon probable cause, supported by oath or affirmation, and particularly describing the place to be searched, and the persons or things to be seized.

Amendment 5

No person shall be held to answer for a capital or otherwise infamous crime, unless on a presentment or indictment of a grand jury, except in cases arising in the land or naval forces, or in the militia, when in actual service in time of war or public danger; nor shall any person be subject for the same offense to be twice put in jeopardy of life or limb; nor shall be compelled in any criminal case to be a witness against himself, nor be deprived of life, liberty, or property, without due process of law; nor shall private property be taken for public use, without just compensation.

Amendment 6

In all criminal prosecutions the accused shall enjoy the right to a speedy and public trial, by an impartial jury of the State and district wherein the crime shall have been committed, which district shall have been previously ascertained by law, and to be informed of the nature and cause of the accusation; to be confronted with the witnesses against him; to have compulsory process for obtaining witnesses in his favor, and to have the assistance of counsel for his defense.

Amendment 7

In suits at common law, where the value in controversy shall exceed twenty dollars, the right of trial by jury shall be preserved, and no fact tried by a jury shall be otherwise reexamined in any court of the United States than according to the rules of the common law.

Amendment 8

Excessive bail shall not be required, nor excessive fines imposed, nor cruel and unusual punishments inflicted.

Amendment 9

The enumeration in the Constitution of certain rights shall not be construed to deny or disparage others retained by the people.

Amendment 10

The powers not delegated to the United States by the Constitution, nor prohibited by it to the States, are reserved to the States respectively, or to the people.

Appendix C

Teachers' Bill of Rights

OF THE PENNSYLVANIA STATE EDUCATION ASSOCIATION

NOTE—The items which have been included in the statement of the Bill of Rights are to be construed as principles, requiring further explanation as to their specific nature and providing for implementation.

1. Size of Class and Pupil Load

Each teacher has the right to classes of such size and a total pupil load of such weight that he may develop the maximum interests, capacities, and skills of individual pupils.

2. Time for Planning and Coordinating Work of a Professional Nature

Each teacher has the right to a class and activity schedule that will allow time during the school day for a thoughtful and effective discharge of his professional duties and for planning and coordinating.

3. Constructive and Sympathetic Supervision

Each teacher has the right to adequate constructive and sympathetic supervision.

4. Good Working Materials

Each teacher has the right to materials and equipment which are of practical necessity to effective teaching.

5. Adequate Physical Conditions in the Building

Each teacher has the right to practice his profession in a school environment that provides physical conditions necessary for good health, good teaching, and good morale.

6. In-service Education

Each teacher has the right to facilities and a program that will encourage in-service improvement, such as a professional library, workshops, group studies, and sabbatical leave.

7. Participation in School Policy and Program

Each teacher has the right to be consulted in the formulation of policies affecting the school and the school program within the framework of the school law.

8. Adequate Contractual Retirement Income

Each teacher has the right to a contractual retirement income based upon the total years of service and total professional earnings, and adequate for him and his dependents.

9. Right to a Position

Each teacher who is properly certified has the right to practice his profession with full contractual status, after an adequately supervised and acceptable probationary period.

10. Right to Engage in Professional Activities

Each teacher has the right to engage in properly recognized professional activities without incurring prejudice.

11. Right to an Adequate Income

Each teacher has the right to receive for his services a financial return, as it becomes due, that will allow him a living standard comparable to that of other professional groups and that will enable him to improve his professional service.

12. Right to Salary When Due

Each teacher has the right to receive his salary when it becomes due.

13. Right to Have Position Defined

Each teacher has the right to have the nature and scope of his professional duties defined.

14. School Day and School Week

Each teacher has the right to decline without prejudice special assignments beyond the normal school day.

15. School Year

Each teacher has the right to proportionate compensation for professional services beyond the minimum mandated school day and/or school term as prescribed by State law.

16. Political Participation

Each teacher has the right to participate in political activities as citizens, consistent with the American way of life, without endangering his professional position.

17. Protection from Discrimination

Each teacher has the right to protection from discrimination on the basis of race, color, creed, sex, political beliefs consistent with American democracy, residence, marital status, economic status, and consanguinity.

THE CODE OF COMPETENCE

The Pennsylvania State Education Association recognizes the opportunities and responsibilities the teacher has in educating children, youth, and adults to be good American citizens. Only a competent person can discharge these responsibilities properly. This Code of Competence is suggested for the guidance of the members of the profession.

Personal Qualifications

Successful teaching depends upon the influence of the teacher's personality.

1. The competent teacher spends his days working with pupils and from these daily relationships he draws deep and lasting satisfaction.
2. The competent teacher can both assemble and interpret facts in socially intelligent and useful ways.
3. The competent teacher places a high value upon physical health and mental health for pupils, imparting a sense of wellbeing and security to pupils.
4. A competent teacher grows professionally and adapts himself to changing conditions.
5. Personal integrity is an essential qualification of a competent teacher.
6. The competent teacher is careful in his grooming, proper in his poise, and accurate in his speech.
7. The competent teacher recognizes that the greatest values of life are those of the spirit and exemplifies them in his character and teaching.
8. The competent teacher evaluates his work in the light of the desirable objectives to be attained.
9. The competent teacher possesses a sense of humor and radiates enthusiasm for his work.

Professional Education

A professionally prepared and competent person is needed in every school position.

1. A teacher builds professional competence upon a broad, cultural background.
2. A competent teacher is educated in a properly accredited institution.
3. The education of the teacher includes those knowledges, skills, and experiences that will make him effective in wholesome teacher-pupil learning situations.
4. A competent teacher continues to study and grow professionally.

Professional Skills

"The primary obligations of the teaching profession are to guide the children, youth, and adults, in the pursuit of knowledge and skills, to prepare them in the way of democracy, and to help them to become happy, useful, and self-supporting citizens."
(NEA Code of Ethics)

1. The competent teacher constantly improves in those professional skills necessary to his position in the total educational program.
2. The competent teacher plans with pupils educational goals to be attained in order to provide for the maximum growth of each pupil.
3. The competent teacher makes the teaching environment as attractive as possible.
4. The competent teacher is concerned with efficient management.
5. The competent teacher utilizes community resources in the development of the educational program.
6. The competent teacher evaluates his own teaching and encourages self-appraisal among pupils.

Professional Opportunities and Responsibilities

The competent teacher regards the profession of teaching as a life career.

1. The competent teacher believes whole-heartedly in the profession of teaching as a great social institution, necessary for the preservation of the American way of life.
2. The competent teacher understands the nature, scope, aims, peculiar characteristics, and problems of teaching, and accepts them as an accompaniment of membership in the profession.
3. The competent teacher strives to achieve maximum development not only in skills for vocational, cultural, and social competence, but also for the development of sound moral character and personal integrity.
4. The competent teacher is willing to participate democratically in the formulation of policies affecting the educational program.
5. The competent teacher engages in professional activities designed to improve the profession as well as himself.

Human Relationships

The teacher's work brings him into constant relationship with many people.

1. The competent teacher strives to understand and apply the techniques of group relationships so that he may work sympathetically with his pupils and their parents, fellow teachers and administrators, and the general public.
2. The competent teacher develops an understanding of his role as a teacher in relation to the objectives and spirit of the whole school system.
3. The competent teacher studies and practices the Code of Ethics of the profession.

Appendix D

PERIODICALS OF VALUE TO TEACHERS AND STUDENTS OF EDUCATION

Adult Education
American Education
American Psychologist
American School Board Journal
American Teacher
Audio-Visual Instruction
Childhood Education
Clearing House
Education
Education Digest
Education Leadership
Elementary School Journal
English Journal
Exceptional Children
Grade Teacher
High School Journal
Higher Education
Journal of Education
Journal of Educational Psychology
Journal of Educational Research
Journal of Experimental Education
Journal of General Education
Journal of Health, Physical Education, and Recreation
Journal of Higher Education
Journal of Secondary Education
Journal of Teacher Education
Junior College Journal
Library Journal
Mathematics Teacher
Modern Language Journal
Music Educators Journal
NEA Department of Secondary School Principal's Bulletin
NEA Journal
NEA Research Bulletin
Nations Schools

Peabody Journal of Education
Personnel and Guidance Journal
Phi Delta Kappan
Reading Teacher
Review of Educational Research
Saturday Review—(one issue monthly with educational section)
School Activities
School and Society
School Arts Magazine
School Review
Science Education
Science Teacher
Sociology of Education
Speech Teacher
Teachers College Journal
The Instructor
The Social Studies
Theory Into Practice
U.S. Department of Health, Education, and Welfare: Office of Education
    Publications
Young Children

In addition to the above, worthwhile periodicals are published by the various state education associations and by the schools of education at many colleges and universities.

Students of education should be aware of the fact that many magazines of high caliber, such as *The Atlantic Monthly* and *Harper's Magazine,* frequently devote considerable attention to matters of educational importance.

Index